Praxis® Elementary Education

with **Online Practice Tests**

for
dummies®
A Wiley Brand

Praxis® Elementary Education

with Online Practice Tests

for
dummies®
A Wiley Brand

by Carla Kirkland and Chan Cleveland

Praxis® Elementary Education For Dummies® with Online Practice Tests

Published by:
John Wiley & Sons, Inc.,
111 River Street,
Hoboken, NJ 07030-5774
www.wiley.com

Copyright © 2016 by John Wiley & Sons, Inc., Hoboken, New Jersey

Published simultaneously in Canada

For general information on our other products and services, please contact our Customer Care Department within the U.S. at 877-762-2974, outside the U.S. at 317-572-3993, or fax 317-572-4002. For technical support, please visit www.wiley.com/techsupport.

Wiley publishes in a variety of print and electronic formats and by print-on-demand. Some material included with standard print versions of this book may not be included in e-books or in print-on-demand. If this book refers to media such as a CD or DVD that is not included in the version you purchased, you may download this material at http://booksupport.wiley.com. For more information about Wiley products, visit www.wiley.com.

Library of Congress Control Number: 2016935257

ISBN 978-1-119-18786-8 (pbk); ISBN 978-1-119-18788-2 (ebk); ISBN 978-1-119-18787-5 (ebk)

Manufactured in the United States of America

10 9 8 7 6 5 4 3 2 1

Contents at a Glance

Table of Contents

Introduction

You probably already know that if you hope to become a teacher, you'll have to take and pass an entry exam. The ones you'll most likely take are the Praxis exams. Many colleges and universities require that students who want to complete an undergraduate degree in education take a Praxis Core exam that tests their knowledge of reading, writing, and math. After that, many aspiring teachers have to take another Praxis exam to obtain licensure. "Wait, what? More than one test?" Yes, we're afraid so. It might be a repeat of the Core exam or it might be a subject test—or depending on your goals, more than one subject test.

The *Praxis Elementary Education: Curriculum, Instruction, and Assessment* (5017) is indeed a subject test. As the name suggests, this particular test covers a pretty broad span of what you need to know regarding elementary education. Also reviewed in this book is the *Praxis Elementary Education: Content Knowledge* (5018) exam. It restricts its coverage to the content of the main four subject areas that an elementary teacher should have mastered: Reading and Language Arts, Mathematics, Social Studies, and Science.

The goal of this book is to refresh your existing knowledge or develop new understanding on what you need to know in preparation for the Praxis exams. We don't cover every topic that is tested in detail; instead, we offer an overview of those topics. The overview allows you to review a topic and say to yourself either, "Yep, got it! I can move onto the next topic" or "I don't get it. I'd better focus on math a little more." While you may be required to successfully pass the Praxis Elementary Education test in order to get a teaching license in your state, don't panic! You have your hands on the right book to help you ace this exam.

About This Book

Praxis Elementary Education For Dummies breaks down the exam's main objectives into understandable sections. This book is organized into subsections so that you can quickly navigate through subject areas. For example, if you're struggling with math, you can find all those topics grouped together. If science makes you want to pull your hair out, you can get a comprehensive overview in Chapter 6. In addition, this book offers helpful tips and strategies that you can practice so you don't fall for the booby traps others seem to. They say practice makes perfect. This book provides two practice tests and an additional two practice tests can be found online. You may want to practice before you read any of the chapters to discover your strengths and areas that could use improvement. Once you have mastered the material, you can practice again to put your skills to the "test."

Foolish Assumptions

In writing this book, we've made some assumptions about you. The biggest assumption we've made applies to all readers: You have decided to become a teacher, which is one of the most rewarding professions known to man. Then, we assume you fall into one of the following categories:

>> **You are a first time test-taker:** You want to take and pass the test on your first try.

>> **You are a retester:** You've taken the test before but didn't get the score you needed or wanted. You can still successfully reach the passing score goal. You're actually in a better situation than the first-time test-taker because you possess a detailed report that outlines your strengths and weaknesses. That way you can truly attack the sections that give you the most difficulty.

>> **You are a traditional teacher candidate:** You're currently working on or have recently completed an undergraduate or graduate education degree. You need to pass this test to get licensed.

>> **You are an alternative route teacher candidate:** You already possess a four-year degree and you need to pass this test as one of your first steps toward certification.

If you're in one (or more!) of these categories, good for you. We have written this book to fit *your* specific needs.

Icons Used in This Book

Icons are the drawings in the margins of this book, and we use several icons to call out special kinds of information.

Examples are sample test questions that appear at the ends of sections and that highlight particular ideas that you should be familiar with. We provide an answer and explanation immediately after the question.

The Remember icon points out something you should keep in mind while you're taking the exam.

A Tip is a suggestion that usually points out a test-taking strategy or a trick for remembering information for the test.

The Warning icon flags traps and tricks that the creators of the Praxis often employ to trip you up when it comes to choosing the correct answer. Pay special heed to these paragraphs.

Beyond the Book

In addition to the material in the print or e-book you're reading right now, this product also comes with some access-anywhere goodies:

>> **Cheat Sheet:** (http://www.dummies.com/cheatsheet/praxiselementaryeducation): When you're down to the last few days before the test, not only do you have to remember everything you've studied for the test, but you have to remember what to take with you to the testing site. Check out the online Cheat Sheet for a handy list of what to take with you. You'll also find some general tips for succeeding on the Praxis. Review this a week or so before you're scheduled to take the test so you can make sure you're as prepared as you can be.

>> **Online practice and study aids:** In addition to the two complete practice exams contained in this book, your book purchase also comes with a free one-year subscription to two additional practice tests that appear online for you to access whenever and from wherever you want. With all of these practice questions at your disposal, you can take entire timed exams or just practice with a handful of questions at a time.

To gain access to the online practice, all you have to do is register. Just follow these simple steps:

1. **Find your PIN access code.**

   • **Print book users:** If you purchased a hard copy of this book, turn to the front of this book to find your access code.

   • **E-book users:** If you purchased this book as an e-book, you can get your access code by registering your e-book at www.dummies.com/go/getaccess. Go to this website, find your book and click it, and answer the security question to verify your purchase. Then you'll receive an email with your access code.

2. **Go to** Dummies.com **and click** Activate Now.

3. **Find your product (*Praxis Elementary Education For Dummies*) and then follow the on-screen prompts to activate your PIN.**

Now you're ready to go! You can come back to the program as often as you want—simply log on with the username and password you created during your initial login. No need to enter the access code a second time.

TIP

For Technical Support, please visit http://wiley.custhelp.com or call Wiley at 1-800-762-2974 (U.S.), +1-317-572-3994 (international).

Where to Go from Here

You don't need to read this book from front to back. Instead, use it as a reference. Skip around to the sections that you find most useful. If you can't decide, begin with Chapters 1 and 2. They present overviews of the Praxis 5017 and 5018 exams. If you know that math (Chapter 5) is your Achilles heel or that language arts questions (Chapter 4) make your eyes cross, go straight to the corresponding chapter. We also give you an index at the back of the book to help you find specific information. Or, if you like, start by taking one of the tests in Part IV to target the material you need to brush up on.

1

Getting the Ball Rolling

IN THIS PART . . .

Get the details about who takes the Praxis 5017 and 5018, what's on the tests, and how your score is calculated.

Figure out how to schedule your study time in advance of test day, figure out what to expect on test day, and get some pointers if you're retaking the test.

Try out some practice questions to identify your strengths and weaknesses.

Develop a study plan to make your weaknesses your strengths.

Chapter 1

The Praxis Elementary Education: CIA Test (5017)

For decades, teacher candidates have been taking assessments in order to meet certification requirements. You may have taken a Praxis Core exam (or some earlier version) to get into a teaching program at a college or university. Once you completed it, perhaps you thought that was the last you would see of Praxis.

Not so fast! If you want to become a teacher, you are likely to encounter more Praxis exams on your road to certification. Many states use the Praxis Core and/or one or more Praxis subject exams as certification tests to show that you've mastered the skills needed to be a highly competent teacher. Praxis Elementary Education: Curriculum, Instruction, and Assessment (5017) (or Praxis Elementary Education: CIA) is one of these subject exams. Teaching licenses often are directly tied to passing this exam and perhaps other subject tests as well. This chapter gives you an overview of what you need to know about this exam.

According to the Educational Testing Service (ETS) this exam is designed for prospective teachers in the elementary grades. It covers the breadth of material a new teacher needs to know while assessing content knowledge, pedagogical principles, and processes. To be successful on this exam, candidates must show mastery of curriculum planning, instructional planning, and assessment planning in the areas of reading and language arts, mathematics, science, social studies, art, music, and physical education. Luckily, you have this book to help you make the Praxis Elementary Education: CIA exam a milestone rather than a roadblock.

REMEMBER

Also included in this book is the preparation for the Praxis Elementary Education: Content Knowledge (5018). This exam differs from the 5017 designation in that candidates must show mastery of content in four areas: reading and language arts, mathematics, social studies, and science. This knowledge is exhibited through questions assessing conceptual understanding, procedural awareness, interpretation, integration, and application.

The items presented on both exams will be aligned to the appropriate state and national standards for that subject area. Examinees should also note that the tests may contain some questions that will not count toward their score. Almost every state in the country uses some form of the Praxis. Contact your state department of education for specific licensure details.

TIP

For details on preparing for the Praxis Elementary Education: Content Knowledge, proceed to Chapter 2. Content review chapters for this test are 4, 5, 6, and 7. The practice test and explanations are Chapters 17 and 18.

Analyzing the Format of the Test

The newly developed Praxis Elementary Education: CIA exam uses 120 questions to evaluate your curriculum development, instructional, and assessment abilities in five subject-area groups:

>> Reading and language arts

>> Mathematics

>> Science

>> Social studies

>> Art, music, and physical education

To date, all 120 questions are selected-response type questions. However, it doesn't necessarily mean the questions are easy!

The topics the test covers

According to the Educational Testing Service (ETS), the 120 questions of the Praxis Elementary Education: CIA exam are divided among five subject-area groups according to the proportions you see in Table 1-1.

TABLE 1-1 **Breakdown of Praxis Elementary Education**

Test Subject	Approximate Number of Questions	Approximate Percentage of the Exam
Reading and language arts	37	31%
Mathematics	31	26%
Science	20	16%
Social studies	17	14%
Art, music, and physical education	15	13%

In each of the five subject areas, questions are related to relevant national standards and test your knowledge of how to help students develop an understanding of particular areas of knowledge or how to help them acquire and use key skills.

The questions about each subject are focused on curriculum, instruction, or assessment.

>> **Curriculum:** Curriculum questions require you to show that you understand developmentally appropriate curriculum planning. Specifically, you need to be ready to demonstrate that you can sequence lessons; plan strategies to enhance students' understanding and, inevitably, correct their misunderstandings; and make connections to and from one subject and other subject areas, such as connecting reading and math concepts, or social studies and science.

>> **Instruction:** Instruction questions require you to show that you understand how to design instruction to meet the culturally and academically diverse needs of your students. They also test your ability to select and use developmentally appropriate instructional methods, strategies, and resources that support learning in the major focus areas of each subject.

>> **Assessment:** The assessment questions for every subject area require you to show that you know how to evaluate the effectiveness of your instruction and your students' progress in each subject area. To answer these questions correctly, you need to be ready to show that you can design, use, and interpret a variety of formative and summative assessments. You must be able to recognize the misconceptions students may develop and devise ways to reteach in order to correct those misconceptions.

Reading and language arts

The topics addressed by questions in the reading and language arts section reflect the state and national standards for language arts. You'll see questions about:

>> **Reading foundational skills:** These questions test your understanding of how to help students develop concepts of print, phonological awareness, phonics and word-analysis skills, and fluency.

>> **Reading literature and informational texts:** These questions test your understanding of how to help students comprehend literature and informational texts; ask and answer questions about texts; identify and organize main ideas and details; use text features; identify point of view; distinguish among fact, opinion, and reasoned judgment; compare texts and different formats; select appropriate texts; and progress toward independent reading.

>> **Writing:** These questions test your knowledge of how to help students do research and develop their writing skills in a variety of genres.

>> **Language:** These questions require you to show your knowledge of how to help students understand conventions of English, build their vocabularies, and interpret figurative language.

>> **Speaking and listening:** These questions test your knowledge of how to help students develop active listening skills, oral presentation speaking and listening skills, and skills in using multimedia in presentations.

Mathematics

The topics addressed in the math section also reflect state and national standards. You'll see questions about:

» **Numbers and operations:** These questions test your knowledge of how to help students develop their understanding of and ability to use natural numbers, whole numbers, integers, and rational numbers; proportional relationships; and number theory.

» **Algebraic thinking:** These questions test your knowledge of how to help students develop their understanding of and ability to use expressions, equations, and formulas, as well as linear equations and inequalities.

» **Geometry and measurement:** These questions test your knowledge of how to help students develop their understanding of one-, two-, and three-dimensional figures; coordinate planes; and measurement.

» **Data, statistics, and probability:** These questions test your knowledge of how to help students develop their understanding of and ability to use measures of center, data collection and display, and probability.

Science

In the science section of the exam, you'll see questions about instructing students in the following topics:

» **Science concepts, inquiry, and processes:** These questions test your knowledge of how to help students develop their understanding of science and science disciplines; scientific inquiry; how to plan, conduct, and observe investigations; and how to choose the appropriate tools to gather data, organize and analyze information, communicate results, and come up with reasonable explanations.

» **Life science:** These questions test your knowledge of how to help students learn about the characteristics, life cycles, and environments of organisms.

» **Earth and space science:** These questions test your knowledge of how to help students develop their understanding of the interrelationships among Earth and space systems; astronomy; Earth patterns, cycles, and change; geology; hydrology; meteorology; oceanography; and soil science.

» **Physical science:** These questions test your knowledge of how to help students develop their understanding of physical and chemical changes, temperature and heat, sound, light, electricity, magnetism, force, motion, energy, and matter.

» **Health:** These questions test your knowledge of how to help students develop their knowledge of healthy living, including growth, nutrition, safety, and well-being, as well their knowledge of communicable and common diseases and substance abuse.

Social studies

In the social studies section of the exam, you'll see questions about the following topics:

» **Information processing skills:** These questions test your knowledge of how to help students develop their understanding of how to locate, analyze, and synthesize social-studies information and how to select and use appropriate materials and equipment.

- » **Geography:** These questions test your knowledge of how to help students learn about relationships among human and physical systems, the environment, and society, as well as learn about states, regions, the United States, and the world.

- » **History:** These questions test your knowledge of how to help students develop their understanding of the interrelationships between the past and the present, causes and effects of historical events, U.S. history, and classical societies.

- » **Government, civics, and economics:** These questions test your knowledge of how to help students develop their understanding of basic economic concepts; governments' roles in economics, democracy, and politics; and U.S. government.

- » **Anthropology and sociology:** These questions test your knowledge of how to help students develop their understanding of how groups and individuals are affected by conditions and events; how people from different cultures interact with their physical environments and social environments; as well as communication, transportation, and technology.

Art, music, and physical education

This section of the exam tests your understanding of how to teach three very different subjects:

- » **Art:** These questions test how well you develop students' understanding of elements and principles of art; visual communication and production; and art history, criticism, and aesthetics.

- » **Music:** These questions test your understanding of how to help students develop their understanding of elements of music, such as texture, harmony, melody, and rhythm; their knowledge of music notation and terminology; and their ability to compose music.

- » **Physical education:** These questions test your ability to help students exercise and develop physical fitness, game and sports skills, and body management and locomotor skills, as well as develop their knowledge of safety, social discipline, and healthy lifestyles.

The types of questions asked

Praxis Elementary Education: CIA is composed entirely of selected-response questions, also known as multiple-choice questions. You don't have to write any essays or even short answers. You've probably been answering multiple-choice questions since you were old enough to wield a No. 2 pencil on your first standardized test. So you may think you know all there is to know about them. But, Praxis puts new twists on a few of these old favorites in two ways: first, by changing the numbers of correct answers, and second, by varying the type of response you need to make. It's not all just clicking the correct ovals.

Number of correct answers

A huge majority of the questions on the Praxis Elementary Education: CIA exam have a single correct answer. The remainder have more than one correct answer. Occasionally, questions with more than one correct answer specify how many answers you should pick, but far more often, this type of question doesn't tell you how many of the choices are correct. The following sections take a closer look.

SINGLE CORRECT RESPONSE

You can think of these as the basic, no-frills model of the multiple-choice question. They have one and only one correct answer. On the Praxis, the question typically includes an instruction to remind you that the question has only one correct answer, such as, "Answer the question by clicking the correct response."

TIP

ETS suggests an effective approach for answering multiple-choice questions that have a single answer. Eliminate any answers you know are incorrect to narrow down the choices before picking a possible answer. Then, try out your preliminary answer by referring back to the question. For example, suppose a question shows a student-generated graph that is supposed to plot the student's answers to several equations. Does it make sense to say that giving the student extra instruction about the horizontal and vertical axes of a graph would address the misunderstanding shown in the student's work sample? If not, eliminate that option and decipher the remaining choices similarly until you find the one that fits.

MORE THAN ONE CORRECT RESPONSE

This souped-up version of a multiple-choice question has two or more correct answers, instead of just one. A few of these will helpfully tell you the number of correct answers, often emphasized in capital or boldfaced letters. For example, you might find a question like this accompanying an example of a paragraph a student is supposed to peer edit: "Which TWO types of errors can a peer editor find in this paragraph?"

TIP

To get points for answering a question that tells you the number of correct answers, following the instructions is essential. Click the specified number of answers, whether it is two answers, three answers, or some other number.

Most of the time, however, the question does not tell you how many correct responses to choose. One of these may look like a no-frills multiple-choice question at first glance, but then you may notice the instruction, "Click on your choices." How many choices? Well, that's up to you. Maybe the question only has one correct answer. Maybe it has two or three. It's possible that every single option is correct.

TIP

When a question tells you to "Click on your choices" but does not tell you how many choices are correct, you need to examine each answer option individually and decide whether or not it is correct.

Different types of answers

The vast majority of items on the official Praxis practice test and the actual test itself are the multiple-choice format you're probably most familiar with. You read the question and click on the oval next to the correct answer choice (or choices). However, you may also encounter items that ask you to indicate your choice in some other fashion. Sometimes, the difference may be subtle; you may be asked to click the boxes, rather than the ovals, beside all the correct answers, or you may choose your answer from a drop-down menu of choices. Other times, the task will look quite different from what you see in a standard multiple-choice question. You may be asked to:

>> **Choose an answer by clicking on a part of a graphic.** For example, a question might instruct you to click on a part of a map to indicate where you would direct your students' attention during a lesson on interpreting the scale of a map.

>> **Select a sentence from a passage.** For example, a question may ask you to click on the sentence from a student's opinion paragraph that indicates whether or not the student has supported his opinion with evidence.

>> **Drag answer choices into the correct spots in a table or list.** For example, you might be asked to drag several examples of student writing into a table to show which example indicates that a student needs practice in a particular reading skill.

In the practice tests both in this book and online, you'll find many examples of various multiple-choice questions with varying numbers of answers. Taking all of our practice tests will give you a consistent feel of what you will see on the actual test so that you'll have a chance to refine your own personal strategy for nailing the answers every time.

How the Test Is Scored

Praxis Elementary Education: CIA is divided into five sections, each focused on a specific subject area (or on a group of subjects) that you're likely to teach: reading and language arts; mathematics; science; social studies; and art, music, and physical education. When you receive your score report, you will see a breakdown of raw points for each section and a total score. The total score is calculated from your raw points and adjusted to a scale that ranges from 100 to 200 points.

Racking up raw points

Your total score on the exam is based on the number of raw points you earn in each section. The available numbers of raw points are very similar to the percentages of the exam represented by each subject area:

>> **Reading and language arts:** 31 raw points available

>> **Math:** 26 raw points available

>> **Science:** 16 raw points available

>> **Social studies:** 14 raw points available

>> **Art, music, and physical education:** 12 raw points available

Your raw score is based on the number of questions you answer correctly. ETS points out in its preparation materials that your test may contain some questions that do not count toward your score. "Which questions?" you ask. Well, if they told you that, you probably wouldn't bother answering them, would you? Nope, and that's why they don't tell you. You need to try and answer every single question on your exam.

TIP

You don't lose any points for answering a question incorrectly. If you were to answer every single question incorrectly, your raw score would be 0, which is exactly what it would be if you didn't answer any questions at all. That's why you have nothing to lose by guessing if you don't know the answer to a question.

Making sense of your score

The number that may interest you the most when you get your score report is your final score, which ETS simply calls "your score." Your score determines whether or not you pass the test. No wonder it gets so much attention!

Your score will be a number from 100 to 200. It is calculated by taking your raw points—which are based on the number of questions you answer correctly—and comparing them to the number of questions on the test. This conversion of your raw points to your total score also adapts to the level of rigor of that particular testing edition.

To achieve a total score that is considered passing by most states, you must answer at least 60 percent of the questions correctly. This gives you a benchmark to measure yourself against as you go through the practice tests in this book or online.

If you fail the Praxis the first time you take it (or if you've already failed it), you can look at your scores for each content category to see where you did well and where you struggled. Use those scores to help you target what to study most before you take the exam again.

Remember, though, that each state that requires passing the exam has its own minimum score. What constitutes a passing score in one state may not be a passing score in another state. Contact your state or local department of education for the minimum passing score.

Getting a Very Early Taste of 5017

In a moment, this chapter will lead you to some practice questions that will give you a basic idea of what to expect on the Praxis Elementary Education: CIA test. This is an ideal time for you to begin studying actual test material.

Because the practice questions that are coming right up will prepare you for the practice questions later in the book, what you are really about to do is practice for practice. You can use these first sets of practice results to help you determine what you need to focus on in the rest of your preparation. You might realize that you have a firm grasp on math instruction but know very little about science curriculum or perhaps that you need to focus on learning social studies content knowledge. However, no matter what you realize from looking at your practice question results, you should thoroughly study all areas to achieve the best possible real test score.

Although the big test you are preparing for is timed, we do not recommend timing yourself when you try the practice questions in this chapter. You should first learn to do something well before you learn to do it fast.

Because time will not be a factor for these questions, you don't need to worry about timing techniques. Pace yourself and do your best to answer every question. Keep in mind that leaving exam questions blank does not benefit you. On the test you are preparing for, there is no penalty for guessing and getting a wrong answer, aside from not getting the points a right answer would have gotten you.

We also encourage you not to check your answers as you go through these practice questions. Knowing for sure that you missed several questions in a row can be discouraging and tempt you to give up too easily. Perhaps, knowing that you are on a roll at this stage can make you worry about jinxing your winning streak. Plus, when you look up one answer, you can easily see the other ones. That makes the practice less of a practice.

Okay, here are the questions. Good luck!

Reading and Language Arts practice questions

These practice questions are similar to the reading and language arts questions that you'll encounter on the Praxis Elementary Education: CIA test.

1. **Answer the question by choosing the correct response.**

   A teacher observes that a student is having difficulty reading a list of words that includes "chow," "shot," "whip," and "then." The teacher can best address this student's needs by adding instruction in which of these phonetic elements?

   (A) diphthongs

   (B) vowel blends

   (C) consonant blends

   (D) consonant digraphs

2. **Answer by choosing all the correct responses.**

   A student writes the following and reads aloud, "It was very cold and dark in the cave, but I could see a lot of bats."

   > It wz vr kld dk n cv bt I kd c lt v btz

   Which skills is this student demonstrating the ability to perform?

   Select **all** that apply.

   (A) Use spaces between words.

   (B) Partially include medial vowels.

   (C) Partially spell consonant blends.

   (D) Use correct directionality of print.

3. **Answer the question by choosing the correct response.**

   Third-grade students are reading informational text that describes the migration patterns of gray whales. Which is the best graphic organizer for students to complete in order to help them understand the sequence of the whales' yearly travels?

   (A) a T-chart

   (B) a K-W-L chart

   (C) a content map

   (D) a Venn diagram

Questions 4 and 5 refer to the following passage.

During a discussion after reading one of Aesop's fables to first-graders, a teacher asks students the following questions:

1. Why didn't the lion think the mouse would ever help him?

2. Can mice and lions really talk?

4. **Answer the question by choosing the correct response.**

   Which comprehension task does answering Question 1 require students to do?

   (A) identify key details

   (B) sequence specific events

   (C) understand the central lesson

   (D) describe character motivations

5. **Answer the question by choosing the correct response.**

   Discussion of students' answers to Question 2 is likely to help the teacher introduce students to which type of figurative language?

   (A) personification

   (B) onomatopoeia

   (C) metaphor

   (D) simile

6. **Answer the question by choosing the correct response.**

   A teacher thinks aloud, "I wonder what this word, *caterwauling,* could possibly mean? I see before that word it says Gemma was very loud and in the next sentence it says the high pitch of her voice was annoying. Maybe *caterwauling* means 'shrill yelling.'" Which technique for determining word meaning is the teacher modeling?

   (A) word sort

   (B) context clues

   (C) structural analysis

   (D) reference materials

7. **Answer the question by choosing the correct response.**

A teacher has students work in pairs to brainstorm possible topics for an upcoming paper. Which stage of the writing process are the students working on?

(A) prewriting

(B) drafting

(C) revising

(D) publishing

8. **Answer the question by choosing the correct response.**

A teacher and student look at several examples of the student's writing collected from the beginning of the school term. They discuss areas in which the student's writing has improved and target areas for further improvement during the rest of the term. Which method is the teacher using to assess the student?

(A) observation

(B) retelling rubric

(C) running record

(D) portfolio review

9. **Answer by choosing all the correct responses.**

A teacher assigns fourth-grade students to prepare and present a class presentation about an endangered species. Which of the following speaking and listening skills should the teacher include on the rubric used to grade the presentations?

Select **all** that apply.

(A) use appropriate descriptive details

(B) take turns speaking and listening

(C) speak clearly at an understandable pace

(D) listen actively and paraphrase key points

10. **Answer the question by choosing the correct response.**

A group of fourth-graders meet to discuss a chapter of a book they have been reading. One student leads the group and calls on the other group members, one at a time, to give their opinion about the main character's actions. This structured method of interaction helps group members develop skills in

(A) paraphrasing each other's speech.

(B) asking questions to get information.

(C) reviewing and summarizing key ideas.

(D) following rules for taking turns speaking.

Answers to practice Reading and Language Arts questions

Use this answer key to score the practice reading and language arts questions in this chapter.

1. **D. consonant digraphs.** This question requires an understanding of the roles of phonics in learning reading fundamentals. *Consonant digraphs* are pairs of consonants that together make a combined sound different from the sound of each letter read separately. Choice (A) is incorrect because *diphthongs* are pairs of vowels that together make a combined sound different from the sound of each letter read separately. Choice (B) is incorrect because not all the example words include vowel blends. Choice (C) is incorrect because *consonant blends* are groups of consonants that appear together but are pronounced more or less individually.

2. **A. Use spaces between words, C. Partially spell consonant blends, and D. Use correct directionality of print.** This question requires an understanding of the roles of print awareness, phonics, and word recognition in learning reading fundamentals. Spaces between words and directionality of print (writing from left to right) are print concepts this student is demonstrating. The student's writing also demonstrates mastery of consonant blends, which are groups of consonants that appear together but are pronounced more or less individually. Choice (B) is incorrect because the student is not using vowels between consonants.

3. **C. a content map.** This question requires an understanding of ways to promote comprehension of a text. A content map is a visual representation of the major events or ideas in a text. Choice (A) is incorrect because a T-chart is more useful for helping students compare and contrast information or ideas. Choice (B) is incorrect because a K–W–L chart is more useful for helping students set a purpose for reading and what they've learned. Choice (D) is incorrect because a Venn diagram also helps students compare and contrast information or ideas.

4. **D. describe character motivations.** This question requires an understanding of ways to promote comprehension of a text. Understanding characters is an important skill for comprehending literature. Choice (A) is incorrect because although the question may seem like a detail, it is actually more closely related to understanding the characters. Choice (B) is incorrect because the teacher's question does not ask students about the events of the fable. Choice (C) is incorrect because although the question may contribute to an understanding of the fable's central lesson, it is more immediately useful in helping students understand the characters.

5. **A. personification.** This question requires an understanding of ways to promote comprehension of figurative language. *Personification* is figurative language that imparts human characteristics, such as speaking, to nonhuman objects or animals. Choice (B) is incorrect because *onomatopoeia* is figurative language that involves using words that sound similar to their meanings. Choices (C) and (D) are incorrect because *similes* and *metaphors* are figurative language used to make comparisons.

6. **B. context clues.** This question requires an understanding of basic components of vocabulary and strategies to determine the meaning of new words. *Context clues* are information from the surrounding words or other material that help students figure out the meaning of a word. Choice (A) is incorrect because a *word sort* is a method of categorizing known or unknown words. Choice (C) is incorrect because *structural analysis* involves looking at prefixes, suffixes, and word bases to determine a word's meaning. Choice (D) is incorrect because the teacher is not modeling using *reference materials,* such as a dictionary.

7. **A. prewriting.** This question requires an understanding of how to help students produce clear and coherent writing using the steps of the writing process. The students are discussing topics before beginning to write, which indicates that they are in the prewriting stage. Choice (B) is incorrect because the draft step involves writing the paper, a step beyond planning. Choice (C) is incorrect because the revision phase involves making changes to a complete or partial draft. Choice (D) is also incorrect because the publishing phase is the final step when students share their finished writing.

8. **D. portfolio review.** This question requires an understanding of how to assess students' writing progress. The teacher and student are reviewing a portfolio, Choice (D), of the student's writing, collected over time. Choice (A) is incorrect because the teacher is not observing the student during the process of writing. Choice (B) is incorrect because retelling is used to evaluate students' listening skills or comprehension. Choice (C) is incorrect because a running record is used to tally students' skills or mistakes as they read or speak aloud.

9. **A. use appropriate descriptive details, and C. speak clearly at an understandable pace.** This question requires an understanding of the skills necessary for speaking, listening, and presenting. Students should include appropriate descriptive details, Choice (A), and speak at an appropriate rate, Choice (C), in their presentations. Choice (B) is incorrect because although students do need to listen while others give their presentations, turn-taking is not a presentation skill that should be graded. Choice (D) is also incorrect because although students do need to listen while others give their presentations, they do not need to paraphrase others' presentations.

10. **D. following rules for taking turns speaking.** This question requires an understanding of the skills necessary for speaking, listening, and presenting. This group's structured discussions scaffold students' ability to take turns speaking and listening, Choice (D). Choice (A) is incorrect because the students were not described as paraphrasing or retelling using their own words from either the book or each other's comments. Choice (B) is incorrect because neither the leader nor the other group members are described as asking any questions. Choice (C) is incorrect because group members are giving their opinions rather than summarizing key ideas.

Mathematics practice questions

These practice questions are similar to the mathematics questions that you'll encounter on the Praxis Elementary Education: CIA test.

1. Mark is trying to multiply 11×14. Which of the following would be the best method for finding the product?

    (A) determining the greatest common factor of the two numbers

    (B) rounding both numbers to the nearest 10 and multiplying the resulting numbers

    (C) adding 11 14 times

    (D) writing one of the factors as the sum of 10 and a number and using the distributive property to multiply by the other factor

2. A teacher gives students a set of square tiles and asks them to make 3 rows of 7 tiles. She then has the students count the number of tiles. Which of the following concepts is the teacher helping the students understand?

    (A) volume

    (B) area

    (C) perimeter

    (D) squaring

3. Fred worked the three following fraction addition problems.

$$\frac{2}{7}+\frac{1}{7}=\frac{3}{14}$$

$$\frac{1}{8}+\frac{3}{8}=\frac{4}{16}=\frac{1}{4}$$

$$\frac{5}{9}+\frac{7}{9}=\frac{12}{18}=\frac{2}{3}$$

The strategy he used suggests that Fred needs instruction in which of the following areas?

(A) making common denominators the denominators of sums until sums are simplified

(B) simplifying fractions

(C) adding numerators

(D) adding denominators

4. A teacher plans to give her students an introductory lesson on using long division. Which of the following do the students need to have learned before the lesson?

(A) prime factorization

(B) properties of equality

(C) single-digit multiplication tables

(D) multiplying fractions

5. A teacher assessed the work of four students she asked to use two figures each to demonstrate a certain geometric concept. Each of the following sets of figures represents the work of the student whose name corresponds to the set. Three of the students correctly demonstrated the geometric concept, and one student did not. The student with the incorrect answer demonstrated which of the following?

Mark: Janet: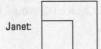

Alex:    Tim:

© John Wiley & Sons, Inc.

(A) reflection instead of dilation

(B) translation instead of reflection

(C) dilation instead of reflection

(D) translation instead of rotation

6. A student wrote the following equations in a class assignment. Which of the following does the student need to be retaught?

$$3(5 + 2) = 15 + 2 = 17$$

$$7(2 + 6) = 14 + 6 = 20$$

(A) the distributive property

(B) factoring

(C) exponents

(D) unit rates

7. The following figure was created by tiles that are 1 square unit each. Every student in a math class wrote an expression to represent the area of the figure. Which of the following student responses shows an incorrect understanding of area?

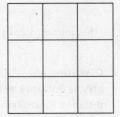

Select **all** that apply.

(A) $1 \cdot 9$

(B) $3 \cdot 3$

(C) $3 + 3 + 3 + 3$

(D) $12 - 3$

8. A teacher plans to introduce her class to the concept of factoring. Which of the following concepts do the students need to have been taught first?

(A) cubing

(B) common denominators

(C) multiplication

(D) associative property of addition

9. A teacher gives his students a list of all whole numbers from 1 to 50. He asks the students to circle the number 2 and then cross out all of the other even numbers. He then asks them to circle 3 and cross out all of its multiples in the list, and then to do the same thing for 5. The major concept the teacher is most likely teaching his students is which of the following?

(A) prime numbers

(B) even numbers

(C) factoring

(D) least common multiple

10. The following word problem is most likely designed to teach which of the following concepts?

A pie is divided into seven pieces of equal size. Johnny took one piece, and then he went back and took another piece. Then, he took his last piece. What portion of the pie did Johnny take?

(A) $1 - 4/7 = 3/7$

(B) Adding a fraction to itself is the same as subtracting its opposite.

(C) Some fractions can be expressed as whole numbers.

(D) $3/7 = 3$ of $1/7$

Answers to Mathematics practice questions

Use this answer key to score the practice mathematics questions in this chapter.

1. **D. writing one of the factors as the sum of 10 and a number and using the distributive property to multiply by the other factor.** Either factor can be written as the sum of 10 and another number. Multiplying this form by the other factor and using the distributive property involve multiplying the factor by 10, which simply involves putting a zero after the factor and multiplying the factor by the other number in the derived sum. That other number is a single-digit number, which is easier to multiply by than a two-digit number. The sum of the two resulting products is the correct answer to the student's problem.

$$11 \times 14 = 11(10+4)$$
$$= 11(10) + 11(4)$$
$$= 110 + 44$$
$$= 154$$

Choices (A) and (B) would not result in the correct product, though Choice (B) would be a good method for getting a broad estimate. Choice (C) would be much more tedious and time-consuming than Choice (D).

2. **B. area.** Each tile represents a square unit. Arranging the tiles with a certain number in each row for a number of rows demonstrates that the number of tiles in each row times the number of rows equals the total number of tiles, which is the number of square units in the area of the arrangement. Choice (A) is incorrect because the arrangement represents two dimensions and volume is three-dimensional, Choice (C) is incorrect because the number of tiles in the arrangement is not the same as the distance around it, and Choice (D) is incorrect because squaring is multiplying a number by itself.

3. **A. making common denominators the denominators of sums until sums are simplified.** Fred made the mistake of adding denominators instead of making the common denominator the denominator of the sum, until sum simplification, in each problem. Choice (B) is incorrect because Fred showed that he could simplify fractions. Choice (C) is incorrect because Fred correctly added numerators. Choice (D) is incorrect because adding fractions does not involve adding denominators.

4. **C. single-digit multiplication tables.** Introductory long division involves multiplying single-digit numbers, and students need to know all of the two single-digit products to correctly engage in the long division process, even at the initial level. Choices (A), (B), and (D) are not involved in the long division process.

5. **A. reflection instead of dilation.** *Reflection* involves a figure's transformation to a position in which it forms the reverse image of its original position in relation to a line. The line does not have to be illustrated. *Dilation* involves a figure's transformation to a similar figure of a different size. Alex demonstrated reflection, while the other three students demonstrated dilation.

6. **A. the distributive property.** Correct application of the distributive property gives the correct values in both cases. Both equations show that the student understands part of the distributive property, but they show that he thinks the outside number is supposed to be multiplied by only the first inside number and that the second inside number is supposed to be added instead of the product of it and the outside number. Choice (B) is incorrect because although the mere multiplication of quantities involves factors, it is not the process of factoring. Choice (C) is incorrect because exponents are not used at all in the equations. Choice (D) is incorrect because neither units nor rates are presented by the equations.

7. **C. 3 + 3 + 3 + 3 and D. 12 − 3.** Choice (C) shows an incorrect understanding of area because the area of the figure formed by the tiles is 9, not 12. It is 3 by 3, not 3 by 4. Choice (D) is incorrect, although its value is the area of the figure. That is because 12 is not relevant to the calculation of the area of the figure. Choice (A) is a true representation of the area of the figure, in terms of both value and principle, so Choice (A) is not a correct answer to the question. Choice (B) is another correct representation of the basis for the area of the figure because the figure is 9 tiles that are 1 square unit each.

8. **C. multiplication.** The concept of factoring is about what whole numbers multiply by each other to get other whole numbers. It is a multiplication principle. Without an understanding of multiplication, factoring cannot be understood. Choice (A) can be part of factoring but does not have to be. Factoring can be comprehended without knowledge of cubing. Choice (B) is a concept that can entail factoring, but understanding factoring does not depend on knowledge of common denominators. Choice (D) is incorrect because the associative property of addition is about adding numbers in different grouping arrangements, and that concept is not an automatic component of factoring.

9. **A. prime numbers.** The two numbers that are circled are both prime. Beyond that, numbers the process is designed to eliminate are composite numbers. Multiples of whole numbers other than 1 cannot possibly be prime, by definition. Choice (B) is incorrect because the exercise creates the elimination of both even and odd numbers, and 2 is an even number that is circled. Choice (C) is incorrect because, although factors are multiplied, factoring does not take place. Choice (D) is not correct because the process does not involve identification of common multiples at all.

10. **D. 3/7 = 3 of 1/7.** The story is about 1/7 being taken 3 times, resulting in 3/7 of the pie being taken. The problem illustrates that those expressions are the same. Choice (A) is a true equation that is shown by the story in the problem, but it is not the focus. The remaining 4/7 of the pie is not mentioned in the problem or even referred to indirectly. Choices (B) and (C) are not at all suggested by the story.

Science practice questions

These practice questions are similar to the science questions that you'll encounter on the Praxis Elementary Education: CIA test.

1. For a science fair project that explores the question, "Which type of fertilizer works best to grow plants?", the independent variable would be:

   (A) growth of the plant measured by height.

   (B) using different amounts of water.

   (C) growth of the plant measured by the number of leaves.

   (D) using different types of fertilizer.

2. When teaching a unit on habitats, the teacher wants to show why certain animals are better suited for a particular climate or type of vegetation. To be proficient in this unit, the student would need to have a grasp of all of the following EXCEPT which of the following?

   (A) knows about the diversity and unity that characterizes life

   (B) understands how species depend on one another and on the environment for survival

   (C) understands the stages of development of a butterfly

   (D) understands the characteristics of ecosystems on Earth's surface

3. In studying the structure and function of living systems, which of the following shows a higher level of understanding on the part of the student?

   (A) The student describes interdependence of one system on another.

   (B) The student identifies and describes each body system.

   (C) The student identifies each system and labels parts.

   (D) The student is able to sketch blood flow into and out of the heart from memory.

4. Which of the following does NOT show differentiation of instruction in the science classroom?

   (A) allowing students to work in groups to answer sample questions

   (B) incorporating labs to make sure tactile learners connect concepts

   (C) using the approved textbook and assigning homework from it each night

   (D) reteaching/remediation for those students who did not pass the last assessment

5. Which of the following is the order of the process of scientific inquiry?

   (A) design, test, research, communicate

   (B) communicate, design, research, test

   (C) research, design, test, communicate

   (D) design, research, communicate, test

Answers to Science practice questions

Here are the answers to the science practice questions in the preceding section.

1. **D. using different types of fertilizer.** The independent variable is the variable that the experimenter changes to test the dependent variable. The effect on the dependent variable is measured and recorded. In this case, what the experimenter is changing is the type of fertilizer, Choice (D). Choice (A) is wrong because it is actually the dependent variable, the entity that would be affected by the type of fertilizer. Choice (B) is wrong because the effect water has on growth is not being tested. Water amount would actually be a constant in the particular experiment. Choice (C) is wrong because the number of leaves is not a measure of its growth. Although the health and number of the leaves can be an indication of the strength of the fertilizer, it is not the tested variable in this case.

2. **C. understands the stages of development of a butterfly.** This is the correct answer because it is the only one that contains information that the student would NOT need in discussing habitats. Choices (A), (B), and (D) are all necessary because the student must understand the characteristics of life, how species depend on the environment for survival, and the main characteristics of each ecosystem. Therefore, they are incorrect for this question.

3. **A. The student describes interdependence of one system on another.** This concept requires the student to combine several objectives to grasp its importance and thus has the highest understanding of the options given. It involves the understanding of the structure and function of each system and then how they interrelate to maintain a healthy organism. Choice (B) requires less understanding than (A); it involves the structure and function of body systems. Choice (C) only involves identification of the systems and their parts. Choice (D) is wrong because it asks about a specific organ, the heart, and thus involves very limited understanding.

4. **C. using the approved textbook and assigning homework from it each night.** Choice (C) is correct because it is the only one that does NOT show differentiation. *Differentiation* is a model of teaching that incorporates more than one type of learning strategy during instruction. This model takes into consideration varied races, cultures, genders, and learning styles. Choice (A) is not correct because working in groups is a way students learn in a differentiated setting. Choice (B) is not correct because making sure tactile/kinesthetic learners get hands-on experience is important in this classroom. Choice (D) is not correct because it makes sure that the students who did not adequately grasp the material are not left behind.

5. **C. research, design, test, communicate.** Choice (C) is correct because in scientific inquiry it is necessary to research the topic you want to explore first. You must then decide which aspect of that topic you want to test. After proposing a hypothesis or educated guess about what you expect the outcome of your experiment to be, you then test it. Finally, the results of that test are communicated with peers in the scientific community. Choices (A), (B), and (D) have these headings in an incorrect order.

Social Studies practice questions

These practice questions are similar to the social studies questions that you'll encounter on the Praxis Elementary Education: CIA test.

1. A third-grade class is exploring a unit on the Land and People Before Columbus. Which of the following would be most effective in understanding gender roles and family life among tribes?

   (A) working in groups to build a teepee and clay models of each family member

   (B) using concept maps to outline daily activities and chores for each member of the family

   (C) reading a book on the interactions between the Cherokee Indians and early European explorers

   (D) watching *Pocahontas* and writing a one-page essay on her role in the tribe

2. A second-grade social studies teacher has the objective of examining civic responsibility in the community. Which of the following will best help her get that point across to the students?

   (A) explaining the various cultural heritages within their community

   (B) using a map to locate and label their city and major landmarks

   (C) explaining why schools have rules and the importance of each leader in their school

   (D) identifying and participating in a local civic activity, such as recycling or a walkathon

3. A fifth-grade teacher is presenting a unit on the five themes of geography. The class is exploring the concept of ecology. Which of the following themes would that concept fall under?

   (A) location

   (B) human interaction with the environment

   (C) movement and connections

   (D) regions, processes, and patterns

4. A social studies class is reviewing the Civil War and its effect on the South. The teacher has given them a project where they can only use primary sources to find information. Which of the following could they use? Check **all** that apply.

   (A) diaries

   (B) encyclopedias

   (C) letters

   (D) biographies

5. A sixth-grade teacher wants to make sure his students are able to integrate knowledge and ideas in their understanding of an article on how a bill becomes a law. Which of the following would show him that the students are able to do that?

   (A) distinguishing among fact, opinion, and reasoned judgment in the article

   (B) describing how a passage on the topic presents its information (sequentially, comparatively, and so forth)

   (C) determining the meaning of words and phrases in the article

   (D) identifying the steps of how a bill becomes a law

Answers to Social Studies practice questions

Use this answer key to score the practice social studies questions in this chapter.

1. **B. using concept maps to outline daily activities and chores for each member of the family.** Using concept maps to divide the responsibilities of men, women, and children will help students understand the expectations of the tribes. Choice (A) is not correct because although hands-on, group projects are a great instructional tool, in this case, such a project wouldn't bring to life the significance of the roles the family members play. Choice (C) is not correct because interactions between Indians and explorers may not provide detail regarding gender roles and family life. Choice (D) is not correct because although the movie can be shown at the end of the unit for pleasure or reinforcement, it can't be depended upon to give an accurate depiction of the era.

2. **D. identifying and participating in a local civic activity, such as recycling or a walkathon.** Participating in a local community activity helps the students see the importance of each citizen and his responsibility to make that community thrive. Choice (A) is not correct because being able to explore the various cultural heritages does not give the students a sense of their responsibility. Choice (B), locating their city on a map, while useful, wouldn't give the students a sense of community. Choice (C) is not correct because it would involve a different unit of study, whereby students would understand how each student, faculty, or staff member has a vital role in the school.

3. **B. human interaction with the environment.** The theme of human interaction with the environment includes how human beings make use of, change, and are limited by the environment, including ecology. Choice (A) is not correct because it involves the absolute versus relative location. Choice (C) is not correct because it includes how transportation and communication connect people all over the world and how these connections have grown and changed. Choice (D) is not correct because it includes the variations in the economy, climate, politics, and culture within specific regions, including sociology, politics, and economics.

4. **A. diaries and C. letters.** *Primary sources* are those written in the historical period being studied or by the historical figure being studied. Diaries and letters would have been written during that time period. Choice (B) is not correct because it would have been written about the period, as a secondary source. Choice (D) is not correct because it would have been written by someone else, making it a secondary source also.

5. **A. distinguishing among fact, opinion, and reasoned judgment in the article.** Distinguishing among fact, opinion, and reasoned judgment allows for connecting several ideas. The students would have to decipher through context clues and identify what information sounded true based on factual evidence versus that which is merely a statement of opinion. Choice (B) is not correct because how a text is organized is an understanding of structure and does not involve integration. Choice (C) is not correct because determining the meaning of words and phrases only involves vocabulary in context and not an integration of ideas. Choice (D) is not correct because identification of steps only requires a basic level of skill and is not, generally speaking, a multilevel task.

Art, Music, and Physical Education practice questions

These practice questions are similar to the art, music, and physical education questions that you'll encounter on the Praxis Elementary Education: CIA test.

Art

1. For a class art project, David created an oil painting that involves heavy use of juxta-positions and bizarre, dream-like imagery. In which of the following genres of art can David's painting best be classified?

   (A) abstract expressionism

   (B) pointillism

   (C) surrealism

   (D) realism

2. A teacher wants to increase her students' understanding of the impressionist art movement of the 1800s. Which of the following instructions would be most effective toward achieving that goal?

   (A) Sprinkle paint drops on a spinning board.

   (B) Paint living room scenery with as much detail as possible.

   (C) Use blocks of varying sizes to create abstract designs.

   (D) Open your eyes and immediately shut them as you face an object and its surroundings, and then paint the visual image you had of the scenery.

3. During which era of art history did Michelangelo create his famous works?

   (A) Italian Renaissance

   (B) neoclassical

   (C) romantic

   (D) modern

Music

1. Melody bells and simple flutes fall into the category of

   (A) orchestral instruments.

   (B) rhythmic instruments.

   (C) melodic instruments.

   (D) harmonic instruments.

2. The spirit of humanism and rationalism pervaded polyphonic music and music began to be seen as a mark of culture during which era?

   (A) Renaissance

   (B) early Christian

   (C) later Middle Ages

   (D) 17th and early 18th centuries

3. Which activities would show how music would be beneficial in exploring other cultures?
   Select **all** that apply.

   (A) having students recite the words to "America the Beautiful"

   (B) having students listen to music from China as they study the culture of the country

   (C) having students view live or videotaped performances of the music and dance of various cultures using traditional costumes and instruments

   (D) having students listen to pop-culture music during a social studies lesson

Physical education

1. Body management in the area of physical education includes all of the following EXCEPT

   (A) body parts.

   (B) sportsmanship.

   (C) concept of directions.

   (D) extensions in space.

2. In which of the following physical education curricula do the students learn about outdoor recreation safety and development of life-long interests?

   (A) movement education

   (B) social-developmental model

   (C) sports-education model

   (D) adventure-education approach

3. Which of the following activities would be most developmentally appropriate for a first-grade student?

   (A) dodgeball

   (B) basketball

   (C) soccer

   (D) tennis

Answers to Art, Music, and Physical Education practice questions

Use this answer key to score the art, music, and physical education questions in this chapter.

Art

1. **C. surrealism.** Surrealist art involves heavy use of *juxtapositions*—concepts that have very little to do with each other and are typically not found together in reality—and imagery that is bizarre and dream-like. Choice (A) does not typically involve a strong degree of realistic imagery to be dream-like or involve juxtapositions. Choice (B) is defined by the method involved in creating the art and not what it depicts. Although pointillist art could possibly be surreal, it generally is not, and it is not characterized by surrealist qualities. Choice (D) does not fit the description because realism is about depictions of actual reality and not concepts of the unreal.

2. **D. Open your eyes and immediately shut them as you face an object and its surroundings, and then paint the visual image you had of the scenery.** This instruction would lead students to create art that lacks detail but still realistically focuses on colors and outlines of objects. Those are the main defining characteristics of impressionism. Choices (A) and (C) would lack the level of realistic depiction necessary for impressionist art, and Choice (B) would tend to result in too much detail.

3. **A. Italian Renaissance.** Michelangelo was the premier painter and sculptor of the Italian Renaissance. He did not create art during any of the other periods that are listed as choices.

Music

1. **C. Melodic instruments.** These are instruments that bring melody to a selection. The definitions for the others are as follows: *Orchestral instruments,* Choice (A), are those found in an orchestra falling under the categories of brass, woodwinds, percussion, and so on. *Rhythmic instruments,* Choice (B), in an elementary classroom are triangles, tambourines, blocks, and sticks. *Harmonic instruments,* Choice (D), are chording instruments like the autoharp.

2. **A. Renaissance.** Music was a part of the evolution taking place in society at that time, so it involved the same theme of humanism and rational thought characteristic of that era. Choice (B) is incorrect because plain song and unaccompanied religious chant were important during the early Christian era. Choice (C) is incorrect because religious and secular polyphonic music were composed throughout the later Middle Ages. Choice (D) is incorrect because Baroque music categorized the 17th and early 18th centuries.

3. **B. having students listen to music from China as they study the culture of the country, and C. having students view live or videotaped performances of the music and dance of various cultures using traditional costumes and instruments.** Exposing the students to music from other cultures either through listening or watching enhances their learning experience. Choice (A) is incorrect because reciting lyrics to an American song does not assist students in learning about other cultures. Choice (D) is incorrect because it is not adequate in building on students' cultural experience.

Physical education

1. **B. sportsmanship.** Body management focuses on the ability of an individual to control his or her physical self, personal movements, spatial conditions, and body-space relationships. These are included in Choices (A), (C), and (D).

2. **D. adventure-education approach.** In adventure-education, students explore a wide variety of outdoor recreational pursuits and learn about the career opportunities available in this field. Choice (A) is incorrect because in movement education, the focus is literally on the basic aspects of human body movement and how it can be incorporated into many aspects of the educational process. Choice (B) is incorrect because the social-developmental model guides students through personal growth and social skills. Choice (C) is incorrect because the sports-education model helps students build knowledge about sports and seasons.

3. **A. dodgeball.** Developmentally appropriate activities for students in grades 1 to 3 involve them throwing a ball because they're better at throwing than catching. Dodgeball is the best choice over basketball, Choice (B); soccer, Choice (C); or tennis, Choice (D); which require more skill and involve more rules.

Analyzing Your Practice Question Results

If you just finished taking the practice test and reviewing your results, you have come to the right place. Your results are a good indicator of what you need to study the most. If you missed some questions, let that become a strength. Incorrect answers tell you what you need to do now to get prepared for the big test. In fact, future practice questions will give indications of where you are at any stage of the preparation process. For now, you are still in the early part of the game, and this is just the first round.

Identifying what you missed

The areas where you struggled the most are most likely the areas where you need to study the most. To get a really precise idea of where you need to put the most focus, you can make an outline based on your results. Write brief descriptions of what you missed and look for patterns. Look for categories within categories, and then look for specific problem areas within those categories. The table of contents for this book can help you identify the specific names of the categories and the divisions within them. You can create a category called "Other" for areas that do not seem to fit into any of the other categories.

You can also look into the subject-area chapters and find category patterns. For example, Chapter 11 is about mathematics curriculum, instruction, and assessment. The instruction part of the chapter gives details on many approaches to teaching elementary-level mathematics. The instruction principles and methods discussed in the chapter are divided into the categories of numbers and operations, algebra, geometry and measurement, and statistics and probability. Each of those categories has smaller categories within it. For example, the geometry and measurement section has a part about having students create diagrams to understand definitions, similarities, and differences among geometric shapes. Also within the category of geometric shapes is the smaller category of the major types of polygons that include parallelograms and an explanation of how one type of parallelogram is a rectangle and one type of rectangle is a square. The system is complex, and you can look through it to determine very specific areas to which you need to give extra focus.

After you identify the areas you need to focus on, look at which of your answers were incorrect. You may not have had any, but that is rare at this stage. If you did have wrong answers, contrast them with the right answers and work to understand why you did not get the correct answers.

Analyzing how to get the right answers can also help you. It can allow you to see areas where you can become strong and increase your ability to understand key components of your areas of weakness. It can also help you identify wrong answer choices so you can mark them out and have a greater chance of getting the right answers.

Determining the why of what you missed

We just mentioned the need to understand why you missed certain questions on your practice test. Now, we are going to further explain the importance of this issue.

When you identify your wrong answer choices, you can ask yourself important questions like the following ones:

>> Did I make simple errors?

>> Do I lack in-depth knowledge of a particular subject?

>> Was my answer incorrect because I lacked focus while answering it?

>> Did I confuse my answer with something else?

>> Is there a strategy that I could have used that would have made the difference?

Think about those questions and ones like them and make a list of your answers. Keep those answers in mind as you study, in order to gain the knowledge, skills, and test-taking strategies necessary to succeed on the real test.

Something else you can do is look for patterns in the reasons for your wrong answers. If you can find patterns, you can be more mindful of your mistakes. For math questions in particular, it is very often helpful to look at any work you may have done in your effort to get right answers. On the real test, you have to apply math knowledge to teaching strategies, and knowledge of math content is the foundation of the answers to the questions. Because of that, you are likely to work out some problems while taking practice tests and are very likely to have done so when you answered practice questions earlier. If you did, your work can tell you further details about where you need to improve. As you improve your math knowledge and skills, your ability to do that will grow.

With the other subject-area questions, perhaps mostly with those in the social studies category, people often have easily correctable tendencies that can lead to wrong answers. For example, you may choose an answer simply because it has big words in it, which gives you the impression that the answer is a good one and the right one. Keep in mind that big words can be wrong words. You may be drawn to answer choices that say interesting things or sound optimistic. The bias involved in such circumstances can give false attractiveness to answers. It is also possible to give up on a question too soon without realizing it because a question seems especially difficult. That is most likely when you remember the advice that you should pick Choice (C) when in doubt. That view can somewhat draw you to select Choice (C) when you have not yet fully evaluated and eliminated any of the other answer choices. Giving up too soon can lead to preventable incorrectness.

Test-prep teachers and tutors have an old saying: "I can tell you how to get a question right, but only you can tell yourself why you got one wrong." Well, okay, maybe it's not an old saying. It's from another *For Dummies* Praxis prep book we wrote. Technically, it will eventually be an old saying. For the remainder of this book, your goal is to build content and develop strategies that will improve your performance on the Praxis Elementary Education: CIA exam.

IN THIS CHAPTER

Finding out what's on the Praxis

Seeing how the Praxis is scored

Trying some sample Praxis questions

Seeing which of your answers are correct and which are incorrect

Chapter 2

The Praxis Elementary Education: Content Knowledge Test (5018)

The Praxis Elementary Education: Content Knowledge (5018) exam is the most recent version of the teacher-candidate certification test. It assesses your grasp of the knowledge and analysis necessary for teaching English language arts, mathematics, science, and social studies.

Perhaps you've already taken a Praxis Core exam in order to enter a teaching program at a college or university. Further challenges lie ahead! Your path to certification will most likely include more Praxis exams.

Many states use the Praxis Core and/or one or more Praxis subject exams as certification tests to show that you've mastered the knowledge and application needed to be a highly competent teacher. Praxis Elementary Education: Content Knowledge is one of the subject area tests. Luckily, you have this book to help you make this exam a mile-marker instead of a danger sign. With this chapter, you'll be able to review the information needed to prepare for the exam.

TIP

Almost every state in the country uses some form of the Praxis. Contact your state department of education for specific licensure details.

Analyzing the Format of the Test

The newly developed Praxis Elementary Education: Content Knowledge exam uses 140 questions to evaluate your understanding, application, analysis, and evaluation in four subject-area groups:

>> Reading and Language Arts

>> Mathematics

>> Science

>> Social Studies

To date, the 140 questions are selected-response type questions as well as numeric-entry. At least for some, you'll be provided with a calculator!

It's important to become familiar with the use of the on-screen scientific calculator. Visit the Praxis Calculator Use web page and view the tutorial.

The topics the test covers

According to the Educational Testing Service (ETS), the 140 questions of the Praxis Elementary Education: Content Knowledge exam are divided among four subject-area groups according to the proportions you see in Table 2-1.

TABLE 2-1 **Breakdown of Praxis Elementary Education: Content Knowledge**

Test Subject	Approximate Number of Questions	Approximate Percentage of the Exam
Reading and language arts	49	35%
Mathematics	41	29%
Science	25	18%
Social studies	25	18%

The questions are in sync with state and national standards for English Language Arts and Mathematics, as well as with the content standards for science and social studies.

Students have 150 minutes to complete 140 questions. For timing and other test-taking strategies, review Chapter 3.

Reading and language arts

The topics addressed by questions in the reading and language arts section reflect the framework of state and national standards for language arts. You'll see questions about these topics:

>> **Reading foundational skills:** These questions test your grasp of how each of the following play an important role in literary development: phonological awareness, phonics and word-analysis skills, and fluency.

>> **Reading literature and informational texts:** These questions test your ability to use key details to analyze literature and informational texts; identify and analyze text features and structures; evaluate point of view; analyze a text's claims and evidence; integrate and compare texts and different formats; and understand text complexity and appropriately leveled texts.

- **Writing:** These questions test your ability to grasp the characteristics and purposes of different types of writing; understand the effectiveness of different structures and styles; understand the importance of revisions; recognize the developmental stages and grade-appropriate continuum of writing; identify factors and tools involved in digitally producing and sharing writing; and understand the research process.

- **Language:** These questions require you to show your knowledge of the conventions of English grammar and usage; arrive at the meaning of unknown words and phrases and of figurative language; and distinguish between conversational, academic, and domain-specific language.

- **Speaking and listening:** These questions test your knowledge of how to develop active listening skills, oral presentation speaking and listening skills, and skills in using multimedia in presentations.

Reading and Language arts content is reviewed in depth in Chapter 4.

Mathematics

The topics addressed in the math section also reflect state and national standards:

- **Numbers and operations:** These questions test your knowledge of the place value system, operations and properties of rational numbers, ratio and percent, number theory, and reasonableness of results.

- **Algebraic thinking:** These questions test your knowledge of expressions, equations, and formulas; linear equations and inequalities; and patterns.

- **Geometry and measurement:** These questions test your understanding of one-, two-, and three-dimensional figures; coordinate planes; nets, area, perimeter, and volume; and measurement.

- **Data, statistics, and probability:** These questions test your grasp of statistical concepts; ability to present and interpret data; and understanding of probability.

Mathematics content is reviewed in greater detail in Chapter 5

Science

In the science section of the exam, you'll see questions involving the following topics:

- **Science concepts, inquiry, and processes:** These questions test your knowledge of scientific inquiry, including the role of hypotheses, models, variables, and evidence; different means of measurement; presentation, understanding, and interpretation of data; and how to be safety-conscious as well as safety-prepared.

- **Life science:** These questions test your knowledge of the structure and function of plant and animal organs and systems, from cells to reproduction and life cycles; hierarchical classifications and characteristics of groups of organisms, including amphibians and reptiles; factors of evolution and genetics; and basics of ecology and ecosystems.

- **Earth and space science:** These questions test your knowledge of Earth's geology, including rocks, erosion, soil, plate tectonics, and fossils; Earth's hydrosphere and atmosphere, including the water cycle, oceans and tides, and weather and climate; and astronomy, including aspects of the solar system, the Moon, and the universe.

» **Physical science:** These questions test your knowledge of matter's structure and properties, from atoms and the periodic table to mixtures and solutions; relationships between matter and energy and what happens to each when changes are involved, including heat transfer and changes in states of matter; fundamentals of chemical reactions, from covalent bonds to combustion; and fundamentals of magnetism, electricity, and waves.

» **Science and technology in society:** These questions test your understanding of the effects of using different energy sources; approaches to pollution, conservation, and recycling; and impacts of science in health, including advances in technology, agriculture, medicine, and nutrition.

Science content is explored in Chapter 6.

Social studies

In the social studies section of the exam, you'll see questions about these topics:

» **Information processing skills:** These questions test your knowledge of primary and secondary sources as well as gathering and evaluating data; differences between fact and opinion; types of information; and how to select and use appropriate materials and equipment.

» **Geography:** These questions test your knowledge of features and patterns of places and regions around the world as well as the concepts and uses of location (such as coordinates and map-reading).

» **History:** These questions test your grasp of cause and effect in world history, from contributions of ancient civilizations, to significant matters of the twentieth century, to the nature of instruction relative to culture; and in U.S. history, from European explorers and Native cultures through the growth, founding, and development of the country to recent economic and technical developments.

» **Government, civics, and economics:** These questions test your knowledge of basic economic concepts, such as supply and demand, as well as governments' roles in economics; different forms and functions of governments; important documents and speeches in U.S. history; and the rights and responsibilities of citizenship.

» **Anthropology and sociology:** These questions test your knowledge of human systems, how groups and individuals are affected by conditions and events; the interconnectedness of humans and their physical environment; and how people from different cultures interact with their physical and social environments.

Social Studies content is reviewed in Chapter 7.

The types of questions asked

Praxis Elementary Education: Content Knowledge is composed of selected-response and numeric-entry questions. Selected-response are also known as multiple-choice questions. You don't have to write any essays or even short answers. You've probably been answering multiple-choice questions since you were old enough to wield a No. 2 pencil on your first standardized test. So you may think you know all there is to know about them. But Praxis puts new twists on a few of these old favorites in two ways: first, by changing the numbers of correct answers, and second, by varying the type of response you need to make. It's not all just clicking the correct ovals.

Number of correct answers

A huge majority of the questions on this exam have a single correct answer. The remainder have more than one correct answer. Occasionally, questions with more than one correct answer specify how many answers you should pick, but far more often, this type of question doesn't tell you how many of the choices are correct. The following sections take a closer look.

SINGLE CORRECT RESPONSE

You can think of these as the basic, no-frills model of the multiple-choice question. They have one and only one correct answer. On the Praxis, the question typically includes an instruction to remind you that the question has only one correct answer, such as, "Answer the question by clicking the correct response."

TIP

ETS suggests an effective approach for answering multiple-choice questions that have a single answer. Eliminate any answers you know are incorrect to narrow down the choices before picking a possible answer. Then, try out your preliminary answer by referring back to the question. For example, suppose a question shows a student-generated graph that is supposed to plot the student's answers to several equations. Does it make sense to say that giving the student extra instruction about the horizontal and vertical axes of a graph would address the misunderstanding shown in the student's work sample? If not, eliminate that option and decipher the remaining choices similarly until you find the one that fits.

MORE THAN ONE CORRECT RESPONSE

This souped-up version of a multiple-choice question has two or more correct answers, instead of just one. A few of these will helpfully tell you the number of correct answers, often emphasized in capital or boldfaced letters. For example, you might find a question like this accompanying an example of a paragraph a student is supposed to peer edit: "Which TWO types of errors can a peer editor find in this paragraph?"

TIP

To get points for answering a question that tells you the number of correct answers, following the instructions is essential. Click the specified number of answers, whether it is two answers, three answers, or some other number.

Most of the time, however, the question does not tell you how many correct responses to choose. One of these may look like a no-frills multiple-choice question at first glance, but then you may notice the instruction, "Click on your choices." How many choices? Well, that's up to you. Maybe the question only has one correct answer. Maybe it has two or three. It's possible that every single option is correct.

TIP

When a question tells you to "Click on your choices" but does not tell you how many choices are correct, you need to examine each answer option individually and decide whether or not it is correct.

Different types of answers

The vast majority of items on the official Praxis practice test and the actual test itself are the multiple-choice format you're probably most familiar with. You read the question and click on the oval next to the correct answer choice (or choices). However, you may also encounter items that ask you to indicate your choice in some other fashion. Sometimes, the difference may be subtle; you may be asked to click the boxes, rather than the ovals, beside all the correct answers, or you may choose your answer from a drop-down menu of choices. Other times, the task will look quite different from what you see in a standard multiple-choice question. You may be asked to:

>> **Choose an answer by clicking on a part of a graphic.** For example, a question might instruct you to click on a part of a map to indicate where you would direct your students' attention during a lesson on interpreting the scale of a map.

>> **Select a sentence from a passage.** For example, a question may ask you to click on the sentence from a student's opinion paragraph that indicates whether or not the student has supported his opinion with evidence.

>> **Drag answer choices into the correct spots in a table or list.** For example, you might be asked to drag several examples of student writing into a table to show which example indicates that a student needs practice in a particular reading skill.

In the practice tests both in this book and online, you'll find many examples of various multiple-choice questions with varying numbers of answers. Taking all of our practice tests will give you a consistent feel of what you will see on the actual test so that you'll have a chance to refine your own personal strategy for nailing the answers every time.

Numeric-entry questions

These questions require you to type in the number that answers the question. You will have access to the on-screen scientific calculator. Even if you've used one in the past, you'll probably want to refresh your skills.

How the Test Is Scored

Praxis Elementary Education: Content Knowledge is divided into four sections, each focused on a specific subject area (or on a group of subjects) that you're likely to teach: reading and language arts; mathematics; science; and social studies. When you receive your score report, you will see a breakdown of raw points for each section and a total score. The total score is calculated from your raw points and adjusted to a scale that ranges from 100 to 200 points.

Earning your raw score

Your raw score is based on the number of questions you answer correctly. ETS points out in its preparation materials that your test may contain some questions that do not count toward your score. "Which questions?" you ask. Well, if they told you that, you probably wouldn't bother answering them, would you? Nope, and that's why they don't tell you. You need to try and answer every single question on your exam.

TIP

You don't lose any points for answering a question incorrectly. If you were to answer every single question incorrectly, your raw score would be 0, which is exactly what it would be if you didn't answer any questions at all. That's why you have nothing to lose by guessing if you don't know the answer to a question.

Making sense of your score

The number that may interest you the most when you get your score report is your final score, which ETS simply calls "your score." Your score determines whether or not you pass the test. No wonder it gets so much attention!

Your score will be a number from 100 to 200. It is calculated by taking your raw points—which are based on the number of questions you answer correctly—and comparing them to the number of questions on the test. This conversion of your raw points to your total score also adapts to the level of rigor of that particular testing edition.

To achieve a total score that is considered passing by most states, you must answer at least 60 percent of the questions correctly. This gives you a benchmark to measure yourself against as you go through the practice tests in this book or online.

TIP

If you fail the Praxis the first time you take it (or if you've already failed it), you can look at your scores for each content category to see where you did well and where you struggled. Use those scores to help you target what to study most before you take the exam again.

Remember, though, that each state that requires passing the exam has its own minimum score. What constitutes a passing score in one state may not be a passing score in another state. Contact your state or local department of education for the minimum passing score.

Getting Started on Taking the Test

In a moment, this chapter will lead you to some practice questions that will give you a basic idea of what to expect on the Praxis II Elementary Education: Content Knowledge test. This is an ideal time for you to begin studying actual test material.

Because the practice questions that are coming right up will prepare you for the practice questions later in the book, what you are really about to do is practice for practice. You can use these first sets of practice results to help you determine what you need to focus on in the rest of your preparation. You might realize that you have a firm grasp on math but know very little about science content or perhaps that you need to focus on learning social studies content knowledge. However, no matter what you realize from looking at your practice question results, you should thoroughly study all areas to achieve the best possible real test score.

Although the big test you are preparing for is timed, we do not recommend timing yourself when you try the practice questions in this chapter. You should first learn to do something well before you learn to do it fast.

Because time will not be a factor for these questions, you don't need to worry about timing techniques. Pace yourself and do your best to answer every question. Keep in mind that leaving exam questions blank does not benefit you. On the test you are preparing for, there is no penalty for guessing and getting a wrong answer, aside from not getting the points a right answer would have gotten you.

We also encourage you not to check your answers as you go through these practice questions. Knowing for sure that you missed several questions in a row can be discouraging and tempt you to give up too easily. Perhaps, knowing that you are on a roll at this stage can make you worry about jinxing your winning streak. Plus, when you look up one answer, you can easily see the other ones. That makes the practice less of a practice.

Okay, here are the questions. Good luck!

Reading and Language Arts practice questions

These practice questions are similar to the reading and language arts questions that you'll encounter on the Praxis Elementary Education: Content Knowledge test.

1. For a general category, a teacher is tracking her students' progress in three specific areas: the number of mistakes made when reading, the number of times students slow down to decode or sound-out a word, and how much meaning students give when reading words. What is the general category the teacher is concerned with?

(A) segmentation

(B) error-frequency rate

(C) running record

(D) fluency

2. When shown the word *cat*, a student can say the sounds /k/, /æ/, and /t/. What, specifically, is the student demonstrating?

(A) context clues

(B) phonological awareness

(C) phonemic awareness

(D) comprehension

3. On the first day of school, a teacher asked her students to write the following sentence, which she read out loud: "Some day I want to go to the moon." One student wrote, "Sow bay I mant fo og teh noom." Judging from this one sample, the student may be

(A) better off with a different teacher.

(B) an English Language Learner (ELL).

(C) dyslexic.

(D) lazy.

4. **Questions 4–6 are based on the following poem. Answer each question by choosing the correct response.**

Easter Wings
By George Herbert

Lord, who createdst man in wealth and store,
　Though foolishly he lost the same,
　　Decaying more and more,
　　　Till he became
　　　　Most poore:
　　　　With thee
　　　O let me rise
　　As larks, harmoniously,

And sing this day thy victories:
Then shall the fall further the flight in me.

My tender age in sorrow did beginne
　And still with sicknesses and shame.
　　Thou didst so punish sinne,
　　　That I became
　　　　Most thinne.
　　　　With thee
　　　Let me combine,
　　And feel thy victorie:
　For, if I imp my wing on thine,
Affliction shall advance the flight in me.

"Easter Wings" is an example of which kind of poetry?

(A) argumentative

(B) concrete

(C) narrative

(D) imagistic

5. What is the meaning of the word "imp" in the second-to-last line?

(A) attach

(B) mimic

(C) lower

(D) redesign

6. In each of the poem's two "wings," the lines go from long to short to long again. How do the line lengths specifically reinforce the poem's meaning?

(A) The pattern of the poem strengthens the meaning that wings have to beat in order for there to be flight.

(B) The pattern of the poem strengthens what can be interpreted from the meaning of the lines in both stanzas.

(C) Each stanza is in the shape of a wing, and the lines describe what the wings are made of.

(D) Each stanza traces a fall, a steady loss, until hardly anything is left of the poet, and then a rise as the poet turns to his faith.

7. Questions 7 and 8 are based on the following introduction from a student's draft:

There are many reasons that led the workers to go on strike. But how many knew they'd end up in jail?

The most likely organizational pattern of this essay is

(A) problem and solution.

(B) cause and effect.

(C) comparison and contrast.

(D) order of importance.

8. When the student goes to revise the draft, which of the following will be a necessary change?

(A) change a pronoun from masculine to feminine

(B) change a verb from plural to singular

(C) change a pronoun from plural to singular

(D) change a verb from present tense to past

9. A few students in a class of 3rd graders are reading a 4th-grade text about a subject they're very familiar with. Which strategies will the teacher most likely use to make sure the students comprehend the material?

Select **all** that apply.

(A) scaffolding

(B) the alphabetic principle

(C) K–W–L

(D) shared reading

10. All of the following are active listening skills EXCEPT

(A) focusing on the speaker.

(B) giving advice.

(C) asking questions.

(D) creating a summary.

Answers to practice Reading and Language Arts questions

Use this answer key to score the practice reading and language arts questions in this chapter.

1. **D. fluency.** The teacher is tracking the students' ability to read with accuracy, automaticity, and prosody. Choice (A) is incorrect because *segmentation* is breaking down words into their component sounds. Choice (B) is incorrect because *error-frequency rate* is a comparison of words read correctly to words read incorrectly. Choice (C) is incorrect because a *running record* tracks accuracy and is used to calculate a text's level for the student (*independent, instructional,* or *frustrational*).

2. **C. phonemic awareness.** The student can identify the individual sounds, or phonemes, of the word. Choice (A) is incorrect because *context clues* refer to words around an unknown word that help a reader establish its meaning. Choice (B) is incorrect because *phonological awareness* is a broad category (involving sound units) that includes, and so is not as specific as, phonemic awareness. Choice (D) is incorrect because *comprehension* refers to a reader's ability to understand the meaning of the text as a whole.

3. **C. dyslexic.** Symptoms of dyslexia include directional confusion, such as writing "d" as "b" or "m" as "w"; sequencing difficulties, such as writing "the" as "teh"; and difficulties with little words, such as omitting "to." Choice (A) is incorrect because the teacher, in all likelihood, used the task as an assessment, and, knowing the issues her students may face, will do all she can to adapt lessons to their needs or get them additional help. Choice (B) is incorrect because, in general, ELL (English Language Learner) errors tend to occur on a broader level than spelling, such as the omission of articles or misuse of prepositions. Choice (D) is incorrect because the mistakes form patterns associated with dyslexia. Some dyslexic children, having experienced failure in the past, may have a tendency to stop trying and so appear to be lazy, but that willful condition is not what is at work here.

4. **B. concrete.** This is a poem whose physical, concrete shape reinforces the theme—here, that of religion's power ("wings") to lift up the believer. While there are elements of the other choices in the poem, as a whole it is best described by Choice (B). Choice (A) is incorrect because this type of poetry's chief function is to discuss an idea, such as fear or courage. Choice (C) is incorrect because this type of poetry's chief function is to tell a story. Choice (D) is incorrect because this type of poetry's chief function is to encapsulate a moment in time through the use of a sensory image.

5. **A. attach.** The word *imp* comes from falconry and means to *graft* or literally *attach* part of one feather to another. Herbert is saying that if he attaches his wing to the Lord's, he (Herbert) will then be able to be lifted up. Choice (B) is incorrect because Herbert does not say he can imitate the Lord's power. Choice (C) is incorrect because Herbert does not say he is above the Lord. Choice (D) is incorrect because Herbert does not say the Lord's wing needs to be remade in a different way.

6. **D. Each stanza traces a fall, a steady loss, until hardly anything is left of the poet, and then a rise as the poet turns to his faith.** Both stanzas turn on the phrase "With thee," as the poet turns from the lows of being "Most poore" and "Most thinne." Choice (A) is incorrect because, while true regarding the mechanics of flight, it does not reflect the poem's meaning. Herbert is not saying that action *per se* is needed, but that specific actions are. Choice (B) is incorrect because it is not *specific*: It is a general statement that confirms the question but does little else. Choice (C) is incorrect because the lines do not describe wings but the poet's losses (of wealth and health) and understanding of how to rise up.

7. **B. cause and effect.** The essay will examine a cause, why something happened ("reasons that led the workers to go on strike"), and an effect, what happened as a result ("end up in jail"). Choice (A) is incorrect because an issue is not being resolved here. Choice (C) is incorrect because similarities and differences of two things are not being compared here. Choice (D) is also incorrect because supporting points (usually in a persuasive essay) are not being listed in increasing or decreasing importance.

8. **D. change a verb from present tense to past.** The introduction should begin "There *were* many reasons" in order to match the past tense of the rest *(led, knew, would)*. Choice (A) is incorrect because *workers* requires the gender-neutral pronoun *they*. Choice (B) is incorrect because the verbs agree with their subjects *(are/reasons; workers/knew)*. Choice (C) is incorrect because the pronoun *they* agrees with the noun *workers*.

9. **A. scaffolding, and C. K-W-L.** Here, the scaffolding (extra support that might be removed later as students gain more independence) might be a graphic organizer or a glossary. The strategy of K-W-L has students activate prior learning by saying or recording what they already KNOW, then what they WANT to learn, and finally going over what they LEARNED. Choice (B) is incorrect because the students will already have learned that words are made of letters and that letters represent sounds. Choice (D) is incorrect because this strategy is *most likely* to be used by a teacher reading, from a big book, together with a whole class of emergent readers, so that she models what good readers do. Older students, even through high school, may benefit from shared reading, but it is not used *per se* as a comprehension strategy.

10. **A. focusing on the speaker, C. asking questions, and D. creating a summary.** Only Choice (B) turns the focus away from the speaker and makes it about the listener's ideas (instead of the listener's listening skills).

Mathematics practice questions

These practice questions are similar to the mathematics questions that you'll encounter on the Praxis Elementary Education: Content Knowledge test.

1. Cindy went to a store and saw a purse that was priced at \$40. The next week, she went to the same store a second time and saw the purse priced at \$50. What was the percent of change in the price of the purse from Cindy's first visit to the store to the second?

  (A) 25% decrease

  (B) 20% increase

  (C) 25% increase

  (D) 20% decrease

2. What type of polygon is the following figure?

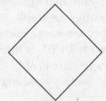

  (A) concave hexagon

  (B) concave quadrilateral

  (C) convex pentagon

  (D) convex quadrilateral

3. What is the coefficient of the term $9wx^4$?

  (A) 9

  (B) w

  (C) x

  (D) 4

4. Ira rolls 2 dice, each having 6 faces, with each face representing a whole number from 1 to 6. All whole numbers from 1 to 6 are represented by each die. What is the probability that both dice will land on 5?

  (A) $\frac{1}{6}$

  (B) $\frac{1}{3}$

  (C) $\frac{1}{36}$

  (D) $\frac{1}{18}$

5. What is the value of the following expression?

$$15 - (4 + 5 \times 2) + 3$$

  (A) 0

  (B) 24

  (C) 35

  (D) 4

6. In which quadrant of the coordinate plane is the point $(8, -7)$?

  (A) Quadrant I

  (B) Quadrant II

  (C) Quadrant III

  (D) Quadrant IV

7. If $3p - 4 = 17$, what is the value of $8p + 5$?

  (A) 7

  (B) 61

  (C) 56

  (D) 12

8. What is the median of the following set of data?

4 10 0 6 20

  (A) 8

  (B) 20

  (C) 6

  (D) 0

9. Which of the following is true about the numbers $\frac{25}{2}$ and 12.51?

(A) $\frac{25}{2}$ is the greater number.

(B) 12.51 is the greater number.

(C) The two numbers are equal.

(D) Which number is greater cannot be determined.

10. Lisa has 5 more than 3 times the number of baseball cards Talbot has. Together, Lisa and Talbot have 21 baseball cards. How many baseball cards does Lisa have?

(A) 17

(B) 4

(C) 21

(D) 13

Answers to Mathematics practice questions

Use this answer key to score the practice mathematics questions in this chapter.

1. **C. 25% increase.** The purse was $40 on the first visit and $50 on the second. Since the price went up, the change was an increase. The next issue is what percent the increase was. It was a $10 increase because $50 − $40 is $10, and $10 is 25% of the original price, $40. You can determine that by dividing 10 by 40. The result is 0.25. To convert a decimal number to a fraction, move the decimal point two places to the right and put a % after the result. The percent form of 0.25 is 25%. Choices (A) and (D) are decreases, and they are wrong because of that alone. Choices (B) and (D) have the wrong percent. That means Choice (D) is incorrect for two reasons. The false figure 20% can be reached by dividing 10 by 50 instead of 40. Percent of change involves percent of the original number, not the number resulting from the change.

2. **D. Convex quadrilateral.** The polygon is convex because none of its adjacent sides join together to point inward. There is no "cave" in the figure. Also, the polygon has four sides, and a four-sided polygon is a quadrilateral. The polygon is, therefore, a convex quadrilateral. Since the figure is convex and cannot have four sides and also some other number of sides, it cannot possibly be any of the other choices.

3. **A. 9.** The coefficient of a term is the number that comes before and is multiplied by the variable or variables, if there are any. In this case, that number is 9. A variable cannot be a coefficient, so Choices (B) and (C) are incorrect. Choice (D) is wrong because the 4 in the term is a variable exponent and not a coefficient.

4. **C. $\frac{1}{36}$.** Each die has 6 faces, with each face having a different whole number from 1 to 6. The probability of an event is the ratio of the number of favorable outcomes, or potential outcomes that would qualify as what is in question, to the total number of possible outcomes. The only number that can qualify as a 5 is 5, so there is 1 favorable outcome. The number of possible outcomes is 6. Thus, the probability of a given die landing on 5 is $\frac{1}{6}$. The probability of the other die landing on 5 is also $\frac{1}{6}$, for the same reasons. The probability of two events both happening is the product of their probabilities. The product of $\frac{1}{6} \times \frac{1}{6}$ is $\frac{1}{36}$, so that is the probability of both dice landing on 5. Choice (A) is the probability of one die landing on 5. Choice (B) is twice the probability of one die landing on 5. Choice (D) is twice the probability of both dice landing on 5.

5. **D. 4.** Determining the value of the expression involves performing multiple operations, and doing that requires following the order of operations. That order is represented by the

acronym PEMDAS, which stands for "parentheses and other grouping symbols, exponents, multiplication and division from left to right, addition and subtraction from left to right."

$$15-(4+5\times2)+3 = 15-(4+10)+3$$
$$= 15-14+3$$
$$= 1+3$$
$$= 4$$

The other choices can result from following false orders of operations.

6. **D. Quadrant IV.** For the point (8, −7), 8 is the x-coordinate, or the horizontal coordinate. The −7 in the coordinate pair is the y-coordinate, or vertical coordinate. Remember that up and right are positive directions on the coordinate plane and down and left are negative directions. To get to the point (8, −7), you can sketch a not very detailed representation of the coordinate plane and move 8 horizontal units from the origin, which is the point (0, 0). In other words, move 8 units to the right from where the x-axis and y-axis intersect. Next, move −7 units vertically. That is 7 units down. If you follow that method, you will reach the point and see that (8, −7) is in the bottom right section of the coordinate plane. That is Quadrant IV. The ordering of the quadrants starts in the upper right section, which is Quadrant I, and goes counterclockwise. A quadrant cannot be Quadrant I and also another one, so the other choices are wrong.

7. **B. 61.** To determine the value of $8p+5$, you must first find the value of p. To do that, solve the equation $3p-4=17$ by getting p by itself on one side. You can achieve that by doing the opposite of what is being done to p, on both sides of the equation.

$$3p-4 = 17$$
$$3p-4+4 = 17+4$$
$$3p = 21$$
$$\frac{3p}{3} = \frac{21}{3}$$
$$p = 7$$

The value of p is 7, so put 7 in for p in $8p+5$ to determine the value of $8p+5$.

$$8p+5 = 8(7)+5$$
$$= 56+5$$
$$= 61$$

Choice (A) is the value of p. Choice (C) is the value of $8p$. Choice (D) is the value of $p+5$.

8. **C. 6.** The median of a set of data is the middle number when the data is in order, or else the mean of the two middle numbers. This set of data has one middle number when it is in order. It also has one middle number when it is out of order, but that is neither here nor there. When the data is in order, the middle number is 6. That is the number of middle value in the set. Choice (A) is the mean of the set of data. Choice (B) is the highest number in the set and is also the range. Choice (D) is the lowest number and also the middle number in the out-of-order presentation of the data.

9. **B. 12.51 is the greater number.** To compare numbers that are not in the same form, put them in the same form. You can change the two numbers in question here to fraction or decimal form, but decimal form may be the easier to work with in this case. The fraction $\frac{25}{2}$ can be converted to decimal form after it is changed to mixed number form. To do that, divide 25 by 2. The quotient is 12 with a remainder of 1. That means the integer part of the mixed fraction is 12. The remainder of 1 will be the numerator of the fraction part of the mixed number.

The denominator of the original fraction is the denominator of the fraction in the mixed number. It is 2. Therefore, the mixed number form of $\frac{25}{2}$ is $12\frac{1}{2}$. Next, convert that mixed number to decimal form by determining what $\frac{1}{2}$ is in decimal form. You can find that by dividing the numerator by the denominator. The quotient is 0.5. Therefore, $12\frac{1}{2}$ is the same as 12.5. The other number in question, 12.51, is already in decimal form. You may want to write 12.5 as 12.50 to get the same number of digits after the decimal for both numbers. That can make them easier to compare. You can then see that 12.50 is less than 12.51, which tells you that $\frac{25}{2}$ is less than 12.51. That makes the other choices impossible.

10. **A. 17.** The number of baseball cards Lisa has is described as based on the number Talbot has, so you should use a variable to represent Talbot's number of cards and write an expression using that variable to represent the number Lisa has. If Talbot has x cards, Lisa has 5 more than 3 times that, so she has $3x + 5$ cards. The sum of their numbers of baseball cards is 21, so $x + 3x + 5 = 21$. You can solve that equation to determine the number of cards Talbot has.

$$x + 3x + 5 = 21$$
$$4x + 5 = 21$$
$$4x + 5 - 5 = 21 - 5$$
$$4x = 16$$
$$\frac{4x}{4} = \frac{16}{4}$$
$$x = 4$$

Since x is 4, Talbot has 4 baseball cards. Lisa, therefore, has $3(4) + 5$ baseball cards, so she has 17. Choice (B) is the number of baseball cards Talbot has. Choice (C) is the total number of cards Lisa and Talbot have. Choice (D) is the number of cards Lisa has minus the number Talbot has.

Science practice questions

These practice questions are similar to the science questions that you'll encounter on the Praxis Elementary Education: Content Knowledge test.

1. Obsidian is a hard, glassy rock. Which TWO of the following pertain to obsidian?

   (A) igneous

   (B) intrusive

   (C) metamorphic

   (D) extrusive

2. Cattle egrets are birds that live near cattle. When the cattle graze, the birds feed on insects that are aroused and thus relatively easy for the birds to see. The relationship between the cattle egrets and the cattle is one of

   (A) mutualism.

   (B) commensalism.

   (C) predation.

   (D) competition.

3. Which of the following is true regarding an atom of the element carbon?

   (A) Its atomic number is 6, it has 6 protons, and it has 6 electrons.

   (B) Its atomic number is 8, it has 8 protons, and it has 8 electrons.

   (C) Its atomic number is 6, it has 8 protons, and it has 8 electrons.

   (D) Its atomic number is 8, it has 6 protons, and it has 6 electrons.

4. Select all of the following that are true regarding the use of solar power.

   (A) Solar power is pollution-free.

   (B) Solar power is essentially silent.

   (C) The U.S. leads the world in countries using solar power.

   (D) Solar power is a renewable resource.

5. Some students are conducting an experiment to determine the effect of different organic food waste on the growth of basil plants. The students' design involves six plants. The three plants in Group A will be in one kind of soil in one part of the room. These plants will get ground eggshells. The three plants in Group B will be in the same kind of soil and another part of the room. These plants will get coffee grounds. When the teacher reviews the students' design, which of the following will need to be attended to? Select all that apply.

   (A) control

   (B) variables

   (C) Type I error

   (D) hypothesis

Answers to Science practice questions

Here are the answers to the science practice questions in the preceding section.

1. **A. igneous and D. extrusive.** As with all igneous rocks, obsidian is made from cooling and hardening. Because it is made from lava, cooling outside the volcano, obsidian is extrusive. Extrusive rocks cool quickly (outside the volcano) and have very fine grains. Choice (B) is wrong because intrusive rocks cool inside the volcano—slowly—and have large grains, such as granite has. Choice (C) is wrong because a metamorphic rock is made from the forces of heat and pressure on an existing igneous or sedimentary rock. Granite, for example, under heat and pressure, becomes the metamorphic rock, gneiss.

2. **B. commensalism.** This relationship benefits the cattle egrets but does not affect the cattle. Choice (A) describes a relationship where both species benefit. For example, some birds eat organisms ON animals, and they benefit as well as the birds. Choice (C) describes one organism feeding off another, such as the relationship between the cattle egrets and the insects. Choice (D) describes a relationship where two organisms are competing for the same food, which does not apply here since the cattle are not eating the insects.

3. **A. Its atomic number is 6, it has 6 protons, and it has 6 electrons.** Carbon's atomic number is 6, which is the number of protons in its nucleus. Since an atom has no electrical charge, the number of (positively charged) protons must equal the number of (negatively charged) electrons. Choice (B) describes an atom of the element oxygen. Choices (C) and (D) do not describe either carbon or oxygen since an element's atomic number is by definition the number of protons in its nucleus.

4. **B. Solar power is essentially silent, and D. Solar power is a renewable resource.** There is no noise associated with the generating of solar power, in contrast to that of wind turbines, for example. Solar energy is renewable, as opposed to such fossil fuels as coal, oil, and gas. Choice (A) is not correct because two greenhouse gases, nitrogen trifluoride and sulfur hexafluoride, are involved in the production of solar panels. Choice (C) is not correct because Germany leads the world in this category, followed by Spain, Italy, and Japan. The U.S. is fifth.

5. **A. control, B. variables, and D. hypothesis.** The problem with the "control" is that there is none. There should be a third group of plants which do not receive any organic food waste. The problem with "variables" is that there should be only one independent variable, but there are two independent variables here: type of food waste and location in the room (affecting the amount of light each group receives). The problem with "hypothesis" is that there isn't one. Most hypotheses follow an if-then pattern: *If* [something is done]*, then* [something will result]. Choice C is incorrect because there aren't any conclusions yet, and a Type I error, also known as a *false positive,* is a conclusion that incorrectly attributes a result to a cause, that cause not in fact being responsible for the result.

Social Studies practice questions

These practice questions are similar to the social studies questions that you'll encounter on the Praxis Elementary Education: Content Knowledge test.

1. For a team project, a group of students has been researching changes in acreage of farmland owned by families compared to corporate-owned farmland in the U.S. over the last thirty years. Which type of map would be best for the students to produce?

   (A) physical

   (B) political

   (C) concept

   (D) thematic

2. Which of the following describes the Old Copper Complex?

   (A) collections of ancient Egyptian artifacts often associated with tradesmen

   (B) Native American cultures of the Great Lakes region that made extensive use of copper in weaponry and tools.

   (C) a bronze foundry used in ancient China where the desired copper-tin ratios were specified

   (D) none of the above

3. The precedent for a U.S. president serving only two terms was established by which of the following?

   (A) the Bill of Rights (1791)

   (B) President George Washington's *Farewell Address* (1796)

   (C) President Franklin Delano Roosevelt's *Third Inaugural Address* (1941)

   (D) the 22nd Amendment to the Constitution (1947)

4. Which of the following was NOT a cause of the War of 1812?

   (A) British impressment of U.S. seamen

   (B) British efforts to hamper U.S. trade

   (C) U.S. Federalist Party power

   (D) U.S. policy of expansionism

5. Opportunity costs may be viewed in light of

   (A) funds not available because of a choice made.

   (B) wants exceeding available resources.

   (C) how much something costs versus how much it will benefit you.

   (D) the difference between basic pay and total earnings.

Answers to Social Studies practice questions

Use this answer key to score the practice social studies questions in this chapter.

1. **D. thematic.** While a thematic map may include characteristics of other types of maps, these characteristics are background information. In this case, the students will most likely use a political map as a reference, showing states where there has been a significant change. However, the main focus of the map is thematic: how there has been a significant change. Choice (A) is not correct because a physical map features natural structures, such as mountains and lakes. Choice (B) is not correct because a political map features human (territorial) boundaries, such as between countries, states, or provinces. Choice (C) is not correct because a concept map, a kind of graphic organizer, shows how different ideas and details are connected to each other.

2. **B. Native American cultures of the Great Lakes region that made extensive use of copper in weaponry and tools.** Evidence shows that aboriginal use of copper began 6,000 years ago during the Copper Age and continues today, although present use is chiefly ornamental. Choice (A) does not pertain to the "Old Copper Complex," although the ancient Egyptians did make extensive use of copper in tools. Choice (C) does not pertain to the "Old Copper Complex," although the ancient Chinese did have specific ratios of copper-tin for use in making such bronze items as cauldrons, spears, swords, and arrows. Choice (D) is incorrect because Choice (B) is correct.

3. **B. President George Washington's *Farewell Address* (1796).** Washington wrote that "choice and prudence" compelled him to "retire" at the end of his second term. Since then, the two-term presidential limit became a *de facto* (in effect) policy. Choice (A), the first ten Amendments to the Constitution, do not address term limits. Choice (C) is not correct—it by nature went against the two-term limit. Choice (D) is not correct: It goes beyond precedent, making it a law that "No person shall be elected to the office of the President more than twice."

4. **C. U.S. Federalist Party power.** The *loss* of the Federalist Party's power was, in fact, an *effect* of the war, as that party's antiwar stance was more unpopular after the war than it had been before. Choice (A) reflects the British practice of stopping U.S. ships and forcing sailors to serve in the Royal Navy. Choice (B) reflects British efforts to restrict U.S. trade with France, which was at war with Britain. Choice (D) reflects the desire of the U.S. to expand westward, and the British were supporting Native Americans against that expansion.

5. **A. funds not available because of a choice made.** Also known as the *value of foregone alternatives*, an *opportunity cost* is an effect of choosing something else (alternative) at an earlier (foregone) time. Every choice has an opportunity cost: an opportunity you've lost because you've chosen something else. For example, an opportunity cost of going to college is the loss of wages due to being in school and not working. Choice (B) is *scarcity*. Choice (C) is a *cost-benefit analysis*. Choice (D) is *wage drift* and includes such things as bonus pay and overtime pay.

Analyzing Your Practice Question Results

Your results are a good indicator of what you need to study the most. If you missed some questions, let that become a strength. Incorrect answers tell you what you need to do now to get prepared for the big test. In fact, future practice questions will give indications of where you are at any stage of the preparation process. For now, you are still in the early part of the game, and this is just the first round.

Identifying what you missed

The areas where you struggled the most are most likely the areas where you need to study the most. To get a really precise idea of where you need to put the most focus, you can make an outline based on your results. Write brief descriptions of what you missed and look for patterns. Look for categories within categories, and then look for specific problem areas within those categories. The table of contents for this book can help you identify the specific names of the categories and the divisions within them. You can create a category called "Other" for areas that do not seem to fit into any of the other categories.

After you identify the areas you need to focus on, look at which of your answers were incorrect. You may not have had any, but that is rare at this stage. If you did have wrong answers, contrast them with the right answers and work to understand why you did not get the correct answers.

Analyzing how to get the right answers can also help you. It can allow you to see areas where you can become strong and increase your ability to understand key components of your areas of weakness. It can also help you identify wrong answer choices so you can mark them out and have a greater chance of getting the right answers.

Determining the why of what you missed

We just mentioned the need to understand why you missed certain questions on your practice test. Now, we are going to further explain the importance of this issue.

When you identify your wrong answer choices, you can ask yourself important questions like the following ones:

>> Did I make simple errors?

>> Do I lack in-depth knowledge of a particular subject?

>> Was my answer incorrect because I lacked focus while answering it?

>> Did I confuse my answer with something else?

>> Is there a strategy that I could have used that would have made the difference?

Think about those questions and ones like them and make a list of your answers. Keep those answers in mind as you study, in order to gain the knowledge, skills, and test-taking strategies necessary to succeed on the real test.

Something else you can do is look for patterns in the reasons for your wrong answers. If you can find patterns, you can be more mindful of your mistakes. For math questions in particular, it is very often helpful to look at any work you may have done in your effort to get right answers. If you did work out some problems, your work can tell you further details about where you need to improve. As you improve your math knowledge and skills, your ability to do that will grow.

With the other subject-area questions, perhaps mostly with those in the social studies category, people often have easily correctable tendencies that can lead to wrong answers. For example, you may choose an answer simply because it has big words in it, which gives you the impression that the answer is a good one and the right one. Keep in mind that big words can be wrong words. You may be drawn to answer choices that say interesting things or sound optimistic. The bias involved in such circumstances can give false attractiveness to answers. It is also possible to give up on a question too soon without realizing it because a question seems especially difficult. That is most likely when you remember the advice that you should pick Choice (C) when in doubt. That view can somewhat draw you to select Choice (C) when you have not yet fully evaluated and eliminated any of the other answer choices. Giving up too soon can lead to preventable incorrectness.

Test-prep teachers and tutors have an old saying: "I can tell you how to get a question right, but only you can tell yourself why you got one wrong." Well, okay, maybe it's not an old saying. It's from another *For Dummies* Praxis prep book we wrote. Technically, it will eventually be an old saying. For the remainder of this book, your goal is to build content and develop strategies that will improve your performance on the Praxis Elementary Education: Content Knowledge exam.

Chapter 3

Getting Ready for Test Day

Think of taking the Praxis like running a marathon. You wouldn't run a marathon without training for the race, would you? No, you probably wouldn't. Just like training for a marathon, you should follow a training regimen to get yourself into top form for the Praxis Elementary Education: Curriculum, Instruction, and Assessment (Praxis Elementary Education: CIA) or Praxis Elementary Education: Content Knowledge. In this chapter, we offer suggestions you can use to "shape up" for your test, whether you're taking it for the first time or taking it again.

Ideally, you'll give yourself a couple of months to get ready for the test. In that time you'll study and review concepts the test covers, take practice tests to familiarize yourself with the format and timing of the test, and brush up in areas that need improvement so you can ace the test. During that time, you'll also familiarize yourself with the test-taking situation, register for the test, and make arrangements for any accommodations you may need.

Registering for the Test

Before you register to take the Praxis, check with your local department of education to make sure you're taking the right test. Don't ask Educational Testing Service (ETS) or your mom or anyone else who isn't in a position to grant you a teaching license; you may get wrong information, which can lead to wasted time and money.

You can find out how to register for any of the Praxis Subject Assessments by going to the ETS website at www.ets.org. These are offered during testing windows at more than 300 testing sites across the country. Refer to the ETS website for specific questions regarding testing windows and locations.

Test-takers must register at least three days prior to their intended test date, and you must pay the testing fee online. At the time of this writing, the fee for either test in this book is $120.

After you register, completely review your entire admission ticket and its information to make sure all the content is correct.

TIP

Organizing Study Time Wisely

You bought this book, and now you're ready to dive in and study, right? Well, you may want to hold off just a bit longer before diving in. First, you need to *plan* your study time. You can expect to spend many hours over the next several weeks reviewing the material that could be on the test, and setting up a study schedule helps you use those hours as efficiently as possible. Your investment in study-planning can pay off big-time. When you budget your study time ahead of your test date, you increase your chances of passing the first time. Do you really want to face the Praxis more than once to enroll in a teacher education program? We didn't think so.

Forming a schedule

The best way to prepare to take the Praxis is to set up a study schedule and then stick to it: Plan your work, and work your plan. It's important to establish times when you can focus. Block off 1-2 hours per sitting during which you will do nothing but prepare for the test. You may need to ask your sister to babysit the kids, or you may need to turn down drinks with friends for a few weeks, but it will be worth it. Studying for this test will suck up your extra time for a relatively short period, but passing the test will benefit you for a long time to come.

What should you do during your allotted daily study time? We recommend that you devote an early session (or two) to taking a practice test. This book includes two full-length tests in Part IV and three more online. You can take a test now and save the others to take in the days leading up to the exam.

When you take the practice tests, take them under timed conditions in a quiet setting where you won't be disturbed. Taking the practice tests in a test-like environment gives you a better sense of how you'll perform on the Praxis when it counts.

TIP

After you take a practice test, spend another study session (or a few sessions) carefully analyzing your performance. Did you do well on the reading and language arts questions? Great. That may let you assign more of your study time to the other subject areas. But, to be sure, do a more detailed analysis. Even if you did well on the reading and language arts questions as a group, did you have trouble with the ones about teaching writing? If so, you'll want to be sure to schedule some study time to review how to teach writing. Review the answer explanations of all the questions on your practice test. These help you see what you did right or where you went wrong. For example, maybe you're having more trouble mastering a particular question type than the subject material.

After all this detailed analysis, you should have a pretty specific list of what you need to study. Divide the topics among your available blocks of time. For instance, if you decide you need to learn more about teaching social studies, you might devote a couple of your sessions to reviewing your old class notes and textbooks on the topic or doing some Internet research to get up to speed on the current methods and standards. Different subjects call for different study habits. If the subject is math, then learn how to analyze students' work on math problems. If it's science, study the methods and standards you learned for teaching science.

ETS provides a sample worksheet in its free preparation materials for the Praxis Elementary Education Subject Assessments (available online at www.ets.org) that you may find helpful in putting together your study schedule.

During your study sessions, familiarize yourself with the question types for each section as well as content matter. Not all the questions are straightforward, multiple-choice questions. Some of them ask you to choose *all* the right answers. Other questions may require you to click a sentence from a passage or part of a graphic, or to drag answers to the correct places in a list or table. Knowing the variations in question types gives you a better chance of answering them correctly. As you get familiar with the question types, also pay attention to the test's directions. Understanding the directions ahead of time can save you valuable time on test day and can reduce test anxiety.

Create an adjustable timetable that you can revise to best meet your needs as test time gets closer.

Compensating for lost study time

You may have noticed us tossing around suggestions like "Take a few study sessions to analyze your practice test" and wondered just how many sessions you should be planning. Our suggestion is that you begin studying four to six weeks before the test. This allows you some time to take and analyze one (or better yet, several) practice tests, as well as to devote at least two or three study sessions to each subject area.

What if it's already less than four weeks before the test, and you haven't started studying yet? You may be able to make up some time by scheduling more study sessions per day. For example, you might study by yourself for a couple hours and meet with a study group daily. We recommend adding more sessions, rather than planning longer ones.

We don't recommend cramming for this test or planning hours-long, grueling practice sessions. Not only will it make you (and your loved ones) miserable, it probably won't help that much.

In general, spreading your practice over more, shorter sessions and frequently testing yourself results in a much better ability to remember the material than does trying to learn it all during fewer monster study sessions.

If you've waited so long, or gotten so far behind your planned schedule, that you can't put in adequate study time before taking the test, seriously consider rescheduling. The Praxis is given several times each year at local testing centers. Rather than taking the test with no preparation, contact the testing center near you or go online to reschedule to take the test at a later date.

Studying with other people

Sometimes people gain more knowledge when they study with others. Others may know more about teaching principles of algebra or approaches for teaching science, and their explanations may help you learn what you need for the test. So consider creating or joining a study group. You can learn from study partners who are strong in your weaker areas and make yourself even more test-ready in your areas of strength by prepping in a group.

If you find yourself slipping behind your study schedule, becoming part of a study group may help you get back on track, because the social rewards of learning together—as well as the accountability of having group members who need you to show up—can motivate you to put in practice time more regularly.

If you can't find a group to study with, look for a Praxis prep course. The instructors of these courses know the ins and outs of what's on the test, and during the class they review material that you're likely to encounter. Yes, you'll have to pay for the course, but the advantage is that the instructor should know the material in depth and be able to answer your questions or explain the material in a way that suits your learning preference. The Kirkland Group has been conducting Praxis workshops for several years. For more details, go to www.kirklandgroup.org.

TIP

Take the test within a week after the prep class ends. This will increase your chances of remembering the information until you take the test. Don't wait six months after completing the course before you take the test, or you may risk not getting the scores that you want.

Doing Some Fine-Tuning

Sufficient content knowledge alone is not enough to ensure a passing score on test day. Even in all of your gain in content, there are still other strategies that can help increase your overall score. Some of them are listed below:

Using bonus study materials and techniques

Even when you're not formally studying, try to sneak in some additional learning or review. Pull out your old textbooks and class notes to review how to teach grammar, reading, and math; skim through them during lunch or while you're on the treadmill. Look over any student work you may have copies of from your practice teaching or clinical experiences. The info in these old materials may jog your memory about something you previously learned.

REMEMBER

ETS offers free *Preparing to Take a Praxis Test* webinars that may be useful. Find the webinar schedule or access recorded webinars at www.ets.org.

Familiarizing yourself with computer testing

You will take the Praxis on a computer. This allows you to take the test any day of the week and almost on demand at the local Prometric testing center. It also allows for faster scoring of your test, which means you'll get your results faster than you would if the test were administered on paper.

Before you take the test, ETS gives you 30 minutes of practice time during which you can figure out how the computer test works. Take advantage of this time because it's the real deal once the test starts. Pay particular attention to tips about how to use the computer, answer questions, and review previous questions.

TIP

Understanding the basics of computerized testing before you even show up at the testing center can help you feel more calm and in control when you take the test. ETS offers an online, interactive Computer-Delivered Testing Demonstration that you can access from its website, www.ets.org.

Preparing the Night Before the Test

On the night before you take the test, you can reduce your stress and improve your chances of doing well by taking these simple steps:

- **Gather test-day essentials:** Make sure you have directions to the testing center, your valid picture ID (not expired), your admission ticket, and your positive attitude.

- **Get a good night's sleep:** Your body and mind will appreciate it. You can party after the high score.

- **Eat right:** Avoid salty and sugary foods the night before and the morning of the test. These can drain your energy. Instead, studies show that fruits and vegetables along with the proper balance of protein, good carbohydrates, and fats are just what the doctor ordered.

Using Test Time Wisely

On test day, it's all about pacing yourself. You can have a mastery of all the necessary content, but without the appropriate timing strategies, your score can suffer greatly. Knowing how much time to spend on the questions is an asset to test-taking.

TIP

Review the specific timing for your test and then the general strategies we recommend.

- **5017:** There are 120 questions on the test, and you will have 130 minutes to answer them. If you were to simply answer all the questions and submit your answers without checking any of them, you would have just over one minute to answer each question.

- **5018:** There are 140 questions on the test, and you will have 150 minutes to answer them. If you were simply to answer all the questions and submit your answers without checking any of them, you would have just over one minute to answer each question.

Don't just plan to use all of your time getting the questions completed. Smart test-takers allow some time to review their answers and revisit any questions they have marked to revisit. And, we know you're a smart test-taker! We recommend that you leave about ten minutes to check answers and revisit questions. This means you'll have about one minute to answer each question.

You may look at those numbers and think, "There's no way I can answer questions that quickly!" But fear not. Here are some tips that can help you shave seconds off the amount of time it takes you to answer many of the questions:

- **Monitor the clock on the computer screen.** With just one minute per question, you need to use that time wisely. You may want to check the clock to be sure you are on track after you finish each major section of the exam. This means if a section has 40 questions, it should take you 40 minutes to complete. Too much over that time could mean you won't have time to get to all the questions in another section, even if you know the answers.

- **Don't make time your sole focus.** Don't get so caught up on timing that you aren't paying attention to what the questions are asking. Strike a balance between monitoring the time and concentrating on the task at hand.

- **Read all possible answers.** Sift through each answer choice to ensure that you aren't overlooking a better answer. Don't select Choice (A) before looking at the alternative answer choices.

- **Use the process of elimination.** If you don't know the answer immediately after reading the answer choices, try to eliminate as many answers as possible. Then guess at the answer. Your chances of guessing correctly increase as you eliminate more answer choices.

TIP

It's especially important to consider each answer choice carefully on questions that have more than one correct answer.

>> **Mark questions you want to revisit later.** Occasionally, you'll come to an item that you aren't sure about. Don't spend a lot of time puzzling over it. If you can't figure out the answer (or answers) quickly, use the "Mark" button at the top of your screen to mark the question as one you will look at again during your review time. Then move on. You can mark questions that you have answered, too, if you think you may want to change the answer later.

TIP

When you use the online demonstration at home or at the testing center, make sure to figure out how to mark questions.

>> **Save time for review.** Praxis Elementary Education offers you the opportunity to review the status of all of your questions. Clicking the Review button at the top of your screen brings you a chart that shows you at a glance which test questions you've seen, which ones you've answered, and which ones you've marked to revisit. You can also navigate from the Review screen directly back to any question you want to look at again.

Getting Extra Advice If You Have Taken the Test

The reality is that sometimes you study for, prepare for, and focus on the Praxis Elementary Education exams only to receive the bad news that you didn't achieve a passing score. Don't panic. According to ETS, you can take the test once per calendar month, but no more than six times within a 12-month period.

If you do need to retake the test, spend some time analyzing the areas where you fell short and then create a plan to improve your score the next time. Examine your previous test scores. The numbers can tell you how close you were to passing each section of the test so you know which subject areas you need to learn more about in order to bring up your overall score. If you didn't pass because you just don't understand how to teach phonics or art history, spend extra time studying those areas.

Some people miss passing the test by 15 points or more. If that's the case, don't rush to retake the test. Enroll in a review course in order to increase your chances of passing the test on your next try. You may spend a little money on the class, but you'll save money in the long run because you won't have to take the test repeatedly. Sometimes test-takers who work together, are or were in the same college program, or go to the same church can form a study group. You can even look into hiring a personal tutor.

You may have argued with your spouse on the morning you took the test the first time. Maybe the baby contracted diarrhea the night before, or perhaps the chicken salad you ate didn't agree with your stomach. These factors may have contributed to your failure to pass the test. When test day rolls around again, try to minimize negative circumstances and know that the same ones aren't likely to reoccur. Take it again and the circumstances will probably be better.

WARNING

Don't take the test while you are fatigued. Sleep deprivation can lead to failing test scores. Make sure you get a good night's sleep the night before you're scheduled to take the test.

Looking into Test Accommodations

The rules of the testing center usually forbid such comforts as bringing a snack or drink, taking extra breaks, or working in a room by yourself. However, if you have a health problem or disability, or if English is not your first language, you may be able to arrange extra time to take the test, for help with reading and writing, or for accommodations such as snacks, breaks, or solitude. ETS provides a list of the accommodations available for the Praxis as well as detailed instructions about how to request accommodations at its website. Visit www.ets.org/praxis/register/disabilities.

WARNING

If you need accommodations for the Praxis Elementary Education exam, you must plan way, way, *way* ahead. You cannot register online. You need to gather the paperwork that ETS requires to verify your level of need and submit that request *by mail.* ETS will then spend six weeks reviewing your documentation before approving or rejecting your request. If you're asked to provide additional information, the process may take an additional six weeks. Read the instructions carefully to make sure your accommodation request is granted with the least amount of delay possible.

REMEMBER

For 5017: Go to Chapters 4–8 for content review; Chapters 9–14 for Curriculum, Instruction, and Assessment review; and Chapters 15 and 16 for practice.

For 5018: Go to Chapters 4–7 for content review and Chapters 17 and 18 for practice.

2

Subject Area Content Knowledge

Chapter 4

Reading and Language Arts Subject Content

Yes, the material you're required to know for the Language Arts section of the Praxis Elementary Education: Curriculum, Instruction, and Assessment or Content Knowledge test can seem mountainous, and you may wonder if you'll ever get up and over to the end. As the ancient Chinese philosopher and poet Lao-Tzu said, however, "A journey of a thousand miles begins with a single step." Congratulations on taking that first momentous step. Now, let's dig in!

REMEMBER

This chapter includes Reading and Language Arts content knowledge necessary for both tests. However, students taking Test 5017 don't require all of the details found here and should spend more time on Chapter 10 and then come back here for a refresher.

Some material requires memorization, and some material requires analysis. In fact, you'll likely achieve all the cognitive objectives in *Bloom's taxonomy*, a classification system used to define and distinguish various levels of learning objectives, by the end of the chapter. For beginnings, there's no time like the present.

Reading into the English Language

The foundations of literacy involve four major areas: print concepts, phonological awareness, phonics and word recognition, and fluency and comprehension. Descriptions of these four areas follow, as well as instructional strategies useful in helping students form these foundations.

Print concepts

When readers are *emerging,* or just developing, they may see letters and punctuation merely as shapes. These beginning readers need to learn about *print concepts,* including the following:

>> A certain shape stands for a letter.

>> Printed letters go together to make words.

>> Printed words go together to make sentences.

>> Words have spaces between them.

>> Text is read from left to right and top to bottom.

>> Texts have a front, back, title, and author.

How can students acquire these foundational skills? Some strategies include the *alphabetic principle,* the relationship between a letter and the sound it makes, as well as *direct instruction,* where the teacher teaches from a script and works directly with the students while instructing them.

Phonological awareness

Phonological awareness is a broad skill involving sound recognition. Included in this broad skill is that of phonemic awareness. Beginning readers start by learning the individual sounds, or *phonemes,* in spoken words. For example, the word *cat* has three phonemes: /c/ /a/ /t/. A beginning reader learns to hear and repeat each sound in isolation and then to repeat a sound heard within a word. Putting sounds together, or *blending* them, follows. As readers progress, they learn to make new words from existing words by adding or switching sounds.

A related skill involves *segmenting* the sounds. Beginning readers learn to segment a word into all its sounds—for *cat,* that would be /c/ /a/ and /t/. Readers also work with larger parts of a word, blending the beginning, or *onset,* /c/, with the vowel + consonant, or *rime,* /at/.

TIP

The familiar word "rhyme" refers to words sounding alike, such as *kale* and *pail.* But these words do not have the same "rime." The word *rime* refers to a part of a word, the part that begins with a vowel sound and ends before the next vowel sound. The rime of *kale* is /ale/; the rime of *pail* is /ail/.

What other strategies might you use to help students gain phonological awareness? In addition to direct instruction, *scaffolding* may be very useful. Scaffolding begins with the teacher instructing the student and then gradually moving from occasional prompts to a release, where the students can blend and segment on their own, with previously learned phonemes. When new phonemes are learned, the teacher may need to begin the scaffolding process from the start, depending on the student.

Other useful strategies to help students with phonics include oral language games involving *rhymes* and saying *nursery rhymes* together.

EXAMPLE

A kindergarten teacher reads aloud to her students from a book, which she holds so the students can see the text. She moves her finger steadily along from line to line as she reads. Which print concept is she teaching?

(A) Printed letters go together to make words.

(B) Printed words go together to make sentences.

(C) Text is read from left to right and top to bottom.

(D) Words have spaces between them.

The correct answer is Choice (C). The teacher demonstrates that texts are read from left to right and from top to bottom. Choice (A) is wrong because she is not pointing out individual letters as she reads steadily across. Choice (B) is wrong because she is not pointing out individual words. Choice (D) is wrong because she is not stopping after each word and then pointing to the space while she pauses.

Phonics and word recognition

In addition to letters, readers learn letter combinations or **consonant blends** such as *pl* and *st*, and **digraphs** such as *sh* and *th*.

When readers can look at a printed word and say it out loud, they are *decoding* it. Beginning readers learn to recognize, or *decode*, many words, including word families and high-frequency words. So, having learned to read *cat*, readers may learn other words in the *at* family, including *bat, fat, hat, mat, sat*, and *that*. Written language games involving rhyme can help students learn phonics.

High-frequency words are often **sight words;** that is, readers need to decode them by sight rather than rely on how the sounds in the words are put together. Such words as *the, you,* and *said* are examples of frequently used words that readers learn by sight. A strategy that may work here is **shared reading,** where students read along with the teacher, or, once initial learning has taken place, where students read in peer groups. Once students have a firm basis, **independent reading** can serve as a helpful strategy.

In addition to memorizing high-frequency words and using the strategy of **instant recognition,** students may use different **context clues**—in a text itself—to help them know what they're reading. These clues may be **semantic,** based on the general *meaning* of the story or sentence; **syntactic,** based on word order in a sentence; and picture or **symbolic,** based on illustrations.

You can keep track of a student's word-recognition skills by using a **running record.** Here, following along as a student reads, the teacher makes a mark or note above each word to show whether it was read correctly or not. The teacher then arrives at the student's **accuracy rate** using this formula: (total words read − total errors) / total words read × 100. To analyze the results, use these text terms and percentages:

>> **Independent:** The student can read 95 to 100 percent of the text.

>> **Instructional:** The student can read 90 to 95 percent of the text.

>> **Frustrational:** The student can read less than 90 percent; the text is too difficult.

EXAMPLE

In a first-grade class, the teacher checks each word as a student reads. Out of 200 total words, the student makes 34 errors. Which category is the student in?

(A) Running record independent

(B) Running record instructional

(C) Instant recognition instructional

(D) Running record frustrational

The correct answer is Choice (D). A total of 200 words read − 34 errors = 166. 166 / 200 = 0.83. Multiplied by 100, this decimal = 83 percent, which is below 90 percent and in the running record *frustrational* category. Choice (A) would require the percentage to be from 95 to 100 percent. Choice (B) would require the percentage to be from 90 to 95 percent. Choice (C) refers to a category that does not exist. The formula pertains to a *running record.*

Fluency

A *fluent* reader can read a grade-level text with accuracy, quickness, and expression. It is important for readers to have lots of practice and feedback all along (from learning print concepts to phonemes to words) so that they can become fluent readers at their grade level.

Ultimately, fluent readers read well enough to let themselves focus on not just what the text *says*, but on what the text *means*. Fluency leads to comprehension.

There are many strategies to help students with comprehension of a passage. These strategies include the following:

>> **Annotating (questioning):** The student asks questions about the text, defines hard or new words, analyzes images and other figurative language, and notes main ideas and supporting details.

>> **Using graphic organizers (visualizing):** The student uses such tools as time lines, Venn diagrams, story webs, plot diagrams, graphs, and charts.

The *KWL chart* is a specific and effective graphic organizer, where the student fills in three columns before and after reading: K = What do I *know?*; W = What do I *want* to find out?; L = What did I *learn?*

>> **Grasping concepts with guided reading:** The student silently reads a book chosen by the teacher, who helps the student and analyzes the results as necessary.

>> **Making inferences (inferring):** Students use prior knowledge or evidence in the text (actions, events, or facts) to make a prediction, draw a conclusion, or "read between the lines."

>> **Developing metacognition:** Students start thinking about thinking. They pay attention to areas they understand or find difficult, and they are aware of why they are reading and how (for example, how quickly or slowly) they are reading.

>> **Employing prior knowledge:** Students comprehend better by utilizing prior knowledge they have related to the text.

>> **Rereading:** Students read the text again; making notes or additional notes (annotating) is a good companion strategy.

>> **Retelling:** Students describe what happened or what they learned in their own words.

>> **Summarizing (determining importance):** Students identify main ideas from supporting details.

EXAMPLE

A third-grade teacher's students are working in groups, drawing a story web about the fable they just read. Which strategy are the students engaged in?

(A) using graphic organizers

(B) metacognition

(C) KWL chart

(D) retelling

The correct answer is Choice (A). The students are using the story web as a visualization tool. Choice (B) involves students thinking about thinking, such as talking about parts of a text that were hard to read. Choice (C) involves making a chart before and after reading to record what a student *knows*, what he *wants* to find out, and what he *learned.* Choice (D) involves the students describing in their own words what happened in the story.

The ABC's of Writing

Writers need to be aware of many things, from having good support details to a clear structure to a strong introduction and conclusion. They need to know that a finished product is the result of many stages and may involve research and the use of sources. And finally, writers need to know how to choose the best words and how to check for errors.

Using what you think, find, and imagine

You need to know how to write different kinds of essays. Three of the most common types of essays are

>> **Informational:** Writing about what you find or discover

>> **Opinion (position or argument):** Writing about what you think

>> **Narrative:** Writing about what you imagine or have experienced. Narrative pieces include poetry.

Informational essays

When you wish to share information in a clear and concise way, you write an informative piece. It might compare and contrast two schools or cultures. It might define and explain a method or the categories of a system. It might be a how-to describing the steps of a procedure. Whatever information you share, that is what you are sharing: the facts.

Opinion essays

Facts are things that can be shown to be true or have happened; their reasons or claims often include numbers or references to time. Opinions, on the other hand, are believed to be true or believed to have happened; their supporting reasons or claims often include one or more of the following words: *think, believe, should, must, good, better, best, worse, worst, more important, most important, of greatest significance.*

Which of the following does NOT show a good closing statement for an opinion piece?

EXAMPLE

(A) Everybody should recycle, even if they don't want to.

(B) We will spend twice as much money later if we don't recycle now.

(C) It isn't fair to make people recycle.

(D) If we don't recycle, we're going to be in the worst shape ever.

The correct answer is Choice (B). It states a fact shown to be true, and it references numbers *(twice)* and time *(later, now)*. Choice (A) states an opinion that could be true, including the word *should*. Choice (C) states an opinion that is believed to be true and includes the clue word *think*. Choice (D) states an opinion that could be true, including the word *worst*.

Before actually writing an opinion essay, it's important to jot down/write out three things:

>> The ***thesis statement*** (main point or primary purpose)/opinion you want to convince your reader of

>> Two or three reasons or claims that support that opinion

>> Examples, details, or facts that support each of the reasons

Now, outline the order in which you want to present your reasons. Put "introduction" above the reasons and "conclusion" below them. Now you have your outline for a four- or five-paragraph essay: one introduction; two or three body paragraphs, one for each reason; and one conclusion. Ultimately, your essay should have

>> An introduction that engages the reader and presents the issue

>> Well-ordered supporting reasons and each reason in a body paragraph with its own supporting details

>> Appropriate linking words, such as those previously listed as well as some of the following: *because, since, for example, for instance, in order to, one reason, another, consequently, specifically*

>> A conclusion that restates the thesis/opinion and rephrases the reasons for it in a memorable way

EXAMPLE

Which of the following would be the start of a good body paragraph for an opinion piece?

(A) One problem with modern art is trying to decide what you're looking at. How do some of these art works get funded? Who gets to decide?

(B) Not every student has a smartphone. Some students could do the assignment, and some couldn't.

(C) Sugar is one of the biggest reasons junk food should be banned. For example, sugar should not be in school cafeterias. There should not even be sugar in vending machines the school might have.

(D) One reason I think school uniforms are a good idea is that they can help kids feel equal. For instance, if everyone wears the same outfit, then no one has to feel left out because of what he or she is wearing.

The correct answer is Choice (D). The opinion *(school uniforms are a good idea)* is supported with a reason *(they can help kids feel equal)* that is supported with a following example/detail. The linking words *one reason* and *for instance* are used. Choice (A) uses the linking words *one problem* and states an opinion *(problem with modern art)* and a supporting reason *(trying to decide what you're looking at)*. But the reason has no supporting detail. Choice (B) does not offer an opinion. Choice (C) includes linking words *(one of the biggest reasons; for example)* and states a reason *(sugar)* to support the opinion *(junk food should be banned)*. But there is no support detail to show why or how sugar is a problem. What follows "for example" doesn't support the reason.

Narrative pieces

Both opinion and informational pieces are expository (they explain) and *nonfiction:* Their details are real. Narratives, on the other hand, are *fiction:* not real. There are many types of narratives a student may write or read about:

>> **Adventure:** A story that's characterized by a lot of action

>> **Allegory:** A story in which the characters and events stand for someone or something else; usually has a moral or political meaning

>> **Drama (play):** A story that's meant to be acted on a stage; uses dialogue to deliver its message

>> **Fable:** A short tale using animals or plants to deliver its message, often a moral one

>> **Fairy tale:** A kind of folk tale with magical beings, including dragons

>> **Fantasy:** A story that takes place in a made-up world

- » **Folk tale:** A traditional story often passed down through many generations; usually has a teaching purpose or moral message

- » **Historical fiction:** A story that takes place in a real time and place from the past and often involves real people; parts of the narrative have been imagined, or *fictionalized*

- » **Legend:** A story grounded in something that really happened or in the life of someone who once lived; stretches the truth as it goes beyond what most likely really happened

- » **Myth:** A tale that often involves gods or animals; created to explain a natural phenomenon, such as lightning or tidal waves

- » **Novel:** A book-length story with fictionalized content

- » **Science fiction:** Often futuristic; characterized by creative scientific developments or technology

- » **Short story:** A chapter-length story with fictionalized content

- » **Tall tale:** A legend with humorous, very far-fetched descriptions

Poetry

In addition to the types of narratives, students need to be aware of types of poems they may write or read about. The main difference between a narrative, or *prose*, and poetry is that the latter is condensed. It might rhyme, it might be set up in short lines and stanzas; it might not rhyme, it might have long lines—but its message, its impact, will be delivered more quickly than a prose piece on the same topic.

Poems that rhyme usually have a *rhyme scheme:* a pattern to the rhyme that runs throughout the poem. To describe the rhyme scheme, you assign the first rhyming words the letter *a*, the next *b*, and so on. This little poem has a rhyme scheme of *aabba*:

What would you like to do today?	*a*
Would you like to come outside and play?	*a*
We could look for treasure	*b*
or carefully measure	*b*
the height of the new-stacked hay.	*a*

If another verse followed using new rhymes (in other words, not rhyming with *today* or *measure*), that *stanza* (verse) would have a rhyme scheme of *ccddc*, following the pattern established in the first stanza.

Some of the many types of poems, rhymed and unrhymed, include the following:

- » **Ballad:** Often tells a story, is written in *quat*rains (*four* lines per stanza), has multiple stanzas, and is meant to be sung; usually has a rhyme scheme of *abcb, defe,* and so on

- » **Concrete (shaped):** Made up of words that are spaced so they make a shape on the page

- » **Couplet:** Consists of two lines, often rhyming

- » **Elegy:** A lament or memorial for someone who has died

- » **Free verse:** Lacks a rhyme scheme or regular *meter* (rhythm pattern)

- » **Haiku:** Consists of three lines, with syllable counts of 5-7-5 for the first, second, and third lines, respectively; of Japanese origin and usually reflecting on nature

- >> **Imagistic:** Focuses on description—of one or more images—rather than abstract thoughts, philosophies, and so on; founded in the early part of the 20th century

- >> **Limerick:** Consists of five lines with a rhyme scheme of *aabba;* meant to be funny

- >> **Lyric:** Song-like, rhythmic, and short; often used in contrast to the term *narrative*

- >> **Narrative:** Story-like, somewhat drawn out; often used in contrast to the term *lyric*

- >> **Ode:** A lyric poem, traditionally in three long stanzas; usually dedicated to someone or something

- >> **Quatrain:** General description of a verse consisting of four lines *(quarto-* means *four).*

- >> **Sonnet:** Consists of 14 lines, usually structured in one of two ways: a *Shakespearean* sonnet has three quatrains plus a couplet and a rhyme scheme of *abab cdcd efef gg;* a *Petrarchan* sonnet has an *octave* (eight lines) plus a *sestet* (six lines) and a rhyme scheme of *abba abba cdecde.*

- >> **Villanelle:** Consists of five *tercets* (three lines) plus a quatrain, all with an intricate use of repeating rhymes and of repeating lines. The tercets all rhyme *aba* and the quatrain *abaa.*

EXAMPLE

Which one best describes the following poem?

"The Purple Cow" by Gellett Burgess

I never saw a Purple Cow,
I never hope to see one,
But I can tell you, anyhow,
I'd rather see than be one!

(A) limerick; rhyme scheme *abab*

(B) ode; rhyme scheme *abba*

(C) ballad; rhyme scheme *abba*

(D) quatrain; rhyme scheme *abab*

The correct answer is Choice (D). The poem is not a specific type but rather falls into the general category of quatrain and has an *a* (cow) *b* (see one) *a* (anyhow) *b* (be one) rhyme scheme. Choice (A) is wrong because a limerick has five lines with an *aabba* rhyme scheme. Choice (B) is wrong because an ode has much longer stanzas; the rhyme scheme here is wrong. Choice (C) is wrong because a ballad tells a story and has multiple stanzas; the rhyme scheme here is wrong.

EXAMPLE

Which answer best describes this poem?

Not marble, nor the gilded monuments
Of princes shall outlive this powerful rhyme,
But you shall shine more bright in these contents
Than unswept stone, besmeared with sluttish time.
(05) When wasteful war shall statues overturn,
And broils root out the work of masonry,
Nor Mars his sword, nor war's quick fire shall burn:
The living record of your memory.
'Gainst death, and all–oblivious enmity
(10) Shall you pace forth, your praise shall still find room,
Even in the eyes of all posterity
That wear this world out to the ending doom.
So till the judgment that your self arise,
You live in this, and dwell in lovers' eyes.

(A) Shakespearean (or Elizabethan) sonnet; rhyme scheme *abba abba cdecde*

(B) Petrarchan (or Italian) sonnet; rhyme scheme *abba abba cdecde*

(C) Shakespearean (or Elizabethan) sonnet; rhyme scheme *abab cdcd efef gg*

(D) ballad; rhyme scheme *abab cdcd efef gg*

The correct answer is Choice (C). The poem has three quatrains of subject matter, a concluding couplet, and a rhyme scheme of *a (monuments) b (rhyme) a (contents) b (time)*, and so forth. Choice (A) has the wrong rhyme scheme. Choice (B) is wrong because a Petrarchan sonnet's subject matter is presented in an octave and a sestet. Choice (D) is wrong because a ballad tells a story in a song-like fashion, and has multiple stanzas written in quatrains.

Writing through the stages

Students will work with the craft and structure of writing, paying careful attention to organization. The stages of the writing process help all writers as they work through a piece.

There are different ways to organize a piece of writing. Table 4-1 lists some common structures, when they are used, and linking words that are often used with them.

TABLE 4-1 **Common Writing Structures**

Structure	When Used	Linking Words
Cause and effect	To explain what caused something to happen	*because of, as a result of, for this reason, thus, consequently*
Chronological	To describe events in the order they happened; used most often in narrative writing	*first, then, now, at last, once, next, when, later, before, after*
Compare and contrast	To look at the similarities and differences between two or more objects, texts, ideas, and so forth	*similarly, likewise, in the same way, in contrast, on the other hand, however, alternatively*
Conflict/resolution	To describe a conflict within a person or between people and how it was resolved; used in narrative writing; may include an *epiphany* or "aha!" moment when a character "sees the light"	Most likely to be chronological linking words, used as the story unfolds
Emphatic (order of importance)	To show relation of (at least) three things to each other	*more, most, first, greatest, better, best, worse, worst*
Problem/solution	To explain how to solve a problem; used in expository writing	*one solution, another possibility, hence, therefore, furthermore, in addition, mainly, more importantly, most importantly*
Spatial	To describe the various parts of something in relation to the location of other parts	*above, over, behind, next to, underneath, to the right of, to the left of*

Each of the following stages of the writing process can be a tremendous help to students:

>> **Pre-writing:** Jotting down ideas regarding the central idea *(thesis)* and two or three main points to support it

>> **Generating ideas:** Brainstorming details (making clusters or lists, or freewriting) to support each main point

>> **Organizing:** Outlining

>> **Writing:** Expressing first thoughts, reasons for them, and closing thoughts

EXAMPLE

A fifth-grade teacher is using a sample, anonymous student essay-in-progress to clarify a point. The problem she is addressing in the student's work is that it seems choppy; it's hard to follow the flow. Which one best describes the problem as well as the stage in the writing process the student has just completed?

(A) lack of linking words; writing

(B) lack of support detail; generating ideas

(C) unclear thesis (central idea); outlining

(D) grammatical errors; final draft

The correct answer is Choice (A). Linking words connect ideas and help make the essay flow smoothly within and between paragraphs. Linking words are usually added in the *revise* stage, after the student has completed his initial thoughts in the *writing* stage. Choice (B) is wrong because support details create conviction, not flow; these details *would* most likely be flushed out in the *idea-generating* stage. Choice (C) is wrong because the problem isn't an uncertainty about the essay's focus; the thesis would be settled on before the *outlining* stage. Choice (D) is wrong because grammatical errors may cause confusion but not choppiness; most, if not all, of these error corrections should have been completed during the *second draft* stage.

Using and citing sources

Students need to know how and where to find information about a topic they want to research, and then how to document their sources. The Internet has become a mainstay of research, and students need to know minimal navigation skills, such as keyboard searches and scrolling, as well as be aware of possible bias on some sites. More traditional sources include the *almanac,* which has yearly weather and sun/moon information; *atlas,* which has maps with ample geographical information; and *encyclopedia,* which has general and in-depth information on a wide range of subjects, from biography to history to zoology.

There are two main kinds of sources: primary and secondary. *Primary sources* are firsthand accounts, those where the information begins. They include autobiographies, diaries, interviews, journals, letters, observations, and presentations.

Secondary sources give secondhand accounts and often include opinions, interpretations, or analysis. It's up to the reader to determine whether a secondary source is reliable. For example, an assessment made by a noted historian in a respectable magazine is probably reliable, but a comment made by an anonymous person on a political website may not be. Writers should stay away from secondary sources that may be uninformed or biased.

Whether a source of information is primary or secondary, it must be correctly acknowledged, or *credited,* in the essay. *Citations* must be provided for *direct quotations,* which require quotation marks, as well as for *paraphrases,* which require you to use your own words and sentence structure to accurately restate the author's opinion. These in-text citations are found within parentheses at the end of the quotation or paraphrase and include the author's last name, unless you have already mentioned it, and the page number, if there is one. Here are a few sample citations:

>> Louise Sampson believes that children who receive instruction in preschool "are not being rushed" (37).

>> In the words of one researcher, preschool children receiving instruction "are not being rushed" (Sampson 37).

>> Preschool is not too soon for children to receive instruction (Sampson 37).

Students may use *footnotes,* which appear at the end of the page that the reference is on; or *end-notes,* which appear all together, in numerical order, at the end of the research paper. A *bibliography* comes at the very end and lists all the sources in alphabetical order. Footnotes, endnotes, and the bibliography have very specific rules for their listings. Here is the format for some common types of sources:

>> **Books:** Author's last name, first name and middle name/initial. *Title of Book.* Place of Publication: Publishing company, year of publication.

>> **Encyclopedias:** Author's last name, first name and middle name/initial. "Article Name." *Title of Encyclopedia.* Edition number. Year of publication.

>> **Magazines:** Author's last name, first name and middle name/initial. "Article Name." *Title of Magazine.* Day of month (if applicable) Month year: page number(s) of article.

>> **Websites:** Author's last name, first name and middle name/initial. "Title of Article/Document." *Title of Site.* Ed. Name of editor (first name last name). Date of publication or most recent update. Name of organization associated with site. Date you accessed the document.

EXAMPLE

A student decides to research and write about the childhood of a famous person. Which of the following would NOT be a concern of the student?

(A) using a primary source such as a diary, citing a quotation from it in the endnotes, and listing the diary in the bibliography

(B) using a description of the person's early life found on the Internet, on a site that the teacher has helped the student verify as objective and well-researched, and listing the site in the bibliography

(C) using a secondary source written by a childhood friend of the famous person, properly paraphrasing it, and listing the article in the bibliography

(D) using the part of an encyclopedic entry under the *Early life* heading, properly paraphrasing it, and listing the volume in the bibliography

The correct answer is Choice (D). The first two parts of this choice would be concerns of the student, but the last part would not be: The bibliographic entry for an encyclopedia does not include the volume because the entries are listed alphabetically and are so easy to find. Choice (A) lists an important primary source and how to properly reference it. Choice (B) lists a legitimate source and an important consideration when using the Internet. Choice (C) lists a legitimate source and how to use and reference it.

Building strength through practice

Writing development occurs in stages as students' skills evolve. An important vocabulary word associated with writing and spelling is **orthography** (*ortho-* means *straight* or *correct*). Orthography is the study of a language's *spelling* system. Orthography involves how letters go together to make sounds and form words.

The stages of writing development are:

>> **Scribbles or drawings:** Marks or pictures the child makes to show ideas; may seem random and do not look like print

>> **Letter-like symbols:** Some marks look like letters; numbers may be present as well; marks may seem random, but the child can tell a story from them

>> **Strings of letters:** Some letters recognizable, usually in capitals; sense of phonics (letter-sound relationship) developing

>> **Beginning sounds:** A greater connection between what the child writes and draws to go with it; child begins noting difference between a letter and a word; spacing may be irregular

>> **Consonants representing words:** Spacing (between words) becomes more regular; lower-case letters appear; some sentences convey ideas

>> **Initial, middle, and final sounds:** Writing makes sense and most is legible; spelling of sight words and known names is correct, but that of most other words is phonetic

>> **Transitional phrases:** Writing is legible and more spelling is correct; the child begins to write in standard form

>> **Standard spelling:** Most spelling is correct; child begins to understand root words, compound words, and contractions

EXAMPLE

A first-grade teacher observes that some students are starting to put spaces between words on a consistent basis. In which stage of development is their writing?

(A) strings of letters

(B) consonants represent words

(C) transitional phrases

(D) standard spelling

The correct answer is Choice (B). The spacing between words becomes more regular. Choice (A) is wrong because students are still focused on shaping letters at this stage. Choice (C) is wrong because students have moved beyond the sense of what a word is and how words are spaced to thinking about correct spelling. Choice (D) is wrong because students have, by this final stage, moved on to an understanding of different kinds of words, such as root words, compound words, and contractions.

Just as students gain confidence and strength as they learn and practice, so will you. To write a clear and detailed essay requires research (or review) and practice.

Assign yourself a topic for an opinion essay, reread the parts of this section about opinions and organization, and go through the stages of the writing process until you have a four- or five-paragraph essay. Review the four bullet points introduced by "Ultimately, your essay should have" in the "Opinion essays" section earlier in this chapter.

Keeping up with rules and words

You need to know many of the ins and outs of the English language, including parts of speech, parts of sentences, and types of sentences, including proper grammar and proper use of words. Table 4-2 lists definitions and some examples of the parts of speech.

TABLE 4-2   Parts of Speech

Part of Speech	Definition	Examples
Noun	A specific person, place, or thing	*astonishment, Belfast, chemistry, king, Marietta, telescope, window*
Pronoun	Takes the place of and refers to a specific person, place, or thing	*anyone, each, he, hers, I, it, many, me, ours, someone, they, this, us, which, whose, you*
Verb	The action, what happens	*learned, may be, ruminates, is, sees, studies, wandered*
Adjective	Modifies a noun or pronoun	*difficult, good, sunny, vast*
Adverb	Modifies a verb, adjective, or other adverb	*amazingly, fondly, very, well*
Preposition	Shows how things are set in time or space	*about, above, at, before, by, during, for, in, of, through, to, under, with*
Conjunction	Makes a connection between words	*and, but, for, nor, or, so, yet*
Interjection	Expresses an emotion	*oh!, look out!, ah, whoopee, oops*

Understanding sentence structure

The two main parts of a sentence are the subject and predicate. The *subject* is who or what the sentence is about; it is a noun or pronoun, person, place, or thing. Here is a sentence: *The unexpected nature of baseball means that nothing might happen or anything might happen.* The *simple subject* is *nature*; the *complete subject* contains all the modifiers (descriptors) of *nature: the unexpected nature of baseball.*

The *predicate* of a sentence is the verb, or the action: what the subject does or what happens to the subject. Look at this sentence: *My Great Aunt Charlotte liked making her own jams and jellies.* The simple predicate is the verb, *liked.* The complete predicate is everything that goes with *liked: liked making her own jams and jellies.*

A *clause* is a group of words, the smallest grammatical unit that has a subject and a verb, such as *after the rain came.* A clause may be *dependent,* as it is in the previous example: It cannot stand on its own because the rest of the thought/sentence is missing. An *independent* clause *can* stand on its own, such as *the rain came after dinner.*

A complete sentence must have at least one independent clause; if it doesn't, it is a sentence *fragment.* The second, underlined part of the following is a fragment: *It is a fact that sometimes students have to memorize things. Because if they don't, they won't remember them.* Sentence fragments show up more and more in modern life, from advertising to Twitter, but they are still considered errors in formal, expository writing. In narrative writing, fragments may be used for effect.

A *compound sentence* has more than one independent clause: *It is a fact that sometimes students have to memorize things, so students need to make time for memorization.* A *complex sentence* has one independent clause and at least one dependent clause: *When students want to take a break, they might go for a brisk walk.* A *compound-complex sentence* has more than one independent clause and at least one dependent clause: *Guiding the young, elementary school teachers juggle time with all the skills and strategies they have to impart; teaching is not a simple job.*

A sentence may be one of four types. A *declarative* sentence makes a statement and ends with a period: *I found my baseball.* An *exclamatory* sentence shows excitement and ends with an exclamation point: *I found my baseball!* An *interrogative* sentence asks a question and ends with a question mark: *Have you seen my baseball?* An *imperative* sentence makes a command or request and can end with an exclamation point or a period: *Go find my baseball! Please help me find my baseball.*

EXAMPLE

What words would you use to describe the following sentence: *In March, when snow still covers some fields, I wonder: Will spring ever come?*

(A) declarative; compound-complex

(B) imperative; compound

(C) interrogative; compound-complex

(D) exclamatory; complex

The correct answer is Choice (C). The sentence is a question (the writer asks it of him- or herself); there are two independent clauses (*I wonder* and *will spring ever come*) and one dependent clause (*In march, when snow still covers some fields*). Choice (A) is wrong because the sentence asks a question and does not make a statement. The sentence *is* compound-complex. Choice (B) is wrong in the first part as well as the second: The sentence is not a command, and it has a dependent clause as well as two independent clauses. Choice (D) is wrong in the first part as well as the second: There is no exclamation point, and it has more than one independent clause as well as a dependent one.

Noun-verb agreement

In order to avoid errors in writing, students need to be aware of *agreement.* There must be *subject-verb agreement,* either both singular or both plural. When you see, *the grasses waves in the wind,* you know there is an error: *grasses* is a plural noun but *waves* is a singular verb. Some errors in subject-verb agreement are more difficult to spot. Look closely for the error in this sentence: *I don't know why it's so difficult to learn about gardening, there is some wonderful books about it.* If you think *is* is wrong and should be *are* because the subject is the plural, *books,* you're right. Try this one: *At the edge of the property, the old barn, roof collapsing yet still keeping its boards, stand in memory to past times.* The simple subject of the sentence is in the singular, *barn* (not *boards*), so the verb needs to be in the singular: *stands.*

A noun and its pronoun also need to be in agreement, in both number and in case. Subject pronouns—*I, we, he, she, they*—are in the nominative case. Object pronouns, functioning as objects (of prepositions), are in the objective case: *me, us, him, her, them.*

Look at this example: *Sarah and me tried very hard to stay out of trouble.* The speaker is one of the two subjects (including *Sarah*) and so the pronoun should be *I.* A handy way to recognize this error is to mentally drop the first subject and see just the pronoun: *Me tried very hard to stay out of trouble* makes the error easier to spot.

One thing to remember about pronoun agreement is the pronoun *each* is singular (as in *each one*), along with *none (no one)* and *either (one).* Also, *they* and *their* are plural, so this sentence has a pronoun agreement error: *A student should know the difference between singular and plural if <u>they</u> want to avoid grammatical errors.* To fix this error, make both subject and pronoun plural (*students. . .they*) or singular (*student. . .he or she*).

EXAMPLE

Which word is incorrect in the following sentence: *After drafting, the students read them aloud to each other.*

(A) After

(B) drafting

(C) them

(D) each

The correct answer is Choice (C). This is a situation where the pronoun *them*'s noun is unclear. What does *them* refer to? A good fix is to use a noun such as *(the or their) drafts*. Choice (A) is a preposition and not part of the noun-pronoun connection. Choice (B) is a verb and not part of the noun-pronoun connection; because it suggests the missing noun *(drafts)*, it can make the error hard to spot. Choice (D) is a pronoun but not part of the noun-pronoun connection in question.

Using words correctly

Usage errors occur when a word is incorrectly used, generally mistaken for another. When, for example, do you use *affect* versus *effect*? What's the difference between *loose* and *lose*? Table 4-3 lists some commonly confused word pairs.

TABLE 4-3 **Commonly Confused Word Pairs**

Word 1	Description	Word 2	Description
accept	*to receive*—a verb	except	*excluding*—preposition
adapt	*to adjust*	adopt	*to take as one's own*
affect	*to cause a change*—a verb	effect	*something caused by a change*—a noun
all ready	*completely prepared*	already	*earlier*
all right	written as two words	alright	nonstandard
beside	*next to*	besides	*in addition to; also*
cite	*to quote*—a verb	site	*a place*—a noun
conscience	*moral sense*—a noun	conscious	*aware*—an adjective
elicit	*to draw out*—a verb	illicit	*unlawful*— an adjective
farther	used to describe distances *(beyond)*	further	used for degree or amount *(in addition)*
fewer	used with item that can be counted	less	used for general amounts
immigrate to	to enter and settle into a country from another	emigrate from	to leave a country and settle into another
it's	*it is; a contraction*	its	*belonging to; a possessive pronoun*
lie	*to rest or recline*	lay	*to put or place*
loose	*not attached*—an adjective	lose	*to misplace*—a verb
media	*more than one form*—plural	medium	*one form*—singular
precede	*to come before*	proceed	*to go forward*
principal	*head of a school; most important*	principle	*essential truth*
than	used in comparisons—a conjunction	then	used to show time—an adverb
to	a preposition	too	*overmuch*—an adverb

Choosing the appropriate writing style

In addition to choosing correctly between two confusing words, writers need to choose the right words for the time and place. Just as you might talk formally to a stranger and casually to a close friend, the *style* of your writing needs to match your *audience.*

Almost all academic and professional writing is formal. In this type of writing, the use of *idioms,* which are usually colorful expressions that don't translate literally, is generally inappropriate. "Keep your eyes peeled" (in other words, *Stay watchful*) is an idiom, as is "A penny for your thoughts" (meaning *What is on your mind?*).

EXAMPLE

Which of the following sentences contains a usage error?

(A) The research team for the revised usage dictionary had the following sentence as an example for the new entry, *dis: The student stood up and angrily shouted, "Don't dis me!"*

(B) Having fully studied the affects of fluoride in drinking water, the team compiled and released its findings.

(C) The television medium is one that has been studied for over fifty years.

(D) There is no overriding reason for Juanita and Carlos to attend their reunion if they're dreading it.

The correct answer is Choice (B). The word *affects* should be the word *effects.* Choice (A) is correct because *dis* is being entered as a word, not being used as slang. Choice (C) is correct because the singular *medium* goes with *one* and *television.* Choice (D) is correct (although some would argue that using a contraction is not) and is yet another example of words that may be confused *(they're* vs. *there, their).*

EXAMPLE

For each of the following three example questions, choose the best answer based on this passage:

1. Far from agreeing with each other, each of the twins have a distinctive opinion about two forms of inner-city transit. **2.** Lawrence feels the bus is a more cost-efficient way to get around in the city, but Trevor thinks the subway makes more sense because it saves time. **3.** Regarding the experience of travel, Lawrence prefers the bus because he likes to see what's going on and doesn't feel trapped. **4.** Trevor says the transit goes amazing fast and that getting to the destination is the point of the experience for him. **5.** One thing you can say about the twins' opinions are that they show reason.

Which word or words in Sentences 1 and 2 contain an error?

(A) each

(B) have

(C) more

(D) sense

The correct answer is Choice (B). The subject *each* (one) is singular and so requires the singular verb *has.* Choice (A) does not contain an error. Choice (C) does not contain an error: The use of *more* is correct when comparing two things; *most* is used if there are more than two. Choice (D) does not contain an error.

Which revision should be made to Sentences 3 or 4 to correct an error?

(A) Remove the comma after *travel* in Sentence 3.

(B) Change *he* to *one* in Sentence 3.

(C) Change *amazing* to *amazingly* in Sentence 4.

(D) Add the word *whole* just before the word *experience* in Sentence 4.

The correct answer is Choice (C). The word *amazing* is an adjective. The sentence calls for the adverb *amazingly* to describe how fast the subway goes. Choice (A) would create confusion as the comma after travel creates a necessary pause. Choice (B) is wrong because the pronoun *he* agrees with the noun *Lawrence.* Choice (D) may be a good suggestion, but there is no error in omitting it.

What is the error in Sentence 5?

(A) The subject and verb are not in agreement.

(B) The noun and pronoun are not in agreement.

(C) There is a proper noun that needs to be capitalized.

(D) The sentence is declarative, so it needs an exclamation point.

The correct answer is Choice (A). The subject of the sentence is *one* (not *opinions*), so it takes the singular verb *is*. Choice (B) is wrong because the noun *opinions* is in agreement with the pronoun *they*. Choice (C) is wrong because twins is a common noun, not a proper noun such as Lawrence or Trevor. Choice (D) is wrong because, while the sentence is declarative, it does not require an exclamation point. The use of an exclamation point here would not in and of itself be wrong.

Using figurative language

In addition to idioms, another type of language that is not to be read literally is *figurative language*. While you may not use it in your academic writing, you or your students will when writing prose and poetry. Here are some figurative language terms to be familiar with:

>> **Alliteration:** Repetition of the initial consonant sounds (for example, *such sweet sorrow*)

>> **Hyperbole:** Exaggeration (for example, my tears could fill *an ocean*)

>> **Imagery:** Descriptions that appeal to the senses

>> **Metaphor:** A direct comparison (without the word *like* or *as*), such as *my love is a rose*

>> **Onomatopoeia:** Words that sound like what they represent, such as *boom* or *squish*

>> **Oxymoron:** An apparent contradiction, such as a loud silence

>> **Personification:** Giving human qualities to something that isn't human, such as a *kind rainfall*

>> **Simile:** A comparison (weaker than a metaphor) that uses the words *like* or *as,* such as *my love is like a rose*

>> **Symbol:** Something used to represent something else

Understanding morphology

Along with *orthography* (the study of a language's spelling system), an important vocabulary word is *morphology,* which means the forms of words (*morph-* means *form* or *shape*). Related to orthography and morphology are these words:

>> **Root:** The basic form of a word, with no element added *(affixed)* to it

>> **Affix:** An element added to a word to change its meaning; includes both prefixes and suffixes

>> **Prefix:** An element (such as *multi-* or *tele-*) added to the beginning of a word

>> **Suffix:** An element (such as *-ment* or *-ship*) added to the end of a word

Determining the meaning of words

Students need to understand the meanings of the following terms:

>> **Homonyms:** Two (or more) words that are spelled the same but have different meanings, such as *left* (not taken) and *left* (not right)

>> **Homophones:** Two (or more) words that are pronounced (that *sound*) the same but have different meanings, such as *you* and *yew*

>> **Antonyms:** Words that are opposite in meaning

>> **Synonyms:** Words that are similar in meaning

When needing to determine the meaning of a word in a story or an essay, a reader may find several types of clues. In addition to syntactical (based on the order/place of the word in the sentence) and semantic (based on the general meaning of the story or sentence) clues mentioned earlier, readers may find more specific clues:

>> **Antonym clues:** Suggest an opposite meaning and are indicated by such words as *but, in contrast,* and *unlike*

>> **Synonym clues:** Suggest a similar meaning and are indicated by such words as *that is* (or the use of *i.e.*), *in other words,* and *also referred to as*

>> **Definition clues:** Follow the unknown word and explain it, indicated by such words as *means* and *defined as* and formatted in boldface or italics

>> **General knowledge clues:** Come from a reader's background knowledge

>> **Word analysis clues:** Arrived at by analyzing the root and affixes of a word

EXAMPLE

A student reads the following in an article: *The imagery is harsh and often hard to think about.* The student has never seen the word *imagery* before but decides it means *pictures suggested by the words* and goes on reading. Was the student's definition okay? What vocabulary clue did the student use?

(A) The student's definition is okay; he or she used word analysis.

(B) The student's definition is okay; he or she used definition clues.

(C) The student's definition is not okay; he or she used antonym clues.

(D) The student's definition is not okay; he or she used synonym clues.

The correct answer is Choice (A). Imagery can create a mental picture, pertaining to the sense of seeing; the student knew that the root word, *image*, meant *picture*. The first part of Choice (B) is correct, but the second is not: There is no definition of *imagery* in the sentence. The first part of Choice (C) is incorrect, as is the second: There is no word in the sentence that means the opposite of *imagery*. The first part of Choice (D) is incorrect, as is the second: There is no word in the sentence that has a meaning similar to *imagery*.

Analyzing Literature and Informational Texts

There are many parts of literature and informational texts to consider when analyzing them. From little pictures or images that lead to the bigger picture, from the things characters say to the way they say them, and from the overall structure to the purpose behind it, all things work together in a well-written text.

Finding and connecting the dots

Readers are often asked to note details and make *inferences,* finding unstated but intended meanings, and to draw conclusions. Many factors need to be considered when analyzing literature.

A central factor of most novels is the main character. A character may be the story's hero, or *protagonist,* or the character or force set against the hero, the *antagonist.* You may learn about characters through thoughts, action, or *dialogue* (speech).

Where a story takes place is its *setting,* and the feeling or mood of the story is its *tone.* The tone may be eerie (think Edgar Allan Poe's *The Tell-Tale Heart*) or satiric (think George Orwell's *Animal Farm*), happy, humorous, serious, or anywhere in between. How fast the story moves along is its *pace.*

When character recollections or third-person narrations take the story back in time, altering the straightforward chronology of the tale, it is called a *flashback.* A story's *plot,* its series or sequence of events, usually follows a five-part pattern. This pattern may be represented by a graph or pyramid showing a beginning, a rise in action/pace, a climax/high point, a fall in action/pace, and a further fall or slowing down that represents the story's conclusion. The five parts are usually labeled as follows:

>> **Exposition:** The introduction of the character(s), setting, and tone.

>> **Conflict (complication) and rising action:** People or events complicate or work against the protagonist and lead to a rise in action and usually in pace.

>> **Climax:** Conflicting forces come to a head; the high point of the story, usually with the most emotion or tension.

>> **Falling action:** The pace slows; unknown things are revealed.

>> **Resolution:** Any remaining questions are answered (usually); conflicts are resolved or somehow put to the side in a concluding manner.

All of these story components go together to create the *theme,* or main idea. When considering a theme, ask yourself what the components add up to—what message the author wants you to get. Many works of literature have more than one theme. For example, many works of Charles Dickens, set in impoverished sections of newly industrialized London, have themes portraying the dirt and squalor that industrialization produced as well as of how superficial the class system was.

EXAMPLE

Use the following excerpt to answer the next three questions. Look for details to connect the dots and make inferences about character, events, and theme.

Moby Dick
—Herman Melville

Chapter I Loomings

Call me Ishmael. Some years ago—never mind how long precisely—having little or no money in my purse, and nothing particular to interest me on shore, I thought I would sail about a little and see the watery part of the world. It is a way I have of driving off the spleen, and regulating the circulation. Whenever I find myself growing grim about the mouth; whenever it is a damp, drizzly November in my soul; whenever I find myself involuntarily pausing (05) before coffin warehouses, and bringing up the rear of every funeral I meet; and especially whenever my hypos get such an upper hand of me, that it requires a strong moral principle to prevent me from deliberately stepping into the street, and methodically knocking people's hats off—then, I account it high time to get to sea as soon as I can.

Which best describes the organization of the passage?

(A) chronological, with a flashback

(B) chronological, with two flashbacks

(C) straightforwardly chronological

(D) compare and contrast

The correct answer is Choice (A). The description traces events and feelings in the narrator's life. The passage starts in the present (Call me Ishmael), the second sentence is a flashback, and the third and final sentences resume in the present. Choice (B) is wrong because there is just one flashback. Choice (C) is wrong because it does not account for the flashback. Choice (D) is wrong because the passage does not methodically describe the similarities and differences of two things.

What do Lines 5–9 convey regarding the passage's tone?

(A) It's completely unhappy and distressing.

(B) It's completely full of sarcasm and discontent.

(C) It combines a longing for the sea with a fear of it.

(D) It combines bleakness and self-reflective humor.

The correct answer is Choice (D). The bleakness is conveyed by such details as "a damp, drizzly November," "coffin warehouses," and "funeral." The phrase "methodically knocking people's hats off" has a slapstick humor to it, and "then I account it high time" is self-reflective. Choice (A) is wrong because it does not account for the self-reflective humor. Choice (B) is wrong because Ishmael is not mocking himself throughout nor expressing discontent throughout. Choice (C) is wrong because there are no details of life at sea.

What is the main purpose of the passage?

(A) to show why Ishmael needed to be at sea

(B) to show the reader how grim life in the city could be

(C) to introduce Ishmael and the mood and setting of the story

(D) to introduce the theme of life at sea by writing in a long, wavering style

The correct answer is Choice (C). The reader learns initial information about the speaker as well as about the setting and tone of the story. Choice (A) covers part of the passage but does not grasp the larger picture or purpose. Choice (B) covers a portion of the passage but leaves out Ishmael. Choice (D) may have been in Melville's mind, but it does not account for what is shown about Ishmael.

Looking at how and why the work was made

Writers make conscious choices regarding how they tell a story and how a character thinks, speaks, and acts. These choices usually align with the author's purpose.

The way a character speaks should reflect his experience and cultural environment. For example, a character with little formal education from a rural or isolated place will most likely have a unique *dialect* that includes regional *slang*.

The imagery of the piece also contributes greatly to its impact. What pictures does the author paint? What do readers see, hear, smell, and so on through the characters' senses? How much space does the author allot for each picture? Answers to these questions tell you what is important to the author and how important it is.

Another consideration is the *point of view* of the text—who is the *narrator*? From whose point of view is the story being told? *First person* uses the pronouns *I, me,* and *mine* and thus presents a very personal, inner voice, the narrator's own, such as in the previous excerpt from *Moby Dick*. *Second person* uses the pronoun *you* and thus includes or involves the reader directly. *Third person* uses the pronouns *he, she,* and *they*, thereby distancing the narrator or speaker. A third-person narrator may be *omniscient (omni-* means *all)*, knowing all the characters' thoughts and feelings, or *limited omniscient*, knowing just one character's thoughts and feelings.

An *author's purpose* may be, generally, to entertain, to inform, or to persuade. Quite often more than one of these purposes appears in a story. As a reader, you most likely want a narrative to entertain you and engage your attention, or you may not purchase it, let alone read it. You may read a newspaper for information or an editorial to be persuaded . . . or not.

EXAMPLE

Use the excerpt from Adventures of Huckleberry Finn to answer the questions that follow.

Adventures of Huckleberry Finn
—Mark Twain

Chapter I

YOU don't know about me without you have read a book by the name of The Adventures of Tom Sawyer; but that ain't no matter. That book was made by Mr. Mark Twain, and he told the truth, mainly. There was things which he stretched, but mainly he told the truth. That is nothing. I never seen anybody but lied one time or another, without it was Aunt Polly, or the widow, or maybe Mary. Aunt Polly—Tom's Aunt Polly, she is—and Mary, and the Widow (05) Douglas is all told about in that book, which is mostly a true book, with some stretchers, as I said before.

Now the way that the book winds up is this: Tom and me found the money that the robbers hid in the cave, and it made us rich. We got six thousand dollars apiece—all gold. It was an awful sight of money when it was piled up. Well, Judge Thatcher he took it and put it out at (10) interest, and it fetched us a dollar a day apiece all the year round—more than a body could tell what to do with. The Widow Douglas she took me for her son, and allowed she would sivilize me; but it was rough living in the house all the time, considering how dismal regular and decent the widow was in all her ways; and so when I couldn't stand it no longer I lit out. I got into my old rags and my sugar-hogshead [a large barrel Huck sleeps in] again, and was free (15) and satisfied. But Tom Sawyer he hunted me up and said he was going to start a band of robbers, and I might join if I would go back to the widow and be respectable. So I went back.

What is the point of view of the story?

(A) first person
(B) second person
(C) third person limited
(D) third person omniscient

The correct answer is Choice (A). Huckleberry Finn tells the story in his own voice, using *I*, *me*, and *my* throughout. Choice (B) is wrong even though the initial word, *you*, seems to indicate otherwise at first. Choice (C) is wrong because there is not a narrator referring to Huck using *he*, *him*, and *his*. Choice (D) is wrong because there is not a narrator referring to Huck as well as all the other characters using *he*, *him*, and *his*.

Which of the following is NOT true about the passage?

(A) The many examples of grammatical errors in Huck's narrative are clues to his rough upbringing; additionally, they instill trust in a reader because they suggest Huck is being true to himself and speaking honestly.

(B) Mark Twain uses Lines 14–16 to show the reader how much Huck liked living in the comfort of the Widow Douglas.

(C) Mark Twain is laughing at himself in Lines 2–3 and thereby setting a humorous tone.

(D) The very shortness of the final sentence adds a touch of humor in its matter-of-factness and simplicity, contrasting with the preceding, longer reflections.

The correct answer is Choice (B). The images of Lines 14–16 pertain to Huck's chosen comforts, which are ragged and not like the life he'd know with the Widow Douglas. Choice (A) is true as we hear the forthright words, incorrect though they may be, and so believe Huck. Choice (C) is true as Twain has Huck, the wise roughneck, say he (Twain) is mostly reliable. Choice (D) is true, especially as it is the rough equivalent of a sigh: Huck did not want to give up his freedom (see Lines 14–16).

What is the purpose of these first two paragraphs of the story?

(A) to entertain and persuade

(B) to entertain and inform

(C) to persuade and inform

(D) to entertain, persuade, and inform

The correct answer is Choice (B). Mark Twain gives readers a humorous, entertaining picture of Huck while filling readers in on what happened in the earlier story *(The Adventures of Tom Sawyer)*. Choice (A) is wrong because Twain is not trying to convince readers regarding one of the sides of an issue; rather, he is trying to give them background information. Choice (C) is wrong because Twain is attempting to entertain readers but not trying to convince them regarding one of the sides of an issue. Choice (D) is wrong because Twain is not trying to convince readers regarding one of the sides of an issue.

Thinking further about structure and logic

When analyzing informational text, it's a good idea to keep structure and purpose in mind. How is the text organized? How does the organization affect the author's purpose? What was the author thinking?

Additionally, ask yourself how convinced you are of the author's logic. Is there enough evidence to support the points? Do the points add up to convince you of the main idea/thesis?

Use the following passage to answer the questions that follow it.

EXAMPLE

Has any one ever met, in real life, the woman who screams and jumps on a chair at the sight of a mouse? I have never heard of her out of the servants' hall, where ladies' maids appear to carry on the traditions of sensibility kept up by their betters two or three generations since, when nerves, swoonings, and burnt feathers played a prominent part in the lives of fashionable women. A little mouse has nothing terrible about it, vermin though it be in strict classification. (05) Now, if it had been a rat! Or a black beetle! A large, long-legged, rattling cockroach! Truly, these are awesome things, and even the strongest-minded of women hate the sight of them. Very few women, I take it, are afraid of mice. And yet, as the world rolls on, that little story of a small grey mouse and screeching women will reappear again and again, dressed up in fresh fancy costumes, when news is scarce and a corner of the paper has to be filled up. (10)

Which one best describes the essay's unconventional structure?

(A) all chronological

(B) some compare/contrast; some conflict/resolution

(C) some problem/solution; mostly spatial

(D) all emphatic

The correct answer is Choice (B). The writer compares and contrasts mice to other vermin, and poses the conflict of old ways (*nerves, swoonings*) with her present, and the conflict of what she takes as a silly notion, *dressed up in fresh fancy costumes,* with a resolution that she somewhat despairs of finding. Choice (A) is wrong because the essay is not built on a timeline, other than the world rolling on. Choice (C) is wrong because, while you may argue that there is a problem— equating women with being afraid of mice—there is no solution; further, there is no spatial description other than a woman being on top of a chair. Choice (D) is wrong because an emphatic structure is organized by points being listed in the order of importance. The rat, black beetle, and cockroach do not (except humorously) qualify as points.

Why do you think the author chose her unconventional structural approach?

(A) It supports her purpose of undermining the conventional attitude regarding women and mice.

(B) It supports her purpose of showing there are worse things than mice to be afraid of.

(C) It supports her purpose of showing how silly women used to be.

(D) It supports her purpose of laughing at women who are afraid of mice.

The correct answer is Choice (A). The author clearly has a tongue-in-cheek attitude toward the whole fear-of-vermin stereotype and wants to put it in its place. Choice (B) is wrong because, although this point was mentioned, it does not speak to the overall purpose of the author's approach. Choice (C) is wrong because it does not address the larger point that the attitudes toward women are outdated, not just customs such as swooning. Choice (D) is wrong because the author doesn't so much laugh at such women as question whether they (still) exist.

Which lines support the author's purpose, and why?

(A) Lines 1–4, because they establish the point that equating women with fearing mice is outdated.

(B) Lines 6–7, because their tongue-in-cheek, part truth/part exaggeration nature functions as satire. The word *awesome*, until recently, meant inspiring awe or reverence—not a word used to describe vermin.

(C) Lines 8–10, because they show how much significance, or, literally, space in the paper, the author thinks should be given to the women-afraid-of-mice story: very little.

(D) all of the above

The correct answer is Choice (D). Choice (A) is wrong because it omits the lines listed in Choices (B) and (C). Choice (B) is wrong because it omits the lines listed in Choices (A) and (C). Choice (C) is wrong because it omits the lines listed in Choices (A) and (B).

TIP

Often, readers are asked to compare texts. Whether comparing two texts for a reading analysis or for an essay, you'll want to examine the question or writing prompt first. Doing so will save time as you can then focus your thoughts on the question or prompt as you read the texts. You may want to make notes or annotations in the margins or on a scrap piece of paper. This is a way of helping you pay attention, of engaging with the material.

If you're writing an essay, underline specific details or facts that strike you as particularly effective: You many want to quote or paraphrase them as support for your argument. Review the stages of the writing process covered earlier in this chapter. Using an abbreviated version of them may be very helpful. Jot down any ideas you get, for either details or main points, as you read. When you finish reading, make a list of two or three main points and put them in the order in which you want to cover them. Decide on your thesis. Then start writing. Remember to wrap things up strongly in your conclusion, and then to proofread, correcting any errors.

Reading deeply, reading strong

It's important for readers to go beyond their comfort zone in both subject matter and grade level. Going beyond both the former and the latter may require scaffolding or support of some sort, but pushing the boundaries of levels, including levels of awareness, is not a bad thing.

In addition to textual aids such as *glossaries* and reading comprehension strategies such as those noted in the earlier section "Fluency" (annotating, KWL, making connections, and so forth), there are many visual aids available to help students understand informational texts. Public organizations have free material on the Internet, such as the National Oceanic and Atmospheric Administration's video on the tsunami warning system (www.tsunami.noaa.gov), and photographs and videos of Babe Ruth (at www.baseballhall.org/hof/ruth-babe).

EXAMPLE

Use the following passage to answer the questions that follow it.

Four score and seven years ago our fathers brought forth on this continent, a new nation, conceived in Liberty, and dedicated to the proposition that all men are created equal.

Now we are engaged in a great civil war, testing whether that nation, or any nation so conceived and dedicated, can long endure. We are met on a great battle-field of that war. We have come to dedicate a portion of that field, as a final resting place for those who here gave their lives that that nation might live. It is altogether fitting and proper that we should do this.

But, in a larger sense, we can not dedicate—we can not consecrate—we can not hallow—this ground. The brave men, living and dead, who struggled here, have consecrated it, far above our poor power to add or detract. The world will little note, nor long remember what we say here, but it can never forget what they did here. It is for us the living, rather, to be dedicated here to the unfinished work which they who fought here have thus far so nobly advanced. It is rather for us to be here dedicated to the great task remaining before us—that from these honored dead we take increased devotion to that cause for which they gave the last full measure of devotion—that we here highly resolve that these dead shall not have died in vain—that this nation, under God, shall have a new birth of freedom—and that government of the people, by the people, for the people, shall not perish from the earth.

People in Lincoln's time, or at least politicians, knew that the Constitution made no reference to "all men [being] created equal," but that the Declaration of Independence, written earlier, did. Keeping that information in mind, what do you think was the purpose of the first paragraph?

(A) to maneuver around the Constitution and stress that the Founding Fathers' main achievement was the Declaration of Independence

(B) to stress the importance of the Constitution in the fight to keep the Union together

(C) to let people know how he felt about slavery

(D) to let people know he was an educated man and was well aware of the exact number of years that had passed since the signing of the Declaration of Independence

The correct answer is Choice (A). Politicians at the time, particularly some from the South, used the Constitution as a defense of slavery, and Lincoln wanted to override that defense. Choice (B) is wrong because the first paragraph references the Declaration of Independence. Choice (C) is wrong because most people already knew how Lincoln felt and because it does not address Lincoln's Declaration of Independence reference. Choice (D) is wrong because it does not address the significance of Lincoln's reference to the Declaration of Independence.

When the speech was delivered in 1863, the war had been going on for two very bloody years with no end in sight, both sides having lost well over 20,000 soldiers each during the three days of the Battle of Gettysburg alone. In retrospect, we know General Robert E. Lee's forces never recovered from their losses at Gettysburg, but people then had no way of knowing when the war would be over.

What was the purpose of the second paragraph and the start of the third?

(A) to encourage more young men to enter the army, knowing they would be fighting for a worthy cause

(B) to acknowledge the union manufacturers who put up a lot of the money and supplies Lincoln needed to keep the living troops going

(C) to confess how little power Lincoln felt he had to make a proper dedication because it was not he who had died

(D) to acknowledge the deaths and how they are part of the ongoing test and cost of keeping a nation, and its adherence to the ideal of independence, alive

The correct answer is Choice (D). The literal purpose of those gathered then at Gettysburg was to dedicate a national cemetery there. Lincoln elevated the purpose by saying those who died dedicated their lives to the nation—a worthy sacrifice that would continue to be needed. Choice (A) is wrong because, while dwindling volunteers was a concern for Lincoln, addressing that issue was not his only concern. Choice (B) is wrong because nothing is said here about manufacturers. Choice (C) is wrong because, while Lincoln does express that sentiment at the start of the third paragraph, the sentiment does not cover all of his intent in that section and the second paragraph.

Lincoln's speech lasted less than three minutes. Do you think there's enough to convince a listener today of Lincoln's purpose? Why or why not?

(A) Yes; the many concrete details and facts provide good support for Lincoln's purpose of convincing people of the great worth of the idea behind the American government.

(B) Yes; the beauty and logic of the speech are moving and convincing. The shortness of it may have been unusual for its time, but in today's world, shortness is an advantage.

(C) No; Lincoln's speech needs more concrete details and facts to support his opinion.

(D) No; Lincoln's speech is too hard to read, and the difficulty of it undermines its purpose.

The question is open to discussion. Two students might each write excellent arguments, each student taking a different stance. However, for the purposes of comparison, here are the thoughts of the question's author: The correct answer is Choice (B). Poetry is moving, and there is poetry in Lincoln's use of repetition, alliteration, and parallel structure (". . . that from . . . that we . . . that this . . . "; "of the people, by the people, for the people"). Today's world *is* a world of sound bytes. Choice (A) is wrong because there aren't very many supporting details at all, the only hard fact being the opening "Four score [4 × 20] and seven years ago. . . ." Choice (C) is wrong because Lincoln was trying to convince his audience not with concrete details but with abstract ideals. Choice (D) is wrong because a speech is meant to be heard, not read, and the difficulty—one might say craft—of it *underlies* its purpose, that supporting the cause of independence is by no means easy.

Speaking and Listening Styles

From pair and group discussions to formal speeches, consideration must be given to speaking and listening skills. Additionally, implications regarding viewing and evaluating different media must be considered.

Talking and listening together

Surely, we all know the importance of talking and listening together. While some students—and teachers—may find it a challenge, or at least new, to incorporate these skills in the classroom, speaking and listening skills help students gain a deeper understanding of texts, not to mention help them beyond the language arts, or any, classroom.

One approach for developing talking and listening skills is to first model the behavior with the whole class. Regarding a character in an assigned passage, you may ask, "Why do you think [the main character] did what he did?" Then call on several students and encourage variations in the responses as long as they are plausible. Focus on students' efforts as well as their interpretations.

Next, prepare students for working in pairs with a set of ground rules. Here are a few:

>> Read the question to your partner out loud.

>> Sit quietly and listen carefully as your partner answers.

>> Agree or disagree with your partner.

>> Give specific examples or details from the passage as to why you agree or disagree.

>> Listen carefully again, letting your partner respond to what you've said.

Once you've gone over the ground rules (and it's a good idea to have them printed out or on the board, at least for the first several sessions), assign specific discussion questions to the pairs. Keep an ear open as to how the pairs are working but don't hover: Students need to try out their new skills, to make mistakes and correct them. Positive reinforcement works best: You want to grow skills and confidence.

Later in the school year, change from pairs to groups of three to five. The same ground rules apply, with one addition: *Take turns.* The same ground rules apply for you too: Be aware of what each group is saying, and intervene if you must, but give the students room.

TIP

Here, as well as in other areas of instruction, you may need to be prepared for English Language Learners, or ELL students. If you model patience with and understanding toward these students in the course of teaching, other students will behave similarly in pair or group work. It is important to remember that ELL students are not slow learners. They are most likely juggling many things, including having to learn the ins and outs of a new language and culture while simultaneously having to learn your curriculum.

EXAMPLE

A sixth-grade teacher has an ELL student in his class who has not offered an opinion after the first two discussions that the teacher has modeled for later pair and group work. What approach would be most helpful for the student at this point?

(A) ignoring the student and leaving her alone, waiting for the student to volunteer when ready

(B) asking the question louder, making sure that the student can hear you

(C) calling on the student and giving the student time to respond, asking a follow-up, prompting question if the student remains silent

(D) providing the student with possible answers and asking the student to choose the best one

The correct answer is Choice (C). The student needs a hand extended to her, figuratively speaking, and time to stand up. Choice (A) might be an initial approach, but the student should not be ignored or let be beyond a session or two. Choice (B) is more likely to have the effect of distressing the student than enlightening her. Choice (D) prevents the student from coming up with the answer on her own and does not prepare her for later pair and group work.

Being clear to your audience

More formal than group discussion, oral presentations have their own set of rules for both speaker and listener. Whether speaking, listening to a speaker, or watching a video on the Internet, students need to be mindful and observant.

The stress on giving oral presentations in class has increased. Here are several considerations for the speaker to keep in mind:

>> **Audience:** Who they are? What do they already know? Do you need to give them any background information?

>> **Occasion:** What is it? Is it somber? Happy? It should affect what you say and how you say it.

>> **Opening and closing statements:** These should be short and strong; the opening should at least imply the thesis, and the closing should state it directly.

>> **Organization:** The main points should be clear, support the thesis, and flow in a logical manner/structure.

>> **Support details:** These should be specific; there should be at least three per main point.

>> **Eye contact:** Look directly at your listeners from time to time.

>> **Looking lively:** Stand in a relaxed yet energized manner; make hand gestures where appropriate.

>> **Speaking lively:** Considering your audience and purpose as you do so, use an appropriate tone; vary the volume and pitch in appropriate places so that you're not using a monotone.

>> **Humor:** Especially at the start, a pertinent, humorous anecdote or joke can help relax an audience—and you. Keep in mind, however, that humor may not be appropriate for some occasions.

>> **Visual aids:** Use these as added support details where appropriate and possible.

EXAMPLE

A student has prepared a speech on the importance of funding for the space program. She first delivers the speech to her Science class at the end of their section on space travel. The following week, she is scheduled to present the speech in her Language Arts class. What change in her presentation is most likely necessary?

(A) the addition of background information

(B) the removal of the visual aids

(C) a conversion from an emphatic structure to a problem/solution one

(D) the taking of a very rigid approach, avoiding any eye contact

The correct answer is Choice (A). Her new audience, the Language Arts class, most likely does not know some necessary background information that her Science class studied. Choice (B) is wrong because visual aids help the audience understand. Choice (C) is wrong because the essence of the speech is the importance of funding, and the best structure to support content emphasizing importance is emphatic. Choice (D) is wrong because a rigid approach is never helpful and making eye contact is always a good idea.

Being a good listener

There are also several considerations for the listener to keep in mind when assessing an oral presentation. To be active listeners, students should be aware of the following, jotting down notes during the speech and after as it helps them:

>> **Approach:** Have your notepad and pen or pencil ready before the speaker begins; sit up straight; focus your attention on the speaker. Listen carefully.

>> **Opinion:** Do you agree or disagree with the speaker's thesis or opinion?

>> **Summary:** Make a list of the speaker's main points.

>> **Details:** Be able to repeat a fact or supporting detail the speaker used.

>> **Visual aids:** What were they? Did they help or hinder the speech? How?

>> **Reactions:** How do you feel about the speech? How do others in the audience feel?

>> **Tone:** What tone did the speaker use? What was the effect of the tone? Did it hurt or help the speaker's efforts?

>> **Questions:** What would you ask the speaker in order to clear up any uncertainties you have?

EXAMPLE

Which of the following lists best covers active listening?

(A) approaching, listening, questioning

(B) listing, annotating, reacting

(C) approaching, hearing, reacting

(D) hearing, understanding, evaluating

The correct answer is Choice (D). It best encompasses the eight bullet points. While it doesn't specifically say *approaching*, one can assume there was some kind of approach if the student is *hearing*. Choice (A) is wrong because *questioning* does not best suggest the more complete act of evaluating. Choice (B) is wrong because it covers neither careful listening nor judging. Choice (C) is wrong because it omits the judging or evaluating required.

Using visuals

Many visual tools are available for teachers today. You need to know how to incorporate them into the classroom so that they enhance or support whatever material you present, not take over your allotted instruction time.

REMEMBER

For assessing whatever is presented in the media, students should take an approach similar to that of assessing a speech. They still need to be good listeners as well as pay attention to what they're seeing and hearing in order to better evaluate the effects of the oral and visual material after the presentation. The guidelines listed previously for active listeners may also serve as a checklist when viewing media presentations.

EXAMPLE

A fourth-grade teacher uses an interactive white board to enlarge an Internet video on the screen. Following the video, the students are to meet in groups and answer four questions the teacher has prepared. What suggestions, if any, should she make before the video begins?

(A) No suggestions are necessary.

(B) She should tell each student to review the active listening guidelines before the video begins and to be aware of them during the group discussion.

(C) She should tell the students to relax and enjoy the video because they've been studying very hard.

(D) She should show the video first, and then hand out or put on the board the active listening guidelines for the students to use in group discussion.

The correct answer is Choice (B). Students will not assume they can use the guidelines in a different situation. They need to be told they can apply the same guidelines to the video as they have been using for texts. Choice (A) is wrong because, with the change in medium from text to video, the students will need, at the very least, a prompt to follow the guidelines. Choice (C) makes the use of the video a reward. While a reward has its place, it will not help students in group discussions answer questions about the video. Choice (D) is wrong because the students will not know they need to be active listeners during the video and so will most likely not pay careful attention.

Chapter 5

Mathematics Content Knowledge

O n your warpath toward acquiring full preparation for the Praxis Elementary Education: Curriculum, Instruction, and Assessment test and the Praxis Elementary Education: Content Knowledge test, you just entered the basic math weapons warehouse. In this warehouse, you find the artillery you need to really advance your level in the later math chapters. Although the math part of the Curriculum, Instruction, and Assessment test will generally ask you about teaching and assessment issues, you must have knowledge of the foundational math principles that are taught in a math classroom before you can get a firm grip on how to teach their application effectively.

Securing the knowledge that is presented here is a major part of the battle. It is the foundation level of your mental picture of how mathematics curriculum material is connected and ordered. In addition, it explores why students have various misconceptions about math, what certain assessment answers and actions indicate about student understanding, and why the many modern math tools and teaching methods work the way they do. The specific material on those issues cannot make sense—and you cannot understand what the questions on the test are asking—until you understand the basics of the language. You must know what the words mean. This chapter is a course on math language and also a course on math principles and math application. You have already taken these courses, but here they are again for your review and knowledge security. Conceptualizing the large body of information will improve your number sense and can help you develop number sense in future students. *Number sense* is a broad understanding of what numbers mean, how they are connected to each other, how operations with them can be performed, and their applications to real-world situations.

Although this chapter is extremely detailed, taking the practice tests in this book will help solidify your ability to apply content knowledge to different types of scenarios, including various types of word problems. This chapter can help you better understand what to do on the practice tests, and the practice tests can help you better understand the material in this chapter.

Numbers and Operations Content

In this section we talk about the very basics of math. A basic, foundational level of math, beyond counting with natural numbers, is categorizing numbers and calling them things like natural numbers. Although preschool children tend to skip that level and get to it later, the next level involves performing the basic operations—adding, subtracting, multiplying, and dividing. After that comes analyzing what numbers are made of, and from there students can get into understanding and working with the different forms of numbers, which is what we are about to cover here before getting into the crazier stuff.

Classifying numbers

We mention *natural numbers* in the preceding paragraph. The first numbers you ever learned are categorized as natural numbers. What is generally referred to as "counting" involves only natural numbers. They start with 1 and go on forever. Each natural number is 1 apart from the previous number and 1 apart from the next one, with one exception: 1 does not have a previous natural number since it is the first. The following represents the set of natural numbers:

1, 2, 3, 4, 5, 6, 7, 8, 9, 10. . .

The *whole numbers* consist of the natural numbers and also 0. The number 0 is not a natural number, but it is a whole number. The following represents the set of whole numbers:

0, 1, 2, 3, 4, 5, 6, 7, 8, 9, 10. . .

The natural numbers, or the whole numbers other than 0, have *opposites*. Those opposites are types of *negative numbers*, which are real numbers that are less than 0, and they are represented in mathematical language with the use of negative signs. Numbers such as -3 and -92 are negative numbers. So are $\frac{-3}{4}$ and -198.432, but we haven't gotten into how to classify those numbers yet. We will in a minute. Anyway, the natural numbers, their opposites, and 0 compose the set of what are called *integers*. In other words, the integers are the whole numbers and their opposites. That does not mean every whole number has an opposite. The one that does not is 0. These are the integers:

. . . $-3, -2, -1, 0, 1, 2, 3$. . .

TIP The sum of a number and its opposite is 0. For example, $-8 + 8 = 0$.

A *ratio* is a comparison of two numbers. Ratios are generally written as *fractions*, which are numbers that, when written in math language form, are presented as one quantity over another, such as $\frac{2}{5}$ and $\frac{71}{113}$. The top part of a fraction is the *numerator*, and the bottom part is the *denominator*. A ratio can also be expressed with words or with the use of a colon, as in 5:7, which represents that for every 5 of one thing there are 7 of another.

A *rational number* is a number that can be written as a ratio of two integers. All integers are rational numbers because they can be written over 1. All the numbers we have discussed so far in this chapter are rational numbers. Numbers that cannot be written as ratios of two integers are *irrational numbers*. Numbers such as π and $\sqrt{3}$ are irrational numbers. We are going a bit beyond the scope of elementary school math here, but you may come across the term somewhere in your adventures.

A summary of number classifications is in Table 5-1.

TABLE 5-1 **Classifications of Numbers**

Classification	Definition	Examples
Natural numbers	The numbers used for counting, beginning with 1 and with each spaced 1 apart from the next	1, 2, 3, 4, 5, 6, 7. . .
Whole numbers	The natural numbers and 0	0, 1, 2, 3, 4, 5, 6, 7. . .
Integers	The whole numbers and their opposites	. . . –2, –1, 0, 1, 2. . .
Rational numbers	Numbers that can be expressed as ratios of two integers	$-5, -\dfrac{3}{8}, 0, 4, \dfrac{17}{2}, 28.49$

All the numbers in the table are rational numbers. Rational numbers plus irrational numbers make up the *real numbers*, which are basically numbers that are not imaginary. We are still in an era of history when elementary school students generally do not have to learn about imaginary numbers at all, so we don't need to get far into what they are in this book. We just mention them to help define real numbers so we can tell you that the numbers elementary school students work with can be represented on the *real number line*, more commonly referred to as just the *number line*, which is a line that goes infinitely in two opposite directions and represents all real numbers in both directions (see Figure 5-1). The numbers that are specifically indicated on a number line are called *coordinates*.

FIGURE 5-1:
Numbers on
a number
line.

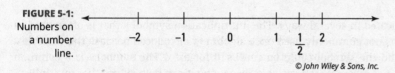

© John Wiley & Sons, Inc.

Base 10

Numbers, as you are probably most accustomed to them, involve ten digits, 0 through 9, in various combinations. A system that uses ten digits is a *base ten number system*. In the base ten number system we use, the whole numbers begin with 0 and are single-digit numbers through 9, and the next whole number (10) has two digits. Ten sets of 10 make up 100, the first whole number with three digits, and ten sets of 100 compose 1,000, the first whole number with four digits. Since that is the format of our number system, many of the tools used to represent numbers and calculations in elementary math are based on this format.

Operating with numbers

The four major operations with numbers are adding, subtracting, multiplying, and dividing. You are of course very familiar with all four of those operations, but it's good to keep in mind the major terms and finer principles involved with them.

Addition (Figure 5-2) is the combining of numbers. The numbers that are combined are *addends*, and they combine to form a *sum*. Thus, a sum is the answer to an addition problem. A sum can also be referred to as a *total* or a *sum total*.

FIGURE 5-2:
Addition.

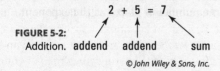

© John Wiley & Sons, Inc.

Subtraction (Figure 5-3) is the taking away of one number from another. The number from which another one is taken is the *minuend,* and the number that is taken away is the *subtrahend.* The result is the *difference.*

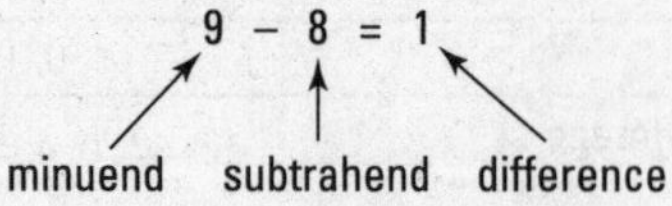

FIGURE 5-3:
Subtraction.

$$9 - 8 = 1$$

minuend   subtrahend   difference

© *John Wiley & Sons, Inc.*

Multiplication (Figure 5-4) is really a form of addition, but with a shortcut. It is the combining of a number with itself a certain number of times. The numbers that are multiplied are *factors,* and the result is their *product.*

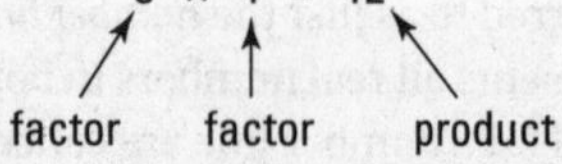

FIGURE 5-4:
Multiplication.

$$3 \times 4 = 12$$

factor   factor   product

© *John Wiley & Sons, Inc.*

Multiplication can be indicated in several ways. The multiplication symbol × that is often used in lower elementary school is not commonly used once algebra is introduced because the variable *x* looks too much like it, and the symbol could be confused for an *x*. The symbol ⋅ is a common replacement for ×. It does not resemble the variable *x*, so using it can help clarify that multiplication is represented. Multiplication can also be indicated by sets of parentheses next to numbers or each other.

$$3 \times 4 = 12$$
$$3 \cdot 4 = 12$$
$$3(4) = 12$$
$$(3)(4) = 12$$

However, parentheses do not symbolize multiplication when they are next to addition or subtraction signs. When larger expressions are used and parentheses must exist within other grouping symbols, brackets are typically used to represent multiplication.

Exponents also symbolize multiplication. They are numbers that represent how many times a number is multiplied by itself. For example, in 2^3, the 3 is an exponent. It symbolizes that 2 is a factor 3 times in the multiplication of itself.

$$2^3 = 2 \cdot 2 \cdot 2$$
$$= 8$$

The value of an expression that has 0 for an exponent is 1.

$$5^0 = 1$$

When a number is multiplied by 10 with an exponent that is an integer, the resulting value is equal to what you get when you move the decimal the same number of places as the exponent.

$$3.758 \times 10^2 = 375.8$$
$$7,485.3804 \times 10^{-3} = 7.4853804$$

Division (Figure 5-5) is the splitting of a number into a certain number of parts. Just as a pizza can be divided up six ways, a number can be divided up into portions. One number divided by another is the number of times the second one goes into the first. That first number is the *dividend*, and the number that is set to go into it is the *divisor*. The resulting number, or the answer to a division problem, is the *quotient*. Division is also a reversal of a process of multiplication.

$$15 \div 3 = 5$$

FIGURE 5-5:
Division.   dividend   divisor   quotient

© John Wiley & Sons, Inc.

That *equation*, or statement that one quantity is equal to another, is correct because $5 \times 3 = 15$. 3 of 5 is 15, so the number of times 3 goes into 15 is 5. Division can be represented in other ways. Fractions represent division, and a fraction bar is a division symbol (see Figure 5-6).

FIGURE 5-6:
Other ways
to represent
division.

$$3\overline{)15}$$ with 5 above

$$\frac{15}{3} = 5$$

$$15/3 = 5$$

© John Wiley & Sons, Inc.

When multiple operations are used in the working of a problem, there is an order in which the operations must take place. False orders can cause false answers, but the true order of operations, which is called the *order of operations*, results in true answers when the calculations involved are correct. The order of operations is often represented by the acronym PEMDAS, which represents the following order: parentheses and other grouping symbols (such as brackets and fraction bars), exponents, multiplication and division from left to right, addition and subtraction from left to right. The acronym PEMDAS has a long history of successfully helping students remember the order of operations.

$$[(5-2)^2 + 3 \bullet 4 - 6] \bullet 2 = [3^2 + 3 \bullet 4 - 6] \bullet 2$$
$$= [9 + 3 \bullet 4 - 6] \bullet 2$$
$$= [9 + 12 - 6] \bullet 2$$
$$= [21 - 6] \bullet 2$$
$$= 15 \bullet 2$$
$$= 30$$

Properties of operations

The discussion about operations needs to continue for just a little bit longer before we take a break from it and get back to it in Chapter 11. Certain principles are involved in operation combinations with more than two numbers. The principles are called *properties.* The four major properties of operations that are taught in elementary math courses are the commutative, associative, distributive, and substitution properties. The commutative and associative properties have versions for both addition and multiplication.

When three or more numbers are added, the order in which they are added does not matter. The sum will be the same no matter what the order is. That is the *commutative property of addition.*

$$8 + 2 + 7 = 2 + 7 + 8$$

The same principle applies to multiplication, and it's called the *commutative property of multiplication.*

$$8 \cdot 2 \cdot 7 = 2 \cdot 7 \cdot 8$$

The root of the word "commutative" is "commute," which means to move from one place to another. If a student attending classes at a college lives off campus, he commutes to class. The commutative properties are about the moving of three or more numbers when only addition or only multiplication is used.

The associative properties are like the commutative properties, but they do not pertain to changes in order. They apply to changes in the ways numbers are associated. Notice the "associate" word root in "associative." The way numbers are grouped is irrelevant when two or more numbers are added or multiplied.

The *associative property of addition* applies to the addition of three or more numbers, as demonstrated in this example:

$$(8 + 2) + 7 = 8 + (2 + 7)$$

The *associative property of multiplication* concerns the multiplication of three or more numbers:

$$(8 \cdot 2) \cdot 7 = 2 \cdot (7 \cdot 8)$$

The *distributive property* is the principle that multiplying a number by a sum or difference has the same result as multiplying the number by each of the numbers involved in the sum or difference and applying the other indicated operation. Portions of the value in parentheses are distributed in the multiplication process.

$$
\begin{aligned}
5(10 + 1) &= 5(10) + 5(1) \\
&= 50 + 5 \\
&= 55
\end{aligned}
$$

$$
\begin{aligned}
3(7 - 2) &= 3(7) - 3(2) \\
&= 21 - 6 \\
&= 15
\end{aligned}
$$

Think about it. If you have five sets of four marbles, you have three sets of four marbles plus another two sets of four marbles. Thus, you have twelve marbles plus another eight (see Figure 5-7).

$$
\begin{aligned}
4(5) &= 4(3 + 2) \\
&= 4(3) + 4(2) \\
&= 12 + 8 \\
&= 20
\end{aligned}
$$

When the distributive property involves multiplying by a sum, it is *distributive property of multiplication over addition.* When the expression in the parentheses is a difference, the more specific name of the property is *distributive property of multiplication over subtraction.*

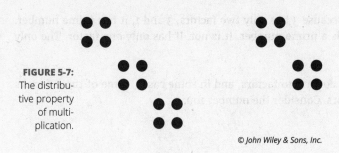

FIGURE 5-7:
The distributive property of multiplication.

© John Wiley & Sons, Inc.

The substitution property says that if two or more number representations are equal, one can replace any of the others without changing the quantity of which the first one is part. Since 7 + 3 and 10 are equal, 5 + 10 = 5 + 7 + 3. In that example, 7 + 3 replaces 10 without causing a change in overall value because the two quantities are equal. One works as a substitute for the other.

Properties of operations are summarized in Table 5-2.

TABLE 5-2   Properties of Operations

Property	Meaning	Example
Commutative property of addition	When two or more numbers are added, their sum does not depend on the order in which they are added.	$5 + 3 + 2 = 3 + 5 + 2$
Commutative property of multiplication	When two or more numbers are multiplied, their product does not depend on the order in which they are multiplied.	$5 \cdot 3 \cdot 2 = 3 \cdot 5 \cdot 2$
Associative property of addition	When two or more numbers are added, their sum does not depend on how they are grouped.	$(5 + 3) + 2 = 5 + (3 + 2)$
Associative property of multiplication	When two or more numbers are multiplied, their product does not depend on how they are grouped.	$(5 \cdot 3) \cdot 2 = 5 \cdot (3 \cdot 2)$
Distributive property	The product of a number and a sum is equal to the sum of the products obtained by multiplying the first number by each addend. The product of a number and a difference is equal to the product of the first number and the minuend, minus the product of the first number and the subtrahend.	$5(3 + 2) = 5(3) + 5(2)$
Substitution property	If two or more number representations are equal, one can be replaced by any of the others without changing the quantity of which it is part.	$12 = 8 + 4$, so $3 + 12 = 3 + 8 + 4$.

Factors and multiples

Factors are numbers that are multiplied by each other to get a product, so numbers that can be multiplied to get a certain number are factors of that number. Okay, we have a confession to make. We said that just to make some sense of what we are about to say. The word "factor" is used in two different senses in math, though one is based on the other. Actually, what are referred to in elementary math as the *factors* of a whole number are only the whole numbers that can be multiplied by other whole numbers to get that number. Higher math levels include negative numbers, complex numbers, and algebraic expressions in what can qualify as factors, but you don't need to worry about that for the Praxis Elementary Education test. On the elementary level, factors of a number are whole numbers.

For example, the factors of 10 are 1, 2, 5, and 10. Every whole number has 1 for a factor, and every whole number has itself for a factor. In the case of the number 1, itself and 1 are the same number, so it is the only whole number with only one factor. All of the rest have at least two. Any whole number that has only two factors is a *prime number*. Those two factors may only be the number itself and 1. A whole number with more than two factors is a *composite number*. Because 10 has four factors, it is a composite number. Because 3 has only two factors, 3 and 1, it is a prime number. A common misconception is that 1 is a prime number. It is not. It has only one factor. The only even prime number is 2.

A composite number can be broken down into factors, and in some cases, some of those factors can be broken down into other factors. Consider the number 100.

$$100 = 10 \cdot 10$$
$$= 5 \cdot 2 \cdot 5 \cdot 2$$

From that breakdown, you can see that the factors of 10 are 10, 5, and 2, and 1 (keep in mind that 1 is a factor of every whole number). The last line of the factoring involves only 2 and 5, both of which are prime numbers. Therefore, the factoring cannot proceed past that line. The line shows the *prime factorization,* or the situation in which all the prime numbers multiplied by each other equal the given number of 100. The factors, other than 1, of any whole number are the products of combinations of numbers in the prime factorization and their products.

The greatest common factor (GCF) of two or more whole numbers is the highest of all the numbers that are factors of each. The highest number that is a factor of both 24 and 32 is 8, so 8 is the greatest common factor (GCF) of 24 and 32.

Factors of 24: 1, 2, 3, 4, 6, <u>8</u>, 12, 24

Factors of 32: 1, 2, 4, <u>8</u>, 16, 32

The multiples of a number are the numbers that result from multiplying it by whole numbers. For example, the multiples of 5 are 5, 10, 15, 20, 25, 30, and so on. The *least common multiple* (LCM) of two or more numbers is the lowest number that is a multiple of each. The least common multiple (LCM) of 6 and 4 is 12.

Multiples of 6: 6, <u>12</u>, 18, 24, 30...

Multiples of 4: 4, 8, <u>12</u>, 16, 20, 24...

TIP

Greatest common factor and least common multiple are easily and commonly confused with each other. Focus on the first word in each term. That will help you remember the difference. The least common factor of any two whole numbers is 1, and greatest common multiple is a nonsense concept because whole numbers other than 0 have an infinite number of multiples. Let 1 and infinity be red flags suggesting that you probably went in the wrong direction when looking for GCF or LCM.

Sequences

A *sequence* is a list of numbers in a certain type of order. Have you ever heard a person talk about doing something in sequence? It means doing the parts of it in order. We will explain the concept in sequence. Many types of orders of numbers exist. For example, a sequence can be a list of prime numbers in which order increases. One of the most common classifications is the *arithmetic sequence,* in which the same quantity is added to each number to get the next. In the following arithmetic sequence, 4 is added to each number to determine the next number.

3, 7, 11, 15, 19, 23, 27...

Another is the *geometric sequence,* for which each number is multiplied by the same quantity to get the next.

2, 6, 18, 54, 162, 486...

On the Praxis exam, you may be asked to determine a number that should appear in a certain position in a sequence. To make the determination, first decide what is done to each number in order to create the value of the one that follows. Then make the calculation for each number up to the position in question.

Fractions, decimals, and percents

Not all real numbers are integers. Some of them—well, actually an infinite number of them—are between integers. Such numbers are often expressed as fractions and decimals.

The major operations can be performed with fractions. They can be added when their denominators are the same. If the denominators are not the same, that can be changed. It requires writing at least one of the fractions in a different form so that it has the same denominator as the other fractions. Think about how one fraction can equal another. As you can see in Figure 5-8, if a pizza is divided into 8 pieces of the same size and you eat 4 of the pieces, you have eaten half of the pizza. In other words, the portion you have eaten is $\frac{1}{2}$ of the pizza. You have also eaten 4 of the 8 pieces, or $\frac{4}{8}$ of the pizza. Thus, $\frac{1}{2} = \frac{4}{8}$.

FIGURE 5-8:
Fractions as slices of pizza.

© John Wiley & Sons, Inc.

Suppose you need to add $\frac{1}{2}$ and $\frac{3}{8}$. The fractions do not have a *common denominator*, or the same denominator, and that needs to be changed so the fractions can be added. You could write $\frac{1}{2}$ as $\frac{4}{8}$ and add it to $\frac{3}{8}$. Then, all you have to do is add the numerators and keep the common denominator. Four apples plus three apples is seven apples, four cars plus three cars is seven cars, and four eighths plus three eighths is seven eighths.

$$\frac{4}{8} + \frac{3}{8} = \frac{7}{8}$$

The same principle applies to subtraction of fractions.

Although $\frac{1}{2}$ was converted to $\frac{4}{8}$ in the previous problem so addition of fractions could happen, $\frac{1}{2}$ is the *simplest form* of the quantity expressed as a fraction. That means the numerator and denominator have a greatest common factor of 1. To get a fraction in simplest form, divide the numerator and denominator by their greatest common factor.

$$\frac{8}{12} = \frac{2}{3}$$

A fraction that has been converted to simplest form has been *reduced*. Fractions must be in simplest form to be correct answers to problems unless instructions say otherwise.

To get a common denominator when combining fractions, determine the least common multiple of the denominators in the problem. You can use any common multiple, but the LCM is the easiest with which to work. Multiply the denominator of a fraction by the number necessary to get the common denominator, and multiply the numerator by the same number. When you do that, you multiply by a number over itself, which is equal to 1 in every case. Multiplying by 1 does not result in a new value.

$$\frac{1}{4} + \frac{1}{3} = \frac{1(3)}{2(3)} + \frac{1(2)}{3(2)}$$

$$= \frac{3}{6} + \frac{2}{6}$$

$$= \frac{5}{6}$$

A statement in which one fraction (or any ratio) is set equal to another is a *proportion*. In a proportion, the cross products are equal. When two fractions are equal, the product of the numerator of one fraction and the denominator of the other fraction is equal to the product of the denominator of the first fraction and the numerator of the second.

$$\frac{3}{5} = \frac{6}{10}$$

$$3(10) = 6(5)$$

$$30 = 30$$

A *mixed number* is a number written as an integer followed by a fraction. For example, $3\frac{5}{8}$ is a mixed number. It can be written as $\frac{29}{8}$. To convert a mixed number to a fraction, multiply the denominator of the fraction by the integer (except ignore the negative sign until the end if there is one), add the numerator to that product, and write the result over the denominator of the fraction.

$$3\frac{5}{8} = \frac{8(3)+5}{8}$$

$$= \frac{29}{8}$$

You can convert an improper fraction to a mixed number by dividing the numerator by the denominator. The whole number you get will be the whole number in the mixed number. The remainder will be the numerator in the fraction part of the mixed number, and the denominator will be the same as the denominator in the improper fraction.

$$\frac{29}{8} = 3\frac{5}{8}$$

A *decimal* is a symbol used to separate digits in a number. It looks identical to a period, like the one at the end of this sentence. A *decimal* is also a number that has a decimal symbol in it. Really, the first use of the word is short for "decimal point," and the second use is short for "decimal number." A decimal point separates two digits in a decimal number. It separates the ones place from the tenths place. After the decimal point, the digits represent quantities that are less than 1, beginning with representations of tenths. The next digit represents hundredths, the next thousandths, and so forth.

$$485.3 = 485\frac{3}{10}$$

$$19.27 = 19\frac{27}{100}$$

$$88.413 = 88\frac{413}{1000}$$

Every digit in an integer or decimal number has a *place value*, which is the type of unit a digit represents in the larger number. In 584.937, the 5 represents the number of hundreds, 8 is the number of tens, 4 is the number of ones, 9 expresses tenths, 3 represents the number of hundredths, and 7 says how many thousandths follow all of that. The 5 is thus in the hundreds place, the 8 is in the tens place, and so on. Those places are the bases of the term "place value."

A *percent* represents a number of hundredths. It is a number followed by the word "percent" or the symbol %, both of which mean "hundredths." The decimal number 0.75 is seventy-five hundredths, or $\frac{75}{100}$, which can be written as 75 percent or 75%. This shows the connections among fraction form, decimal form, and percent form. Any rational number can be expressed in all three forms. Converting numbers to like forms can help you determine whether a number is greater than, less than, or equal to another number.

To convert a percent to a fraction, drop the % and write the number over 100. Then simplify if necessary.

$$50\% = \frac{50}{100}$$
$$= \frac{1}{2}$$

Converting a fraction to a decimal is simply a matter of dividing the numerator by the denominator.

$$\frac{4}{5} = 4 \div 5$$
$$= 0.8$$

If you need to change a fraction to a percent, divide the numerator by the denominator and get a decimal form of the number. From there, you can write the number in percent form by moving the decimal point two places to the right and putting a % after the number.

$$\frac{3}{4} = 0.75$$
$$= 75\%$$

Since the % symbol means "hundredths," dropping it gets rid of dividing by 100. Undoing dividing by 100 is the same as multiplying by 100. Putting a % by a number is the same as dividing by 100. To write a number in a new form, you must keep the same value. The way to balance multiplying by 100 is to divide by 100, and vice-versa. Moving a decimal point two places to the left is dividing by 100, and moving a decimal point two places to the right is multiplying by 100. Keep that in mind when you make conversions involving percents.

$$0.45 = 45\%$$
$$78\% = 0.78$$

You can work with those kinds of conversions of mixed numbers by first converting the mixed numbers to improper fractions and going from there.

$$\frac{11}{4} = 2\frac{3}{4}$$
$$= 2.75$$
$$= 275\%$$
$$= \frac{275}{100}$$
$$= \frac{11}{4}$$

With that knowledge, you can make any kind of conversion necessary among mixed number, fraction, decimal, and percent forms.

If you are comparing numbers that are not in the same form, the best thing to do is put all of the numbers in the same form. Then you can see which numbers are greater than others. Suppose you want to determine whether 48% is greater than or less than $\frac{11}{25}$. You can write 48% in fraction form and simplify, and you can also write $\frac{11}{25}$ as a percent. Then you can easily compare the numbers.

$$48\% = \frac{48}{100}$$
$$= \frac{12}{25}$$

Since $\frac{12}{25}$ is greater than $\frac{11}{25}$, 48% is greater than $\frac{11}{25}$. Fractions need to have a common denominator for you to compare them with clarity. In some cases, you will need to find a common denominator when comparing fractions.

Percent increase and decrease

Percent increase is the percent of an original number an increase is. *Percent decrease* is the same thing except it involves a decrease instead of an increase.

Suppose a dress is $20 one day and $25 the next day. The price of the dress increased by $5. Since 5 is 25% of 20 (you can divide 5 by 20 to determine that), the price of the dress had a 25% increase. If the dress price were to go back down to $20, it would undergo a 20% decrease since 5 is 20% of 25.

Rounding and estimating

When students perform operations, it is often a good idea for them to *estimate* the answer, which means to get an idea of the general ballpark area where it can be found, by working with *rounded* numbers. If a student multiplies 12 and 18, she can round both of them to the nearest 10, since they are two-digit numbers, and multiply the results. This will tell her that the answer is somewhere in the vicinity of 200, so if she ends up with an answer of 35 or 4,800, she can know that she made a mistake and needs to try again.

Numbers can be rounded to different places. Simply put, rounding a number to a given place is about putting a 0 in the next place immediately to the right and all places after it. Of course, 0's after a decimal point are understood after the last non-zero digit.

To round a number to the nearest 10 means to determine the nearest multiple of 10. Rounding a number to the nearest hundredth is rounding with the final digit being in the hundredths place. When rounding to a nearest place, if the digit in the place to the right is 5 or greater, a student should round up by increasing the value of the place to which he is rounding by 1. If the digit to the right is 4 or lower, one should keep the value of the place to which he is rounding.

58 rounded to the nearest 10 is 60.

53 rounded to the nearest 10 is 50.

14.53 rounded to the nearest tenth is 14.50, which equals 14.5.

Absolute value

The *absolute value* of a number is its positive distance from 0. A positive number's absolute value is the number itself, and the absolute value of a negative number is its opposite, or what results when you drop the negative sign. Absolute value is represented by pipe symbols, which look like this: $|\ |$.

$|12| = 12$

$|-12| = 12$

Knowing Algebra Content Down to the Letter

In the preceding section, we talk a lot about numbers. Now we are going to talk about letters. However, the letters we're talking about represent numbers. A letter used to represent a number is a *variable*. The most commonly used variable is x, but y, z, a, b, p, q, and many other letters are also used as variables. Consider the equation $x + 2 = 5$. The value of x in the equation is 3 because $3 + 2 = 5$. The branch of math that focuses on the use of variables is *algebra*.

Terms and other expressions

A *term* is a variable, number, or combination of numbers and variables multiplied by each other. For example, $8y$ is a term. It represents 8 times y. $54xyz$ is a term too. The number 4 alone is also a term. Variables in terms can be shown to have exponents. The number that is presented in numerical form in a term that has at least one variable is the term's *coefficient*. In the term $5q$, 5 is the coefficient. A number that is not next to a variable is a *constant*. If a term does not involve division by a variable and the variable exponents are only whole numbers, the term is a *monomial*. The sum of the variable exponents in a monomial is the monomial's *degree*.

Like terms have exactly the same variables, with each variable having the same exponent in every case. (If a variable's exponent is not indicated, it is understood to be 1.) For example, $12a$ and $3a$ are like terms because their variable combination is the same. $14pq$ and $11pq$ are also like terms.

Like terms can be added to and subtracted from each other. However, unlike terms cannot be combined. To combine like terms, combine the numbers and keep the variable combinations the same. The variable combinations work like denominators in that way. If you have 3 of something and add another 2 of the same thing, you have 5 of that thing, whether it is an apple, an eighth, or an x.

> 3 apples plus 2 apples = 5 apples
>
> $3\,x$'s $+ 2\,x$'s $= 5\,x$'s
>
> $3x + 2x = 5x$

An *expression* can be a single term or a set of terms. Terms that are part of a larger expression are separated by addition or subtraction. $14g + 7h$ is an expression. $22xy + 9yz - 54ab$ is also an expression. So is $3x$. All terms are expressions, but not all expressions are terms. If an expression consists only of monomials separated by addition or subtraction, the expression is a *polynomial*. The highest degree of a monomial in a polynomial is the degree of the polynomial.

An *equation* is a statement that one expression is equal to another. To *solve* an algebraic equation is to determine the value of a variable in it.

> $a - 3 = 12$

The *solution* to the equation is 15 because $15 - 3 = 12$; thus, the value of a is 15.

Solving equations

To solve an equation, get the variable by itself on one side of the equals sign. The goal is to end up with the variable followed by the equals sign and then what the variable equals. You can get the variable by itself by undoing everything that is being done to it, by doing the opposite. Addition and subtraction are opposite operations, or *inverse operations*. Multiplication and division are inverse operations. Also, you want to keep the two sides of the equation equal, so anything you do to one side, you must do to the other. Suppose you want to solve the equation $3x + 5 = 26$. You would first subtract 5 from both sides so the 5 can be removed from the left side. Then you would need to divide both sides by 3 to cancel the 3 by which the x is multiplied.

$$3x + 5 = 26$$
$$3x + 5 - 5 = 26 - 5$$
$$3x = 21$$
$$\frac{3x}{3} = \frac{21}{3}$$
$$x = 7$$

You can check the answer by putting 7 in for x in the original equation and seeing that it makes the equation true.

$$3x + 5 = 26$$
$$3(7) + 5 = 26$$
$$21 + 5 = 26$$
$$26 = 26$$

As stated earlier, with any proportion, the cross products are equal. You can use that principle to solve algebraic proportions.

$$\frac{8}{w} = \frac{20}{5}$$
$$8(5) = 20(w)$$
$$40 = 20w$$
$$\frac{40}{20} = \frac{20w}{20}$$
$$2 = w$$
$$w = 2$$

You can write algebraic equations derived from written language. If a problem says that four more than three times a number is 19, two sides of an equation are presented. One side is four more than three times a number, and the other side is 19. The first step in deciding how to translate English wording about an unknown quantity into an algebraic equation is to decide what is unknown. A variable can be used to represent it.

n: the number

Then, the English wording can be directly translated into mathematical language to show what is being done to the variable. What is described in the situation here is four added to three times n.

$3n + 4$

That is what is equal to 19.

$3n + 4 = 19$

From there, you can solve the equation.

An *inequality* is like an equation, but it uses symbols to indicate that one side is or could be greater than or less than the other. The following symbols are used in inequalities:

> means "greater than"

< means "less than"

≥ means "greater than or equal to"

≤ means "less than or equal to"

This is an example of an inequality:

$$a - 3 < 12$$

The solution to the inequality is not an exact number. It is a statement of what the value of a could be, based on what it is less than. The solution is $a < 15$. If the < had been = instead, the correct conclusion would have been $a = 15$.

Solving inequalities entails using the same principles as solving equations, except you must change the direction of the inequality sign if you switch the sides or multiply or divide both sides by a negative number.

$$14 < 4x - 2$$
$$14 + 2 < 4x - 2 + 2$$
$$16 < 4x$$
$$\frac{16}{4} < \frac{4x}{4}$$
$$4 < x$$
$$x > 4$$

Notice how the direction of the inequality sign was changed when the sides were switched. The formal way to express the solution to such an inequality is to have the variable on the left side.

Graphing solutions

To graph the solution to an inequality on a number line, put a dot on the number in the solution. If the symbol is > or <, then "or equal to" is not part of the solution, so you use a hollow dot to show that the number is just the boundary of a range of numbers and is not part of it. If $\geq$ or $\leq$ is used, "or equal to" is part of the solution, so you put a darkened in dot on the number to show that it is included in the range of numbers. Suppose you want to graph the solution to the inequality in the recent example, $x > 4$. Put a hollow dot on 4 on the number line, and then shade the number line in the direction that includes all numbers greater than 4 (see Figure 5-9).

FIGURE 5-9:
The solution to an inequality.

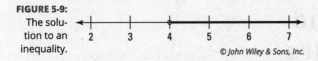

© John Wiley & Sons, Inc.

Working with formulas

A *formula* is a universally true algebraic equation. Formulas are used a great deal in math as well as physics and related branches of science. For example, $A = lw$ is the formula for the area of a rectangle. In the formula, A represents area, l stands for length, and w symbolizes width. The area of a rectangle is the measure of its length times the measure of its width. When the values of two of those variables are known, the value of the other variable can be determined. We realize that we're not in the geometry section yet, but we're on the outskirts. In the next section, we enter it together.

When a formula or other equation has two variables and one variable is by itself on a side, the variable by itself is generally called the dependent variable. Its value depends on the value of the other variable, which is called the independent variable. Basically, the value of the independent variable precedes and determines the value of the dependent variable. Consider the equation $y = 3x + 4$.

In that equation, x is the independent variable, and y is the dependent variable. The value of y depends on what value is put in for x.

Relationships between variables can be determined and represented by equations. An algebraic equation can be a formula that represents a pattern. Consider an example of someone who makes $25 for babysitting plus another $10 for each hour of babysitting. A question could ask how much money the babysitter would make for 5 hours on the job. The student could answer the question by making a table.

Number of Hours	Number of Dollars Earned
0	25
1	35
2	45
3	55
4	65
5	75

The table shows that the money earned for 5 hours of babysitting would be $75. Another question that could be asked about the pay pattern is what formula could represent it. Two major components of the formula are the numbers 25 and 10 because they are part of what determines the amount of money earned. Also, the number of hours worked is part of what determines an amount of money earned, so it is part of the formula and must be represented by a variable, since it varies and is unknown until a specific number is given for a particular situation. So, three parts of the formula are 25, 10, and a variable representing hours worked, which could be h. The amounts of money are in terms of dollars earned, so d would make a good variable for representing that quantity. The other terms come together and determine its value. Since 25 is always added, the formula involves + 25. To what is it added? It is always added to the product of 10 and the number of hours. All of that together equals the value of d. Therefore, a formula that can represent the number of dollars earned for a number of hours of babysitting is $d = 10h + 25$. You can check every example in the table to see that the formula works.

Sizing Up Geometry and Measurement Principles

Geometry is basically the study of shapes. The major geometry issues covered on the Praxis Elementary Education test concern various types of two- and three-dimensional shapes and categories of measurement that apply to them. The test also covers certain principles of measurement that are not geometry issues.

The building blocks of geometry

The most basic concept in geometry is the *point*, which is an infinitely small, exact location. Points are represented by dots and usually named by single letters. A series of points going infinitely in two opposite directions is a line. Finite parts of lines are called *segments*, which are named by their *endpoints*, or the points on the ends. A *ray* is also part of a line. A ray has one endpoint and goes infinitely in only one direction. When two lines, or parts of lines, intersect, they form *angles*, which are figures that have two sides that are parts of lines. Figure 5-10 shows angle ABC, or < ABC. The B is in the middle of the name because it is where the two sides meet, a point called the *vertex*. Point A is on one side of the angle, and point C is on the other side. That is a common way of naming angles. An angle can also be named by a number that is presented inside it, so the angle can also be called < 1. Also, since this angle has a vertex that is the vertex of only one angle that is shown, the angle can be named by the vertex only. Another name for the angle is thus < B.

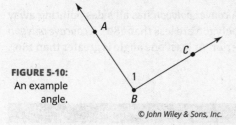

FIGURE 5-10:
An example angle.

© John Wiley & Sons, Inc.

An angle in which one side runs straight into the other side head on is a right angle, which has a measure of 90 degrees. An angle with a measure between 0 and 90 degrees is an acute angle. An angle that is a straight line is a straight angle and has a measure of 180 degrees, and an angle with a measure between 90 and 180 degrees is an obtuse angle. Check out Figure 5-11 for examples of these different types of angles. Degrees can be represented by the ° symbol.

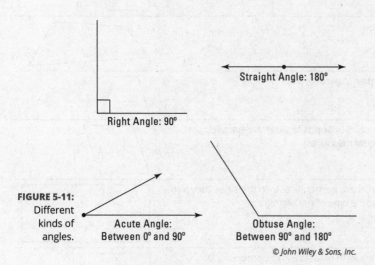

FIGURE 5-11:
Different kinds of angles.

© John Wiley & Sons, Inc.

If two angles share a side and a vertex and form a right angle together, or if their measures merely add up to 90°, they are *complementary angles*. If two angles share a vertex and a side and form a straight line, or their measures have a sum of 180°, they are *supplementary angles*.

Shapes

We start this part of the exploration in the second dimension and move on to the third in a little bit. By "second dimension," we mean "where everything is completely flat." Things that take up space are three-dimensional. Most of the *two-dimensional* shapes (flat shapes) you need to understand are *polygons,* which are completely enclosed, two-dimensional figures with all sides being segments joined to the ones next to them at their endpoints. The point where two sides of a polygon are joined is a *vertex,* the plural of which is *vertices*.

A *triangle* is a three-sided polygon, and a *quadrilateral* is a four-sided polygon. A rectangle is an example of a quadrilateral. Classifications of quadrilaterals typically depend on whether the shapes have sides that are *parallel*, which means that they are the same distance away from each other at all points, and whether sides that join are *perpendicular*, meaning that they go straight into each other to form *right angles*. Table 5-3 defines and gives examples of the major types of polygons covered in elementary-level math. Keep in mind that some of the categories exist within other listed categories.

Polygons can be convex or concave (see Figure 5-12). A *convex polygon* has all sides pointing away from the interior. All of the interior angles of a convex polygon are less than 180°. A *concave polygon* has at least one set of two sides pointing toward the interior. At least one angle is greater than 180°.

TABLE 5-3 ## Types of Polygons

Name	Definition	Example
Triangle	Three-sided polygon	
Right triangle	Triangle with two sides perpendicular (one right angle)	
Quadrilateral	Four-sided polygon	
Trapezoid	Quadrilateral with just one pair of parallel sides	
Parallelogram	Quadrilateral in which both pairs of opposite sides are parallel (opposite sides also have equal measures)	
Rectangle	Quadrilateral in which all sides are perpendicular to the sides they join (this creates four right angles); a type of parallelogram	
Square	Quadrilateral with all sides equal in measure and perpendicular to the sides they join; a type of rectangle and therefore a type of parallelogram.	
Pentagon	Five-sided polygon	
Hexagon	Six-sided polygon	

© *John Wiley & Sons, Inc.*

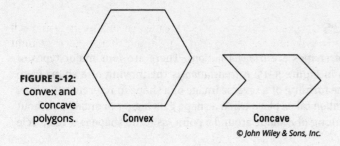

FIGURE 5-12:
Convex and
concave
polygons.

A polygon in which all of the sides have the same measure and all of the angles have the same measure is a *regular polygon*. A polygon in which not all sides have the same measure or not all angles have the same measure is an *irregular polygon*.

Two-dimensional shapes can come together to form *three-dimensional* shapes, which take up space, unlike those that are two-dimensional. A major example of a three-dimensional shape is a *right rectangular prism*, an enclosed figure in which all of the faces are rectangles that are perpendicular to the joining faces (see Figure 5-13). The *faces*, which are two-dimensional shapes that form the surface of the figure, are rectangles that are joined at their sides. A *cube* is a right rectangular prism in which all of the faces are squares. Keep in mind that a square is a type of rectangle.

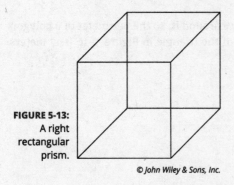

FIGURE 5-13:
A right
rectangular
prism.

Composite shapes

Shapes can come together and form other shapes that don't tend to have specific names. In general terms, such shapes are called *composite shapes*. The composite shape in Figure 5-14 is formed by two rectangles and a triangle.

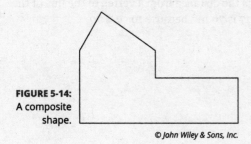

FIGURE 5-14:
A composite
shape.

Transforming shapes

Changes in the positions or sizes of shapes are *transformations.* There are four major types of transformations, which you can see in Figure 5-15. A *translation* is the moving of a shape from one place to another. A *reflection* is the forming of a reverse image of a shape in reference to a line, which does not have to be shown. *Dilation* takes place when a shape gets bigger or smaller without changing shape. A *rotation* is the spinning of a shape around a point, as if the shape is on a bicycle spoke of a tire that is being spun.

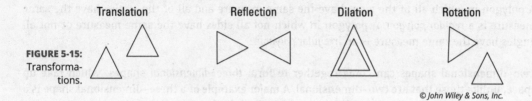

Translation   Reflection   Dilation   Rotation

FIGURE 5-15: Transformations.

© John Wiley & Sons, Inc.

Shape measurements

Shapes can be measured in various ways. First we look at two-dimensional shapes.

The *perimeter* of a two-dimensional shape is the distance around it, so the perimeter of a polygon is the sum of the measures of its sides. The perimeter of the triangle in Figure 5-16 is 17 meters because that is the sum of its side measures.

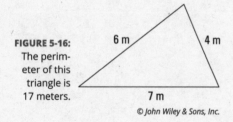

FIGURE 5-16: The perimeter of this triangle is 17 meters.

6 m   4 m   7 m

© John Wiley & Sons, Inc.

The *area* of a two-dimensional shape is the amount of two-dimensional room inside it. Area is how much surface a shape takes up. As discussed previously, the area of a rectangle is the product of its length and width. The area of a triangle is half of the measure of one of its sides (called a *base*) times the height that corresponds to that side. The base of a triangle can be any side, but the height that is used is based on that base, and height is the distance from a vertex to the line of the opposite side. The area of the rectangle in Figure 5-17 is 70 in.² because $10 \cdot 7 = 70$.

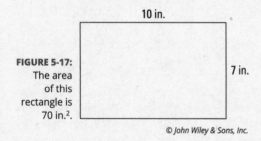

10 in.   7 in.

FIGURE 5-17: The area of this rectangle is 70 in.².

© John Wiley & Sons, Inc.

The area of the triangle in Figure 5-18 is 27 cm² since $\frac{1}{2} \cdot 9 \cdot 6 = 27$.

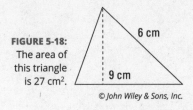

FIGURE 5-18: The area of this triangle is 27 cm².

6 cm

9 cm

© John Wiley & Sons, Inc.

Now consider the third dimension. The *volume* of a three-dimensional figure is how much space it takes up. It is how much room is inside an object that takes up space. The volume of a right rectangular prism is the product of its length, width, and height.

The *surface area* of a three-dimensional figure is the amount of area on its surface. For a right rectangular prism, the surface area is the sum of the areas of the faces. Although surface area pertains to three-dimensional figures, it is a two-dimensional measurement because faces are two-dimensional.

The volume of the cube in Figure 5-19 is 125 ft.³ since 5 · 5 · 5 = 125, and the cube's surface area is 150 ft.² because each face has an area of 25 ft.² and the sum of the areas of the faces is 150 ft.².

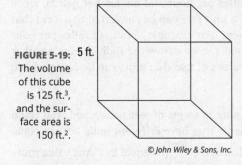

FIGURE 5-19: The volume of this cube is 125 ft.³, and the surface area is 150 ft.².

5 ft.

© John Wiley & Sons, Inc.

REMEMBER

Although surface area concerns three-dimensional figures, it is a two-dimensional measurement because surfaces are two-dimensional.

Forms of measurement

Measurements can be described in various types of units. English system units for distance include inches, feet, yards, and miles. They are based on each other. A foot is 12 inches, a yard is three feet, and a mile is 5,280 feet. Area measurements are given in those units *squared,* or to the second power (having an exponent of 2), and volume can be given in those units *cubed* (to the third power) or in another subsystem of English units based on the cup. A cup is about the size of a small drink that goes in the type of object called a cup, a pint is two cups, a quart is two pints, and a gallon is four quarts.

The metric system's basic unit for distance is the meter, and other distance units are based on the meter. For example, a centimeter is one-hundredth of a meter, and a kilometer is 1,000 meters. Those are one-dimensional measurements. Two-dimensional units are the squares of one-dimensional units. For example, a rectangle with a length of 5 centimeters (cm) and a width of 2 cm would have an area of 10 cm². Volume often involves the same kinds of distance units with an exponent of 3 because volume is three-dimensional. However, the metric system also uses the *liter* for measures of volume. One liter is equal to 1,000 cm³. Table 5-4 lists metric prefixes.

TABLE 5-4   **Metric Prefixes**

Metric Prefix	Meaning
Milli	1/1000
Centi	1/100
Deci	1/10
(no prefix)	1
Deca	10
Hecto	100
Kilo	1000

Things other than geometric shapes can be measured, and various types of units can be used. For example, money can be measured in dollars and euros. Time can also be measured. The amount of time that passes between two events is *elapsed time.* Some measurements involve ratios of measurements. The price of gasoline per gallon is a ratio of money to volume. Such a ratio is called a *unit rate.* Because measures can be expressed in different types of units, unit rates can be represented in various types of ratios.

Unit rates involve ratios of measurements, such as miles per hour and dollars per gallon. Since multiple systems exist for each type of measurement, a unit rate can be converted to a form that uses a different system for each individual measurement. For example, a ratio of miles per hour can be converted to feet per second. Each measurement can be converted individually. Another method entails multiplying units by ratios that have values of 1 so that units can be canceled and the desired units can remain.

Suppose you want to find the value of 11 yards per minute in terms of feet per second. You could multiply by fractions that present ratios of measurements that have different units but are equal in value. For example, 3 feet is equal to 1 yard, so the fraction $\frac{3\,\text{feet}}{1\,\text{yard}}$ is equal to 1. Any value multiplied by 1 is equal to the original value. Anything times 1 is itself. Therefore, multiplying by $\frac{3\,\text{feet}}{1\,\text{yard}}$ does not change anything except the way something is written. If you multiply that and $\frac{11\,\text{yards}}{1\,\text{minute}}$, "yards" can be canceled while "feet" remains. That principle is key to the method. You want "feet" to remain, so you want to get rid of "yards." You can follow the same algorithm and get rid of "minutes" and keep "seconds," since you are looking for a value in terms of feet per second.

$$\frac{11\,\text{yards}}{1\,\text{minute}} \times \frac{3\,\text{feet}}{1\,\text{yard}} \times \frac{1\,\text{minute}}{60\,\text{seconds}} = \frac{33\,\text{feet}}{60\,\text{seconds}}$$

$$= \frac{11\,\text{feet}}{20\,\text{seconds}}$$

$$= \frac{11}{20}\,\text{feet / second}$$

11 yards per minute = 11/20 feet per second

When determining elapsed time, remember that our system of time is not completely a base 10 system. A new hour begins after 60 minutes, not 100. You cannot simply subtract one time of day from another. You must make calculations with hours and minutes separately.

Points on the coordinate plane

A number line is one-dimensional. However, different number lines can exist together on *planes*, which are to the second dimension what lines are to the first. A plane is an infinite configuration of lines existing in two dimensions. Imagine a flat sheet with zero depth, consisting of an infinite number of lines going in all directions two-dimensionally. That is a plane.

The *coordinate plane* has a foundation of two number lines that are perpendicular to each other. The horizontal number line is the *x-axis*, and the vertical one is the *y-axis.* All points on the coordinate plane are named by where they exist in reference to the intersection of the *x*-axis and the *y*-axis. Every point has an *x*-coordinate and a *y*-coordinate, taking the form (x, y). The point of intersection of the two axes (the plural of "axis") is the *origin*, and its coordinate pair is $(0, 0)$. The coordinates of every other point are based on a horizontal distance (*x*-coordinate) from the origin followed by a vertical distance (*y*-coordinate) to the point (see Figure 5-20).

Several points are labeled on the following coordinate plane. Notice where the points exist in relation to the origin and why their coordinates are what they are.

Points on the coordinate plane can be vertices of polygons. The segments joining the vertices may be visible or invisible. By plotting the vertices and connecting them, you can determine the types of polygons represented by the vertices.

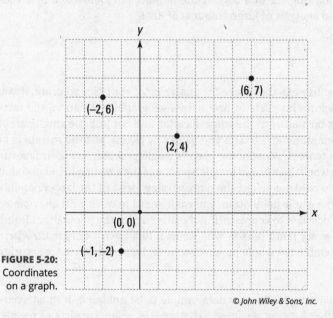

FIGURE 5-20: Coordinates on a graph.

© John Wiley & Sons, Inc.

The coordinate plane is divided into four *quadrants*, or sections, by the two axes (see Figure 5-21). The quadrants are named by Roman numerals as indicated in the following diagram.

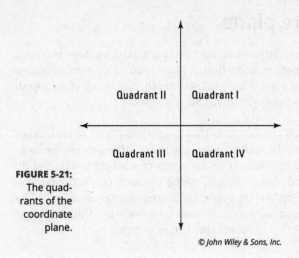

Quadrant II   Quadrant I

Quadrant III   Quadrant IV

FIGURE 5-21:
The quad-
rants of the
coordinate
plane.

© John Wiley & Sons, Inc.

Data, Statistics, and Probability

Facts that are collected and listed for analytical purposes are called *data.* A fact could be the number of male students in a classroom, the size of a dog, or the number of albums sold by a rock group. *Statistics* is the collection and analysis of large amounts of data.

Collecting data

The gathering of data must be done in ways that make the analyzing of statistics accurate. If you want to get an idea of the major sports interests of people in a geographical location, the facts you collect need to correctly reflect the nature of the whole location and not just one small part of it. Would it make sense to base your statistics on data you gather by asking just the members of a football team what their favorite sport is? Most of the players would probably say their favorite sport is football. The football team would be a *biased sample* because of the extreme likelihood that the list of responses you would get would not reflect the more varying views of the larger population. To get a true perspective on the whole population, you would need to work with an *unbiased sample* by trying to get as close as possible to representing the diversity in the population. Doing something like giving a survey to every tenth person who walks into a town's only mall, where all local social divisions closely resemble the whole population, would give a much more accurate reading of the views of the region.

That is one example of an unbiased sample. For any data sample to be unbiased, it must accurately represent the larger group that is being analyzed, whether that group consists of people, animals, automobiles, or rocks.

Data can apply to different types of classifications. *Categorical data* concerns categories that are not based on number intervals or labels that are in order. Data regarding mere cities, movie titles, and types of food are forms of categorical data. *Interval data* applies to intervals of numbers, such as age groups and finishing times in a road race. *Ordinal data* includes classifications based on order, such as military rank and educational degree level, but not mere numerical levels.

Finding measures of center

Some numbers can give really good indications of the general nature of data collections. They are called *measures of center* because they are found near the center of the data or at least strongly affect the center of the data. The *median* of a data set is literally the dead center of the data. If you put every number in order, the median is the one in the middle (if the set contains an odd number of numbers) or the number halfway between the two numbers in the middle (if the set contains an even number of numbers). Suppose the scores a student made on five tests are 98, 84, 98, 72, and 85. Since the data set has five numbers, it has a middle number. However, the median is the middle number in value, not in just any random listing. When the numbers are in order, the median is the one in the very middle.

72 84 85 98 98

The middle number is 85, so it is the median.

The *mean* of a set of data is the average number. It is the sum of the numbers divided by the number of numbers. The mean of the five test scores is calculated like this:

$$\frac{72+84+85+98+98}{5} = \frac{437}{5}$$
$$= 87.4$$

The mean of the data is 87.4.

The *mode* of a set of data is the number that appears the most. The mode of the set of data here is 98 because it is in the data set in two instances, while all of the others are in it once each.

Representing data

Bar graphs are a common and effective form of data presentation. They include bars, which are rectangles that correspond to data that is listed vertically. The categories to which those numbers apply are listed horizontally. The categories can be baseball tickets sold for each team in a year, jaywalking incidents in various cities, average hair lengths at universities, and all kinds of other such matters.

» *Line graphs* are like bar graphs, but line graphs use points connected by lines instead of bars.

» *Circle graphs*, also known as *pie charts*, can be used to represent portions.

» *Scatterplots* use points to represent data involving two measures, such as year and profit. Scatterplot points are a lot like points on the coordinate plane. You can look at the points' patterns and determine how the two measures are related. For example, as one measure increases, the other may tend to increase, decrease, or stay the same. A *line of fit* can be drawn through approximately the middle of the plotted points to indicate the relationships.

» *Box plots* are illustrations placed above number lines to show the lowest number, highest number, and median of a set of data. The full range is divided into *quartiles*, which are quarters of the full ranges of data. Box plots can also indicate *outliers*, or numbers way outside of the general vicinities of the other numbers.

Figuring out probability

The *probability* of an event is a ratio that represents the likelihood that it will happen. It is the number of outcomes that qualify as the event divided by the number of possible outcomes. If a bag contains three yellow ping-pong balls, two orange ones, and four green ping-pong balls, the probability of pulling out an orange ping-pong ball when pulling out a ball randomly is 2 out of 9, or $\frac{2}{9}$. The number of outcomes that could qualify as orange if they happened is 2 because there are two orange balls, and the number of possible outcomes is 9 because there are nine ping-pong balls in the bag.

Now, technically, that is the theoretical probability. It is usually just referred to as "probability," but there is also the principle of *experimental probability,* which is the number of times an event actually does end up occurring divided by the total number of events. If an orange ping pong ball were selected 14 out of 15 times, the experimental probability of selecting one would be $\frac{14}{15}$.

The probability that one of two events will happen is the sum of their individual probabilities. The probability that all of two or more events will happen is the product of their individual probabilities.

Well, that concludes the review crash course on elementary math. You can always go back and take it or parts of it again. You can refer to this chapter as much as you need to when studying the coming chapters on mathematics. Chapter 11 is about mathematics curriculum, instruction, and assessment, but we highly recommend studying the chapter even if you are only studying for the Praxis Elementary Education: Content Knowledge (5018) exam. Chapter 11 can give you deeper perspectives on math content and teach you extra tricks you can use. We hope to see you there no matter which test you are preparing to take.

Chapter 6

Concepts of Science

Memorization helps you through the many terms and principles of the sciences. Visualization also helps, so spending time studying this chapter's illustrations will be of benefit to you.

Be sure to read the answer explanations carefully. You can learn from incorrect responses as well as correct ones.

REMEMBER

This chapter contains Science content material required for both tests. However, those students taking 5017 should focus on Chapter 12 for curriculum, instruction, and assessment and then come back here to refresh the basics.

Life Science Principles

There are many important parts of living things, from cells to organ systems, from reproduction to heredity. Organisms interact with their environment, responding and evolving. Organisms have roles in their ecosystem, their community.

What things are made of

An *organism* is a living thing, and all living things are made of *cells.* Some organisms, such as bacteria, have just one simple cell. Complex organisms, such as trees, horses, and people, have many different kinds of cells which, altogether, number in the trillions.

For an animal, these different cells include blood cells, bone cells, muscle cells, and nerve cells. Plant cells include leaf and root cells. All of these types of cells look different and have different functions; blood cells, for example, carry oxygen to the other cells. But the parts of a cell, for both animals and plants, are surprisingly similar.

The cells of both have a *membrane*, controlling what moves in and out of the cell (nutrients in, waste out). Three types of cell movement are *osmosis*, where water passes through the membrane to even the concentration (of proteins) on both sides; *diffusion*, where molecules move from a place where they are highly concentrated to one where the concentration is lower; and *active transport*, where material moves, with the help of protein energy, from low to high concentration (the opposite of diffusion).

Both animal and plant cells have other things in common: a *nucleus*, which contains DNA and is the "brain"; *cytoplasm*, all the jellylike substance outside of the nucleus where the organelles are; and *organelles*, smaller structures within the cell that have specific roles. Organelles include *mitochondria*, which make energy in the form of *adenosine triphosphate* (ATP); the protein-making *ribosomes*; *lysosomes*, which hold enzymes that can break down molecules (as in digestion); *vacuoles*, which hold water and nutrients; *endoplasmic reticula* (ER), tubes which carry material from the cytoplasm to the nucleus; and the *Golgi apparatus*, which modifies proteins for movement through the cell.

One thing an animal's cell does not have but a plant's does is a *cell wall*, which is made of cellulose and makes a firm surround for the cell while still allowing movement in and out. Another feature unique to plants is the chloroplast organelle. Found mostly in leaves, *chloroplasts* contain chlorophyll and are involved in photosynthesis, using energy from the sun to *produce their own* food in the form of *glucose* (sugar). As such producers, plants are *autotrophs* (*auto-* means *self*; -*troph*, *nourishment*). This reaction describes photosynthesis:

$$6CO_2 + 6H_2O \rightarrow 6O_2 + C_6H_{12}O_6$$
Carbon dioxide + *water* – *produces oxygen and glucose*

Animals, which *consume* food to get energy, are *heterotrophs* (*hetero-* means *other* or *different*).

Both animals and plants have *tissues*, similarly specialized cells grouped together, and *organs*, groups of similarly functioning tissues, which make up *organ systems.* Most organs have very important functions, but some do not, such as a human's appendix, tailbone, and wisdom teeth; these organs are *vestigial*, left over from an evolutionary time.

Some plant organs are the leaves, stems, and roots. A plant's reproductive system, usually in the flower, includes the *stamen* (the male part), which uses *anther* to make *pollen*; and the *pistil* (the female part), which has an ovary and egg cells.

Human organ systems include the following:

>> **Digestive:** Includes the mouth, stomach, and intestines

>> **Respiratory:** Includes the nose, lungs, and diaphragm

>> **Circulatory:** Includes the heart, veins (thin), and arteries (thick)

>> **Integumentary:** Includes skin, nails, and hair

>> **Skeletal:** Includes bones and ligaments

>> **Nervous:** Includes the brain, spinal cord, and sensory organs

>> **Muscular:** Includes skeletal, cardiac, and smooth muscles

>> **Endocrine:** Includes glands

>> **Excretory (renal):** Includes the kidneys

>> **Immunological:** Includes the lymphatic system

>> **Reproductive:** Includes male and female reproductive organs

EXAMPLE

What is the primary function of mitochondria in a cell?

(A) controlling the release of waste material and the entrance of nutrients

(B) combining oxygen and glucose to make/release energy

(C) combining carbon dioxide and water to make oxygen and glucose

(D) sending instructions to the other cells regarding their functions

The correct answer is Choice (B). Mitochondria convert energy from food (glucose) into the chemical ATP. Choice (A) describes the function of the cell membrane. Choice (C) describes the function of chloroplasts (found only in plants). Choice (D) describes the function of the nucleus, which not only controls how and when other cells carry out their functions but also contains chromosomes and DNA, which control reproduction.

The facts of life

Living things reproduce in one of two ways. When reproduction is *asexual* (*a-* means *not* or *without)* the offspring come from a single parent, such as a bacterium or fungus. The parent cell creates two identical chromosome pairs; each pair forms a separate membrane, and then they split into two in the process called *mitosis.*

In *sexual reproduction,* there are two parent cells, a male gamete (sperm) and a female gamete (egg), each with their unique genetic information. Gametes are formed in the process called *meiosis,* where cell division produces four cells, thus accounting in part for genetic variation. Each cell has half the number of chromosomes as the parent cell. A human male gamete has 23 pairs and the female 23, so a human has 46 chromosomes pairs.

Each chromosome has genes and each gene has a trait, or characteristic, that may be *dominant* or *recessive.* The table in Figure 6-1, based on results discovered in the 19th century by Gregor Mendel when experimenting with plants, shows the results of dominant–recessive combinations.

FIGURE 6-1:
Gene
combinations.

if one trait is		and the other is		then the effect will be the trait that is	
	dominant		dominant		dominant
	dominant		recessive		dominant
	recessive		recessive		recessive

© John Wiley & Sons, Inc.

EXAMPLE

An individual with brown eyes, which is a dominant trait, wants to have a child with brown eyes. How can the individual know for sure that his child will have brown eyes?

(A) marry someone with brown eyes

(B) marry someone whose parents both have brown eyes

(C) marry someone whose grandparents both have brown eyes

(D) none of the above

The correct answer is Choice (D). If the individual marries someone with brown eyes, that person may carry one gene with the trait for brown eyes and one for blue eyes, which is a recessive trait. Recessive traits such as blue eyes may lie hidden for generations. Choice (A) would work only in the case of either the individual or the spouse carrying two genes with the dominant trait. Choice (B) would work only in the case of all four parents each carrying two genes with the dominant trait. Choice (C) would *ensure* brown eyes only in the case of all eight grandparents each carrying two genes with the dominant trait.

Short- and long-term changes

To help study and understand organisms, scientists have a way of classifying them, or a *taxonomy* (*tax-* means *arrangement; -nomy, names*). From most general to most specific, the eight classification levels are: Domain, Kingdom, Phylum, Class, Order, Family, Genus, and Species. While there are only three domains and five kingdoms, there are close to eight million species (give or take a million).

For example, the taxonomy for the African lion is Eukaryotes (organisms with cells having a distinct nucleus containing DNA and specialized organelles), Animalia, Chordata (with backbone), Mammalia (with hair; milk-producing glands), Carnivora (meat-eating), Felidae, *Panthera, Panthera leo.* The seven-armed starfish, or southern sand star, has a specific classification of: Eukaryotes, Animalia, Echinodermata, Asteroidea, Paxillosida, Luidiidae, *Luidia, Luidia australiae.*

Organisms change in response to their environment. Short-term changes may involve *homeostasis,* where an organism regulates part of itself in order to maintain stability. Examples of homeostasis include humans sweating in order to maintain a normal body temperature and using hormones to regulate glucose and calcium levels. Chameleons can regulate their skin color. Plants regulate water levels and may lean toward the light *(phototropism).*

Some change involves longer periods of homeostasis, such as in an animal's hibernation or a plant's seed dormancy; some change involves a plant or animal's life cycle, such as a butterfly's egg, larva (caterpillar), pupa, and adult stages. Some change involves external behavior, such as migration. Sometimes, factors in an organism's environment change. The organisms who can best adapt to the change survive, so their genetic traits survive. Charles Darwin is credited with this theory of *natural selection.* Sometimes, a change in traits occurs through genetic mutation over generations, and thus species *evolve.*

EXAMPLE

Which of the following is NOT true?

(A) "Survival of the fittest" is a way to describe natural selection.

(B) A cold-blooded animal such as a snake can regulate its body temperature in an example of homeostasis.

(C) The classification of an organism is Animalia, chordata, reptilia, squamata, eublephari-dae, *Coleonyx, Coleonyx variegatus.* From its species name, you can deduce that its skin or appearance was not a single color.

(D) Chemical changes in a chameleon resulting in a skin-color change are an example of homeostasis.

The correct answer is Choice (B). A cold-blooded animal is not able to *internally* regulate its body temperature. It may regulate its temperature by changing its *environment,* such as when a snake suns itself on a rock. Choice (A) IS true because environmental factors ("nature") cause the survival or selection of the organisms most fit for current situations or changes in the environment. Choice (C) IS true because the *variegatus* of the species name suggests variation; the animal is the banded gecko. Choice (D) IS true because the chameleon is responding to its environment and *internally* regulating itself for protective reasons.

The food chain

In addition to producers (plants producing energy in the form of glucose) and consumers (organisms using that energy), there is a third group of organisms: decomposers. *Decomposers,* such as bacteria and fungi, get their energy from dead plants and animals; in doing so, the decomposers break down the dead organisms and leave remnants in the soil or water, which, in turn, serve as material for the producers. Figure 6-2 shows an example of such a *food web* (a food chain would show only one path; a web contains many chains).

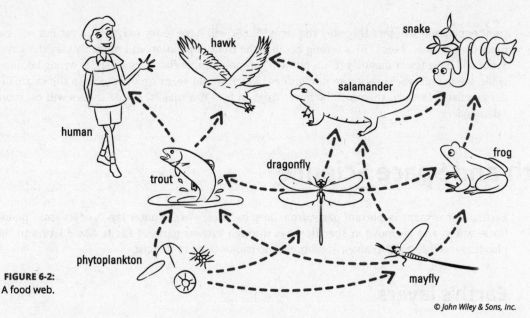

snake

hawk

salamander

human

frog

trout

dragonfly

phytoplankton

FIGURE 6-2:
A food web.

mayfly

© John Wiley & Sons, Inc.

Many such food webs thrive on Earth, each web's organisms being part of the ecosystem, or group of interacting living and nonliving things. Often, many ecosystems can be found in one of Earth's five major *biomes*, which are described in Table 6-1.

TABLE 6-1 ## Earth's Biomes

Biome	Characteristics or Conditions
Aquatic	*Freshwater:* ponds, wetlands, lakes, streams, rivers
	Marine (saltwater): estuaries, bays, coral reefs, oceans
Desert	Extremely dry; may be hot or cold; very little plant life (vegetation)
Forest	*Chaparral:* hot and dry; plants adapted to reaching for (via root system) or conserving water
	Rainforest: warm and wet all year long in *tropics;* not as warm and wet in *temperate* regions; high diversity in organisms
	Taiga: mild, short summer; cold winter; conifer (cone-bearing) most common tree
	Temperate: mild summers and winters; wet; deciduous (leaf-losing) most common tree
Grassland	*Savanna:* warm; wet summer, very dry winter
	Temperate: hot summer, cold winter; soil good for farming
Tundra	Cold, windy, dry; boggy in summer from snowmelt; low diversity in organisms

EXAMPLE

In the food web depicted in Figure 6-2, which is likely to happen if human use of pesticides wipes out the mayfly population?

(A) The trout population will decrease.

(B) The trout population will increase.

(C) The salamander population will decrease.

(D) The salamander population will stay steady.

The correct answer is Choice (C). While it is true that salamanders will eat more dragonflies, which would seem to work to keep the salamander population steady, there will be fewer frogs to feed the snakes, so the snakes will eat more salamanders. Choice (A) is wrong because the trout population will probably stay the same. Trout will have fewer mayflies to eat but will eat more dragonflies. Choice (B) is wrong because the trout population will probably stay the same. Trout will have fewer mayflies to eat but will eat more dragonflies. Choice (D) is wrong because, while salamanders will eat more dragonflies, which would seem to work to keep the salamander population steady, there will be fewer frogs to feed the snakes, so the snakes will eat more salamanders.

Earth and Space Science

Earth also has many important parts, from deep in its core to the outer layers of its atmosphere. Rock, water, and air move in specific ways through various parts of Earth. Some layers in the planet reveal information about conditions and connections in its past.

Earth's layers

A cross-section of Earth's interior shows several layers, as shown in Figure 6-3. Deep inside is the *inner core,* solid and made mostly of iron. Next is the liquid *outer core*, the source of Earth's magnetic field. The *mantle* is the largest layer, being roughly 1,800 miles (2,900 kilometers) thick. It contains the lower asthenosphere, which has a fluidity that makes the plates move, and above that the lithosphere *(litho-* means *stone),* which is solid. Last is the crust, about 5–30 miles (8–50 kilometers) thick.

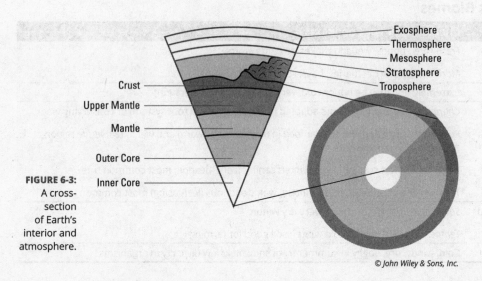

FIGURE 6-3: A cross-section of Earth's interior and atmosphere.

© John Wiley & Sons, Inc.

The ocean floor has levels, from the depths of an ocean trench (the Mariana Trench is the deepest, at 6.8 miles, almost 11 kilometers), to an abyss, to a continental slope, to the continental shelf where water meets land, or continent.

Earth's atmosphere is made up mostly of nitrogen (78 percent) and oxygen (21 percent). The lowest layer of the atmosphere, the *troposphere,* extends about 11 miles (17.7 kilometers) and is the source of most of our weather and most of our clouds. The *stratosphere* extends to about 31 miles (50 kilometers); it contains the ozone layer and, at its lower reaches, a few clouds, planes, and large birds. Next is the *mesosphere,* extending to about 50 miles (80 kilometers). Most meteors burn up in the mesosphere. The *thermosphere* extends to about 430 miles (almost 700 kilometers). It is extremely hot and has satellites, little air, and many ions. The *exosphere* extends to over 6,000 miles (10,000 kilometers) and has very little in it at all.

EXAMPLE

Which of the following is NOT true?

(A) An object falling to the deepest possible part of the ocean would land in the abyss.

(B) A vulture was seen in the stratosphere.

(C) The aurora borealis and aurora australis both occur in the thermosphere.

(D) The tectonic plates of the Earth are in the lithosphere and crust.

The correct answer is Choice (A). The deepest level of the ocean is the oceanic trench. Choice (B) IS true. A large, Rüppell's vulture was found at 11,552 miles, just into the stratosphere. Choice (C) IS true. The aurora borealis and aurora australis (from the north and south polar regions, respectively) occur as a result of charged solar particles (ions) falling through the thermosphere. Choice (D) IS true. The tectonic plates are the hard slabs of Earth's crust (surface) and lithosphere; there are seven or eight large plates and several smaller ones.

The movements of rock

Tectonic plates (the hard slabs of Earth's crust [surface] and lithosphere) move continually under Earth's oceans and continents. Most geologists believe that Earth's continents were all together in one large continent 250 million years ago: *Pangaea* (*pan-* means *all*; *gaea* means *earth*). As the plates moved over the eons (in the general movement of plates called *continental drift*), they arrived at their current shape and location.

There are three specific types of plate movement:

>> **Convergent:** Plates collide into each other; material gets pushed up, resulting in ridges and mountains as well as volcanoes; crust gets recycled

>> **Divergent:** Plates pull apart or separate from each other; new crust forms as well as oceans, lakes, and rivers; volcanoes may also form

>> **Transform:** Plates rub against each other in either a back or forth motion; earthquakes result

As you may suppose, most volcanic eruptions and earthquakes occur along the *fault* lines or boundary areas of the plates. The Pacific Plate's borders have over 400 active volcanoes and over 80 percent of our planet's earthquakes. When volcanic material such as the hot, liquid *magma* cools, rocks are formed. Earthquakes re-form rocks. In fact, rocks are continually being made and remade into one of three types:

>> **Igneous:** Made of cooling and hardening magma (inside the volcano) or lava (outside the volcano)

>> **Sedimentary:** Made of material (animal and plant material, other rocks) broken down and then built back up

>> **Metamorphic:** Made of existing rock material (igneous, sedimentary) that underwent a change due to heat and pressure

Figure 6-4 shows the many ways rocks can change.

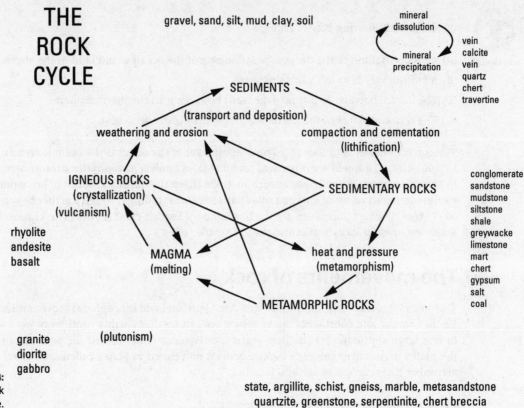

THE ROCK CYCLE

gravel, sand, silt, mud, clay, soil

mineral dissolution
mineral precipitation
vein calcite
vein quartz
chert
travertine

SEDIMENTS

(transport and deposition)

weathering and erosion

compaction and cementation
(lithification)

IGNEOUS ROCKS
(crystallization)

(vulcanism)

SEDIMENTARY ROCKS

conglomerate
sandstone
mudstone
siltstone
shale
greywacke
limestone
mart
chert
gypsum
salt
coal

rhyolite
andesite
basalt

MAGMA
(melting)

heat and pressure
(metamorphism)

METAMORPHIC ROCKS

(plutonism)

granite
diorite
gabbro

FIGURE 6-4:
The rock
cycle.

state, argillite, schist, gneiss, marble, metasandstone
quartzite, greenstone, serpentinite, chert breccia

© *John Wiley & Sons, Inc.*

EXAMPLE

Which of the following is true?

(A) Heat and pressure will, over time, remake some rock into metamorphic rock following convergent tectonic plate movement.

(B) As Pangaea began breaking up, magma moved up and, over time, cooled to form new ocean crust.

(C) The Law of Superposition explains how the oldest rocks are located in the bottom or lowest levels of rock strata.

(D) all of the above

The correct answer is Choice (D). Choice (A) is true because, as the plates collide, part of the crust is recycled. This happens as the forces of heat (friction) and pressure (weight) change previously igneous or sedimentary rock into metamorphic. Choice (B) is true because the plates that the continents rested on began moving away from each other, a divergent movement. Magma rose and cooled as ocean moved in; the hardened surface became oceanic crust. Choice (C) is true because, as rock layers form, the younger ones are deposited or *positioned over* older ones.

Rocks are affected by **weathering** when they are *broken or worn down* by exposure to wind, water, or plants (roots). When these smaller rock pieces are *moved* away by such forces as wind, water, or ice, it is the process of **erosion**. When the pieces are *dropped* or *deposited*, it is called **deposition**.

Other materials besides rocks and soil move on Earth, including *carbon.* Whether in the form of the gas carbon dioxide (CO_2) or the solid calcium carbonate ($CaCO_3$) found in shells, carbon is the element of life: Every living thing on Earth has carbon in it.

Carbon remains in bones long after the living creature has died. Fossils and materials made from fossils—natural gas, oil—contain carbon. When fossil *fuels* are burned, carbon is released in the form of CO_2. Even though plants use CO_2 in photosynthesis, they cannot use all of the CO_2 humans are currently pumping into the atmosphere. The built-up CO_2 traps more and more radiated warmth in the atmosphere, causing the *greenhouse effect.*

The movement of water

Water also is in constant movement on Earth. Ocean currents move on the surface as wind pushes the water. Currents also move underwater from the rising and falling of water temperatures. Even the Earth's rotation, pulling the winds, affects the currents.

In the water or *hydrologic* cycle (as shown in Figure 6-5), the sun's energy *evaporates* water into steam or vapor, which can cool or *condense* into clouds, fog, or dew. When enough condensation builds up in clouds, the heaviness of the water molecules causes them to fall, or *precipitate*. Water molecules may not change but may accumulate and be *stored* for long or short periods of time, including in glaciers, underground, or in the air.

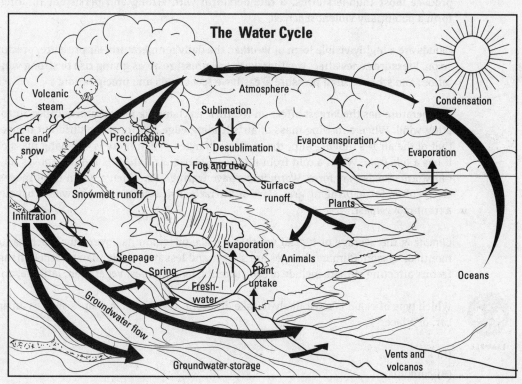

FIGURE 6-5:
The water cycle.

© John Wiley & Sons, Inc.

EXAMPLE

Which of the following explains *transpiration,* or the release of plant moisture into the atmosphere?

(A) weathering

(B) erosion

(C) the carbon cycle

(D) the water cycle

The correct answer is Choice (D). Transpiration is basically excess water from plants *evaporating*. Choice (A) is the breaking down of rock. Choice (B) is rock pieces and soil being carried away. Choice (C) involves the movement of carbon, not water. Plants are involved in the movement of both.

Clouds and weather

When water molecules condense into clouds, they form one of three major types:

» **Stratus:** Low clouds (surface to 2,000 meters); often in layers *(strato-* means *layer);* flat and gray; light rain, drizzle

» **Cumulus:** Middle clouds (2,000–6,000 meters); white and puffy *(cumulus* means *heap);* fair weather

» **Cirrus:** High clouds (6,000–12,000 meters); often feathery *(cirro-* means *curl of hair)*

Sometimes, huge *cumulonimbus* clouds form, spanning the upper two levels. These vertical giants produce most thunderstorms; a thunderstorm with strong and persistent rotating winds can form a potentially violent *supercell.*

Clouds are a highly visible form of *weather:* the daily temperature, air pressure, precipitation, and so on. Pressure zones affect weather, with low pressure areas giving rise to strong winds, precipitation, and storms. High pressure areas have few clouds and precipitation.

Temperature has the largest affect on weather, as changing temperatures cause air to move, creating wind. When a moving mass of air's leading edge, or front, is a different temperature than that of the air it's moving into, the weather changes. When there is a moving mass of cooler air, it has a *cold front.* When a cold front moves in, warm air (which is lighter) moves up over it, and tall storm clouds may form. *Warm fronts* have warmer air. When a warm front moves in, stratus clouds often form, bringing gray skies and drizzle. Fair weather, cool or warm, usually follows as a front moves past.

Climate is the average or typical weather a place or region has over time, such as for a specific month or season. Climate changes are slower and less noticeable than weather changes. Natural factors affecting climate include ocean currents, land masses, vegetation, latitude, and elevation.

Which type of cloud is most likely to take different, recognizable shapes such as an animal, a car, or a face?

EXAMPLE

(A) stratus

(B) cumulus

(C) cirrus

(D) supercell

The correct answer is Choice (B). The heaped and puffy cumulus clouds often take imaginable shapes. Choice (A) is wrong because stratus clouds are usually flat and in layers. Choice (C) is wrong because cirrus clouds are usually wispy and drawn out. Choice (D) is wrong because the clouds of a supercell are the huge cumulonimbus "thunderheads."

EXAMPLE

Can climate change affect an ocean current? Why or why not?

(A) No. The movement of water is not susceptible to temperature.

(B) No. Currents are stable and unchanging.

(C) Yes. Surface ocean currents are pushed by wind, which is an effect of changing temperatures.

(D) Yes. Currents will push warmer air northward.

The correct answer is Choice (C). Rising (and falling) temperatures affect wind patterns, and winds drive surface currents, such as the jet stream. Choice (A) is wrong; the movement of water IS affected by temperature. Choice (B) is wrong; currents DO change. Choice (D) is wrong because it is the warmer air that, in effect, pushes the currents.

Earth's past

In geologic history (*geo-* means *earth*) there are many divisions, shown in Table 6-2.

TABLE 6-2   **Earth's Geologic History**

Eon	Era	Period	Millions of years ago begun	Characteristics
Phanerozoic	Cenozoic	Quaternary	1.6	Modern humans
		Tertiary	65	Plants, insects evolve; large mammals
	Mesozoic	Cretaceous	138	First primates, flowering plants; dinosaurs die out
		Jurassic	205	First birds; dinosaurs dominant
		Triassic	240	First dinosaurs; first mammals
	Paleozoic	Permian	290	Many reptiles
		Pennsylvanian	330	First reptiles; first trees
		Mississippian	360	First four-limbed vertebrates
		Devonian	410	First amphibians
		Silurian	435	First veined land plants
		Ordovician	500	Many multicellular animals
		Cambrian	540	First fishes; first chordates—vast, sudden increase in life forms
Proterozoic	Precambrian		2500	First multi-cellular life (including sponges)
Archean			3800?	First single-celled life (including algae)

Traces or remnants of plants or animals that are at least 10,000 years old are called *fossils*. Paleontologists (*paleo-* means *long ago*) may not know the exact age of a fossil, but fossils found in the same rock stratum of a given geologic period are supposed to have the same *relative* age as each other.

The Earth is believed to be about 4.5 billion years old, forming as a great cloud of gas that solidified into a sea of magma. Gradually the outer parts cooled; a thin crust formed on the surface and water vapor helped form the atmosphere. Roughly 3.8 billion years ago, oceans began forming as the planet continued to cool and condensed water (rain) poured down. It was about that time that the first organisms appeared.

EXAMPLE

A paleontologist finds the fossil of a tree and a crocodile near each other in a stratum of rock that carbon dating has shown to be 350 million years old. Which of the following is the only one the scientist can deduce from her findings?

(A) The crocodile is probably much older than the tree.

(B) The crocodile and the tree come from the Paleozoic Era.

(C) Nothing else was alive at the time of the crocodile and the tree.

(D) The crocodile probably rested by the tree.

The correct answer is Choice (B). The Paleozoic Era ranges from 540 to 240 million years ago. Choice (A) is wrong because the scientist uses relative dating and can deduce only that both fossils are relatively the same age, being found in the same stratum. Choice (C) is wrong. The absence of a fossil in a particular rock formation does not indicate the absence of that species on the planet. Choice (D) is wrong because the scientist has no way of knowing what long range, planetary forces (such as shifting of plates) may have brought the two fossils together or moved them apart over time.

Venturing beyond Earth

A year is the time it takes Earth to make one *revolution* around the sun. A month (the lunar month = 28 days) is the time it takes the moon to make a revolution around Earth.

As Earth revolves, it *rotates* on an axis, resulting in day and night. The moon also rotates on an axis, and it does so at the same rate of speed as Earth's rotation. As a consequence, we only ever see one side of the moon as it's lit by the sun, resulting in the portion of the moon—or phase—we see.

Eclipses happen when either the Earth blocks sunlight from reaching the moon, and it is eclipsed (lunar), or when the moon blocks sunlight from reaching Earth, and the sun is eclipsed (solar).

Earth and its moon are part of our solar system, which includes eight planets and one dwarf planet, Pluto. Mercury, Venus, Earth, and Mars—the inner planets—are made mostly of rock and are the smaller group of planets. The larger group—Jupiter, Saturn, Uranus, and Neptune—all have rings and are made mostly of gas; they're often referred to as the *gas giants*. Also found in our solar system are:

>> **Asteroids:** Large, rock-like objects orbiting the sun; the Asteroid Belt lies between Mars and Jupiter

>> **Meteoroids:** Small, rock-like objects (smaller than 10 meters in diameter) orbiting the Sun

>> **Meteorites:** What's left of a meteoroid that has burned in the atmosphere and fallen to Earth

>> **Comets:** Bodies also orbiting the sun and made of a nucleus surrounded by dust and gas that often forms a *tail*

Beyond our solar, or *sun*, system lie *galaxies* made of systems of stars. Our sun, for example, is one star of roughly 200 billion stars in the *Milky Way* galaxy. Astronomers (*astro-* means *star*) estimate there to be more than 170 billion galaxies.

EXAMPLE

Which explains the main cause of a solar eclipse?

(A) the Big Bang theory

(B) the casting of a shadow

(C) the lunar revolution

(D) the tilt of the Earth's axis

The correct answer is Choice (B). During a solar eclipse, the moon blocks sunlight from, or casts a shadow on, the Earth. Choice (A) is an explanation for how the universe was created, more of an ongoing expansion than an actual explosion. Choice (C) is the 28-day period it takes the moon to make one revolution around the Earth. Choice (D) is the main cause of the seasons.

Physical Science Facts

Physical science involves the condition of substances and how they combine or interact. It also involves different objects and how they interact, as well as different types of energy and how they are involved in interactions. Several laws describe how forces can affect the motion of objects.

States of matter

What is matter in? Everything from rocks to water to air, from mountains to microbes to mist, all objects and substance—anything that has mass and takes up space is *matter*.

As you can see in Table 6-3, there are three basic states of matter, with each state having specific *properties* regarding the shape it takes and the speed at which its molecules move.

TABLE 6-3   ## States of Matter

State	Shape	Volume	Molecules
Solid	Keeps its own	Fixed	Has strong force; slow moving; tightly clustered
Liquid	Takes on that of its container	Fixed	Has weaker force; moves faster; not so tightly clustered
Gas	Takes on that of its container	Takes on that of its container	Has the weakest force; moves fastest; spreads out

Changes in temperature or pressure can cause a change in a state of matter. As temperature increases, molecules move faster. As pressure increases, molecules move slower.

>> **Melting:** An increase in temperature making the molecules move faster; a solid may change to liquid, which may change to gas

>> **Freezing:** A decrease in temperature making the molecules move slower; a gas may change to liquid, which may change to solid

>> **Boiling:** When liquid, having reached its *boiling point,* changes to gas

>> **Sublimation:** When a substance changes from a solid to gas, skipping the liquid state

>> **Deposition:** When a substance changes from a gas to a solid, skipping the liquid state

A change in a *state* of matter, such as ice (solid) melting (becoming liquid), results in a *physical change.* The process can be reversed: The melted liquid can be frozen back into a solid. The substance is still water. When the *substance* of matter changes, it is a *chemical change.* A nail made of iron, when left outside long enough, will rust. The rust is made of iron and oxygen: The substance (iron) changed (to iron and oxygen).

Molecules are made up of two or more atoms. For example, a molecule of water is made up of two hydrogen atoms (H_2) and one oxygen atom (O). Any atom of an element—such as the element iron, hydrogen, or oxygen—looks the same. Scientists have identified 118 elements; each element's atoms have their own characteristics.

O_2, the way oxygen is usually found (that is, with two atoms and not just one), is a molecule of two atoms of the same element bonded together. When two or more *elements* are bonded together, they form a *compound.* A common compound is NaCl: sodium chloride, or table salt.

In a *mixture,* two or more compounds are mixed to form a solution. The compounds are NOT bonded to each other—they can be separated out of the mixture.

Which of the following is NOT true?

(A) Burning wood is an example of a physical change.

(B) On Earth, an empty glass is actually full.

(C) Protons and neutrons are inside the nucleus of an atom.

(D) Carbon dioxide is a compound.

The correct answer is Choice (A). It is a chemical change. When wood burns, new substances are formed (such as carbon dioxide and water vapor) that *cannot be changed back.* The ash in a fireplace where wood is burning cannot be changed back to wood. Choice (B) IS true because, on Earth, the glass has air in it, and air, as matter, takes up space (has volume). Choice (C) IS true. Choice (D) IS true because carbon dioxide, CO_2, is one atom of the element carbon bonded to two atoms of the element oxygen.

Energy

Whether you are sleeping in bed or running a marathon, you have *energy:* the ability to do *work,* a force moving an object. If you are sleeping (and not tossing or turning) your energy is *potential,* or stored, waiting to be used. If you are in motion, your energy is *kinetic.* An acorn still on the oak branch has potential energy; when falling, the acorn's energy is kinetic.

The *chemical energy* of matter is that which is stored in the bonds of compounds (including food, wood, and so on) and released in a chemical reaction.

Thermal energy involves the generating and measuring of *heat.* According to *the first law of thermodynamics* (the law of conservation of energy), energy may change forms, but it cannot naturally be created or destroyed.

Heat is measured in units, including the British thermal unit (BTU), calorie (cal), and joule (J). There are three scales used to measure temperature: Celsius (C), Fahrenheit (F), and Kelvin (K). Kelvin units are based on an absolute scale. Absolute zero is −273.15 degrees Celsius, −459.67 degrees Fahrenheit, and 0 degrees Kelvin.

According to *the second law of thermodynamics,* when energy is transferred or transformed—when work is done—some energy (thermal) is lost to the system. There is less energy for work and more disorder in the system; this situation describes *entropy.*

Other types of movement involving heat include the following:

>> **Conduction:** Heat moving between objects that touch, with the heat moving from the warmer to cooler object, as from a stove burner to a pot resting on it

>> **Convection:** Heat circulating, moving in currents through liquids and gases, as the heated water in the bottom of a pot rises and then the cooler water in the pot moves down to replace it and so on, in a circular motion

>> **Radiation:** Heat moving through space and radiating back off a surface, as the sun's energy radiating off the land or a burning log's energy radiating off the fire

In *mechanical energy,* the power comes from machines. The energy or work (W) is equal to the force (F) times the distance (D) an object moves, or $W = F \times d$. A simple machine works by changing either force or distance. The *wheel and axle* as a unit increase the distance you may go while reducing force. A *lever* is a long bar that pivots around a support, or *fulcrum,* and allows you to lift objects, or *loads.* The fulcrum does not need to be located in the middle. When you swing a ball bat, the fulcrum is the nub of the handle, and the load is the ball. A *pulley* increases distance while reducing force. A *wedge* is an inclined plane (reducing force while increasing distance) that transfers the force from the wide to the narrow end. An *inclined plane* lets you reduce force while increasing distance. A *screw* is an inclined plane around a shaft that affects distance by changing the force from a rotational one to a linear one.

Which of the following is an example of chemical energy?

EXAMPLE

(A) a stretched rubber band

(B) a wheelbarrow

(C) an apple on a table

(D) a grill burning propane

The correct answer is Choice (C). The *stored* energy in food is released during digestion and the new substances formed cannot be changed back into *apple,* but instead are released during the chemical reaction. Choice (B) is an example of mechanical energy. A wheelbarrow is a kind of lever; the fulcrum is located at the wheel-end. Choice (D) is an example of thermal energy as it gives off heat.

Interactions between energy and matter

Energy has a special relationship to matter. As Einstein's theory of special relativity shows, a body's kinetic energy (E) is equal to its increased relativistic mass (M) times the speed of light squared (C^2), or $E = MC^2$.

There are several ways that energy can interact with matter:

>> **Sound:** Waves made by vibration passing through the matter of air. The faster the vibration, the higher the pitch. Shorter (more compressed) wavelengths carry more energy so they vibrate at a higher frequency.

>> **Nuclear energy:** Stored in the nucleus of an atom. The energy may be released through *fusion*, when two or more nuclei are combined (as in a hydrogen bomb), or through *fission*, when the nucleus of an atom is split (as in a reactor or an atomic bomb).

>> **Magnetic energy:** A force that pulls or pushes across a distance by opposing or like poles, respectively. A north pole (N) pulls a south pole (S), and vice versa, but two N poles repel, as do two S poles.

>> **Light:** Electromagnetic waves produced by fast-moving electrons releasing energy. Light waves are *transverse,* occurring in a series of up-and-down oscillations. When the rays of light waves bounce off a surface, it is a *reflection.* When light rays bend passing through a medium, such as water, it is *refraction.* The color we see is the color—frequency—of the spectrum NOT absorbed by an object. A ripe orange absorbs all the colors except orange, reflecting that color back out.

>> **Electric energy:** Produced when electrons move through a conductor along a closed circuit, as shown in Figure 6-6. Because electrons have a negative charge, they move toward a positive charge (opposite charges attract). Electric energy may produce heat, light, motion, or a magnetic force. Static electricity is an accumulation of charges (positive or negative) on an object. Units of measurement include the *voltage* (volt), measuring electrical pressure, and the *ampere* (amp), measuring the rate at which the current flows.

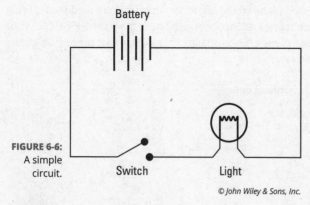

FIGURE 6-6: A simple circuit.

© John Wiley & Sons, Inc.

EXAMPLE

Which of the following is true?

(A) A circuit needs just to be closed and to have a conductor in order for heat or light to be produced.

(B) You can hear sound in outer space.

(C) A prism is an example of reflection.

(D) A compass's North points towards the North (directional) Pole of the planet. So, in reality, Earth's North directional pole is its South magnetic pole.

The correct answer is Choice (D). Earth is a magnet and thus reacts with other magnets in this opposites–attract manner. Choice (A) is not true because there must also be a source (of energy) such as a battery. Choice (B) is not true because there is no matter, no air, for the energy to interact with and produce vibrations (of the air molecules). Choice (C) is not true because when (white) light passes through a prism, the light is *refracted*, or bent, and the different colors, traveling at different frequencies, exit the prism at different speeds. Red light has a longer wavelength and travels faster than violet, so red is refracted the least and comes out on top, followed by orange, yellow, green, blue, and violet.

The laws of force and motion

Isaac *Newton's First Law* states that an object's rate and direction of movement (including being at rest) tend not to change unless an external force acts on them. Because *inertia* is the tendency of an object to stay in motion or at rest, Newton's First Law is also called the *Law of Inertia.*

External forces can affect an object's motion. One such force is *friction,* which is caused when two objects have contact with each other and motion is slowed; the rougher the surface, the slower the motion.

Another important force to consider is gravity. Newton's *Universal Law of Gravitation* states that two objects will exert a force on each other that depends on their mass and how far apart they are. The greater the mass of an object, the greater its gravitational force.

A third force is *electromagnetic.* Electric and magnetic forces can combine in such forms as x-rays, ultraviolet and infrared radiation, microwaves, and radio waves.

Because force is a push or pull, force affects motion. The following terms describe motion:

> » **Speed:** A change in an object's position relative to time.

> » **Velocity:** The speed of an object in a certain direction.

> » **Acceleration:** A change in an object's speed or direction; can be expressed in the equation $F = ma$, or *force = mass × acceleration*, the **Law of Acceleration.**

> » **Momentum:** Can be expressed as *mv*, or *mass × velocity.*

> » **Interaction:** For every action, there is an equal and opposite reaction—Newton's Third Law, the **Law of Interaction.**

EXAMPLE

A piece of plastic jettisoned in outer space has moved along at the same velocity for 27 years. This is an example of

(A) the Law of Gravitation

(B) the Law of Inertia

(C) the Law of Interaction

(D) the Law of Acceleration

The correct answer is Choice (B). The piece of plastic has not come into contact with anything, including air, that would cause friction and slow the piece down if there were air in outer space, but there is not. Choice (A) is wrong because there has been no object close enough to the piece of plastic for the object's mass to pull the plastic toward it and thus change its velocity. Choice (C) is wrong because there has been no second object, such as a space rock or another piece of space "junk," coming into contact with the piece of plastic and changing its velocity. Choice (D) is wrong because there has been no change in the piece of plastic's velocity.

Science Today

An important part of science today is considering how and why scientists go about their work. It's not enough to have a microscope and look into it. Science has an important role to play in society, from an individual's health to that of the planet.

Scientific methods

For a scientist to properly go about his work, several practices of the scientific method are necessary. When beginning an inquiry, a scientist needs a specific *question,* something that can be investigated and answered through experiments. Next, a scientist makes an educated guess, or *hypothesis,* regarding the outcome of the experiments. The scientist *plans* the investigation, making sure fair tests will be used that control each variable (so each is stable, except one) and the number of trials.

During the investigation, the scientist makes careful *observations and measurements,* recording the data accurately. The scientist then uses this data to come up with a *model* **or a** *theory* that explains the results. Finally, the scientist uses the model or theory to *predict* events or behaviors and to design further experiments that could disprove the model or theory.

Over time, scientists have gathered, recorded, and analyzed an incredible amount of data, and they are still doing so. To classify and sort all this information, scientists use systems, order, and organization. They may use *hierarchical* classification, arranged in order from group to increasingly smaller subgroups, as in the case of biology's domain, kingdom, phylum, class, and so forth. They classify machines using systems such as *simple,* *mechanical,* and so forth. *Time* is also a significant classification, such as in the study of fossils and rock strata.

Many scientists study why things change, whether they're studying changes in *temperature* (heat moving from a warmer area/object to a cooler area/object), *pressure* (force applied, causing liquid or gaseous matter to move from higher to lower pressure area), *length* (the distance between two given points), *volume* (the amount of space something takes up), or *mass* (how much material is *in* an object).

To take accurate measurements, a scientist may use a:

>> **Thermometer:** Temperature

>> **Barometer:** Pressure

>> **Calipers:** Distance

>> **Graduated cylinder:** Volume of a liquid; the reading is taken at the bottom of the *meniscus,* the liquid's curved surface

>> **Balance scale:** Mass

EXAMPLE

A student conducted an experiment at home over the weekend. He wanted to determine which would freeze faster, water on its own or water with sugar added. On Monday, the student brought in a graph. This graph is an example of

(A) part of the scientific method.

(B) hypothesis.

(C) hierarchical classification.

(D) frozen sugar-water.

The correct answer is Choice (A). The graph is a model communicating the results. Choice (B) is wrong because the hypothesis stage comes *before* the observation and collection of data that produces a model (here, the graph). Choice (C) is wrong because the display is not an interconnected organization of a group and its subgroups. Choice (D) is wrong because, while it references the time it took the water with sugar to freeze, the graph itself is not an example of frozen sugar-water.

Science and medicine

Science has long played an important role in society. From inventions such as the steam engine to discoveries such as a vaccine for polio, science has made and continues to make significant contributions.

Science tells you just how important *nutrition,* a balance of vitamins and minerals, is to your health. From sweet potatoes, carrots, and dark leafy greens, you can get Vitamin A, which helps your eyes, skin, and immune system. Fish can give you B_1 and B_3 for energy, and B_6 and B_{12} for red blood cells and the nervous system.

Citrus fruits are an important source of Vitamin C, which helps connective tissue such as bones and blood vessels. Your skin can help your bones by making Vitamin D with the aid of the sun. From leafy greens, nuts, and oils, you can get Vitamin E, an *antioxidant,* which helps prevent cell damage.

Minerals help build strong bones, skin, nerves, and muscles. Important *minerals* such as magnesium, potassium, and zinc come from different fruits, vegetables, nuts, and legumes.

Science also helps you understand the importance of exercise and disease prevention. You can help avoid the spread of germs in such *infections* as colds, flu, malaria, and tuberculosis. You can strengthen your immune system and thereby help your body fight a *virus,* which, unlike a bacterial infection, can't be successfully fought with antibiotics. You can help your liver by not drinking too much alcohol and your lungs by not smoking tobacco.

On a larger scale, science can help people understand and prepare for changes in populations or the environment, natural disasters, and the benefits and risks of technological advancements. For example, the draining of wetlands provides space for buildings, but it also creates a loss of natural water filters and storm barriers. The burning of fossil fuels provides energy for cars, furnaces, and washing machines, but it also releases excess CO_2 into the air and contributes to climate change.

EXAMPLE

Which of the following is NOT true:

(A) A diet rich in fruits and vegetables can help prevent cancer.

(B) Exercise can help you by increasing high-density lipoprotein (HDL), or "good" cholesterol.

(C) Antibiotics are effective against viruses.

(D) The most important scientific information regarding tsunamis has to do with real-time models of changes in sea level, not models based on the size of the undersea earthquake causing the tsunami.

The correct answer is Choice (C). Antibiotics are designed to work against bacteria, which can reproduce on their own, but not against viruses, which have to attach themselves to host cells in order to reproduce. Choice (A) IS true: As with antioxidants and cell damage, there is evidence to show a relationship between fruits and vegetables in the diet and lower cancer rates. Choice (B) IS true: Proper exercise usually increases HDL, which helps remove low-density lipoprotein (LDL), or "bad" cholesterol, from the arteries. Choice (D) IS true: The real-time models are quickly produced and very accurate, and, since their increased use following the devastating Indian Ocean tsunami of 2004, have already saved countless lives.

Chapter 7

Studying Social Studies Content Facts

S ocial studies teachers have a complex job; their work involves a content that embraces the entire world and all of history. Because that is what social studies really is—a mixture of government, history, and civics, all seasoned with the culture and geography of the world's inhabitants. The question is, then, just how do you teach the world to youngsters?

After all, life is complicated and sometimes scary. And it's interesting, just like social studies. This chapter looks at the "working parts" of social studies, including the geography, history, government and economics, anthropology, and sociology, and shows readers why these subjects are so vital to education.

A Big-Picture View of Social Studies

When it comes to helping children—and adults, for that matter—understand the world, it's best to start small and build from there. This type of instruction is called the *expanding horizon approach,* or the *widening horizon curriculum.* The teacher starts with what the students know and moves outward from that point to include widening circles within the social studies content framework. For example, kindergarteners and first-graders should learn about their immediate environment at home and in school. In the second grade, the focus expands to the community. By the twelfth grade, students should know the particular geographical and cultural features of the world and be able to understand how geography, history, economics, government, anthropology, and sociology contribute to the daily lives of U.S. citizens, including influencing those people in regards to where they work, where they live, and what they know and can do. Naturally, there is a huge gap between kindergarten and graduation, and it is the job of the teacher to keep widening those circles that are begun, really, before children ever enter the school door.

To fully understand this view of the big, wide world, students must look at different sources and organize the information in their brains, categorizing and sorting it according to their own needs and viewpoints. Then they analyze it. However, the phrase "looking at organizing and analyzing source information" is entirely too long, so the process is instead called *systematic inquiry*.

Systematic inquiry is a research and action strategy that focuses on the problem to solution, or cause to effect, relationship of content—in other words, what happens, or has happened, when a piece of knowledge is introduced into an environment. An example of this might be map-making. Prior to the widespread making and usage of maps in the 1500s, many used geographical and physical features to find their way. When they ran out of land, there was water. After sailing in one direction in the water for a long time, they came upon a different land. While much has changed in the world, this systematic inquiry method is still at play. Man still uses cause and effect to find his way.

This has become even more true, not less so, in the age of technology. Inquiring students must use primary sources like newspapers, letters, diaries, ledgers, oral histories, census reports, photos, journals, and artifacts to understand and evaluate information. Students also need to be taught about secondary sources, usually easier to get, which include encyclopedias, books, textbooks, and journal articles. With so much information out there, students must be taught which information can be trusted.

Of course, life cannot be lived through words alone. Students must also see the importance and purpose of their school library, museums, local libraries, educational exhibits, and historical societies. Social studies is the subject area that introduces these vital community links and encourages that quest to know more. If allowed, school field trips involve furthering knowledge that is often introduced in a social studies classroom.

With budget cuts, social studies is often the first to be targeted, and the subject has often been called the "stepchild" of education, because so little attention is given to it and so little money is spent there. So, then, why is social studies important? Because this is a complex world that keeps changing, and those little people studying the map of the United States in geography class will someday be bigger people responsible for the planet we live on. They need to understand how geography and natural factors affect people and cause them to create the different cultures around the world. Students also need to understand the workings of time and how things change and yet, sometimes, stay the same.

Geography

It is a standard joke in comics and TV shows that men will never ask directions while the woman sits by knowingly with a map. But, we all want to know where we are. We also want to know where to go and how to get there. Man is a nomadic creature. While historical man traveled for food, present man, for the most part, travels to experience the wonders of the Earth we live on. Geography helps us understand this Earth and our place on it; it also helps identify the other people who share our planet—all those different cultures, peoples, areas, and animals. Geography helps us to understand the environment's effect on humanity as well as man's impact on the Earth.

Geography helps us interpret the past, understand the present, and plan for the future. There are three basic geographical ideas:

>> **Physical factors affect cultural factors.** In other words, natural resources affect human civilization. Greece developed differently than Russia, in large part because of the different terrain.

>> **Everything changes, and it changes all the time.** Merely by existing in a region, people bring change to the region. The region also changes them, both physically and culturally.

>> **Humans manipulate the environment to fit their needs.** Controlled burning of forests and the damming of rivers are basic examples of how man changes the environment to better suit the needs of a community.

While many may question the need to know geography with maps and technology available to guide us, there are many ways that the study of geography helps students, including:

>> Discovering how different regions help create different cultures

>> Explaining how historical conditions, such as colonialism, land ownership, and economics, affect humanity and its cultures

>> Understanding how humans adapt to environmental stresses, such as climate or soil fertility, and create architecture, clothing, and food

>> Explaining how technology and the use of tools affect the environment

>> Discussing the purpose of human migrations, in terms of political, economic, physical, and/or cultural factors, both locally and internationally

>> Discussing the similarities and differences of world regions

In essence, geography helps explain the Earth and its inhabitants, how they interact with each other, and what can result from that interaction.

Categories of geography

Geography is the study of the lands, the features, the inhabitants, and the phenomena of this planet we call Earth. Those who learn and study geography seek to understand the relationship between Earth and its human and natural features. Geography is not a static concept, but must be taught so that students understand that there is a relationship between humans and Earth and that each of these affects the other. An example of this is the way the natural features of volcanoes have affected both how and where people live. Another example is air or water pollution and how that misuse of natural resources has caused the Earth to change in ways that affect climate, habitation, and health.

To illustrate this relationship between man and Earth, geography is divided into two broad categories: physical geography and cultural geography.

Physical geography

Physical geography is the study of the Earth's physical features, such as plant life, climate, geological formations, and soil. It includes the Earth's movement and weather patterns, but not man's influence.

For example, why do the La Quebrada Cliff Divers dive 115 feet from the cliffs of Acapulco? Because they have those cliffs (a physical feature). Not every culture has that physical feature. Other cultures are known for other things in their physical environment. The area around Mt. Everest is another example. Sherpa and explorers dedicate their very lives to understanding and conquering this mountain. Its existence is physical geography. Man's attempt to conquer the mountain or create a tourist attraction of cliff diving leads to another branch of geography, cultural geography.

Cultural geography

Cultural geography, or *human geography,* is the study of how man interacts with his environment and the consequences of these interactions. These consequences result in cultural characteristics such as art, music, and language. Other human aspects of cultural geography are religion, economic prosperity, diet, and shelter, among others.

Studying cultural geography leads man to better understand history, the development of different cultures on Earth, politics, and more. While we may take geography for granted, learning how our world works is of the utmost importance for understanding the past, present, and future.

Themes of geography

In order to give some organization to this huge topic, the National Council for Geographic Education and the Association of American Geographers created *five themes of geography.* These themes are discussed in the following sections.

Place

Place is the understanding of the physical and human characteristics of an area. This includes mountains, rivers, beaches, and how man has adapted to living in these areas.

Location

Location is the understanding of where things are physically located, with respect to their connections with other places. Location has two different types:

>> **Absolute location** describes the location of a place based on a fixed place on Earth. This fixed place is commonly identified using pairs of numbers known as coordinates. These pairs of coordinates consist of latitude and longitude:

- **Latitude:** Imaginary lines on earth that start at the *equator,* an imaginary dividing line that separates the planet into two halves which are known as *hemispheres.* Everything north of the equator is known as the *Northern Hemisphere.* Everything south of the equator is known as the *Southern Hemisphere.* The equator is known as 0 degrees latitude. In a paired coordinate, latitude is always written first.

- **Longitude:** Imaginary lines on Earth that run from pole to pole, north to south. The poles are represented as 0 degrees longitude. In a paired coordinate, longitude is always written last.

   An example of a paired coordinate with latitude and longitude would be 38° 53′ 35″ N, 77° 00′ 32″ W. If you were given these coordinates, where would you go? No guess? These coordinates would take you directly to the United States Capitol building in Washington, DC.

>> **Relative location** is the position of a place in relation to another known and named place. It explains the interrelationship between two places. For example, the relative location of Louisville, Kentucky, is 310 miles from Chicago, Illinois. Naturally, this is the type of location that most people use, while absolute location is left to those who rely on being very specific with their directions, like pilots, for example.

Human-environmental interaction

Human-environmental interaction shows how humans affect, adapt to, and modify their environment and how the natural environment helps and hinders humanity. Both interactions can have positive and negative effects. Consider a river. An example of a positive interaction would be that a river is a great mode of transportation and it helps with trade. An example of a negative interaction would be that some rivers flood and can destroy human dwellings.

Movement

Movement and connections show how people and goods traveled in the past and present. Movement gives an understanding of how people communicate and the different networks and methods they use. Ancient Egyptians and ancient Greeks traded and communicated. As you can probably imagine, it is easier to travel via the Mediterranean Sea than to walk through Macedonia, Ionia, Syria, and Phoenicia to get to Egypt.

Regions, patterns, and processes

Regions divide the world into manageable chunks for study. Regions, patterns, and processes identify cultural patterns in the different regions on Earth. This study includes economic, political, and climactic patterns and how these are different from region to region. They can change within a region, too. Regions can have official designations, like the names of states, but they can also include more casual designations, like "the South" and "the Midwest."

The five themes of geography help interpret regions, movement, human-environmental interaction, location, and place. They were developed to facilitate and organize teaching of geography within classroom settings.

Maps, globes, and other tools of geography

Just as a carpenter has a hammer, chisels, and saws, a geography teacher has tools, too. Teaching others to use these tools is also part of teaching geography. The tools that budding geographers need to know how to use are globes, maps, graphs, and charts because these tools organize information so that others can understand it easily and quickly.

Globes

Globes give the student an idea of the shape of the Earth and the interconnectedness of different regions. They also answer the basic question of, "Where are we?" and give students an idea of their location in regards to other peoples, cultures, and land masses.

Students should be able to identify the following parts of a globe:

>> **Equator:** This is an imaginary dividing line that separates the planet into two halves: the northern hemisphere and the southern hemisphere.

>> **North Pole:** As everyone knows, this is the place where Santa Claus lives! While this could certainly be added to any definition in an elementary classroom, for the purposes of geography, the North Pole is the northernmost point on Earth where all lines of longitude meet.

>> **Antarctic Circle:** This is one of five major circles that mark the map of Earth. This circle is the northernmost latitude.

>> **South Pole:** This is the southernmost tip on Earth and is directly opposite from the North Pole.

>> **Arctic Circle:** This is another of five major circles that mark the map of Earth. This circle is the southernmost latitude. The others are the Tropic of Cancer and the Tropic of Capricorn.

>> **Meridian:** This is also known as *line of longitude* and is an imaginary arc on Earth connecting the North Pole and South Pole. Meridians can be thought of as a circle that divides the Earth into two halves at any point, much like slicing an apple.

>> **Parallels:** These are also known as *circles of latitude.* This is an imaginary east-to-west circle connecting all points of latitude of Earth. In other words, if you are still thinking of the apple, just imagine cutting it differently, not sliced down the middle, but sliced from the top, showing the core.

>> **Prime meridian:** This is the spot at which the longitude line is defined at 0°. It divides the Earth into two *hemispheres,* the *Eastern Hemisphere* and the *Western Hemisphere.* Because the meridian is determined by the axis and rotation of the Earth, there are several locations for this around the globe.

>> **International date line:** This is an imaginary line on the surface of the Earth that runs from the North Pole to the South Pole and is used for keeping track of the calendar. Someone traveling, for example, may cross this line and be moved ahead one day or behind one day, according to the calendar.

>> **Time zones:** Regions observe specific times to make it easy for people to understand where they are.

Maps

Maps are like globes, except they provide a two-dimensional view of the Earth. Globes present a three-dimensional view. Think of a map as a globe that has been run over by a steamroller. Because it is a flat representation, it is distorted. There are also maps that provide more accurate scale representations, and some maps are interactive or can appear three-dimensional when coupled with technology. For the purposes of the test, though, think in terms of a flat map, like one you would unfold to find your way on vacation. This kind of map is known as a *road map.* In addition to roads, these maps can also include points of interest in an area, railway tracks, cities, airports, and even, in some cases, rest stops.

Maps are used for many different reasons, not just finding your way if you are lost. There are many kinds of maps, including

>> **Physical maps:** Illustrate rivers, lakes, mountains, and other physical features of an area.

>> **Climate maps:** Show the average weather, rainfall, and snowfall in an area.

>> **Economic or resource maps:** Depict what natural resources are available in a region. They also show the resulting economic activity.

>> **Geological maps:** Give geological features such as faults, stratum, and rock formations.

>> **Topographical maps:** Often show both natural features and those made by man. They are very detailed and use contour lines, as well as other methods of depicting information.

>> **Political maps:** Depict the political boundaries of countries, states, and other political entities. These maps also can include capitols and major cities.

There are many other types of maps. In fact, the possibilities are almost endless.

Students should be able to find the following parts of a map:

>> **Map scale:** This is the *ratio* of the distance on a map corresponding to the actual distance between two locations on the ground. Maps have to be small enough to hold, but the depictions have to become smaller and also have to accurately represent the distances between objects.

>> **Legend:** This is also known as a *key.* Legends contain the symbols of a map and what they represent.

>> **Compass rose:** This displays the cardinal directions of North, South, East, and West for orientation.

>> **Altitudes:** This is the height or depth of an object. While most students think in terms of air space, altitude is also useful to determine how tall mountains are, for example.

Maps also use some labels that are the same as those on globes, including meridians, parallels, latitude, and longitude.

Approaches to Teaching History

How do you teach a subject as big as all of history to elementary school children? Like all instruction, organizing the information into manageable chunks is a necessary first step. There are broad categories to focus on when teaching history to youngsters, such as *chronological thinking,* or the act of putting events in order along a mental timeline, and *historical comprehension,* or reading with a historical perspective and understanding of the past.

Clearly, history requires an understanding of what happened (historical comprehension) and when (chronology). A bigger question may be "Why?". Research and analysis come into play here. In order to gather information and analyze it, students look at time, continuity, and change, as well as how people react in their environment. Lastly, this research and analysis helps the student develop a personal identity and an understanding of others. In order to get to that goal, start small and move outward.

The expanding horizon approach, or widening horizon curriculum

The easiest way to present all this information to elementary students is to use the expanding horizon approach, as mentioned earlier in the chapter, where teachers start with areas of immediate focus and gradually enlarge that circle during instruction to show students more of the world they live in. While particular standards and guidelines may change from state to state, these areas are the particular focus for these grade levels:

>> **Kindergarten to first grade:** Family, home, school

>> **Second grade:** Community

>> **Third grade:** Holidays and U.S. history, or state history and geography

>> **Fourth grade:** State geography and history, or world regions

>> **Fifth grade:** American history and geography

>> **Sixth grade:** World history and geography

>> **Seventh grade:** U.S. history or state history

>> **Eighth grade:** American history and civics

It is important to help students in grades K–3 establish an idea of what order and time are. Stories from the past help them see that different situations resulted in different actions. They help them understand that actions have consequences—something we're all still learning, right?

The further a child advances in school, the heavier social studies content becomes. Remembering history is a focus on understanding the most important events of the past, either the far past or recent past, so that decisions about the present and future can be made in a more knowledgeable way. It is not simply memorizing facts and figures, although everyone can probably remember a high school teacher who taught in this manner. However, instruction in elementary school focuses more on the connections that students can make between the past and their own personal present.

This is considered an *integrative approach*, and combines geography with history. While many facts and figures need to be known, many states focus on a particular curriculum aimed at local influence. This is the only time students learn, or are expected to know, local and state history. After elementary and upper elementary, the guidelines and standards for history become very exact and demanding.

In order to develop the understanding that the past affects the present and future, students need to learn various concepts, including the following:

>> **Time, continuity, and change:** These words practically form the history teacher's mantra. They explain everything a teacher needs to impart and a student needs to learn. Everything changes, and still there is something that remains the same. This allows learners to understand their own historical heritage and to locate themselves in the stream of time. Learning how to read and understand events from the past allows them an understanding of how to connect those events with the present. This understanding also leads to decision-making based on those past experiences. You've probably heard the quote, "Those who do not learn from the past are destined to repeat it." George Santayana, the guy who actually spoke those words, knew what he was talking about, and students who learn this skill will be able to join him and other learned people.

>> **People in the environment:** Another factor is people and how their environments shape them. In this case, the environment is not just the physical environment, but the social and cultural environment, including religious beliefs. A crusading knight had a different environment than a Native American. They were in different places geographically and faced different challenges. Even among American Indians, the terrain a tribe lived in was different from another forest, sea island, or plain. Each environment caused different social and cultural responses. You build this knowledge using students' personal experiences of how their environment has caused them to respond.

>> **Individual identity:** Lastly, individual identity is formed through a culmination of experiences, both in time and through the environmental and cultural influences. Who am I and why am I here? Good questions, right?! History can help answer those questions. For the K–3 crowd, this can lead to an understanding of how they have changed over time, as well as how and why they may feel differently about things than their best friend in the seat next to them. In other words, social studies helps explain how they feel about things and other people and how people respond to them. Higher-level elementary students can focus on how memory and self-identity can color decisions. It helps them see the similarities and the differences in us all.

A fourth-grade teacher is planning a lesson on people in the environment and, specifically, how humans have impact on the physical environment in which they live. Which of the following is the best example to use for showing the most direct impact of human activities on the environment?

(A) The 2004 Indian Ocean earthquake and tsunami

(B) The 1986 Russian Chernobyl nuclear disaster

(C) The current California drought

(D) The yearly effects and cycles of El Niño

The correct answer is Choice (B). This question requires an understanding of how humans have impacts on the conditions and events in the environment. Of all the listed activities and disasters, only the 1986 Chernobyl disaster was caused by and can be directly attributed to human actions. Because of this incident, the living conditions in and around Russia have dramatically changed, and there have been radioactive effects on the rivers, lakes, and soil in the area, which will last for years. The incident also had political and economic consequences. The other answer choices, while affecting human life, are neither associated with nor caused by humans.

Systematic inquiry

Studying history requires going to the source for the best and most unbiased information. Teaching history requires helping students understand and gather information using *systematic inquiry*, a method of research action that can explain and describe the event being studied. Two types of sources are commonly used in systematic inquiry in a social studies classroom:

>> **Primary sources:** These are original materials that have not been changed in any way. Primary sources include artifacts, a diary, a journal, a stone tablet with writing on it, newspapers, magazines from the time, or other artifacts. Ledgers and receipts are primary sources. Museums and the Library of Congress are great options to locate primary sources. People are great primary sources, too! Most of them are not going to be found in a glass case in a museum, but an eyewitness account based on an interview is priceless.

>> **Secondary sources:** Secondary sources are items that were not present when the event occurred. These can be textbooks, encyclopedias, dictionaries, and journal articles. Secondary sources are found in the library, whether a school, county, university, or other type of library. Of these, textbooks are perhaps the least useful, because they cover so much information that they are "thin" in some areas. Some texts are also biased and portray only one point of view.

Both primary and secondary sources can be used in the study of history. Whether studying the distant past or the recent past, students will likely have to rely on secondary sources. Teaching students how to evaluate and analyze those sources is key to getting the most reliable information.

You want to help your students gain personal insight into different sociocultural systems, both past and present. In doing so, you help them understand and appreciate different cultures and how they impact individuals. They learn how point of view can color decisions and long-held beliefs.

Government and Economics

Whenever you get a group of people together, someone has to lead and someone has to follow. The people within that same group are naturally going to barter and trade—and sooner or later, someone will hammer out a coin or print some money. While this is an extremely short form of history, the study of a society will prove that timeline. Government and economics are a result of civilization, and are, in fact, the markers of civilization. In other words, in order for a community to be considered an advanced civilization, it must have an economic and governmental system.

Government

A government is not the same as a political system, although government is what is seen as a result of a political system. Clear as mud?

Government actually concerns two concepts, which work together to form an understanding of how that huge bureaucratic system works:

>> **Civics:** The study of the rights and duties (yes, it's actually a duty) of citizenship.

>> **Political science:** The study of the systems of government and an understanding of general political activity and behavior. While some candidates may seem to defy understanding, there is reason behind all that madness come voting time.

People study government primarily for four reasons:

>> To become informed voters

>> To know their responsibilities under the law

>> To know their Constitutional and other legal rights under the law

>> To improve society by understanding how the process of government works.

Have you ever been told that discussing politics in social circles is a bad idea? Well, here's where you get to bend the rules, because discussing politics is now your job! Regardless of your viewpoint or political affiliation, you must admit that the government controls the country. It creates and enforces national policy. In the United States, this is done on a local level, a state level, and a national level. Using the widening horizon curriculum, the student first examines his local government. He then moves on to the state level and finally the federal government, examining the three branches of the U.S. government:

>> **Legislative:** This branch creates and declares law. The House of Representatives and the Senate join together to form the Congress, which has the power to enact laws.

>> **Executive:** This branch is responsible for implementing laws and running the government on a daily basis. This is where the President and Cabinet operate.

>> **Judicial:** This branch ensures equal justice under the law. The courts work here to ensure each citizen gets a fair trial.

In the study of government, a student sees how voting works, how laws are made, and how documents affect government. The civic rights and responsibilities of a U.S. citizen are outlined in those documents. The students also gain an understanding of the power they have in the three branches of government previously outlined and that the government is a representative of the laws and rules created through circumstances from history. See how this is all starting to work together?

In addition to U.S. government, other political systems are reviewed, such as dictatorships, fascism, oligarchies, absolute monarchies, and constitutional monarchies.

» **Dictatorship:** A form of government in which absolute power is concentrated in a dictator or a small clique, or a government organization or group in which absolute power is concentrated

» **Fascism:** An authoritarian and nationalistic right-wing system of government and social organization

» **Oligarchy:** A small group of people having control of a country, organization, or institution

» **Absolute monarchy:** A country that is ruled by a monarch, such as a king or queen, with the monarch having unlimited power.

» **Constitutional monarchy:** The monarch's power is limited by a constitution.

This "Big Picture" results in students seeing that, while individuals mold government, at times the government is not a completely true representation of the people in an area. Perhaps this insight can help students identify with classmates of different cultural backgrounds. Additionally, by understanding how the U.S. government works, students become better citizens, active in their community, their nation, and the world. That's always a good thing!

EXAMPLE

In a social studies class, the students have just learned about the system of checks and balances that regulates the three branches of government—legislative, executive, and judicial. As part of a lesson, the teacher assigns groups of students to compare the limits of each branch of government and then to contrast those limits. What is the highest level of thinking within Bloom's taxonomy of educational objectives that this assignment requires of students?

(A) Knowledge

(B) Comprehension

(C) Synthesis

(D) Evaluation

The correct answer is Choice (B). Students are required, as part of curriculum, to know the three branches of government and to be able to compare and contrast that content using specific details and main ideas. It involves more than just memorizing the knowledge, Choice (A). For this activity to be at the level of synthesis, Choice (C), students could have been directed to propose ideas for making a better system of checks and balances, or could have been directed to change the system in some way, by adding or detracting a branch, for example. A process of evaluation, Choice (D), would have required the students to give their opinion on how well those systems worked, with examples.

Economics

Money has been called many things—the root of all evil, the most important thing in life, a tool for good, a way to buy peace of mind. Regardless of one's opinion about money, it is important all over the world. It motivates people to leave an area, seeking a better standard of living (geography). It colors our interactions with our international neighbors (anthropology). It has greatly influenced, and still influences, man's decision-making (history). Elementary economics examines the desire for, the manufacture of, and the sale and use of money, both locally and globally. The teaching of economics includes concepts like wants versus needs, costs, and more thought-provoking topics, such as the following:

» Natural, human, and capital resources

» Supply and demand

» Producers and production

- » Consumers and consumption
- » Taxation and spending
- » Inflation and recession

Teaching *economic literacy,* or the ability to understand how money works in the world, can help students understand how the payment of taxes works to keep roads safe, to repair bridges, and to pay for their schooling, for example.

Also, economics brings home the point that the shiny trinket in the store is a result of the use of natural resources, human labor, shipping, wrapping, and overhead. Basically, economics helps the student learn that sometimes people have to make choices based on needs rather than wants.

As you travel through the more complex economic ideas, you can discuss how people make decisions based on their economic status; how they use natural resources to build economic stability; and how rivers and ports help with trade. The end goal is to see that money, indeed, does make our world go round, whether we want it to or not.

EXAMPLE

A social studies teacher shares a graph with her class that shows how home heating costs rise in the local area during winter months because of the reliance on heating oil, a product that has risen in cost. Which economic principles can the teacher be demonstrating by the use of the graph? Check all that apply.

(A) Supply and demand

(B) Consumers and consumption

(C) Natural, human, and capital resources

(D) Inflation and recession

The correct answers are Choices (A) and (B). This question requires that students have an understanding of the basic economic principles governing goods. During the winter months, when the demand for oil is greater, the supply decreases, creating a higher cost, hence, Choice (A). A discussion of the graph can also relate to the amount of money spent by households in an economy. It is usually measured on a monthly basis, hence, Choice (B). The answer is not Choice (C) because the graph does not explore natural, human, and capital resources. Only one type of resource, oil, is mentioned. The answer is not Choice (D) because in a recession (when businesses cease to expand), you would expect inflation (a general rise in the prices of goods and services over a period of time) to decrease. Neither of these is presented in the graph.

Anthropology and Sociology

All the information on place, time, history, and government doesn't really add up to much without the human factor. We are complicated little bundles of internal undercurrents that sometimes reject, and sometimes accept, the rules imposed on us. The best way to "bind" all that information is to wrap it up in anthropology and sociology.

Children come up with the most interesting topics because they look at things in an unfiltered way. A look at geography, history, government, and economy can bring some really interesting questions into the classroom. *Why did ancient Egyptians mummify cats? Why don't we mummify cats?* Great question, and probably one you've never thought of before. We don't mummify cats because . . . we don't want to, culturally. We, as a modern and scientific society, don't view the afterlife as the ancient Egyptians did.

Anthropology and sociology allow us to study the how's and why's of civilization that just can't be easily understood without analysis and reflection. It brings together why people settled in certain areas (geography), how they let that change their customs (history), and how they let those customs evolve into processes that governed their way of life (government and economics). Hopefully, you can see how all this is coming together . . .

Anthropology

Anthropology is the study of humankind. Human culture allows for a wide variety of anthropological study. An anthropologist can focus on modern culture or prehistoric culture, as well as all the cultures in between.

There are a lot of different types of anthropologists, or specialists who study all that culture, including:

>> **Archaeologists:** Archaeologists re-create the lives and cultures of people who died a long time ago. They do this by excavating entire cities, burial grounds, and other areas like wells and garbage dumps. You may be surprised to know what you can find out about people when you look through their garbage.

>> **Biological or physical anthropologists:** Physical or biological anthropologists examine both living and fossilized primates and humans. Yep, these anthropologists dedicate their time and expertise to studying things like rock-hard skulls.

>> **Primatologists:** Primatologists study primates like gorillas and chimpanzees to see how their group behavior matches or differs from human behavior. Gorillas and chimps are mankind's closest relative species; primatologists work to discover just how close.

>> **Linguistic anthropologists:** Linguistic anthropologists study language and how it's used socially. These specialists learn about people by looking at their writings and words.

>> **Ethnographers:** Ethnographers study ethnic groups in the field. They have a firsthand look at how different cultures work by living among the people or primates. This line of work can be fun and even dangerous.

By studying anthropology, students get an understanding of what being a human being means. They learn about the evolution of the human species, not only as a biological creature, but as a thinking and feeling creature. They learn of their heritage and their own potential for greatness as they learn about indigenous peoples and ancient civilizations of their own small, and potentially large, part of the world and in human culture. Anthropology also teaches them that the borders that separate them are really only sets of rules and customs that have been created over time.

EXAMPLE

The emergence and widespread use of the code of Hammurabi from ancient Mesopotamia is most directly connected to which of the following?

(A) Laws concerning economic necessity which brought about the use of a government-controlled banking system

(B) A rise in government-sanctioned religious ceremonies

(C) A focus on the physical and biological needs of all community members, not just the ruling class

(D) The emergence of laws concerning the rights of individuals in matters of personal economics, punishments of crimes, and contractual provisions

The correct answer is Choice (D). The question requires an understanding of the role of the fundamental laws in government and legal rights of citizens in this culture, as well as an understanding that this is one of the oldest primitive constitutions to be found by archeologists. The answer is not Choice (A) because the code was not related solely to economics and did not precipitate a government-controlled banking system. The answer is not Choice (B) because the code was not based on religious ceremonies; it was more political in nature. The answer is not Choice (C) because it was not related to the basic human needs of the society; rather, it was focused on individual *rights*.

Sociology

Sociology is the study of the development, structure, and functions of human societies. *Sociologists* study group behavior. Just as there are many types of anthropologists, there are also many types of sociologists. A few of them include

>> **Medical sociologists:** Medical sociologists study how diseases have impacted and influenced culture. This type of sociologist doesn't look at only history, though, but also at diseases occurring worldwide. She predicts how humans might react to outbreaks, plagues, and epidemics.

>> **Criminologists:** These guys are probably the most popular of the group, thanks to criminologist shows on television. While much of that work done on the TV is scientific, criminologists must also have an understanding of what causes crime and how to prevent criminal behavior.

>> **Social psychologists:** These sociologists study how people's thoughts, feelings, and behaviors influence and are influenced by others. They may tell us why, for example, we behave in a certain way.

>> **Sociobiologists:** These professionals study how social behaviors have been influenced by evolution and biology. For example, they may tell us why human beings learned to communicate verbally while other creatures, such as gorillas and chimpanzees, learned other types of communication.

All these careers start with a basic understanding of sociology and involve studying groups of people, whether those groups are families, workers in large organizations, men, women, children, mobs, or soldiers.

All of these disciplines—geography, history, government, economics, anthropology, and sociology—help to answer the question of why we are who we are. That process has been known to be long and complicated, but understanding that process promotes the importance of family, community, and civic pride, not to mention pride in humanity. In hindsight, it wasn't so very long ago that our ancestors sat around campfires grunting. Today, just a few hundred thousand years later, we're sending representatives to the moon and mapping our own DNA sequences. Look how far we've come!

Chapter 8

Art, Music, and Physical Education Content

Not every school has its own art, music, and physical education teachers, but how important these subjects are for the emotional, intellectual, and physical development of children!

In this chapter, you examine the elements and principles of art, elements of music, and concepts of movement. You look at how all three subjects fit in a time and a place, including your classrooms. And you explore how art, music, and physical education can help students become more socially adept, responsible citizens.

Seeing the Light of Art

Discussions of art involve four major areas: the elements of art, the principles of design, art throughout history and in cultures, and looking at art from an aesthetic as well as an ethical point of view.

The elements of art

The foundations or basic components of art are line, shape, form, color, texture, and space. *Line* is the distance between two points, or the path a point makes as it moves through space. It has direction and length, of course, but it also has width. A line can be thick or thin, as well as curved (curvilinear) or straight, and vertical, horizontal, or diagonal.

Shape is a closed line, or lines making an enclosed area. It is flat or *two-dimensional* (2-D), having length and width. Shapes can be *geometric*, such as circles, triangles, or squares; or they can be *organic*, that is, natural or free-form. When a shape is of a recognizable object, it is *representational* or *figurative* (of a figure or an object). When a shape is not that of a recognizable object, or when it is suggestive of an object, it is *abstract*.

The way the shapes are organized in a work of art, along with its lines and colors, is its *composition*. A *collage* is a 2-D composition comprised of different objects, such as types of paper, photographs, or pieces of fabric grouped (pasted) on a surface. Many collages are of *mixed media*, using more than one medium, such as layered photographs and fabric. *Mixed media* also refers to a work that uses, for example, ink and paint together, or, in sculpture, steel and bronze. When a shape is *three-dimensional* (3-D), having length, width, and depth, it is called a *form.* Forms also may be geometric, such as cylinders, pyramids, or cubes, or forms may be organic. Form is the basis of sculpture, which may be viewed from different sides. An *assemblage* is a 3-D work comprised of different objects affixed together; usually the objects are found objects as opposed to created ones.

Color, which is a product of light, has three main components. *Hue* is the name of the color, such as blue or red. *Intensity* refers to how bright or vivid a color is. A color's *value* refers to how light or dark it is. When white is added to a color, it is called a *tint.* When black is added, it is called a *shade.* Colors may be *cool*, such as the blues and greens, or *warm*, such as the yellows and reds.

>> **Primary colors:** Yellow, blue, and red; these are the only true colors—all other colors are made from them.

>> **Secondary colors:** Green, violet, and orange; these are made by mixing two of the primary colors—yellow + blue = green; yellow + red = orange; blue + red = violet (or purple).

>> **Tertiary/intermediary colors:** Yellow green, blue green, blue violet, red violet, red orange, yellow orange; these are made by mixing a primary color and a secondary color.

>> **Complimentary colors:** Two colors directly opposite each other on the color wheel that have no color in common; when combined, they have the effect of neutralizing each other, producing brown. Pairs include yellow and violet, green and red, and blue and orange.

>> **Analogous colors:** Three colors next to each other on the color wheel, such as yellow, yellow orange, and orange; they usually create a feeling of calm and naturalness.

A work of art's *texture* is the way its surface looks and feels. The feel may be real, such as in a sculpture or in a painting whose surface is rough with paint; or the feel may be implied, as in a painting whose surface *looks* soft.

The *space* in a work of art is how the shapes and forms are situated in relation to each other. Space may be *positive*, where objects actually are, or *negative*, where objects are not—that is, the shape of the area *between* the objects. In 3-D art, the space is real; in 2-D, the space or illusion of depth is created.

In a painting, the space in the front is called the foreground; the space in the back the background; and that in the middle, the middle ground. 2-D art can create the sense of depth or space with *perspective.* Going from foreground to middle to background, objects get smaller; their *aerial perspective* changes as they become paler and less detailed. Their *linear perspective* changes as lines that begin as parallel in the foreground slant toward each other until they converge at a *vanishing point* in the background. A painting with a single vanishing point has a *one-point perspective.*

EXAMPLE

A second-grade teacher is helping her students assemble mobiles with paper and string. She tells the class to make sure there is enough room between the hanging shapes for them to twirl around. Which element of art is she most likely teaching?

(A) line

(B) space

(C) shape and form

(D) texture

The correct answer is Choice (B). There must be enough room or space—negative space—for the objects in the mobile to turn. Choice (A) is wrong because she is not focusing on a visible mark showing the distance between two points. Choice (C) is wrong because her focus is on the space *between* the shapes, not on the shapes themselves. Choice (D) is wrong because her focus is not on how the shapes or string feel (or look) to the touch.

The principles of design

When using various elements of art, artists employ different principles. These principles of design include balance, proportion, scale, emphasis, movement, repetition, unity, and variation.

Balance is how various elements are positioned in a work to give it a sense of equilibrium. When the balance is *symmetrical,* or *formal,* the distribution of elements (color, objects, space, texture) is very similar on both sides. *Asymmetrical* or *informal* balance has an unequal positioning of elements although they still look balanced. *Radial* balance has elements positioned around a central point.

Proportion refers to the relative size of objects to each other, and *scale* to an object's size relative to its real-life counterpart. Some objects in a work may be proportionally bigger than other objects in the work; some works may be *monumental* in scale, such as larger-than-life sculptures, or they may be *miniature,* smaller than their real-life counterparts.

Emphasis is the focal point of the work, the part of the work that catches the viewer's eye. This effect could be created by a contrast in colors, shapes, or other elements, creating an area that stands out, or is in *dominance.* Areas in *subordination* are toned down to deflect emphasis elsewhere.

The *movement* of a piece is its suggestion or feeling of motion, how the viewer's eye travels, as from foreground to background with linear perspective in 2-D. In 3-D, movement can refer to objects that actually move, as in *kinetic* sculpture.

Artists use *repetition* when creating patterns or rhythm. A *pattern* is made by repeating the same elements all through the work; *rhythm* is made by repeating similar elements to give the work a sense of flow, as in music or dance.

When the elements are in harmony with each other, there is **unity;** the work feels complete. When the elements of a piece have interesting differences, there is **variation.**

EXAMPLE

A kindergarten teacher is having her students draw several lines of the same thickness, and then draw one line that is thicker than the others and one that is thinner than the others. Which principles of design is she most likely teaching?

(A) proportion, emphasis

(B) repetition, balance

(C) repetition, variety

(D) unity, movement

The correct answer is Choice (C). The students practice making a pattern, repeating the lines of the same thickness, and then variation, making one line thicker and one thinner. Choice (A) is wrong because, while the thicker and thinner lines are different in proportion to the others, the line-drawing practice is not meant to be a work unto itself, so it has no focal point (emphasis) meant to catch the viewer's eye. Choice (B) is wrong because, while the lines of the same thickness do illustrate repetition, the line-drawing practice is not meant to be a work unto itself. The various lines (elements) are not meant to be seen as part of a whole where the various elements are *positioned* in relation to each other. Choice (D) is wrong because the lines (elements) are not meant to be part of a complete, whole (work), so the principle of movement, where the eye moves from one part of the work to another, is not involved, either.

Art history

Changing over time and from place to place, artistic styles range from lifelike, representational cave drawings to abstract, contemporary acrylics (man-made polymer paints). Table 8-1 shows major art movements, artists, and characteristics.

TABLE 8-1 **Major Art Movements in History**

Period/Movement	Artists/Works	Characteristics
Stone Age (30,000 B.C.–2500 B.C.)	Cave paintings, stone statues, Stonehenge	Human figures and animals; fertility goddesses; megaliths
Mesopotamian (3500 B.C.–539 B.C.)	Gate of Ishtar, Stele of Hammurabi's Code	Glorifies rulers/warriors; tomb art
Egyptian (3100 B.C.–30 B.C.)	Hieroglyphs, pyramids	Centered on the afterlife; symbolic
Greek (850 B.C.–31 B.C.)	Parthenon, Praxiteles	Idealism, perfect in line and proportion
Roman (500 B.C.–A.D. 476)	Augustus of Primaporta, Colosseum	Idealism and realism; the arch
Indian, Chinese, and Japanese (653 B.C.–A.D. 1900)	Gu Kaizhi, Li Cheng, Guo Xi, Hiroshige	Representational; peaceful and thoughtful
Byzantine; Islamic (A.D. 476–1453)	Hagia Sophia, Andrei Rublev, mosque of Córdoba, the Alhambra	Heavenly mosaics; maze-like designs
Middle Ages (500–1400)	St. Sernin, Durham Cathedral, Notre Dame, Chartres, Giotto	Celtic art, Carolingian renaissance, Romanesque, Gothic
Renaissance (1400–1550)	Botticelli, Donatello, Leonardo, Michelangelo, Raphael	Rebirth of classical elements to portray Christian imagery; balanced; harmonious
Mannerism (1520–1580)	Cellini, El Greco, Tintoretto	Unbalanced; unharmonious (as in clashing colors); highly skilled
Baroque (1600–1750)	Caravaggio, Velazquez, Rembrandt, Rubens	Light, vivid colors; realism; landscapes; self-portraits
Romanticism (1780–1850)	Eugène Delacroix, J.M.W. Turner, Benjamin West	Focus on feelings, mood, imagination and mystery; brushwork less precise
Realism (1848–1900)	Gustave Courbet, Thomas Eakins, Adolph von Menzel, Ilya Repin	Focus on accuracy; subjects often working-class people
Impressionism (1865–1885)	Mary Cassatt, Edgar Degas, Claude Monet, Pierre-Auguste Renoir	Focus on accurately depicting different/changing aspects of light; vivid colors; brushwork often small, thin strokes
Post-Impressionism (1885–1910)	Paul Cézanne, Georges Seurat, Vincent Van Gogh	Vivid colors but brushwork thicker; shapes or color sometimes distorted or exaggerated

Period/Movement	Artists/Works	Characteristics
Fauvism; Expressionism (1900–1935)	Henri Matisse, Wassily Kandinski, Edvard Munch	Harsh colors and brushwork; paintings look flat, emotional; focus on emotion as opposed to reality
Cubism (1905–1920)	Georges Braque, Pablo Picasso	Multiple viewpoints in the same picture; fragmented
Dadaism; Surrealism (1917–1950)	Salvador Dali, Max Ernst, Frida Kahlo	Depicting the unreal or ridiculous; exploring dreams and the unconscious
Abstract Expressionism (1940–50)	Helen Frankenthaler, Willem de Kooning, Franz Kline, Jackson Pollock, Mark Rothko	Complete abstraction; freedom of expression and technique
Postmodernism and Deconstructivism (1970–)	Gerhard Richter, Cindy Sherman, Frank Gehry	Collage, performance art; breaking down barriers between high and low art; experimental

Careers in art

It's important for students to know that their interest in art may lead to a profession or career. Here is a list of some of the many opportunities available to students: architect, motion picture producer, animator, web page designer, fashion designer, illustrator, medical illustrator, photographer, videographer, art teacher, urban designer, window designer, interior designer, graphic designer, and landscape designer.

Art and other academic subjects

There are many ways for teachers to integrate art into other subject areas. ELA teachers can have students write reports or research papers that compare and contrast two artists of a particular movement or the difference between two paintings with similar themes but using different elements. Small-group discussions and oral presentations can focus on a particular work of art or art movement. Math teachers can have students examine objects in a (projected) piece of art and work on direct measurements as well as proportions and ratios. Conversions can also be made from imperial (inches, feet, and so on) to metric units. Angles and geometric shapes in art works can be identified and used as a reference point for further study.

Social studies classes can explore the effects of a culture (or events in a culture, such as a revolution) on its artists, and vice versa. Further, an exploration into choices in elements and design between different cultures can shed light onto their differences and similarities. For example, how are Japanese screen paintings and African masks different? How are they similar? In science, classes can conduct experiments in light and shadow by using a moveable light source and a (digital) camera. Experiments can also be conducted by mixing various proportions of primary colors of (liquid) paint.

When using different materials in art, teachers must always be safety-conscious. Many substances can be harmful if they come in contact with skin or eyes, are inhaled, or are ingested. Young children have a tendency to be less conscious than adults of substances on their hands; further, the size and higher metabolic rates of children make them more susceptible than adults to hazardous substances.

Instead of spray or aerosol paints, use liquid or non-aerosol forms. Instead of commercial or powdered dyes, use plant-based dyes, such as cranberries or turmeric. Avoid powdered products in general, products with heavy metals such as lead, and solvent-based products such as permanent markers or rubber cement. Use water-based paints (such as tempera), markers, and glues.

Additionally, make the environment safe. Have proper ventilation, keep art materials away from the eating area, have children wear protective clothing, and clean up spills immediately with a wet cloth.

EXAMPLE

Fifth-grade students are making small turns as they rotate an object around slowly, drawing the basic lines of the object seen in each turning. Which artistic movement are they most likely studying?

(A) Impressionism

(B) Surrealism

(C) Renaissance

(D) Cubism

The correct answer is Choice (D). They are drawing the different, fragmented parts that will show multiple viewpoints of the object in their final drawing/picture. Choice (A) would more likely have students working on their brushstrokes and on depicting different aspects of light. Choice (B) would more likely have students drawing complete images that seem strange or absurd together. Choice (C) would more likely have students focusing on how to show depth and realism in their depictions of structures and the human form, such as how to draw a hand so that it looks 3-D.

EXAMPLE

Select all of the following that are important safety considerations during an art class:

(A) Make sure lunch or snack items are in a separate room or else properly stored away.

(B) Open windows and/or use fans whenever possible.

(C) Have children wear smocks and eye goggles.

(D) Have water and paper towels handy.

The correct answers are Choices (A), (B), (C), and (D). Safety should always be a paramount concern.

Analyzing art

One painting may thrill some viewers while offending others; one artist may receive funding while another does not. These responses and choices are part of a culture's *aesthetics,* how people characterize what is beautiful or in good taste, both emotionally and intellectually. Aesthetics can be individual, varying within a culture, as well as cultural, varying among cultures.

Teachers may begin a discussion involving aesthetics by displaying two works of art that vary, for example, in balance—one being balanced and the other not. Ask students how each work makes them feel. Then lead students in a discussion of each work's elements and design, and how the choices each artist made affect the viewer. Ask students to consider why the artists made those choices.

Finally, it's important for students to understand that while a work of art may be shared and enjoyed by many, it belongs to its creator. Having students create their own artwork will help them understand the importance of respecting and protecting others' creativity. Older students will learn the legal aspects of *copyright,* but elementary students can and should learn about copyright as a basic concept.

EXAMPLE

A third-grade teacher's students are working in groups, talking about which of two paintings they like better and how the colors in one painting make them feel really different than the colors in the other painting. Which set of colors are the students probably studying?

(A) complimentary colors

(B) analogous colors

(C) colors of two different values, one of which is a tint of the other

(D) colors of two different values, one of which is a shade of the other

The correct answer is Choice (A). Complimentary colors are opposite each other on the color wheel and so are likely to have opposite effects, such as the cool effect of blue and the warm effect of orange. Choice (B) involves three colors next to each other on the color wheel; thus, they do not create a different effect but a unified, similar, or calming effect. Choice (C) describes two closely related colors, one of which is the other with white added, such as green and light green; these colors create a similar effect. Choice (D) describes two closely related colors, one of which is the other with black added, such as green and dark green; these colors create a similar effect.

Marching to the Beat of Music

Students of music need to be aware of many things, from the elements and components that make up a work of music to various musical periods and their characteristics. Students need to know how music may help them in a career, how music may be connected to other subject areas, and how music may be approached analytically as well as ethically.

The elements of music

The characteristics of a musical work can be described by different elements of music. These basic aspects include pitch, rhythm, melody, timbre (tone color), dynamics, and texture.

Pitch refers to the highness or lowness of a note. The large double bass produces a note of a lower pitch than a violin does. The distance in pitch between two notes is an *interval.* When guitar players tune their instruments, they listen to the interval between the strings. Pitches and interval patterns can be organized into *scales,* or sequences of notes played in order, up or down. A scale in the key (note) of C, for example, begins with C and ends with C.

Scales are usually major or minor, depending on the combination of whole and half steps. On the piano, a *half step* is the distance from any key to the next closest key, black or white. Two half (H) steps make a *whole* (W) *step.* A *major scale* has a pattern of W-W-H-W-W-W-H. This pattern produces what in western culture is sometimes described as a *happy* or *light* effect. A *minor scale* has a pattern of W-H-W-W-H-W-W. Its effect is often described as *dark* or *heavy.* These scales are based on eight notes. The *pentatonic* scale is based on five notes and does not have half steps. It may be represented by the notes *do, re, mi, so, la.*

Rhythm is the time element, the combination of long and short notes that gives a piece of music its flow or movement. Rhythm has a *tempo,* or speed at which the notes are played, and a beat, or pulse. Rhythm patterns consist of a given number of beats within a *measure,* or unit of beats.

Common durations for notes, each time-length relative to the others, are whole notes, half notes, quarter notes, eighth notes, and sixteenth notes. A measure that has six (6) beats and uses eighth (8) notes is called 6/8 time, or 6/8 meter. A two-beat measure using quarter notes would be 2/4 time.

Meter is a regular pattern of beats. Beats can be weak or strong, as the *thump-THUMP* of a heart beating is weak and then strong. Most rhythms stress the strong beat. In *syncopation*, the weak beat is stressed. When a motif or rhythm is repeated in a musical work, it is called an *ostinato* (from the Italian for *stubborn*).

When music is written or notated, it is done so using a *staff*, or set of horizontal lines, and a bass (lower) or treble (higher) *clef*, the symbol that indicates the pitch. The bass clef and treble clef are written on separate staffs. The duration of a note is also shown on the staff. A whole note looks like this: ○. A half note is the round shape with a line going up from its right side. When the round shape is filled in, it's a quarter note, like this: ♩. An eighth note looks like this: ♪.

When single notes are combined into an organized unit, they produce a *melody*, the combination of pitch and rhythm that functions as the main focus of a piece of music, the basic tune. A short melody, or a short part of a long melody, is called a *motif*. When supporting notes are added to and sounded simultaneously with the melody, they form a counterpoint, or *harmony*. The lead voice or instrument usually plays the melody, while the accompanying voice(s) or instrument(s) play the harmony, the *accompaniment*.

Differences between voices or instruments can be described in terms of *timbre*, or tone color, the quality of the sound. The timbre of a sound may be bright or brassy, reedy or raspy, mellow or shrill. The main *voice* parts are, from highest to lowest, soprano, alto, tenor, and bass.

Instruments, while sometimes including voice, are often classified according to four main groups: brass, woodwind, string, and percussion. The *brass* group includes the trumpet, trombone, saxophone, French horn, and tuba. The *woodwinds* include the flute, clarinet, oboe, and bassoon. The *strings* include the violin, viola, cello, guitar, banjo, and harp. The *percussion* instruments include the drums, tambourine, chimes, marimba, and xylophone.

The *dynamics* of a musical work refer to its varying volume, how loud or soft it is in places. The dynamics are noted by the use of *pp* (*pianissimo* = very soft), *p* (*piano* = soft), *mp* (*mezzo piano* = medium soft), *mf* (*mezzo forte* = medium loud), *f* (*forte* = loud), and *ff* (*fortissimo* = very loud). When the dynamics get louder or increase, it is called a *crescendo*; when they get softer or decrease, it is called a *decrescendo*.

The *texture* of a musical work, or composition, refers to the combination of its melody, harmony, and rhythm; the overall effect of the layers of sound. A *monophonic* texture has one part, usually a single melody. *Polyphony* is the texture of music with more than one part being played at the same time.

EXAMPLE

A first-grade class is playing hide and seek, where an object is hidden and all the students except one know where the object is. The class sings a simple song that may be repeated over and over, such as "Row, Row, Row Your Boat." The one student then moves about the classroom. When the one moves near to the object, the others start singing louder, and when the one moves away from the object, the others sing softer. Select all of the following the teacher may be teaching.

(A) piano and forte

(B) soprano and alto

(C) crescendo and decrescendo

(D) quarter and eighth notes

The correct answers are Choice (A) and Choice (C). Choice (A) relates to softness and loudness. Choice (C) relates to an increase and decrease in volume, or loudness and softness. Choice (B) is wrong because it does not involve dynamics but rather the difference in pitch between two voices, the higher and lower of the female range. Choice (D) is wrong because it does not involve dynamics but rather different tempos a song may have.

EXAMPLE

Which of the following is a percussion instrument?

(A) pan pipes

(B) piano

(C) recorder

(D) double bass

The correct answer is Choice (B). Although a piano does have strings, its sound is produced by hammers striking the strings, so it is fundamentally percussive. Choice (A) is wrong because pan pipes are tubes strung together that produce sound when blown into, so they belong to the woodwinds. Choice (C) is wrong because the recorder is a flute-like instrument and a member of the woodwinds. Choice (D) is wrong because the double bass is a string instrument. It looks similar to a cello but is larger and has longer strings; its pitch is lower than a cello's.

Music history

As in the visual arts, music styles change over time and place. Table 8-2 identifies some of the major styles or periods, composers, and characteristics.

TABLE 8-2 **Music Throughout History**

Period/Movement	Composers/Instruments	Characteristics
Pre-historic (30,000 B.C.–1500 B.C.)	Drums, pipes	Simple melodies and rhythms
Ancient (1500 B.C.–A. D. 500)	Drums, pipes & lyre (Greece), bowed fiddle (India)	Melodies and rhythms more complex
Western: Middle Ages (500–1400)	Roman Catholic Church, Hildegard von Bingen, troubadours, voice more prominent than other instruments	Sacred music, Gregorian chant (monophonic), beginnings of polyphonic music
Western: Renaissance (1400–1600)	Antoine Brumel, John Dowland, Claudin de Sermisy	Increase in emotion in music but rhythm, timbre, and dynamics very calm
Western: Baroque (1600–1760)	Johann Sebastian Bach, Henry Purcell, Antonio Vivaldi	Continuity in rhythms and elaborate melodies
Western: Classical (1730–1820)	Ludwig von Beethoven, Franz Josef Haydn, Wolfgang Amadeus Mozart, Franz Schubert	Contrast in musical elements—more pauses, syncopation, mood changes, and changes in dynamics; melodies balanced
Western: Romantic (1780–1910)	Johannes Brahms, Frederick Chopin, Antonin Dvorak, Felix Mendelssohn, Peter Ilyich Tchaikovsky	Creation of many moods, high emotion; new harmonies and timbres, more swings in dynamics, pitch, and tempo
Western: Impressionist (1875–1925)	Claude Debussy, Maurice Ravel	Focus on mood and atmosphere; melodies not strict, may seem wandering
Western: Modern (1850–present)	Bela Bartok, Leonard Bernstein, Carlos Chavez, Aaron Copeland, George Gershwin, Igor Stravinsky, Arnold Schoenberg	Changes in timbre; increased use of percussion; different rhythms and scales that are more jarring; atonal (lacking a central tone) music

Careers in music

Many people feel they can't live without music, and for students it's important to know that their interest in music may lead to a profession or career. Musicians may play in a band or orchestra, or they may sing in a chorus or choir. They may be arrangers, film-score composers, jingle writers, or conductors. They may be booking agents, business managers, or music publishers. They may consider careers in sound engineering or music therapy. Or they may become music teachers.

Music and other academic subjects

There are many ways for teachers to integrate music into other subject areas. Science teachers can integrate pitch in lessons on sound waves. The slower the frequency of vibration and the bigger the object, the lower the pitch. For example, the pitch of a viola is lower than a violin's because the viola is a little larger and has longer strings.

Math teachers may lead students in a comparison and contrast of time *signatures* (notations), such as 3/4 time, with fractions. Here it is important to remember that the main similarity is a visual one, for 3/4 time—shown on the clef *without* the line or slash—is not a fraction but rather an abbreviation, an expression of the number (3) and type (quarter-note: 4) of beats in a measure. Having visual examples of different times and clapping them out with students helps them grasp the meaning of time signatures.

Both ELA and Social Studies teachers can have students research and report on different composers, instruments, or musical periods. As in the visual arts, different cultures have different ways of expressing themselves through music. Important events in a culture can affect the culture's music, and sometimes a culture's musicians can influence it. Persuasive essays can be assigned that ask students to present opinions on a particular piece of music and why they do or do not like it, using the work's elements as evidence.

Analyzing music

How does a work of music's texture contribute to the emotion it arouses in listeners? What elements make up a work of music's texture? Reflecting on and analyzing such questions helps students make informed aesthetic judgments about the music and how it functions in a given section of a given society. Such processes also help students create and evaluate their own music.

An awareness of musical property rights is extremely important in today's world, when electronic media allow for so much access and replication. While elementary students need not know specific legal terminology, they do need to know what is right and what is wrong when it comes to "borrowing." As in the visual arts, having students compose their own music, even if it's just the lyrics, helps them understand the importance of respecting and protecting others' creativity.

EXAMPLE

A fourth-grade teacher wants students to appreciate the role of a participating choir member who does not sing the melody. Which example would work best for the lesson?

(A) a player on a basketball team whose role is to pass the ball

(B) a player on a soccer team who scores the most goals

(C) a player on a baseball team who sits on the bench, waiting for a turn

(D) a player on a volleyball team who often assists the coach in helping students with their form

The correct answer is Choice (A). The player is not as noticeable as a shooter or scorer but is an integral part of the whole, as is a choir member who sings harmony, which is usually softer than melody. Choice (B) is wrong because the player is the most noticeable, in contrast to someone who does *not* sing melody. Choice (C) is not the best example because the player, while an important part of the team, is not in a situation that is parallel to the participating choir member, who is engaged with the other students (singing). Choice (D) is not the best example because the player, while an important part of the team, is not in a situation that is parallel to the participating choir member, who is engaged with the other students (singing).

Getting in Shape on Physical Education Principles

While it is important to know the terminology associated with physical activities, it is also important to know which activities are appropriate for different age or developmental levels. Learning to move with skill and gaining strength and flexibility should be fun as well as challenging for children, helping them gain a sense of their self-responsibility, the importance of group dynamics and social interactions, and how physical education may help them in career choices.

Movement concepts

Being able to move in different ways, or demonstrating *movement variations,* is an important part of physical development. Children need to learn how, where, and with what their bodies move. For children with physical disabilities, teachers may focus on motor skills to enable successful recreational participation.

Use of the following *movement concepts* are the first steps toward children attaining body management:

>> **Body awareness:** The *what* of the body; learning about body parts, such as eyes, ears, nose, fingers, toes; as they get a bit older, children learn about the shapes their bodies can take, such as curling into a ball or stretching their arms out like a tree.

>> **Space awareness:** Where the body moves; learning about *personal space,* the area where things can be touched without moving, and *general space,* the area beyond, which may be unlimited, as in a park, or limited, as in a room. The *low level* of space awareness is on or near the ground, *middle level* is where the child is when standing, and *high level* is when the child is on tiptoe. Directions such as forward, backward, left, and right are part of space awareness, as are moving through *pathways,* such as going straight, in a circle, or zigzagging.

>> **Effort concepts:** How the body moves; exploring the ways the body moves in terms of speed, force, and flow of movement. *Speed* may be simply slow or fast initially, then slower or faster; *force* is the amount of exertion, how much muscle effort or tension is involved, such as the difference between tiptoeing and foot-stomping; and flow may be free or interrupted, such as the difference between children pretending to be birds flying in the sky or birds on the ground, moving with a hop-hop-stop, hop-hop-stop.

>> **Relationship concepts:** Where body parts are in relation to objects and where a person or people are in relation to another person or persons. Some of the many relationship concepts include: near-far, above-below, over-under, in front-behind, together-apart, leading-following, and unison-opposites.

Following movement concepts, children can focus on *body management*. **Locomotor skills** involve traveling or moving. These basic travel patterns are listed in the order of increasing skill development and are either *even*, where the weight/movement change is equal in time, or *uneven*, where one of the changes is longer or shorter in time than the other(s):

>> **Walking:** Even

>> **Running:** Even

>> **Hopping:** Even

>> **Leaping:** Even

>> **Sliding:** Uneven—long (the step) and short (the landing)

>> **Galloping:** Uneven—long (the step) and short (the landing)

>> **Skipping:** Uneven—long (the step) and short (the hop)

>> **Jumping:** Even

Children's locomotor skills develop as they do. First-graders may roll forward smoothly, in a rounded form; they may jump a swinging rope held by others. Third-graders may perform a full forward roll (from standing to crouch, to a tucked chin and back of the head on the floor, to the push-off, rotation, and then pressing their feet back up to standing); they may jump two ropes, one swinging forward and one backward, held by others. Fifth-graders may jump for height and distance, using proper takeoff and landing forms; they may hop into, jump, and hop out of the space made by a long rope swung by others.

Stability skills, or *non-manipulative skills,* focus on maintaining and keeping balance. They include *static balance* (maintaining a position while performing a task, such as catching a ball), *dynamic balance* (maintaining balance while moving, such as dribbling a ball), bending, curling, stretching, transferring weight, turning, and twisting.

Manipulative skills involve the use of an implement of some kind and include throwing, catching, dribbling, kicking, punting, volleying, and striking. As children develop, they are able to perform increasingly complex skills. First-grade students may throw a ball underhand and overhand; they may catch a self-tossed ball. In third grade, students may work on the distance and accuracy of a thrown ball and catch a ball while they are in motion. In fifth grade, students may throw and catch a ball while avoiding an opponent; they may use a backhand movement to hit a ball (as in tennis); they may stop a kicked ball by trapping it with the foot while moving (as in soccer).

The final skill area is that of **rhythmic skills.** These skills involve music (from a simple drum beat to, with the older children, a syncopated jazz orchestra) and moving in some way to the music. Kindergarteners may begin these skills by clapping in time to a simple, rhythmic beat. In second grade, students may perform the simple rhythmic sequences related to a folk dance, individually or with a partner. By fourth grade, students may perform a series of square-dance steps. They may perform a routine that has even and uneven locomotor patterns, such as the polka, whose pattern is (hop)-step-close-step.

EXAMPLE

Mirroring is an example of which of the following?

(A) relationship concept

(B) effort concept

(C) space awareness

(D) body awareness

The correct answer is Choice (A). *Mirroring* is when parts are reversely arranged (as though in a mirror) in comparison or *relationship* to someone/something. Choice (B) involves the use of how the body itself moves in terms of time, force, or flow. Choice (C) involves knowing where the body itself moves in terms of personal or general space. Choice (D) involves knowing body parts and shapes the body itself may take.

EXAMPLE

Which of the following skills is appropriate for a kindergartener?

(A) kicking a rolled ball from a stationary position

(B) striking a ball with a bat from a tee or a cone

(C) bouncing a ball continuously, using two hands

(D) foot-dribbling a ball continuously while traveling

The correct answer is Choice (C). Choice (A) is first-grade appropriate. Choice (B) is second-grade appropriate. Choice (D) is third-grade appropriate.

Fitness and nutrition

From conditioning to flexibility, from body-awareness to nutrition, students need continuing physical education. Kindergarteners' physical activities should be fun as well as challenging; they may have three or four days each week where the activities increase their heart and breathing rates. They become aware of the different body parts involved when they stretch; they learn that the body is made of bones, organs, fat, and other tissues; and they learn that muscles help the body move.

In second grade, students' physical activities should continue to be fun and challenging, increasing in difficulty and duration. They may perform curl-ups, push-ups, and lunges, and learn how to properly stretch different muscles such as hamstrings and biceps. They may learn that the body needs more fuel during physical activities than during inactivity and that water consumption during activity is important for body temperature and blood volume.

Fourth-grade students may participate in warm-up and cool-down activities. They demonstrate correct body positions for pushing or pulling. They may hang by their hands from an overhead bar with their hips and knees each at a 90-degree angle. They may measure and record changes in aerobic capacity and muscular strength using the proper scientific and health-based assessments. They may explain the principles of physical fitness: F.I.T.T., or frequency, intensity, time, and type. They may understand that the body uses calories and burns fat for energy.

The United States Department of Agriculture (USDA), has an excellent source for teachers to use when focusing on a nutrition unit. The source is the Myplate website (www.choosemyplate.gov), where these four important actions are featured:

>> Focus on variety, amount, and nutrition.

>> Choose foods and beverages with less saturated fat, sodium, and added sugars.

>> Start with small changes to build healthier eating styles.

>> Support healthy eating for everyone.

EXAMPLE

When might a student be expected to describe muscular strength as important in moving heavy objects?

(A) kindergarten

(B) second grade

(C) fourth grade

(D) sixth grade

The correct answer is Choice (B). Choice (A) is wrong because, in kindergarten, students are just learning about muscles. Choice (C) is wrong because, in fourth grade, students have moved beyond the awareness that muscular strength is necessary to move a heavy object to demonstrating a correct body position for doing so. Choice (D) is wrong because, in sixth grade, students have moved beyond muscular- and body-position awareness to describing specific movements using a knowledge of basic anatomy and joint types.

Careers in physical education

Many career opportunities are available in physical education. A few students may become professional athletes. More may be coaches, umpires, referees, or teachers. Other related professions include sports broadcasting, sports management, and sports medicine, as well as nutrition and physical and occupational therapy.

Physical education and other academic subjects

There are also many possibilities when integrating physical education with other subject matter. Math teachers may have students measure different distances, such as for long and high jump, in feet and inches, and then convert the measurements to metrics. Arcs of flexibility may also be measured.

Science teachers may relate the use of simple machines, such as a lever or pulley, and the difference in physical strength or effort when using a simple machine versus not using one. The chemical reactions involved when glucose is used may be integrated with lessons in using physical energy. The scientific method may be studied and applied when students observe and record changes in their muscular strength.

Social studies teachers may have students research and report on the importance of sports in various cultures, from the original Greek Olympic athletes to modern-day professional sports millionaires. ELA teachers may have students write poems or narratives about their own sports' experiences or interview local sports personalities for a research paper using primary sources.

EXAMPLE

Students are working in groups to compare the results of a specific physical activity when they eat different amounts of the same food. The students are most likely working in which class?

(A) English

(B) math

(C) science

(D) social studies

The correct answer is Choice (C). The students are most likely studying dependent (that which doesn't change; here, the activity) and independent (that which does change; here, the amount of food) variables. Choice (A) would be possible if the students were comparing results in order to write a paper, but, given the situation described, they'd more likely be writing up the results of the experiment for a science class, so Choice (C) is better than Choice (A). Choice (B) would be possible if the students were comparing results in order to convert the numbers to a different system or to consider the accuracy of the measurements, but neither situation accounts for the dependent and independent variables, so Choice (C) is better than Choice (B). Choice (D) is wrong as the scenario, while itself part of a culture, does not revolve around a cultural or historical topic.

Psychological and social aspects of physical education

Physical activity provides children with opportunities to experience pleasure, self-expression, and social interaction. They learn to identify their physical and emotional feelings and to participate willingly with others.

In kindergarten, children begin to identify the feelings resulting from physical activity, such as happy, excited, frustrated, or tired. They learn how to share and take turns in physical activities. They experience being both a leader and a follower.

In second grade, students learn how to engage in group activities without interfering with others and how to acknowledge their own behavior. They acknowledge their opponent or partner before and after an activity and provide positive feedback and encouragement. They engage in more diverse types of group activities, including those that rely on cooperation, such as passing the ball in basketball so that another may make a score for the team.

By fourth grade, students set self-improvement goals in health-related fitness and keep records of their progress. They include and invite others in physical activities and learn to respect differences in skill level and motivation. They do not blame others for their own performance and respond to winning and losing with dignity and respect.

EXAMPLE

Which of the following would come first in the development of a student's social responsibility?

(A) an understanding of what a teammate (another) is feeling

(B) an understanding of what he or she (the student) is feeling

(C) an understanding of how a problem on the playground may be solved

(D) an understanding of how to set a personal goal on the playground

The correct answer is Choice (B). Identifying one's feelings, which begins in kindergarten, is the first step toward self-responsibility, which later leads to an understanding of group responsibility. Choice (A) is part of learning to respect differences, which is third- or fourth-grade appropriate. Choice (C) is an ability that is fifth-grade appropriate. Choice (D) does involve self-responsibility but is late-third or fourth-grade appropriate.

3

The Principles of Curriculum, Instruction, and Assessment

Chapter 9

A General Overview of Curriculum, Instruction, and Assessment

Any experienced teacher would say that curriculum, instruction, and assessment are not three separate entities. Rather, they all work together to achieve one aim—that of educating the child. Therefore, any consideration of education cannot consider curriculum, instruction, and assessment separately. Each of those components must always be considered together when planning for any one of them. For instructional purposes, though, we begin with a basic definition of what each word means in regard to education.

>> **Curriculum** is the course of study of a subject.

>> **Instruction** is detailed information telling how that subject should be taught.

>> **Assessment** is the evaluation of how well the instruction enabled the students to learn the curriculum.

It is even difficult to give proper definitions without having the three different terms crop up in the other's definitions. This proves the point that they can't really be considered as three different components, as each influences the other two in remarkable ways. Think of these three components as steps on the three-legged stool of education. Without any one, the stool is destined to fall with the slightest push and cannot support any weight placed upon it. The same is true in a literal sense, as well as with that figurative example.

Also, it is difficult to decide where a teacher should begin teaching, as each are so integral to the aims of education. Rather, it may be best to consider the movement from one to another, as shown in Figure 9-1.

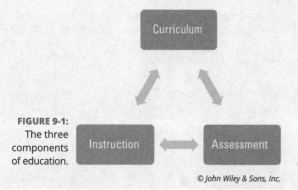

FIGURE 9-1:
The three components of education.

Forming a Curriculum

With the thought in mind that all components of education influence each other, it is necessary to start the whole process at some point. Curriculum is the best way to begin any conversation about teaching, because the specific content often dictates the types of instruction needed and the types of assessment given. Consider, for example, the subject area of mathematics. Any instruction of mathematics has to include different sets of manipulatives so that students can see and understand the concepts being taught. In science, students have to be interactive, influencing and directing changes to understand the changes in nature that are part of each scientific topic. Language arts does not include a large number of manipulates or much interactivity; instead it relies heavily on communication through speaking, reading, and writing. Knowing what a teacher is expected to teach influences the type of instruction primarily given.

Likewise, the type of curriculum often dictates the type of assessment given to any student. Math content on general assessments very rarely includes only multiple choice. Most math assessments allow, or require, students the time and space to work out the problem, showing their thinking. In science and social studies, multiple choice is often the primary method of assessment on standardized tests so that content knowledge can be shown, which must be memorized based on earlier practice in the classroom. Language arts is also frequently assessed through writing tasks, as well as multiple-choice questions.

So, knowing what is to be taught (curriculum) influences the other two components, instruction and assessment. However, each component does have an art and a mastery that can only be achieved when teachers fully understand the finer delicacies of each component separately. Only then can each be seen to fully influence the others. So, can there be an art to teaching curriculum? Of course, and each teacher must consider his or her own small, but vitally important place in the grand scheme of any child's education. Without considering any extraneous circumstances such as special needs or life circumstances, consider what must occur for a child to enter preschool without knowing any letters and exit school after grade 12 knowing how to analyze multiple interpretations of a story, drama, or poem and being able to follow multistep procedures when carrying out an experiment. In order for this to occur, there must be an overall guiding plan so that each child learns what she needs to in a timely manner that takes into account maturity and ability and that allows for a progression of developmental growth and knowledge over the course of this time.

Getting familiar with curriculum guidelines

What each teacher does builds the knowledge and ability base of each child. This gradual building up must be done in ways that are carefully planned. Over decades of discussion and experimentation, guidelines are put in place for teachers so that much of the guesswork is taken out of what to teach and when to teach it. There are several guidelines that must be considered with any talk of curriculum planning. These guidelines are common terminology for educators and those invested in educational programs. These terms, though, are not necessarily used in each school, district, or state. While each school, district, or state does have its own specific curriculum planning guides, an understanding of what each term is and how it relates to the others gives new teachers a broad glimpse of how curriculum is organized for instruction and assessment purposes. These terms include the following:

>> **Curriculum:** All the experiences that occur in an educational process in regard to specific knowledge attained. At the broadest definition, curriculum is the lessons and content taught in a classroom. This includes all content knowledge, intellectual skills, and essential understandings that a student is expected to know or be able to do.

>> **Curriculum guide:** A way of determining what to teach and how to teach it. This is the broadest use of the idea of curriculum and planning. It can reference a teacher's individual plan, a district's overall instructional plan, or even a state or nation's curriculum plans for all students considered. Generally, guides are specific to subjects and take into account instructional methods for the delivery of content.

>> **Curriculum framework:** An organized plan that defines the content to be learned in terms of standards for what a student should know and be able to do.

>> **Academic standards:** Benchmarks of quality in regard to curriculum delivery and assessment of curriculum knowledge. These are also known as ***content standards*** when referencing specific knowledge components.

>> **Core content:** Content that has been identified as essential for all students to know. The core content is not meant to be a curriculum standard nor is it meant to reflect state assessment expectations. Rather, it is the set of knowledge that experts, through research, have determined to be the basic and most important units of knowledge for that subject area in that time frame.

>> **Core content guidelines:** A set of content guidelines. These guidelines show a progression of core content knowledge that can be used for yearly as well as long-term planning in regard to progressions through the entire academic career of a student.

>> **Pacing guide:** A timeline that shows what teachers are expected to teach over the course of a year or over the course of study. Many school districts provide these logically sequenced timelines so that teachers do not repeat areas of instruction, ensuring that all core content is taught over the course of a time frame.

>> **Curriculum maps:** Tools that help educators keep track of standards that are expected to be taught over the course of a time frame. These maps help schools and districts to identify redundancies or gaps in content. Generally, once a curriculum map has been developed by a school or district, plans are made for pacing guides to address those gaps or redundancies.

Realizing the limits of curriculum planning

While many new to education may consider that most of the work of curriculum planning is already done for them in the way of content knowledge planning, that is not the case. All these guidelines and pacing guides are maps to instruction and assessment. Very few of them actually include methods of instruction and assessment. None of them can provide the daily mastery of content that teachers are expected to pass on to their students. Knowing how each part of the content builds on another is the human part of the process that can never be eliminated, no matter the content.

Also, while guidelines and pacing guides are set, very few teachers are given daily sets of lesson plans or are placed in programs that are scripted, as far as curriculum is concerned. Even for those teachers, redirection and reteaching must occur as not every student will master the curriculum during his first experience with any new content. So, while it seems as if the work of curriculum planning is done for the teacher, that actually is not the case. Each teacher must understand how the specific core content fits into the grander scheme of instruction. It is not enough to be masters of a small part of curriculum; rather, teachers must understand the entire process of the timelines and guides so that all content that students are expected to know can be addressed. Teachers must understand the totality of the sequence of instruction.

Mastering content knowledge

Teachers must also become content knowledge masters because of learning differentiation required by *Response to Intervention* (RTI) rules and regulations. In order for instruction to be modified, teachers must know enough of the breadth and depth of the content so that the instruction can be given while keeping core content knowledge intact.

Furthermore, some curricula are designed to specifically address the needs or interests of a community. For example, Indiana has a set of curricula that addresses Indiana state history. This curriculum is addressed within a grade in late elementary school, but teachers of those grades must become experts in a specific content area that other teachers are not accountable for. Knowing the curriculum involves more than just knowledge, though. Curriculum must also address materials and resources available, as well as modern technological developments that may change curriculum or curricular needs.

Answering curriculum questions

General information about curriculum, instruction, and assessment comprises approximately 15 percent of the test. These questions measure a basic understanding of curriculum planning and concern general issues rather than specific content knowledge. On the test, curriculum questions examine the organization, materials, and resources of a content area, without specifically addressing content knowledge in regard to English/language arts, mathematics, history/social studies, science, or technical content such as art, music, or physical education. Questions include

>> The components of curriculum and how curriculum is organized.

>> How that organization of content area addresses concepts within and across content areas. An example would be the implications of literacy in regard to understanding specific social studies or science text.

>> The types of materials, media, and resources required to teach a specific curricula, for example, the use of manipulatives in math or the purpose of the scientific method for science.

These questions also focus on state and national standards, curriculum planning, and sequencing in regard to objectives and standards.

EXAMPLE

In the process of determining the rationale of a lesson, the teacher should ask all of the following, except:

(A) Will this lesson fit the curriculum guide as given by my administrator earlier in the year and as mandated by my district and state?

(B) Will this lesson ensure mastery of the content as measured by end-of-year state standardized assessment?

(C) Does this lesson fit with parental and community approval?

(D) Have my students been adequately prepared to meet the curriculum based on their mastery of similar lessons earlier in the curriculum planning process?

The correct answer is Choice (C). Lessons should always be focused on the curriculum as provided by administrators, districts, or states, Choice (A). Lessons focused on curriculum should also ensure that students have achieved mastery of prior skills needed in order to meet curriculum and content guidelines, Choice (D). Curriculum lessons should always be planned with the mastery of content as a primary focus, with the end aim being state standardized tests, Choice (B), which are designed to measure academic expectations and standards. Parental and community approval is assumed because curriculum maps and guides are generally approved by school boards in a public forum, if not mandated as a condition of hiring a teacher.

Understanding the components of a curriculum

Because so much of the curricular work is already arranged for many teachers, it is helpful to understand where and how the curriculum framework, mapping, and guides have been organized, historically. Currently, there is no national curriculum in the United States. Rather, the United States does have a Department of Education (DOE), which does not specifically mandate that certain curricula should be taught but gives curriculum and content standards. Instead, specific states have the power to enact legislation that specifies what curricula is taught within the schools.

To create those standards, states rely upon many different resources. Certainly, teachers, administrators, parents, and community members are part of that work. These states also rely upon researchers in the field, authors, and official organizations that provide the most up-to-date curricular knowledge, such as the National Council of the Teachers of English, for example. Once a set of standards is decided upon, states enact legislation making each set of standards either guiding curricular principles or state laws that use standardized testing for assessment. These standards, though, are not static mandates. Rather, continuing work is done by teachers and others to ensure that the standards have no gaps, show no redundancies, and model the most current and up-to-date knowledge in each content area. This is why it is in the best interest of every teacher to determine where his curricular guidelines come from. While states do often provide the standards as guideposts for content and skills, they are not the curriculum. Curriculum is often determined at the district level in larger school systems. However, neither standards nor curriculum tell teachers how to teach in order to ensure all the information gets through to every student. These standards and curricula enable each teacher to monitor his or her own work and to decide what other content and skills should be included in order to meet academic expectations and standards so that every student can be successful.

Who is not involved in developing standards and guidelines for curriculum planning?

EXAMPLE

(A) educators

(B) students

(C) the community

(D) curriculum specialists

Choice (B) is the correct answer. While educators and curriculum specialists are most certainly involved in core content and curriculum instruction, students do not have the knowledge or expertise to make any decisions about included curriculum. Also, community members can influence curriculum, especially those who are politically involved with state-mandated committees that discuss curriculum maps, guides, and standards.

A curriculum, though, is more than just content of any given subject. Curriculum involves all the material a teacher uses to impart that content knowledge. Curriculum, then, refers to the following:

>> Objectives for learning

>> Instructional content to be learned, which is a set of knowledge comprising facts, concepts, generalizations, principles, and theories

>> Experiences that take place during content attainment

>> Materials, such as manipulatives, games, flashcards, and so on

>> Resources, such as computer programs, books, libraries, and so on

Additional subject matter in the explicit curriculum

For subject matter and content to be included within a course of study, a plan of action should be taken by the classroom teacher. This plan of action involves a set of key steps that should be taken, regardless of whether the material is for in-class use or for proposals for inclusion outside one classroom. The set of action plans include, in this particular order:

1. Focus on one small part of the content.

This content should focus on only a grade level, a subject area, or a course of study. Furthermore, this content should address a gap within current guidelines or curriculum standards.

2. Collect and gather information to address the curriculum gap.

This information gathering can be composed using community resources, class resources, school resources, or other resources that can help determine whether or not the content inclusion is needed.

3. Organize the information.

Once the collection and gathering of information has occurred, the information needs to be sorted and coded for use if the proposal for inclusion is larger than one classroom.

4. Analyze the information.

Ensure that the content inclusion meets a need, whether that need addresses a gap, eliminates a redundancy, or addresses up-to-date knowledge or technology that is not yet within curriculum guides. In selecting other or additional subject matter for curriculum inclusion, all teachers should take certain criteria, and certain questions, into consideration. This process helps the teacher to both organize and analyze the information for further reporting. Consider these aspects:

- **Significance:** Does the subject matter contribute to basic ideas about the content, and does it develop learning skills?

- **Validity:** Is the content meaningful to the learner, and does it respect maturity level, prior experiences, educational backgrounds, and commonly accepted social values?

- **Utility:** Is the content useful to the learner, either in the present or in the future?

- **Learnability:** Is it possible for the student to learn the material, based on maturity level and educational background of the individual?

- **Feasibility:** Is it possible to be taught with the resources and materials readily available?

5. Report the information, if usage is beyond one classroom.

Reports should be evaluative in nature and should address the needs for curricular inclusion within a given set of standards, guides, or academic expectations.

If curriculum inclusion meets the preceding criteria, then a set of principles should be adopted for the inclusion of the material in teacher lessons. First, the content should be *balanced* and should provide balance to other content. In other words, the content should have both breadth (meaning it pertains to more than one particular lesson) and depth (meaning it can scaffold prior learning). Second, the content should be *sequenced.* This means that the content should have a logical arrangement and should address other learning, both horizontally (meaning that it connects to curriculum already in existence) and vertically (meaning that it connects to curriculum in other grades within the same subject). Lastly, curriculum inclusion should have the principle of *articulation,* meaning that it can be addressed by the subject matter expert, or teacher, to a group of learners who are ready for such knowledge, the students.

This curriculum inclusion process, though, focuses on only one type of curriculum: *explicit* curriculum, curriculum that is formal, stated, and mandated and has stated and expected outcomes. Explicit curriculum contains explicit steps and procedures to follow for proper instruction and assumed assessment expectation. Explicit instruction includes

>> Exact content to be taught, as either knowledge or skills

>> Precise steps for implementation

>> Grade-level mandated texts or programs, such as basal readers, remediation materials, or curriculum resources from textbooks, and so on.

>> Supplemental tasks and activities, if needed

>> Sequencing for material presentation, including a timeline for the specific content to be taught

>> Evaluation and assessment procedures and expectations

Explicit curriculum is the curriculum that is documented and appears in teacher lesson plans.

The role of implicit curriculum

Two other types of curriculum occur in addition to explicit curriculum (see the preceding section). One of these is *implicit curriculum,* often called *hidden* curriculum. This type of curriculum involves all the assumptions that a teacher brings into the learning environment and unconsciously projects into that environment. Every teacher brings into the classroom unique experiences, perspectives, and backgrounds that influence the content. Of course, the same is true for students, as each brings his own unique understanding of the content delivered. For example, the issue of teacher control and student subservience is one that teachers unwittingly or knowingly project when they set up classroom rules and standards of behavior with consequences.

Other examples of implicit curriculum are communication style, the teacher being the knowledge authority, and the value, or marginalization, of particular topics by time spent on topics or topic discussion in the classroom. Often, students know much more about the implicit curriculum than teachers who may unconsciously project opinions and biases into discussions.

Teachers often must make on-the-spot decisions as students bring unique questions to classroom discussions. These spontaneous discussions likely reflect common understandings or misunderstandings from the immediate environment, which directly influence the topic discussed. For example, say teachers are delivering content about immigration. Most adults have very specific views about this topic, and those opinions are often imparted to offspring who repeat messages from home. Teachers then have to make implicit curriculum decisions, decisions that still teach content but also reflect a larger world understanding that reflects diversity acceptance. Often, because teachers know their specific class audiences more fully than outside curricular influences, such as political mandates, implicit curriculum can provide a more realistic context for screening and monitoring students' progress in diagnostic assessments.

Teachers, though, must guard against hidden agendas with topic introductions, especially topics that are potentially controversial. Teachers must always assume the role of an expert, especially when delivering curricular content that is open to interpretation and is not based on accepted scientific fact, for example. Social and emotional needs must always be considered, although those needs must not negate curriculum that is beneficial or mandated. In this way, implicit curriculum often results in hidden practices and procedures that differ from decisions made when attempting to implement explicit curriculum. This often results in unintended outcomes. Hidden curricular choices could have results on state standardized testing outcomes or benchmarks of learning, especially if those benchmarks do not monitor yearly progress, but progress gained in smaller increments, such as every grading period or every semester.

All this, however, does not mean that implicit curriculum is harmful, or potentially harmful, to students. Most common classroom procedures are also forms of hidden curriculum, such as the proximity of the teacher to the students, the tone of voice used during instruction, and student seating choices and grouping choices. Teachers make hundreds of small decisions each day in the best interests of students and class maintenance that affect how well explicit curriculum is learned. This is especially true when teachers are confronted with students who have learning disabilities, as standard curriculum delivery will not result in expected outcomes of the general population. In these cases, implicit curriculum can override explicit curriculum as choices are made about which parts of the curriculum are the most important to learn, or are core for understanding a topic.

Null or absent curriculum

Another type of curriculum is *null* curriculum, also called *absent* curriculum. This is curriculum that exists, but simply isn't taught. An example of this is evolution. While this is an accepted scientific process, many school districts, because of community belief or political affiliation, do not include it in the classroom setting. Another example is the decision of how to teach the topic of Christopher Columbus. Was he truly the explorer who discovered America, or was he, instead, complicit in the destruction of those civilizations he encountered? To teach one makes the other null. In other words, to teach only one aspect of a controversial issue makes the other side, or viewpoint, null. Many null curricular choices are influenced by religious motivations or political affiliations that affect the adoption of standards in district and state guides. Null curriculum, whether intentional or unintentional, can exclude specific aspects of explicit curriculum if these aspects are deemed controversial. For example, specific community or national events may prohibit certain explicit curriculum from being taught fully at a certain time in the year due to considerations of emotional effect on the students. Other examples of null curriculum that are commonly used in daily classrooms include

>> Interventions that are evidence-based on specific student needs

>> Cultural examples that are excluded or included based on specific community or cultural decisions

>> Use of grouping to teach core content, as opposed to direct instructional methods

>> Deviations from lessons of explicit curriculum in order to take advantage of a teachable moment, based on community or national interest

>> Interventions that take place outside the classroom of the highly qualified teacher

>> Supplemental materials that may address explicit curriculum, but also address other topics

Culturally-responsive curriculum

Another consideration is *culturally-responsive curriculum.* This is curriculum that is contextually relevant to all students, whether those students are represented in a classroom or not. This content also specifically addresses the needs and interests of linguistically diverse learners who *are* represented in classrooms. Culturally-responsive curriculum introduces students to culturally relevant content from around the world. Unfortunately, much curriculum, especially curriculum that has been designed by small districts with little diversity, does not deliberately include issues that are culturally relevant to an entire population. America's diversity is no longer represented solely by white and black interests, but also includes interests and needs from students around the world. A lesson in February for the established Black History Month is not the only inclusion in curriculum that should occur during a school year, for any school subject. A review of curriculum focusing on this aspect will surely lead teachers to find large gaps in the way of lessons that will meet the needs and interest of these learners. Consider, also, how a typically white classroom would be ignorant of customs they will encounter in a larger, culturally diverse workforce that does expect cultural norms and attitudes to be reflective of inclusion, rather than exclusion, of global ideas and customs.

EXAMPLE

A fourth-grade social studies teacher feels as if the district curriculum map does not meet the needs of certain diverse learners in the school, particularly as this diverse learner population has rapidly grown only recently. Current curriculum does not address the cultural views or values of this population. To include culturally relevant topics to the current curriculum of the fourth grade, this teacher will need to consider all of the following aspects except

(A) whether the new content is significant to the population as a whole and whether the new content will develop learning skills and academic standards and expectations.

(B) whether the new content is learnable to the age range and maturity level of the fourth-grade students.

(C) whether the content is useful to the population as a whole and will build on present and future educational needs.

(D) whether the principal sees the value of adding such curriculum to the content as the content focuses on diversity in the school.

The answer is Choice (D). All other answers focus on the needs of the learners in including the new content. Content does not need to meet the values and opinions of building administrators.

Furthermore, curriculum must take into account changes that have not yet occurred in content knowledge. A primary example is the demoted planet of Pluto. While academic standards continued to announce the planet's "planethood," Pluto was demoted, according to scientists, many months before the change was seen in the wording of the academic language. While this may seem like a small example, teachers must never forget that the purpose of curriculum is to take into account changes that are occurring in the world. Curriculum must address the rapid increase of knowledge constantly occurring in scientific, political, legal, and technological fields, as well as achievements in culture, arts, music, and physical education events. Knowledge attainment has been accelerated by the Internet, and curriculum must keep pace with any changes that occur that may redirect curriculum or make it moot.

REMEMBER

As well as instructional content, curriculum must also address interventions, management, and monitoring of specific learning styles and learning needs. Therefore, curriculum must be layered, or leveled, so that instruction is able to be given to all learners, regardless of needs or abilities. This *multi-tiered instruction* can provide both duration and intensity during instructional needs. In this way, curriculum implementation also has *curriculum differentiation,* modification or adaptations that meet a variety of learners' needs to provide access to content.

Grasping the Principles of Instruction

Instruction is the heart of teaching. It is the educational process whereby students learn knowledge, skills, values, beliefs, and habits that enable them to become fully-functioning members of society. Instruction involves many different modes and surpasses simply telling or showing students core content, or curriculum. Rather, instruction involves every classroom experience that causes students to grow and learn, including storytelling; reading books; talking with teachers and students, either formally or informally; science experiments; research; computer training; and so forth. The list goes on and on. Basically, any activity that causes a student to grow and mature, to learn and think, or to feel and act can be instructive.

Instruction also involves more than just what is said or read in a classroom. Classmates, teachers, and even the lunchroom can all involve instruction of some type or another. In classrooms, teachers carefully prepare rooms at the beginning of each year to be as instructive as possible, hanging posters, arranging desks, and labeling crates and folders. This is all for one purpose—improving instruction. In addition, classroom practices, such as morning meetings or weekly spelling quizzes, can also be considered part of instruction. While this may all seem to be a random melting pot, great teachers know that each part of each day involves a carefully planned process designed to bring students further along in their knowledge, so that they can understand the curriculum in more depth and be prepared for assessments and further learning. While there also has to be a balance of the three—curriculum, instruction, and assessment—instruction is always what drives the students' and teachers' day and provides purpose to the learning environment.

The elements of instruction

The most important part of a teacher's job is the instructional planning that must take place when making decisions about what is best for the students. While knowing what to teach is important, knowing the teaching method to use is vital as knowledge gathering is going to take place.

Instruction doesn't begin with the teacher, though. Instruction really begins with the students and their willingness and ability to learn. As for instruction, there are some key names and instructional methods and theories that every teacher has to know in order to determine how willing and able students are. Consider the following "fathers of teaching," discussed alphabetically rather than by time period of research:

>> **Benjamin Bloom:** An American educational psychologist who developed a classification of education goals, called *Bloom's Taxonomy.*

>> **Erik Erikson:** An American developmental psychologist who developed theories of personality and development. Erikson's *Theory of Development* states that every human passes through

several different stages in life and that conflicts at any one stage of development may hinder growth and maturity. If teachers know and understand each stage, then instruction can model what a child needs at a particular moment of growth.

>> **Lawrence Kohlberg:** An American psychologist best known for the ***Theory of Stages of Moral Development.*** Kohlberg's Theory of Stages of Moral Development is a continuation of Jean Piaget's work and states that there are also stages for ethical behavior, as well as the development stages that Piaget proposed. The development of moral reasoning is the product of successfully transitioning through all the stages.

>> **Abraham Maslow:** An American psychologist best known for his theory of psychological development according to ***Maslow's Hierarchy of Needs.***

>> **Jean Piaget:** A Swiss biologist who studied the development of how children learned new tasks. Piaget's developmental theory says that children will not learn until they are socially ready to learn in a way that matches their physical maturation state. In other words, kids cannot learn certain tasks until they are old enough and mature enough to do so. His stages of cognitive development became known as ***cognitive constructivism.***

>> **B.F. Skinner:** An American psychologist and behaviorist who studied how reinforcement of certain behaviors leads to consequences. Skinner believed that, in order for a student to learn, that student had to engage in learning. His theories, called ***operant conditioning,*** focus on the influence of using positive reinforcement in classrooms so that students become more engaged in the learning process. Skinner also proposed that behavior in the classroom can be changed when influenced by positive reinforcers rather than punitive punishment.

>> **Edward Thorndike:** An American psychologist who proposed the ***Theory of Connectionism.*** This theory proposes that a connection exists between a stimulus and response to every situation. These consequences can be predicted and manipulated to advance learning situations.

>> **Lev Vygotsky:** A Soviet psychologist who proposed the idea of the ***Zone of Proximal Development,*** which refers to the way new knowledge is acquired. This Zone, or ZPD, states that children gradually learn to do certain tasks without help. This theory is most often used in reading and language arts instruction, as children are guided into appropriate zones so that reading progression can occur.

EXAMPLE

What level of questions, according to Bloom's Taxonomy, is shown in the following: What are the advantages and disadvantages of recycling? How can schools create more opportunities and advantages to recycling without allowing any disadvantages of the consequences?

(A) evaluation

(B) knowledge

(C) analysis

(D) comprehension

The answer is Choice (C), analysis. While the question requires both knowledge and comprehension, there is a deeper level of thinking as the questions direct students to show two sides of an issue. However, this question does not show evaluation because the students are not asked to make a judgement about recycling or about their school's use of recycling. They are simply asked to list advantages and disadvantages and describe ways a school could implement these steps.

EXAMPLE

According to Maslow's Hierarchy of Needs, where is the student located on the triangle in the following situation: Janey missed school the entire first week of October because her family home burned. Janey's mother was gravely injured in the fire, and Janey has suffered some physical trauma as well. Janey has been placed in a foster home until her mother's condition improves or until another family member can be found. Janey is starting to lag behind in her homework and often doesn't pay attention to directions.

(A) Need for love and belonging

(B) Esteem needs

(C) Physiological needs

(D) Safety needs

The answer is Choice (D), safety needs. Janey has all her physiological needs being met as she has a house to live in (the foster home) and food and water (provided by social services, the school, and/or the foster home). However, due to her own injuries (physical safety and health) as well as the traumatic injuries to her mother (well-being), Janey is located only on the second tier of Maslow's Hierarchy. She cannot attend to esteem needs or needs for love and belonging until her safety needs have been met.

EXAMPLE

What does the Zone of Proximal Development, or ZPD, suggest about a student's reading ability?

(A) This equates to the percentile rank of a student and suggests a national placement among scores of other students in the same grade.

(B) This level suggests that students are within a percentage of a norm group who obtained the lowest scores.

(C) This suggests what grade in school the student should be placed in as students cannot learn at levels higher than their zone of learning, or ZPD.

(D) This suggests a readability range from which a student should be reading and should be instructed in order to achieve optimal growth without frustration.

The answer is Choice (D). The Zone of Proximal Development is generally given after students are assessed for reading level. The ZPD corresponds to the instructional reading level, or the level at which a student can independently read a text with some type of support or *scaffolding*. Any reading occurring at levels higher than this number will likely frustrate students. Reading at lower levels will also frustrate students as it presents no challenge or area for learning growth. ZPDs do not equate to percentile rankings or norms. ZPDs should also not be used for grade placement as the assessment often measures only silent reading comprehension and does not indicate whether or not students can learn orally or through listening to teacher instruction. ZPDs are also specific to the skill of reading comprehension, not a broad concept like grade placement.

How students learn

Now that you have determined whether students are willing and able to learn, some attention must be paid to *how* students learn. Not every student learns the same material in the same way or at the same pace as another, even in regard to gender, socio-economic considerations, or geographical placement. Each child is an individual, and those individual brains process information very differently. Being aware of an individual's, and a classroom's, learning style can influence instruction to a great degree. These learning styles are often referred to as learning intelligences, as each represents a preferred mode of learning new information. *Howard Gardner* (another important guy to know) has identified seven different learning intelligences that should be considered when planning instruction. Consider these learning styles:

>> **Visual-Spatial (Picture or Art Smart):** These learners think in terms of physical space and are very aware of their environment. They like to draw, do puzzles, and daydream. They enjoy working with tools and models in the classroom and often excel at technological connections of the content.

» **Bodily-Kinesthetic (Body Smart):** These learners use their bodies effectively and have a keen sense of body awareness. They like to move, make things, and touch, and they communicate well through physical activity. They enjoy working with models in the classroom and enjoy frequent movement throughout the day, especially in regard to learning.

» **Musical (Music Smart):** These students are sensitive to rhythm and sound. They learn best with musical applications or when music is played while they are working. They enjoy working with multimedia equipment that involves sounds.

» **Interpersonal (People Smart):** These students like to interact with others and learn best through interaction, especially in situations resembling social connections. These students are often popular, with many friends, and get along well with others regardless of class placement or group. These students enjoy learning through group activities, dialogue, and writing when shared with others.

» **Intrapersonal (Self Smart):** These students work best alone and tend to shy away from other people. They understand their own motivations, strengths, and weaknesses, often better than their teachers, and have a strong will and strong opinions. They learn best through independent study and reflection, as in journaling. They often enjoy books and reading, journaling, and other creative activities. They are extremely independent.

» **Linguistic (Word Smart):** These learners love to work with words and can use them very effectively, for a variety of purposes. They are also good listeners. They like to read, play word games, and write stories. Favorite classroom activities include reading books, being part of class discussions and classroom lectures by an expert, and working with the computer, especially when conducting research.

» **Logical-Mathematical (Math Smart):** These students are best at reasoning and calculating, especially when dealing with abstract ideas, patterns, and connections. These students like to experiment and solve puzzles and learn best when presented with problems and concepts.

» **Naturalistic (Nature Smart):** This intelligence was added later than the previous ones. Naturalistic learners are very attuned to their natural environment. They enjoy being outside and feel connected to natural processes and classifications. These students enjoy lessons or free time that employs outside time, such as recess or playground time. They also enjoy working with classroom pets, recycling projects, and observing their natural surroundings.

The different types of learners

Unfortunately, no classroom is composed of only one type of learner or one intelligence. Rather, each classroom has a multiplicity of the intelligence types, probably all of them. Also, students often change their intelligence type as they mature and are exposed to different ideas and concepts in content. However, understanding classroom make-up can, and should, influence instructional planning. No one short lesson can include all the intelligences, but any unit of instruction should include opportunities for all the intelligences.

Consider how those intelligences could influence a lesson on the elements of poetry.

» **Visual-Spatial learners** could be assigned to draw and create posters explaining how each element of poetry works. Research on the computer may lead to changes in classroom environment, especially during group discussions.

» **Bodily-kinesthetic learners** could be tasked with performance poetry presentations. For example, they could present the concept of rhyming while dribbling a basketball and reading poems about sports and basketball.

>> **Musical learners** could be assigned research into poetry that has heavy musical influences, especially focusing on song lyrics.

>> **Interpersonal learners** could be asked to work with a group of students and present to the classroom specific elements of poetry found in class books. These students could read a poem aloud each day for class discussion and could be asked to present new poems discovered by others in their group.

>> **Intrapersonal learners** could be assigned the task of an independent project on one element of poetry, which might then be researched. The presentation could be given to the classroom teacher as a multimedia presentation, rather than a classroom presentation.

>> **Linguistic learners** could be tasked with learning about several elements of poetry and conducting research for the class. They could also be tasked with writing poems modeled after famous poets.

>> **Logical-mathematical learners** could be assigned with the task of rhyming, understanding how words rhyme as well as understanding how rhythm occurs because of stressed and unstressed syllables.

>> **Naturalistic learners** could be tasked with reading poems about nature and comparing those poems to actual physical processes that occur. Descriptions and journals of natural reflections could be used as examples of specific detail.

Naturally, these classroom tasks would take much classroom time, but they should be considered tasks of instruction. Instruction does not mean that the teacher always has to be speaking, only that the teacher has planned for the expected outcomes. This method of instruction is often ignored by teachers as a degree of classroom control must be given up. However, behavior management strategies can make this concern irrelevant. When students are involved in their own instruction, the learning outcomes far exceed direct instruction. These intelligences should guide instructive practice and pinpoint specific learning activities that appeal to students within the classroom.

EXAMPLE

What is the best way to incorporate the multiple intelligences theory of instruction so that every type of learner is engaged in the classroom?

(A) The teacher begins each unit with direct instruction, ensuring that core content is delivered. Afterward, the teacher assigns each person free time to explore what interests them most about the content.

(B) The teacher divides the class up into eight different groups and presents each lesson using eight different formats, ensuring that the lesson meets the academic expectations.

(C) The teacher begins each day with direct instruction and core content discussion. Then, students start work at specific centers, in groups, with a focus of activity on different learning styles. Throughout a specified time frame, the students visit each of the centers.

(D) The teacher asks each student how she would like to present the content. Then, time is given for independent or group research or presentation of topics of student interest.

The answer is Choice (C). Choice (A) isn't right because allowing children random free time leads to behavior management concerns, regardless of the age of the students. Choice (B) would be an ideal classroom but is an impossibility due to time constraints. A teacher cannot realistically teach each lesson in eight different ways. Choice (D) is incorrect because it does not ensure that core content is being learned by the students. Only Choice (C) ensures that the curriculum is being addressed and that students can explore the core content in deeper ways through independent, but directed, research.

General models of instruction

After you've addressed the willingness, ability, and interest of the student, instructional procedures can be focused on the classroom and how core content is delivered by the teacher. Classroom teaching strategies can vary by subject matter, teacher instructional style, and other issues related to the school situation. Furthermore, each learning strategy varies depending on the core content to be taught. Some content can only be taught through avenues of exploration, while other content must be simply memorized and learned. There are, though, sets of learning strategies that teachers employ that address all these situations and must be varied according to the content taught and the students to whom it is presented. A great teacher uses a variety of these styles to enhance presentation of content rather than using one style for the sake of convenience. The following sections discuss classroom learning strategies.

Direct, explicit instruction

These activities are teacher-directed and prepare students to construct meaning from the content that is being delivered. Direct, explicit instruction involves lecture of materials and content, teacher-directed practice of content skills, and directed meaning from the reading of text. This strategy also involves modeling of procedures or skills to be learned. Direct instruction often gets a bad reputation, but a certain amount of classroom time must be spent with the expert presenting information to the less knowledgeable. Teachers, though, who rely on only this method of instruction have less favorable results than teachers who embrace all classroom learning strategies. This method is most favored by teachers of high school and higher learning and is referred to in those grades as "lecturing." In this method of instruction, the teacher is always in charge of the environment and the curriculum.

Scaffolding instruction

In this instructional strategy, also called the *gradual release of responsibility,* the teacher acts as a structure and support for student learning. In the beginning of new learning or new curriculum, the teacher is mostly responsible for the skills and content to be learned, much as with direct, explicit instruction. However, in this strategy, control of the curriculum is gradually released until students can work independently. This is not a behavior strategy, though. The instructional part of the strategy means that teachers step away slowly, step-by-step, as students show the ability to comprehend certain tasks or concepts. Teachers, as people, though, are not the only scaffold that can be used. A *scaffold* is any type of instructional support that helps students to accomplish a learning task. Teachers and peers can be scaffolds, but so can computer programs, resources, and manipulatives in the classroom. Any type of aid can be used as a scaffold if it provides a level of support that a student may need to access and understand curriculum concepts and skills that prove difficult to learn at a particular moment in time.

The scaffolding instructional strategy allows a teacher to introduce more difficult curriculum when students are below grade level in skills or have not mastered a certain set of skills or curriculum needed for further learning. This instructional strategy is also a great way to provide different levels and layers of learning for a classroom of students whose different needs—in terms of reading abilities, physical abilities, or other abilities—may interfere with their ability to learn at the pace of the group as a whole. A classroom example would be reading with the use of a graphic organizer to understand the main concepts in a story. A teacher might use the graphic organizer to help students understand the main concepts in a story, such as character, setting, and plot points. As students progress in reading skill, they may no longer need that level of scaffold and could move to a graphic organizer that calls for more critical thinking. For example, math students who do not know their multiplication tables fully could use a chart or calculator for help until they have mastered the memorization of the numbers or internalized the skill required.

Modeling

This instructional strategy, also called *mental modeling, mental mapping,* or *thinking aloud,* is most often used in reading and math where teachers are the experts and show and tell students what is going through their heads as they complete a task or solve a problem. Because much of language arts, reading, and math is skill-based rather than content knowledge–based, understanding how to complete and internalize those skills is best often done by showing students the learning that occurs where no one can see, in the brain, while thinking. Teachers who use this instructional strategy use white boards or other presentation aids to list the steps and cognitive ideas that occur while showing students the skill and how it can be internalized. This strategy makes thinking visible to the set of novices in the classroom. The cognitive modeling process shows the mental maneuvers that are necessary to achieve certain reasoning that is required for a set of skills. This instructional strategy is best used with concepts that need to be explained, demonstrated, or described. For example, the teacher could read a story aloud with a group of students and use inferences to determine what will happen next in the story.

Reciprocal teaching

In this instructional strategy, also called *active learning,* students assume the role of experts, or teachers, in small groups. The teacher models the skills or curriculum objectives for the entire class. Then, in smaller groups, students take turns practicing the skills or curriculum goals with feedback from peers. This instructional strategy blends direct, explicit teaching and modeling and allows students a safe place to practice skills and content before entire class presentations and before assessments. This strategy works best with small chunks of curriculum rather than broad concepts, and with skills that are learned in progression, rather than those that require no prior knowledge or background introduction. This strategy encourages students to think about the processes required for knowledge attainment and gives time and space for practice without assessment, formal or otherwise. This strategy is most often used during reading, but can be used with the reading of text in any subject and has many applications in math, for example, during problem solving that requires several steps.

Facilitative teaching

This instructional strategy relinquishes control of the classroom and allows the teacher to become an expert in some task rather than simply a disseminator of knowledge. In this strategy, the teacher makes the children understand that the knowledge to be gained is interchangeable, for many reasons, such as experimentation, point of view, background knowledge, and so on. The students are viewed as willing participants in the learning process and are given rein for independent thought directed at some skill. The content is usually more concept-based rather than knowledge recalled by rote. Students are free to ask questions, to venture onto new paths of knowledge, and to make mistakes without fear of assessment, formal or otherwise. The purpose of a facilitative teacher is to provide as much valid information as possible to lead students into topics of interest that will broaden and deepen their understanding of core concepts. Such concepts must be based in real-life and real-world examples as opposed to constructed curriculum objectives that expect all students to learn one thing. Facilitative teaching means guiding students and directing their learning in certain paths while sharing learning strategies for mutual understanding. This strategy is especially effective in a science classroom, where the teacher can be seen as a scientist conducting experiments along with the students rather than having students watch the experiment. For example, a teacher might lead the students in creating paper airplanes to see which style flies the farthest. The teacher is the expert and monitors each group, giving suggestions only when failure is leading to frustration. The teacher models the experiment and makes each student understand that there are a variety of "correct" answers, leading to a demonstration from the students of their own work rather than a demonstration of teacher-led knowledge. Another facilitative instruction example is a writing workshop wherein the teacher writes and shares the writing process along with students rather than delivering a final draft of text.

Cooperative learning

This is an instructional strategy in which small groups of students work together on a common task. This instructional strategy is often called "grouping," which is a formal instructional strategy where each member of the group is responsible for a certain task so that content can be learned and teacher directives and expectations can be met. Cooperative learning can also be informal, where each group member is individually accountable for tasks. Cooperative work allows students to critically think independently about the content while also learning to work with others toward a common goal. Successful small group learning incorporates five elements: positive interdependence, communication and interaction, individual and group accountability, group behavior management, and group processing and analysis of ideas. In this method of instruction, the teacher relinquishes control of the environment in order to enhance teaching of the curriculum. With this instructional strategy, students have more opportunities to directly interact with the curriculum rather than being told or shown, as is the case with much direct teaching. Cooperative learning also enhances and builds on the spirit of community within a classroom.

Rehearsal learning

This instructional strategy is used for rote memorization of content. Some content, such as multiplication tables or musical notes, must be learned fully so that future concepts can be learned. This strategy focuses on having children repeat performances of content—whether orally, through writing, or by actual physical manipulation—until the desired content becomes mastered, leading to automaticity. It is best used with foundational information, especially when new concepts are being introduced, before more complex approaches are used. This strategy helps students increase access to and retain curricular content and skills that will be used often and repeatedly. Choral responses, repetition games, and student competitions often make this strategy more engaging for students.

EXAMPLE

Ms. Schroeder, a social studies teacher, notices that students are having difficulty when reading and understanding a new chapter in the textbook that discusses governance and governing principles. As an instructional strategy, she decides to lead the class in a dialogue in which she generates leading questions, summarizes key concepts, and clarifies misunderstandings. Then, she has the students take turns being the teacher in a small group, summarizing key concepts and providing examples from their own daily lives. Which of the following instructional strategies best describes the method of teaching that Ms. Schroeder is using?

(A) scaffolding

(B) reciprocal teaching

(C) direct, explicit instruction

(D) cooperative learning

The answer is Choice (B). While the strategy does have some components of scaffolding and direct, explicit instruction, Choices (A) and (C), these two strategies are only briefly used. The teacher is not using cooperative learning, Choice (D), where the students assume control of a group or project with specific instructions for a commonly created task. Rather, this type of instruction is reciprocal teaching, where the students, after being taught content with which they struggled, are then asked to take on the role of teacher and practice the new content until a level of understanding and mastery has been reached.

EXAMPLE

Cooperative learning allows students to learn content, but also enables them to further develop social skills. Which skills are reinforced during cooperative learning?

(A) Survival of the fittest, in which each group member can show mastery of the task and reveal which students need concepts and skills to be retaught

(B) Developing a rote memory for content because group members rely on each member being an expert

(C) A desire to achieve and be the best in the group, reinforcing healthy competition among peers

(D) Developing collaboration when working with peers and developing problem solving through critically thinking about core content and curriculum

The answer is Choice (D). The purpose of any instruction is to teach the content and curriculum. While many social skills can be reinforced with this strategy, such as a desire to achieve, the development of social skills is not the primary purpose. The purpose of any instruction must be to impart knowledge in ways that will make retention fuller and more lasting. Cooperative learning should not be used as an assessment measure, as in Choice (A), because cooperative learning imparts instruction. Such a measure of assessment must not assume that students do or do not know content. Students who are shy or intrapersonal in nature may not share their knowledge, and that aspect should be considered when assessing for content.

Balance in instructional styles

Each of the instructional strategies should be used in balance in a classroom, without relying on any one strategy because it feels most comfortable or helps to control behavior in the classroom. The choice of instructional strategy should be determined by the needs of the students in the classroom and by the curriculum being taught. Having a balance of instructional styles alleviates boredom for both teachers and students and makes the classroom more engaging, thus also solving many behavior management issues. Teachers should embrace an eclectic, or multifaceted, approach to instruction, which balances the needs of content with the needs of individuals and the demands of school life.

A classroom that does all of these things and practices all of these instructional measures can be considered a *differentiated classroom.* A differentiated classroom is a classroom that contains both the resources and the instructional measures and procedures that enhance learning for all students, regardless of disability or need, such as learning style. A differentiated classroom can embrace the varied factors that students and school demand in terms of time and attention. A differentiated classroom supports a learning environment that respects different learning styles and preferences, different backgrounds and cultures, different language needs, different reading levels, different behavior management concerns, and different abilities of students. These classrooms use instruction in evidence-based ways to provide the best delivery of the content with the needs of individual learners always balanced with the demands of the curriculum.

Which of the following classrooms provides the best example of a differentiated classroom?

EXAMPLE

(A) The teacher begins a lesson with total group instruction to share new information. After the presentation of information, the teacher asks probing questions to determine concept attainment and then directs the class to work in small groups to correct misunderstandings.

(B) The teacher begins the lesson with total group instruction to share new information. Students are then directed to read the chapter that was just discussed and answer questions from the textbook. The teacher also makes time available so that students can have individual time with the teacher to ask questions and clarify misunderstandings before the weekly content quiz.

(C) The teacher begins the lesson by sending each student to a predetermined group in the classroom. The teacher directs the students to instructions at each location in which students are to learn the content. Each group has a different method of content introduction, which may be watching videos, listening to a book on CD, or reading books on the content. The teacher circulates around the room and monitors behavior and content attainment.

(D) The teacher begins the lesson with total group instruction to share new information. Students then move to small groups for guided practice of the newly introduced content. Students are allowed to sit in different areas of the room rather than in only the desk used for instruction. After a set time period has passed, the students are directed to go to predetermined stations in the classroom, which involve computers, a table with articles and manipulatives, a station with TV prompted to a video, and a book station with selected books on the topic being discussed.

The answer is Choice (D). Choice (D) is the only answer that fully incorporates several different instructional styles and methodologies. In this answer, the teacher gives direct instruction, allows cooperative learning, and includes elements of facilitative teaching as some content learning is being relinquished to other curriculum experts, such as computers, videos, and books. Furthermore, the teacher allows movement in the classroom and has different stations to appeal to different learning styles.

Conducting Proper Assessments

When many new teachers hear the word "assessment," the common synonym of "test" comes to mind. While assessments certainly do include tests, they are also inclusive of other types of measurement, including written assessments, performances, and portfolios of work. Basically, an assessment is any type of measurement in which the teacher can determine the level to which curriculum knowledge and skill attainment has occurred. Assessments do not have to be simply the old multiple-choice tests of the standardized variety or the rote memorization of a list of spelling words for a written test or spelling bee in front of a class.

Also, when new teachers consider assessment, they might assume that this process occurs at the conclusion of lessons. Master teachers know differently. Master teachers know that assessment happens throughout instruction. If teachers were to wait until the end of a unit to discover whether students were learning, it would be too late to step in and clear misunderstandings and provide opportunities for reteaching for students who might need extra time or instruction in a different way. Rather, assessments should take place throughout the learning process—at the beginning, middle, and end of instruction. While assessing often may seem time-consuming, it does pay off in the long run. Teachers who assess only at the end of instruction have students who lag far behind the students of teachers who take the time to make careful instructional decisions based on what their assessments reveal. Assessments, after all, are not truly meant for administration, for state officials, or for public presentation. Assessments are designed to give teachers, and schools, an understanding of the minds of the students so that teaching and learning can occur in a progressive way for every student in the school. Because students do not learn at the same pace or in the same way, knowing where and how some students are struggling can provide roadmaps for getting those kids back on the right track.

Designing and using formative assessments

All assessment types can be classified as either formative or summative. *Formative* assessments look at the "form" of learning that has occurred thus far. An easy way to remember formative assessment is by the word itself. Formative means capable of giving form. At this point in the assessment process, students are still capable of forming new growth and new learning, and their learning "formation" is still taking place. Formative assessment does many things, including

>> Helping teachers to plan instruction

>> Guiding teachers in the next steps of instruction

>> Helping teachers to identify areas of misunderstanding so that redirection and reteaching can occur

>> Checking students' understanding of topics, concepts, content, and skills

>> Monitoring student learning during the instructional process

>> Identifying areas where students are struggling

>> Responding to the needs of students

There are many different types of formative assessment, and these assessments must be considered a partner to instruction, because the assessment data often drives instruction and must be included with any planning of curriculum goals and objectives.

Pre-assessments

Since student monitoring is a year-long process, assessment of that progress must begin with discovering where students are prior to any real curriculum planning. Language arts, reading, and math assessments, called *pre-assessments* or *determinative assessments,* are often given at the beginning of each year so that teachers can determine the necessary skills that may be lacking in student knowledge. Knowing where the students are in terms of educational progress is the first step in planning how to deliver the curriculum and which curriculum may need to be redelivered. It doesn't matter whether students were supposed to learn some skill prior to a teacher receiving them. Teachers must meet students where they are and learn who they are so that careful instructional planning can meet their needs. These assessments can also monitor and measure learning at the beginning of a unit with such strategies as exit slips to gauge understanding or a warm-up that can be quickly observed and noted. Even something as simple as a thumbs-up if you get it and a thumbs-down if you need help can be considered an assessment, as teachers can quickly hone in on the students who need individual attention.

Diagnostic assessments

Diagnostic assessments often occur at the beginning of the year or at the beginning of a cycle of learning. This type of assessment is actually a process of assessment and knowledge gathering in which a specific learner's need may be pinpointed for redirection. This assessment often includes an evaluation for a possible disability or other school resource, such as a *Response to Intervention,* or RTI. RTI interventions may include teachers using a variety of instructional strategies to reach these learners, or they may require time spent with a specialist, such as a reading specialist, a speech pathologist, or another specialist for a particular learning need.

Interim assessments

The most important type of assessment does not occur at the end of the year, during standardized testing windows, or even at the end of units. The most important assessment occurs while instruction is occurring on particular pieces of content or just after a skill has been taught. This type of assessment is frequently referred to as *progress monitoring* or *interim assessments* and lets teachers know which students did not fully learn the content or skill. This frequent monitoring may happen monthly, bi-weekly, or daily, depending on the circumstances and the students involved. This assessment provides proof of learning and shows students' progression toward benchmarks, academic expectations, and objectives. The monitoring does not have to be formal with pen and paper, but can be any type of measurement that adequately checks whether a skill or content has been learned. It can be quick and easy, or more involved and timely, as with reading checks that measure comprehension progression.

Other types of assessments

While most people may think of assessment as pencil-and-paper type work, there are many different types of assessments beyond the traditional idea of multiple-choice tests. Progress monitoring and formative assessment can involve many types of assessment, including the following:

>> **Performance-based assessments** show the physical prowess of certain feats, such as musical or choral performances in a music class or miles run or push-ups attained in a physical education class. However, performance-based assessments can also occur in other content-area classes. In language arts and reading, a quick assessment could be having children clap to count syllables. A science class might show knowledge through certain science experiments. Another example would be the creation of a computer project or application to show knowledge gained through the performance of a series of steps taken.

>> **Self- and peer-reflection and evaluation** asks students to judge their own works and the works of peers, in order to determine what has been learned and what students may still be struggling with. Often, these assessments point to hidden thoughts and feelings that can't be measured or assessed with traditional measurements.

>> **Exhibitions and demonstrations,** such as projects, allow students to showcase work they feel is their best example of content learned.

>> **Journals** allow students to share innermost thoughts and feelings about their own work and identify any misunderstandings that may have been missed by the teacher.

Other quick forms of formative assessments include polls, surveys, clickers that check for understanding, quizzes, exit slips, graphic organizers, paired discussion, and wrap-up activities that ask questions directed at content acquisition.

EXAMPLE

Which of the following is NOT an appropriate type of formative assessment?

(A) A mid-term test with multiple-choice and essay questions directed at unit content acquisition

(B) A vocabulary game

(C) Paired collaborative discussion questions

(D) A project on a content concept

The answer is Choice (A). That answer is clearly a more formalized and standard type of assessment that doesn't measure the formation of knowledge. At the end of the unit, such as at a mid-term, the opportunity for the formation of knowledge is gone. All of the other answers are quick ways for teachers to assess small units of content or skill acquisition. These forms allow redirection before the end of a unit and check whether students are forming knowledge during curriculum acquisition.

Which of the following is best to do as part of a formative assessment that is going to evaluate a level of understanding of core curriculum?

(A) Give cumulative assessments at the end of each unit with weighted scores so that students understand how important the core curriculum is.

(B) Give students rewards for each correct answer during a practice quiz. The positive reinforcement will ensure the other students work harder to learn the core curriculum.

(C) Assign portfolios that represent different aspects of the curriculum and showcase the breadth and depth of each student's knowledge acquisition.

(D) Have students revisit assignments after teachers have checked their work and made comments. Direct students to find and revisit mistakes, using classroom resources to help.

The correct answer is Choice (D). Choices (A) and (C) are examples of a different type of assessment, one that measures end-of-content knowledge rather than formative knowledge. Choice (B) is not an assessment of knowledge, but rather a behavior modification strategy. Only Choice (D) allows teachers and students to address small chunks of learned information. Checking work and revisiting the work with student input and retrial allows students more opportunities to interact with curriculum, apply newer skills, and utilize other resources for knowledge attainment.

Creating, using, and interpreting summative assessments

End-of-content assessments, also called *cumulative assessments* and, more often, *summative assessments,* are techniques and tools that evaluate student learning over a course of time or unit of study. Summative assessments, in effect, provide "summaries" of what students have learned over a particular course of study. The word "summative" means total or collective, and this is an indication of the type of data it gives to a classroom teacher, a student, or another interested party. However, that does not mean that summative assessments provide no data that can be used for instruction. Summative assessment data is often used to provide a clearer direction of what is or is not working with the students, with the instructional style, and in regard to the direction and growth of progress. While summative assessments take place at the end of a time frame, such as the end of a unit, the information they provide frequently gives a broader and deeper picture of content knowledge than formative assessments do.

The purpose of these tests is to measure content and skill acquisition. The audience for whom the test is prepared and designed is usually the teacher. This, however, can vary by school, district, and state. Some school districts require that students complete assessments that have been designed by test-makers or other professionals. While the teachers are audience recipients, the results are often shared with administrators to determine content acquisition, among other things.

Summative assessments, often simply called "tests," can include examples other than multiple-choice testing, such as those seen in state standardized testing. Other summative assessments include semester testing, unit testing, and course finals. Summative assessments are often called *high-stakes* or *high-value* testing because the results can be considered as part of evaluative processes for teachers and schools, or because the assessment results in some type of grade for students, usually a grade that will influence a report card or grade-point average, in the higher grades. This type of testing can be informal, but it is more likely to be formal for the purpose of grades and presentation of knowledge to parents and administrators. Teachers also use these assessments to determine what learning has occurred, but if formative assessment is ongoing all year and balanced with instruction, most teachers can make accurate and predictive guesses about how the students will perform on summative assessments.

Types of summative assessment activities

Like formative assessment, summative assessment includes certain types of activities or questions. Unlike formative assessments, these activities and questions are designed to measure overall growth or performance concerning curriculum acquisition. Some examples of summative assessment activities or questions include the following:

>> **Multiple choice questions:** These questions provide students with a stem or starter and a set of answers concerning specific skills or concepts of curriculum. Usually, only one answer choice is correct.

>> **Constructed response questions:** Sometimes called essay questions, written response, or "explain your answer," these questions require a written response to a prompt, usually in the form of a short answer, short essay, or paragraph.

>> **Extended constructed response questions:** These questions, often called "writing prompts," are similar to constructed response questions, except that students are required to perform more difficult writing tasks, such as a multi-paragraph essay. Usually, these assessments are not included on tests until late elementary school or early middle school.

>> **Performance tasks:** These assessments require students to solve a multi-step problem or to create something new. Often these assessments require students to read text, analyze data, and respond to the data with a task, usually in writing.

>> **Holistic rubrics:** These assess student work as a whole when considered as a product of learning, with exemplars and academic expectations. An example is a rubric that measures a written project of a student, such as a short story. Such a project is graded holistically, or as a whole. Consideration is given to the entire work, with particular attention paid to specific academic and content expectations, such as whether the story has a main character, a setting, and so on, as well as how well these characteristics are employed. Another example is an art project that is assessed based on inclusion of particular content and application of concepts.

>> **Student portfolio of work:** This example of summative assessment takes the longest to acquire. In this type of assessment, students collect work that showcases their best attempts at curriculum attainment. After the work is collected during a specified time frame, the entire collection of work is assessed. While this is often used for performance arts, this evaluative procedure is also used by some states, such as Kentucky, for standardized testing in the area of writing.

Other examples of summative assessments include tests, exams, and written papers demanding application of content attained.

In a classroom, summative assessments are most often used to arrive at a grade for a student, as well as to assess curriculum content. These assessments are most effective when dealing with specific content to be learned, rather than a set of skills that must be developed, as in early reading and math, for example. In order to create a summative assessment, teachers must begin with the curriculum, academic expectations, and course goals and objectives. Often, summative assessments are designed prior to instruction and serve as a roadmap, or checklist, for instruction. Authentic summative assessments, though, measure what students were expected to learn as well as what students were taught. The summative assessment serves as proof of content delivery and instructional occurrence should these assessments be used for evaluative purposes, as they are in some districts and states. Rubrics and checklists are also used by classroom teachers to guide students toward comprehensive understanding of the academic expectations and goals set for them and provide roadmaps of study for the students, as well.

A comprehensive assessment program, just like a comprehensive instructional program, has to provide balance. Teachers who use only one form of assessment—formative or summative—are not getting a full picture of student needs, curricular gaps, or instructional directives. Summative assessments should become part of any classroom instructional process, regardless of the age of the child. Again, the tests don't have to be multiple choice and short answer, but should be cumulative so that an idea of student progress is attained. Summative tests should be used as accountability measures for both students and teachers, and should be communicated to parents and other stakeholders. A summative assessment measures that particular moment in time and, if that moment sends off warning signals, proper interventions can be used to scaffold the students until success has been achieved. Summative assessment that occurs too infrequently, such as yearly standardized testing, does not provide the curricular and instructional information needed to make necessary changes. Often, these yearly tests, as well as semester finals, are simply used for grading purposes or to give a snapshot of a student. To be used effectively, summative assessments must take place more regularly, with the specific purpose of making adjustments and intervening for the good of the students. Summative assessments should not be used solely as an accountability measure.

Summative assessment data

Interpreting summative assessments takes a bit of work, and some specific terms must be learned so that student results can be analyzed and used. Here are some terms that are most helpful in understanding and interpreting summative data:

>> **Accountability:** The idea holding students, teachers, schools, and states responsible for test results. Often, state money is tied in to test results, and some teachers, depending on the state and district, can be evaluated based on students' scores.

>> **Benchmark assessments:** Tests given frequently throughout a year, giving immediate feedback as to how students are progressing toward successful learning of curriculum and meeting of academic expectations.

>> **Criterion-referenced tests:** These tests measure student performance against a standard or specific goal, such as a curriculum timeline. Examples are classroom unit tests.

>> **Cut score:** An assessment proficiency level or score that learners are expected to achieve in order to be considered as making progress. These are also referred to as *maximum* and *minimum results scores.*

>> **Indicators:** Labels that provide a guide as to how students perform against a range. For example, on some state tests, students who achieve a certain number of correct answers are deemed "Proficient." Some states use terms such as "Pass +," "Advanced," "Needs Improvement," and so on. Teachers also assign indicators to tests conducted in classrooms, with certain scores earing an "A," and so forth.

>> **Norm-referenced tests:** These tests measure students against a national "norm" or average, and rank students against one another. Examples are the SAT, ACT, and state standardized tests.

>> **Percentile score:** Also called *percentile rank.* This is a converted score that indicates where an individual performs when a group is ranked by percentages. For example, students can be said to be performing within the 90th percentile, meaning their scores are as good as 90 percent of test-takers or within the top 10 percent of those who took the test.

>> **Reliability:** The likelihood that scores and outcomes will be repeated across a population of test-takers. In other words, the test does not favor one type of test-taker over another, but fairly measures learning across a given population.

>> **Standard score:** An indication of where one test lies in comparison to a norm group, such as those who take norm-referenced tests.

>> **Validity:** How the test is analyzed, interpreted, and applied. Tests can be deemed invalid if an analysis reveals that students—or teachers—had access to privileged information or were given too much or too little time, for example.

EXAMPLE

A sixth-grade teacher has students keep all art classwork during the semester in a portfolio for evaluation purposes. This portfolio can best help the teacher determine which of the following things?

(A) How well students understood a particular assignment

(B) How well students will perform in the county-wide juried art fair against other schools

(C) How likely students are to complete all of the next unit's work

(D) How students generally developed in skills over the time period of the unit

The correct answer is Choice (D). This portfolio was being used as a summative assessment for evaluation purposes over a long period of time. As a summative assessment, it does not measure particular assignments, Choice (A), or predict future behavior, Choices (B) and (C). While the teacher might use it to gauge how well students might perform in an art fair, the purpose is to generally get an idea of how well those students understood and performed the curricular concepts and skills introduced.

Using appropriate assessments

With all these assessments listed, how are teachers to determine which assessments are best to use for any specific situation? The best way is to remember what each assessment means and what each measures.

REMEMBER

A formative assessment measures the formation of knowledge. Formative assessments are used when students are still forming ideas about content and learning key skills and core ideas. A summative assessment provides a summary of what has been learned thus far. Summative assessments are used when students have completed some unit of learning.

As with all other types of teaching, a balance should be maintained between the two to get the best overall picture of how students are doing, in regard to progress toward goals. Following are some other things to consider doing when deciding which type of assessment is best to use and how to use each type of assessment:

>> **Vary the types of assessments given.** If students know they are always going to take a certain type of test on Friday—a vocabulary quiz, for example—they may also learn other tricks that may corrupt the results. Using different measures, such as direct and indirect, graded and ungraded, formal and informal, teacher-directed and self-directed, gives teachers and students a better idea of both how and to what degree learning is occurring.

>> **Plan for the assessments.** While some formative assessments necessarily occur on the spot when it becomes obvious that learning has gone off-track, an effective teacher has a careful plan about what kinds of assessments to give and when to give them. Alternative plans should also be made that take into account the results of the assessments. In this way, the assessments provide markers for teachers and tell just as much about instructional effectiveness as student progression. Ideally, both formative assessments and summative assessments should be prepared and planned for as or before instruction begins on a new concept or topic. Assessments should never be used as a behavior modification tool, such as throwing a pop

quiz to see who read the required chapters of a story. Information gathered this way is not valid because the analysis doesn't reveal which students may have comprehension issues.

>> **Make sure that the assessments match what was taught and what was expected to be learned.** While preparing assessment ahead of time is ideal, those plans do not need to be set in concrete. Any teacher who has spent even one hour on the job knows that plans change, based on either internal forces like the students themselves, or outside forces like surprise fire alarms. Teachers should never be held to any plan so rigidly that individual student needs and interests are ignored. Those "teachable moments" should be embraced without derailing overall plans of learning. Those teachable moments also allow more in-depth curricular interest that can greatly affect summative data and should be taken into consideration.

>> **Keep assessment data.** If the only assessment data that is kept is a series of grades on tests, teachers are given no idea as to which students may be struggling with content. Grades are extremely subjective; showing that a student scores 70 percent on comprehension quizzes says only that comprehension is within an average range. Closer examination of the scores may reveal that a student consistently misses questions relating to author's purpose. If this skill is never directly and explicitly taught, this skill will never be learned. Teachers should have some way to record specific data about individual student progress. While charts and folders are always handy, new technological programs and computer apps make this easier than ever before. Most computerized programs, if students use these for assessments, will actually pinpoint particular needs and gaps in student learning. While such programs may be expensive, the time saved in teacher labor may be worth the investment.

>> **Try new assessments.** Teachers should never get so comfortable with one type of assessment that no others are considered. What works for one group in one period may not work for every student in another. Teaching, like learning, is a constant process.

Understanding the purpose of assessments

It is important to understand the appropriate purposes of assessments. Both formative and summative data can, and should, be used by classroom teachers. Formative data, though, is used only by classroom teachers. Generally, administrators want larger pictures of learning. Therefore, on a building, district, and state level, only summative assessments are used. Within a school, other assessments take place. Regardless, all assessments fall within these three purposes:

>> To identify gaps in learning

>> To determine progress toward academic expectations

>> To identify a disability, or reason for failure to progress

While much has been said about the first two purposes, many assessments are given to students who fail to close gaps in learning and fail to progress toward academic expectations. Generally, these tests are for inclusion in a special education program, but that is not always the case. While there are specific tests for specific learning disabilities, other issues also come into play. For example, students may have health concerns that cause them to miss large chunks of school. Other health issues, such as sight, speech, and hearing, are also tested. Reading tests are frequently given, and students may have some specific type of disability, such as dyslexia. Regardless of the type of test given, the assessments and results always influence instruction.

At the beginning of this chapter, Figure 9-1 shows how tightly connected the three areas—curriculum, instruction, and assessment—are. In a closer examination and reflection, again note that the arrows between each go both ways. These three areas cannot be seen as having one beginning (starting with curriculum) and one ending (conclude with an assessment). Rather, learning must be seen as a constantly revolving process where each enhances, influences, and is controlled by the others.

EXAMPLE

Which of the following CANNOT be tested using a formative assessment?

(A) reading for pleasure

(B) a working knowledge of high-frequency words

(C) ability to multiple by 5

(D) governing American principles

The correct answer is Choice (D). All the other answer choices can be measured quickly and are used to determine whether any redirection should immediately take place. Even Choice (A), which may seem like opinion, can be assessed with a quick questionnaire or through journal entries. Only Choice (D) needs a more comprehensive assessment. No quick assessment can conclude the degree or depth to which a student understands such a large and broad concept, one that takes many weeks to teach and develop.

EXAMPLE

Which of the following CANNOT be tested using a summative assessment?

(A) Meaning of core content words and phrases

(B) Capitalization and punctuation rules

(C) An understanding of the writing process

(D) Identifying where colors should be placed on a color wheel

The correct answer is Choice (D). While Choice (D) does involve core concepts and content that children should know and a concept that does take time to develop and learn, this assessment of identification can be done quickly and only provides information on that one skill set. All the other answers provide summative and comprehensive information on how well students have learned and performed with larger concepts and content.

Identifying student misconceptions and correcting them

One of the key purposes of any assessment is to provide information about when students are not learning what they are supposed to when they are supposed to, or when they have learned information incorrectly, leading to misconceptions, that, if not corrected, can interfere with other learning. When students fail to learn, the first step in correcting the problem is figuring out why students are not learning at the pace and in the way that is expected and desired. In this way, teachers are like doctors who diagnose cases based on observations and behaviors. The diagnosis for treatment, though, must rely on what type of learning error has occurred. Most misconceptions fall into one of these categories:

>> **Preconceived notions:** No student arrives at the classroom door fresh out of the box. Rather, each student is a little human being with ideas already established. In the younger ages, some of these preconceived notions may be cute at first, but they can interfere with content acquisition. Consider the phenomenon of Harry Potter. These books and movies have so embedded themselves into the culture that many students actually believe that such creatures and worlds exist. There comes a point in language arts curriculum where students have to be able to identify the difference between fantasy and reality. Similar situations certainly occur in science with science-related "facts" that students see in movies or TV shows, and in social studies curriculum as it involves possible stereotypes surrounding world cultures.

- » **Conceptual misunderstandings:** Often students are confronted with curriculum that causes them to question large concepts and ideas about the world they may have never considered before. While such ideas may be on curriculum guidelines, certain types of reasoning and thinking are certainly dependent on the maturity of the students involved. A good example is inferential thinking. While even the earliest language arts standards include the teaching of inferences, the ability to think inferentially does not fully develop until high school. A similar situation occurs with logic and reasoning skills. While these skills are not fully developed until later, teachers must begin the process of teaching them early. Understanding when the concepts and content are too difficult because of the individual maturity level of a student is helpful when designing alternative instructional tasks.

- » **Alternative conceptions:** Material that is learned incorrectly, for whatever reason, results in alternative conceptions. While it is probably not polite to say so, sometimes students are just wrong, and the material and knowledge they have is incorrect. In order for this type of thinking to be corrected, redirection must occur so that students can correct how they have learned. A primary example is the old rule, "*i* before *e* except after *c*." Students who have internalized this rule, or any other rule about the English language, apply it to every situation, when in reality there are more exceptions to that rule than words that obey it. Learning must occur that shows students tips and strategies for identification of unknown words so that learning can continue.

When teachers have identified areas of misconception, redirection and reteaching must occur. Often, the old knowledge stands in the way of new work and new content that must be learned. Frequent assessments should direct teachers to such misunderstandings. When students encounter misunderstandings and fail to progress, certain actions can be taken:

- » **Initiating remediation and reteaching:** While remediation often has a bad connotation, every child at some point in his academic career will need some type of remediation. This is an instructional strategy where teachers explain or teach the same content in a new and different way. They may try a new learning strategy, take more time, or employ resources and materials, such as computer programs, that foster the necessary skills. Cognitive skills and foundational skills are most often involved in remediation needs.

- » **Identifying intervention strategies:** When students fail to progress, different instructional strategies must be employed. When students are clearly not learning, the educational program must change to meet the students' needs. Schools often have intervention strategies already in place, especially in regard to reading, but each teacher has to also develop a set of strategies to use. They may involve altering time spent on task, changing the classroom arrangement, and even developing individualized education plans for progress.

- » **Involving specialists:** No teacher should have to feel like a captain on a ship set adrift in a sea. A school has a host of specialists who can often diagnose and work with specific students without attaching labels to them. Flexibility is the key. Parents should also be involved and often provide outside resources, such as tutoring, to spend extra time on the needed skills.

Having Subject Area Content Knowledge

The Praxis test takes a page out of Bloom's taxonomy book when it comes to the topics of curriculum, instruction, and assessment. While there are questions concerning general concepts and core content (curriculum) that all teachers should know, most of the test has questions that apply those concepts to specific curricular concerns of instruction and assessment. The majority of test questions are set within the contexts of the subjects taught within most elementary schools: reading and language arts, math, science, social studies, art, music, and physical education. Therefore, teachers must know, be able to understand, and then apply general education principles of curriculum, instruction, and assessment to particular subjects.

Reading and language arts

In **reading and language arts,** teachers are expected to know the following matters regarding curriculum, instruction, and assessment:

>> **Curriculum:** How to sequence lessons, plan for strategies, address misconceptions, and make text connections across other disciplines when dealing with foundational skills, literature and informational texts, writing, language, and speaking and listening.

>> **Instruction:** How to design instruction that differentiates for diverse needs and how to implement appropriate instructional strategies to support learning in reading foundational skills, reading literature and informational texts, writing, language, and speaking and listening

>> **Assessment:** How to evaluate the effectiveness of reading and language arts instruction and student progress using formative, summative, and other assessments and strategies

EXAMPLE

Which of the following teacher activities is designed to assess the listening skills of a primary student?

(A) Asking a student to say and write the word "cat" and then having the student draw a picture of a cat

(B) Asking a student to think of three words that rhyme with "hop"

(C) Showing a student two pictures with the same rime and asking that student to write the rime on paper

(D) Reading a sentence aloud and then asking the student to restate what was just read

The correct answer is Choice (D). Choices (B) and (C) measure content of rhymes and rimes, and Choice (A) measures comprehension and concrete connections of word to printed text. Only Choice (D) involves a listening component.

REMEMBER

"Rhyme" refers to words that sound alike, such as *kale* and *pail*. But these words do not have the same "rime." The word *rime* refers to a part of a word, the part that begins with a vowel sound and ends before the next vowel sound. The rime of *kale* is /ale/; the rime of *pail* is /ail/.

Mathematics

In **mathematics,** teachers are expected to know these matters about curriculum, instruction, and assessment:

>> **Curriculum:** How to plan curriculum by sequencing examples and lessons, developing strategies, and making connections among numbers, operations, algebraic thinking, geometry, and measurement, as well as data, statistics, and probability.

>> **Instruction:** How to design instruction that differentiates for diverse needs and how to implement appropriate instructional strategies to support learning in numbers and operations involving natural numbers, whole numbers, integers, and rational numbers; numbers and operations involving proportional relationships; numbers and operations involving number theory; algebraic thinking involving equations and formulas; algebraic thinking involving

expressions, equations, and formulas; algebraic thinking involving linear equations and inequalities; geometry and measurement involving dimensional figures; geometry and measurement involving coordinate planes; geometry and measurement involving measurement; data, statistics, and probability involving measures of center; and data, statistics, and probability involving data and probability

>> **Assessment:** How to evaluate the effectiveness of mathematics instruction and student progress using formative, summative, and other assessments and strategies

Science

In **science,** teachers are expected to know the following matters about curriculum, instruction, and assessment:

>> **Curriculum:** How to plan curriculum by knowing the broad purposes of teaching science topics both within the subject and as connections occur across other content areas.

>> **Instruction:** How to design instruction that differentiates for diverse needs and how to implement appropriate instructional strategies to support learning in science concepts, inquiry, and processes in the areas of life, earth, space, and physical science, as well as health

>> **Assessment:** How to evaluate the effectiveness of science instruction and student progress using formative, summative, and other assessments and strategies

EXAMPLE

Which of the following skills will students most likely use when grouping different types of clouds and cloud formations?

(A) analyzing

(B) inferring

(C) classifying

(D) predicting

The correct answer is Choice (C). Students have to know that clouds can be classified into a specific system based on appearance and other components.

Social studies

In **social studies,** teachers are expected to know the following matters regarding curriculum, instruction, and assessment:

>> **Curriculum:** How to plan curriculum by knowing the broad purposes of teaching social studies topics both within the subject and as connections across other content areas

>> **Instruction:** How to design instruction that differentiates for diverse needs and how to implement appropriate instructional strategies to support learning in information processing skills; geography; history; government, civics, and economics; and anthropology and sociology

>> **Assessment:** How to evaluate the effectiveness of social studies instruction and student progress using formative, summative, and other assessments and strategies

EXAMPLE

The National Curriculum Standards for Social Studies outlines ten themes. The third theme is people, places, and environment. Which of the following objectives for an upper elementary classroom falls within this theme?

(A) Understanding that the environment would be a healthier place for all humans and animals without urban centers and factories

(B) Understanding that environments without homes and people should be considered wild and unexplored and left untouched so that nature can exist in its natural state

(C) Understanding that humans should live in homes with floors and walls, for safety and hygienic reasons

(D) Understanding that there are many different kinds of habitats for humans around the world and that homes are part of communities

The correct answer is Choice (D). All of the other answers have some type of opinion expressed in them that does not embrace the idea of social studies, which is to introduce topics and develop students' understanding of anthropological and sociological backgrounds and communities.

Art, music, and physical education

In art, music, and physical education, teachers are expected to know the following matters about curriculum, instruction, and assessment:

>> **Curriculum:** How to plan curriculum by knowing the fundamental purposes of teaching art, music, and physical education topics both within the subject and as connections across other content areas

>> **Instruction:** How to design instruction that differentiates for diverse needs and how to implement appropriate instructional strategies to support the development of an understanding of

- Art and design media, techniques, and concepts

- The elements of music, including music notation, terminology, and music making

- Physical education concepts

Test-takers should also understand how to select and use manipulatives from all three contents for applied purposes.

>> **Assessment:** How to evaluate the effectiveness of art, music, and physical education instruction and student progress using formative, summative, and other assessments and strategies

EXAMPLE

During a physical education unit on volleyball, a student must show how to serve a ball to the other team, or side, as the teacher observes the effort and style. Which of the following comments from an elementary physical education teacher provides the student with the most effective feedback on the ability to serve well?

(A) "Wow! You've really improved since last year! Keep up the good work."

(B) "Did you see how the students were looking at you when you served? Make sure to see where their eyes go and then try to place the ball in a surprising spot."

(C) "When you swing back, your elbow bends sharply. If you keep your arm straight both when you swing back and on the upswing, that will give you more strength to hit the ball up and over the net."

(D) "Practice with John. His swing was perfect, and he can show you what you need to do to make it better."

The answer is Choice (C). Only this answer shows an understanding of how to identify and evaluate different types of constructive feedback in order to improve a performance, pointing out specific actions and behaviors to focus on.

Chapter 10

Reading and Language Arts Curriculum, Instruction, and Assessment

L iteracy begins when a child hears his first word, and that literacy learning continues for an entire lifetime. Many children walk through their first classroom door already reading and writing. Some have verbal skills far beyond their years. Some students may never have seen a book or heard a story before. Regardless, literacy instruction must embrace the background of each learner and build on that background to create a masterful reader, writer, and communicator.

The learning of language skills really never starts or stops. It can only be perfected in a gradual way, and instruction in language arts is similar to the old-fashioned apprentice and expert relationship. The students, no matter their age or grade, are the apprentices in the relationship, looking to others around them to learn this difficult task of communication. The teachers, and others in educational and social situations, are the experts—seeking to impart the finer parts of the communication arts, to point out the pitfalls of potential mistakes, and to redirect those apprentices who might stray from the preferred path of learning—helping the student to progress to a higher level of learning and language acquisition.

REMEMBER

As an expert, teachers must also understand that literacy curriculum development and instruction must not begin with a lesson. Rather, any development and instruction must always take into consideration the assessment process, or what it is that students need to understand and do with the knowledge being created.

This chapter shows you how to design curriculum instruction that meets the needs of all developing learners, no matter their background, in order to successfully undertake assessment tasks that measure learning and life-long literacy.

Creating a Reading and Language Arts Curriculum

As a teacher, creating a language arts curriculum must include several components so that the overall effect embraces language instruction in a seamless and realistic way and models the speaking, listening, reading, and writing that the student already uses in her own life. In other words, it is necessary to incorporate and build on language skills that have already begun through communication, language, and reading in the home with family, friends, and other acquaintances. These components, naturally, begin in early education, but must also continue through high school and beyond. The components of literacy instruction that must be included in the development of curriculum design are listening and speaking, language study, using words as vehicles for ideas, and communicating through writing.

Many schools and school districts have purchased or created curriculum that focuses on some of the concepts that follow. Few, if any, have purchased programs that embrace all the concepts needed for complete language development. While many teachers use the curriculum provided by the schools, these packages are not necessarily comprehensive nor do they take into account the needs of all learners. Planning curriculum means taking a look at all the resources and using those that are most applicable to the situation and the needs in the classroom. Relying on only one resource, or one canned program, is certain to cause instructional and assessment situations that will require reteaching of certain concepts.

Listening and speaking

Creating a culture of language immersion in the classroom must first include an understanding that communication is a two-way process, with each side presenting ideas and then considering those ideas before a second round of idea presentation. This component of creating a reading and language arts curriculum involves listening and discussing written words, both on the part of the teacher and the student.

Building and facilitating a classroom where both listening and speaking are practiced involves

» Creating and agreeing upon rules for discussion, where listening is as important as speaking and knowing that those two processes cannot happen at the same time

» Understanding that listening has a purpose and is an important part of *comprehension*, understanding what is spoken or read aloud

» Responding to the statements of the speaker in a way that either moves along the conversation on the same topic, or clarifies the statements with a question to avoid misunderstanding

A primary classroom may seem the only place where these rules and understandings about language need to be taught, but that certainly isn't true. While the first steps in speaking and listening are all about taking turns when communicating, there are standards for listening and communicating through Grade 12. The premise is the same, but the range, quality, and complexity of the skill changes to model the maturity of the students.

Listening and speaking curriculum design should include more than just taking turns speaking out loud, although that first step in a primary classroom may take up a majority of any class time! Curriculum design should also include academic processes, such as listening and responding to stories, drawing conclusions from an exchange of ideas represented in a text, and furthering knowledge based on diverse perspectives. Naturally, this communication exchange promotes learning through many different genres, including fiction in literature and poetry, and nonfiction through articles and research-driven text.

Having discussions and drawing conclusions are the hallmark of any successful listening and speaking curriculum design and should be included in every facet of every lesson. Collaborative discussions should include lessons that involve these facets:

>> One-on-one communication

>> Group communication

>> Teacher-led communication

This is the basis on which all future learning can occur, except for those students with profound hearing loss. Even then, accommodations can be made so that all students are included in language immersion that values the exchange of ideas.

Language study

This component of the curriculum involves an understanding that language has parts, and when those parts are combined, students can use those parts to build sounds, words, sentences, and stories. This is the core of all future work for teaching reading and language arts, and its importance cannot be overemphasized. Mastery of this skill is vital for each and every student. Every lesson must involve assessment and, if needed, redirection and reteaching of concepts and skills so that sounds and words can be successfully used by every student, in both reading and writing, because those are the skills that form the foundation of all communication.

This language study is the center around which all literacy lessons must rely. Future lessons in comprehension, writing, and fluency all involve a mastery of language. At its core, language study involves understanding these concepts:

>> Sounds have meanings *(phonemic awareness)*. For example, hearing or speaking the same set of sounds can produce a meaning, like a baby who learns "mommy" will cause a smile or reaction from a mother, or that "bottle" will produce food.

>> Sounds have meaningful units *(phonemes)*. A phoneme is the smallest unit of sound. For example, the first sound in "mommy" is/m/. Changing that first sound can change the meaning of a word, as in /t/ to "tommy."

>> Sounds can group together to make a unit of sound *(morphemes)*. A morpheme is the smallest unit of language that holds meaning. Fox example, adding "c" to "h" produces a unit, /ch/.

>> Letters are linked to sounds *(the Alphabetic Principle)*. The sound /h/, which is like a breath of air, corresponds to the English letter "h."

>> Sounds are linked to written symbols *(graphemes)*. There are 44 graphemes in the English language, including consonants, which usually make the same sound, except for "c" which can produce either an /s/ or /k/ sound. Other variations include vowels, which can change from long to hard, or which can be changed when doubled, added to another vowel, or placed in front of certain consonants, like "r."

>> There is a relationship between sounds and written symbols *(phonics)*. For example, an "e" at the end of a word changes how the word sounds, as in "ton" versus "tone." Phonics involves manipulation of graphemes, phonemes, and morphemes according to a set of rules.

>> Sounds group together to make words *(phonological awareness)*. For example, words can be changed, or manipulated, and grouped together to make meaning and change meaning. A basic example is "not," which, when added to a sentence, can change its meaning.

These important terms form the basis by which all children learn to read print and become aware of how sounds work together to make words that match the print being read. Children must have the ability to notice, think about, and work with the individual sounds in spoken words before they can begin to read and understand print.

REMEMBER

Understanding the key terms in the previous list and using them in literacy instruction is vital to create a building block on which all further word work takes place. While students don't need to know the terms, the experts, or teachers, do. Furthermore, these terms, in some form, will be on the Praxis test, so make sure to understand how each works.

Phonological awareness

Becoming phonologically aware cannot be overemphasized when planning curriculum instruction. Children who have *phonological awareness* can talk about words they know, words that rhyme, words that can be broken into syllables, and so many other different aspects of how words behave and what they do. This all shows a child's ability to pay attention to, manipulate, and talk about words, building an academic vocabulary that is needed for school life. Phonological awareness is necessary for the next steps in learning to read, which is phonemic awareness and decoding of unknown words. Students who do not learn, or are not taught, this interplay with words and language will be the students who memorize sight word lists or high-frequency lists and have no skills when encountering words that are new or unknown.

Individual student needs

Knowing the individuals in your classroom should also govern curriculum design. Many students have specific troubles with certain areas of language acquisition. While each child is an individual, many of these learning difficulties can be predicted and should be accounted for when designing lessons regarding language learning.

For example, students who have learned another language prior to learning English (ELL, ESL, or ESOL students) have a different set of graphemes from their first language and need to be deliberately taught the specific sounds and letters that could be new or different for them. For example, the letter "j" in Spanish makes no sound in a word, while in English, that sound is /j/, as in "judge." Another predicted group is students with hearing difficulties. These students often don't hear the nuances of each sound a word makes. Likewise, students who have specific learning disabilities such as dyslexia, if identified, can have instruction that meets their specific learning needs. Understanding the makeup of a classroom guides curriculum instruction to ensure that the needs of all learners are met. This also means that curriculum design will change from year to year, as a different group of learners, with different needs, enters the environment. While this may seem to be a huge amount of work, planning for these contingencies within curriculum design can save time during instruction and assessment. If you know certain areas are going to be problematic, planning for them ahead of time can actually save a lot of time in the long run.

Words as vehicles for ideas

Language study is the foundation on which reading and language development, vocabulary development, and structural and conventional understanding of the language must take place. Students must understand that words, when combined with other words, can begin to form sentences, which can then form paragraphs, and so on. An initial understanding of this in primary education allows students to understand basic ideas when reading sentences and continues as students understand the more specific rules that govern literature and nonfiction conventions of speaking, reading, and writing.

While language study is the building block of communication with ideas, it cannot be taught in isolation. The phonics and word work, as previously discussed, must be taught in conjunction with work that furthers using words in ways that deepen comprehension. Even a rudimentary understanding of language study enables a student to understand basic ideas when reading sentences or hearing simple stories.

Word work, including work at a primary level, involves the following:

>> Phonics study

>> Sight words or high-frequency words

>> Vocabulary development

>> Spelling

>> Grammar

>> Decoding words

All of this is for one purpose: to build comprehension of words, whether printed as text or spoken as speech. The ultimate aim of reading and language arts curriculum is to enable a reader to tackle text, at an age- and skill-appropriate level, with no difficulties so that the message of the words is understood. This is comprehension.

This vocabulary, or word work, instruction involves all the words that have to be known in order to communicate effectively, plus word attack strategies that can help when encountering unknown words. This word work plays an important part in learning to read, but is also important for the other communication arts. Word work should focus on

>> **Reading vocabulary:** Words we have to know to understand what we read

>> **Listening vocabulary:** Words we have to know to understand what we hear when others speak

>> **Speaking vocabulary:** Words we have to know and use when we speak

>> **Writing vocabulary:** Words we have to know and use in writing

These four types of vocabulary may seem interchangeable, but research has shown that children learn the meanings of most words indirectly and have a listening vocabulary that's much greater than their reading vocabulary. The language skills of children who engage in daily oral language are much different than those of children who read extensively on their own.

Indirect vocabulary learning

Understanding that vocabulary learning can be indirect must also mean that teachers must directly teach academic vocabulary very specifically, because it is learned primarily in the classroom. It isn't spoken in a child's environment, in conversations with friends or at home. Therefore, specific word instruction must occur, and that instruction must be planned before the lesson. Pre-teaching vocabulary words helps both vocabulary learning and, ultimately, reading comprehension. Planned, extended, and repeated instruction ensures that necessary concepts are understood. Skipping this vital step in curriculum design can doom any lesson to failure. While you may tell students that certain words are important, it is necessary for specific instructional steps to be taken if you want those words to become part of the students' long-term knowledge and usage.

As comprehension is built, more difficult work can be added. For example, fluency is also word work. *Any* activity that engages a child with words for the purpose of understanding meaning is word work. It has literal and figurative meanings that often can't be separated.

Word work with other core curriculum and learning outside the classroom

Word work needs to take into consideration all core content and standards that a child is expected to learn. Word work is the perfect way to incorporate different standards and content that isn't based in language arts curriculum. Primary teachers, which can vary by state and grade, are also expected to teach content from social studies, science, and perhaps even more subjects depending on particular schools and needs.

Word work involves deepening a child's understanding of how the world works and incorporates ideas—and words—from outside the classroom. These ideas can be fiction-based, but they can also be based on nonfiction, research-based topics. Understanding that words have meaning and that this meaning is not limited to print in stories but also reaches to print online, on TV, and from the radio, deepens an understanding about communication and its uses and meanings.

Starting with a basic understanding, word work continues throughout a child's entire career in school and beyond. As students progress in school, they learn and understand the more specific rules that govern literature and nonfiction. These rules include the conventions of speaking, reading, and writing, such that students can make meaning for themselves, others, and the world around them. This communication is not limited to a language arts classroom, and curriculum design should always look at the larger picture of assessment, which is, "What is the child expected to learn and do?" Curriculum planning must involve the whole picture.

Communicating through writing

As students become more versed in each of the former components of language, they can begin to structure their own form of communication through writing. Early writing may not resemble what the world would consider a story; yet, those beginning steps in crafting a story with pictures and attempts at letters are vital for understanding how words are needed for communication of ideas to take place.

Emergent literacy also means emergent writing development, where students become adept at retelling stories, or telling new stories, using a growing list of skills. Curriculum design should not skip this necessary component in primary classrooms with the thought that the students cannot write full words or sentences. Playing with words also means that students should be allowed to express themselves on their own. Writing development, in many ways, is easier than reading development because students are not necessarily learning unknown symbols, but are creating their own. Developing writing literacy must encompass this first step so that students can see the full picture of communication. In other words, they should come to understand that having ideas, giving them sounds, and, finally, transferring those sounds into symbols is how we humans exchange information.

It is necessary to build opportunities into each day so that students can begin to synthesize all the knowledge coming their way. Reading and writing, listening and speaking—these concepts should always be taught together. One is simply not possible without the other. Students who don't practice one won't be able to develop the other. Connections with the outside world—with literature, TV, movies, and radio—occur only if an interactive classroom is planned. Any language arts and reading curriculum must address these components. Writing often gets left out or is thrown on the end as an assessment.

Writing is a crucial skill that all students must learn how to do well for a variety of reasons. Most, if not all, communication regarding student academic work is in the form of writing, especially as students progress throughout their academic career. Writing is an important part of every class, every subject, and every grade. Furthermore, writing becomes an important vehicle for communication on standardized tests, especially state standardized tests. Many tests have written components that measure the ability to communicate ideas through writing, but writing also becomes the vehicle for the content knowledge of other subjects. Students cannot be expected to write for assessments if they are never taught the processes and procedures for this type of communication. Assessments show students who are not learning to communicate through writing and cannot write about the knowledge that may be trapped in their head. The value of that knowledge must be expressed in some way, and many tests include written parts, in addition to multiple-choice questions.

It may seem this section doesn't address comprehension at all. Yet, each of the former components is necessary in order for comprehension to take place. Each component builds on a child's comprehension, whether oral, listening, or reading comprehension. If any of these steps are skipped in order to focus solely on comprehension, re-teaching of concepts and skills will have to take place. Comprehension can only be built when students understand that communication involves many parts:

>> Listening and speaking

>> Language study

>> Words as vehicles for ideas

>> Communicating through writing

Dealing with apprehension about teaching writing

Many teachers feel as if they should be a published writer before teaching writing. Others feel that they do not have the skills necessary for writing instruction; yet this couldn't be further from the truth. A good rule of thumb is this: If you are asking students to read and comprehend text, they should be able to write text in a similar way. Sure, their efforts won't be as polished, but the concept is the same. Always remember, the teacher is the expert, and the student is the apprentice. Apprentices must be able to work on writing if they are ever going to be able to use written words with any proficiency. Do not wait to teach it, thinking that next year's teacher can pick it up.

Giving Reading and Language Arts Instruction

Standards-based education reform has been at the forefront of national and state news for years. Such reforms set measurable goals for outcomes in order to improve educational processes and results. The 2001 No Child Left Behind Act precipitated the nationwide reform movement. The act requires increased accountability for teachers and schools and instruction grounded in scientifically based research. For reading and language arts, the National Reading Panel responded to a Congressional mandate that was designed to help parents, teachers, and policymakers identify the key skills central to the teaching of reading and language. The panel examined more than 100,000 studies and developed several criteria that addressed reading success and achievement. Part of that guide focused on five specific areas of reading: phonemic awareness, phonics, fluency, vocabulary, and text comprehension.

Each skill must be taught using proven methods so that all students, regardless of prior knowledge, disability, or first language learned, have the opportunity to learn to read and to read proficiently. This act led to further reforms within different states, but all follow a prescribed method, because it is based in scientifically proven research methods. Regardless of the state you are employed by, you will find these five specific areas of reading to be the main focus of any curriculum and instruction.

Phonemic awareness instruction

When a child has phonemic awareness, he has the ability to notice, think about, and work with the individual sounds of words, primarily spoken words, in the beginning of instructional practices. Before children can learn to read words, they have to be able to identify the sounds, or *phonemes,* that make up those words.

Phonemic awareness instruction should not happen in isolation. The best way to ensure that children are learning to read is to create a learning environment that is rich in print and sound. Stories should be read aloud often, and the same stories should be available to children to touch and practice with. Matching words that are spoken and heard to words that are printed, both in specific lessons and from stories, ensures that children develop phonemic awareness.

Example lessons

Simply having a print-rich environment doesn't ensure that every child is able to read. Specific lessons must be taught concerning phonemic awareness. Lessons should include having children manipulate and play with words and the sounds in words. Following are some examples of lessons to develop phonemic awareness.

TEACHING PHONEME ISOLATION

Purpose: Children will recognize a sound in a word.

Example: Directing a student to tell the sound, usually beginning or ending, in a word, as in, "What is the first sound in the word 'bird'?" The answer is /b/. If children can answer these types of questions repeatedly, they have mastered phoneme isolation.

TEACHING PHONEME IDENTIFICATION

Purpose: Children will recognize the same sounds that occur in different words.

Example: Directing a student to tell the sound, usually beginning or ending, in a series of words with the same sounds, as in "What is the same sound in the words, 'bird, bug, bus'?" The answer is /b/. If children can answer these types of questions repeatedly, they have mastered phoneme identification.

TEACHING PHONEME CATEGORIZATION

Purpose: Children will recognize which word does not belong in a set of words, categorizing similar sounds internally.

Example: Directing a student to tell which word doesn't fit in a group of words, as in, "Which word doesn't belong in this group of words, 'bird, bus, bug, tub'?" The answer is "tub." If children can answer these types of questions repeatedly, they have mastered phoneme categorization.

TEACHING PHONEME BLENDS

Purpose: Children will combine a set of phonemes to make a word.

Example: Directing a student to tell which word a set of sounds makes, as in, "What word is /b/, /u/, /s/?" The answer is "bus." If children can answer these types of questions repeatedly, they have mastered phoneme blending.

TEACHING PHONEME SEGMENTATION

Purpose: Children will break a word into separate sounds.

Example: Directing a student to tell how many sounds are in a word, as in, "How many sounds are in the word 'tug'?" The answer is three: /t/, /u/, /g/. If children can answer these types of questions repeatedly, they have mastered phoneme segmentation.

TEACHING PHONEME DELETION

Purpose: Children will recognize a word that remains when a sound, or phoneme, is removed.

Example: Directing a student to tell the word that remains when only one sound is removed, usually a beginning or ending sound, as in, "What is 'cart' without the /t/ sound?" The answer is "car." If children can answer these types of questions repeatedly, they have mastered phoneme deletion.

TEACHING PHONEME ADDITION

Purpose: Children will make a new word by adding a sound to an already existing word.

Example: Directing a student to make a new word by adding a specific sound to the word, usually at the beginning or ending of the word, as in, "What word do you get if you add the sound /s/ to the beginning of the word 'and'?" The answer is "sand." If children can answer these types of questions repeatedly, they have mastered phoneme addition.

TEACHING PHONEME SUBSTITUTION

Purpose: Children will recognize that changing one sound in a word can make a new word.

Example: Directing a student to tell the new word that can be made when a sound is substituted, usually at the beginning or ending of a word, as in, "The word I have is 'mat.' What would happen if we changed the /m/ in 'mat' to /b/?" The answer is "bat." If children can answer these types of questions repeatedly, they have mastered phoneme substitution.

Activities and assessment

Children's phonemic instruction should include various activities with words and sounds, and should provide opportunities for children to work with these sounds and words manipulatively. While direct instruction is important, small-group instruction is the fastest way to teach these lessons and ensure that every child masters the skills.

It is important to assess students as instruction is being given. This type of assessment must occur regularly, with each skill taught, so that redirection and reteaching can immediately follow instruction. Students who master phonemic awareness have a much easier time learning to read and spell. Students who do not master these skills, or do not master specific skills, struggle in learning to read and have difficulties comprehending text, either printed or when writing.

Phonemic awareness and phonological awareness are part of many state standards, and most limit the teaching of those skills to kindergarten through second grade. Students who do not master these skills by the end of second grade most likely have some life event, such as a specific disability, that prevents the learning of these sounds.

Phonics instruction

When a child masters phonemic awareness and understands that words are composed of different sounds and that these sounds can be manipulated, the next step is to teach the relationships between those sounds and the written letters represented by those sounds, also known as *the Alphabetic Principle.* Children need to understand that these symbols can also be manipulated to create ideas, words, sentences, and more. When enough symbols are known, children are able to look at a word and decode it, just as an Egyptologist might look at hieroglyphics and decode a message. The process is exactly the same and, for new learners, exactly as time-consuming, until all symbols and sounds are known.

For this reason, phonics instruction, or *phonemic decoding,* is not left solely upon the shoulders of primary, or early, education teachers. Phonics instruction can last longer, into middle-school grades, where the manipulations of sounds become more skilled and more difficult, as in rhyming, syllabification, and roots of words, like Greek and Latin roots. Many of the students in the later grades who require daily, regular phonics instruction are those students who are behind grade-level in reading, who have a disability that prevents learning of phonics, or who are categorized as ESL, ELL, or ESOL students.

Phonics instruction, like phonemic instruction, should not happen in isolation, but should be part of a print-rich educational environment, where students can play with words and language. Listening to stories, writing stories, and telling stories are all important and enhance the direct instruction of the teaching of phonics.

Phonics and word recognition standards are a part of the College and Career Readiness Standards as well as most state standards. While phonics is generally not a tested item on any state standardized test, specific word strategies and content often are. These standards have specific and targeted phonics instruction through fifth grade, which focuses on learning roots and affixes in order to decode and comprehend words in text.

Specific phonics instruction begins with developing *graphophonemic* relationships, the relationship between spoken sounds and written words. Learning to write the letters for the sounds students hear transitions to writing and reading longer words, then sentences, and then longer spans of ideas and information. Phonics instruction must be very systematic and explicit, so that the direct teaching of one skill is mastered by a student before a more difficult skill is attempted. Systematic and explicit phonics instruction benefits

>> A beginning reader's word recognition skills

>> A beginning writer's spelling skills

>> Reading comprehension, including oral, listening, and silent comprehension

>> Children from all social and economic levels, especially ones where homes are not rich in printed text

>> Children who are having trouble learning to read or who have been identified with a specific learning disability that inhibits learning to read

Many school districts purchase programs that do not offer specific phonics instruction. Schools that purchase literature-based programs, basal reading programs, whole-word programs, or sight-word programs need to add phonics instruction to that curriculum. Phonics instruction can be given to either a whole group or small groups, but it should be assessed on an individual basis so that specific skill needs can be met.

Vocabulary acquisition instruction

Each child comes to the classroom with a set of vocabulary words already learned. These are the words that children have learned socially, at home, and around friends. At school, children begin to work with an academic vocabulary, words that are learned at school and pertain to educational topics. These two types of vocabulary are not always separated. While it is true that students will have a different set of words they use around friends and at home, the words they learn at school will enhance the vocabulary they use on a regular and daily basis. As a matter of fact, studies have shown that people with larger vocabularies are thought to be more intelligent. Think of the life applications for students with richer vocabulary: They most certainly will test better on any given test; they will apply for scholarships using vocabulary more likely to appeal to admission officers; and they will more likely impress any potential employer during interviews. A strong and broad vocabulary is an important skill for every student to cultivate, regardless of future academic goals.

Many teachers assume that vocabulary instruction resembles memorizing word lists and taking a test, or using a set of random words in a story. Effective vocabulary acquisition instruction, though, must be taught as deliberately and explicitly as phonemic awareness and phonics. If vocabulary is to be remembered long-term—longer than for a test or for a class—then instruction must model those methods most likely to result in long-term knowledge storage.

The true goal of phonics and phonemic instruction is to give students skills they need to decode and understand new words they encounter. If the basic foundational reading skills are not mastered, independent vocabulary acquisition is unlikely to occur. These students will not be able to tackle new words and will not have a working vocabulary that is academic in nature. They will have to rely solely on a social vocabulary, words they learn in social situations. Students who do not build an academic vocabulary will be unable to read fluently and to comprehend text.

Three specific strategies allow for a beginning instruction in vocabulary acquisition. These are

>> Teaching students strategies to decode words into smaller word parts, or even into phonemes. This is a strategy that even adults use when encountering new and unknown words.

>> Providing ample practice with academic vocabulary learned at school. If you want students to know and use social studies and science words, then those words must become part of a working vocabulary. That will only happen with practice. Think of a football team learning

a new play. If the only place they hear and see the play is during a coach's speech, they are unlikely to do it well. Instead, they must practice repeatedly until the play is learned. Academic vocabulary follows the same principle. The harder the words are, the more time and work is needed for long-term memory storage and *automaticity,* using the word automatically without thinking about it.

>> Teaching students strategies that lead to vocabulary independence. If students always rely on teachers to give them sets of words to memorize, they aren't likely to enlarge their academic vocabulary very much by the end of any class year. Instead, students must be deliberately and explicitly taught what to do when they encounter an unknown word to discover what the word means and how it sounds. If students don't know how the word sounds, they are unlikely to learn and use it. Most words are learned this way, indirectly, when students are reading or just living life.

Four different types of vocabulary must be considered when providing instruction:

>> **Listening vocabulary:** Words a person recognizes and understands when listening to speech or to text being read aloud

>> **Reading vocabulary:** Words a person recognizes and understands when reading aloud or silently

>> **Speaking vocabulary:** Words a person knows when speaking aloud

>> **Writing vocabulary:** Words a person knows when writing, either formally or informally

Students generally have larger listening vocabularies than any other kind of vocabulary, and, if assessed, can be seen to have listening vocabularies perhaps grades ahead of their current life situation. This is because students learn words by listening to others talk around them, by listening to TV and radio, and by listening to the words read to them by teachers. While they might never use a word in reading or writing, they might add it to their speaking vocabulary.

Specific vocabulary acquisition instruction should focus on effective word-learning strategies, such as:

>> Developing word walls in classrooms to expose students to how words look, not just how they sound (furthering the graphophonemic connections)

>> Teaching specific sets of words that must be known for a unit and that may be unknown in a story

>> Allowing students to play with words by creating their own sets of dictionaries or playing word games

>> Using academic words often, not just during a lesson or as an assignment

>> Having students read aloud

>> Having discussions about printed text, whether from books, newspaper, or the Internet

>> Giving students time to practice silent reading

>> Teaching students how to use dictionaries, especially online dictionaries that provide spoken pronunciation, and other reference aids to assist in unknown word meanings

>> Teaching word families and, later, word parts, such as Greek and Latin root words, to aid in decoding harder words as students progress through school

>> Using context clues to figure out the meanings of unknown words from clues in the surrounding text

>> Repeatedly exposing students to new words

>> Reading stories aloud to students beyond the early elementary years

Reading aloud to students must never be considered a waste of time, even as students progress through ages and grades. As students mature, many become less likely to read for pleasure. It is entirely possible that the only stories some children experience are those stories read aloud to them at school. Studies show that the vocabulary in fiction stories is much more difficult and expansive than the words in nonfiction text, which is often focused on a single topic.

Assessment of vocabulary is often conducted as vocabulary quizzes. You want to ensure, though, that long-term storage of important academic words occurs so that students will be able to read and write these words on state standardized tests. Vocabulary quizzes are not the best type of assessment to ensure vocabulary acquisition is taking place. Rather, students' usage of the words in reading, writing, and speaking is a much better measure of word knowledge.

Reading with fluency

For the most part, students must master the previously mentioned foundational reading skills before they will be able to read text with fluency. Reading with fluency means that a student is able to read a given text clearly, quickly, and accurately. A student who gets stuck on a word and has to decode it slowly is not reading fluently. Reading with fluency is important. It allows students to stop focusing so much on decoding words and more on comprehending the text. Fluent readers can both comprehend and decode words at the same time.

Being a fluent reader means recognizing words automatically, pronouncing words correctly and without hesitation, reading aloud effortlessly, reading with expression, and sounding natural as reading occurs.

Therefore, students should have already mastered phonemic awareness and, on some level, phonics instruction and vocabulary acquisition, before they can read fluently. However, since the given text is on grade-level, even young students can read some text fluently.

Reading with fluency, like all the other foundational reading skills, must be explicitly and directly taught to students. While a few students may have naturally beautiful reading voices and habits, the vast majority of students will have to be taught the skills that are inherent in reading out loud. Instructional classroom activities to practice fluency include reading aloud to an adult or more competent reader, reading chorally with a group, reading along with a prerecorded voice, reading with a partner, and participating in a readers' theatre.

Reading with fluency is an instructional skill that should begin as soon as a child can read and should continue in early middle grades. It may take longer for some students, particularly those with developmental delays, identified reading problems, or who read below grade level. Reading with fluency is not the same as merely oral reading, or reading out loud. Instructions should be focused on having a child read a text multiple times so that comprehension is improved and familiarity with the text leads to better reading. Fluency is not necessarily a surprise reading task where an unknown text is given to a student who has never seen it before. Rather, fluency is checking to see that students can fluidly read text on a certain reading level independently, modeling the kind of reading that should occur within a student's brain when she is reading silently.

There are three different levels of text, for the purpose of fluency. These are

> » **Independent reading level text:** Text that is easy for a student to read, or text where no more than one mistake in 20 words is made.
>
> » **Instructional level text:** Text that is challenging but manageable, where one mistake is made for each ten words.
>
> » **Frustration level text:** Text that is difficult for the reader, where more than one mistake for each ten words occurs.

Texts given to students should not be on grade level, but should instead be on a student's independent reading level. When students repeatedly read on or above grade level with no mistakes and comprehend what they read, fluency no longer needs to be an instructional practice in a classroom.

Comprehension of text instruction

All of the previous foundational reading skills discussed build to this, the top of the mountain for readers—understanding text and speech. Comprehension is the reason for reading, the reason for learning to read, and the reason that educational reforms exist in the first place. When assessments are given and results are measured, what is being tested is comprehension.

However, the teaching of comprehension and comprehension strategies can't wait until students have mastered all the previous foundational reading skills. Rather, students should be taught comprehension skills and strategies while they are learning the other foundational reading skills. Even students who do not know any letters, any graphemes to correspond with the phonemes they are learning, can still comprehend words that are spoken to them, stories that are read to them, and even symbols that they see. Any toddler who has ever eaten at McDonald's can probably recognize the "M" in the McDonald's sign and knows that it signifies food.

When teaching comprehension, it's important to know that there are three different kinds of comprehension, and all of them are measured and addressed by College and Career Readiness Standards in some way. The types of comprehension are

> » **Listening comprehension:** What is understood when listening to a speaker or a text being read aloud. It is understanding words that are spoken.
>
> » **Oral comprehension:** What is understood when speaking or reading aloud. Some students can understand a story if another person reads it aloud, but if they read the same story themselves, even if they make no decoding mistakes, they often don't understand much of what they read. In this way, fluency is often mistaken for *automaticity*. Automaticity is best understood like the functions of a robot—while speaking is occurring, the brain just isn't comprehending what is being read.
>
> » **Reading comprehension:** What is understood when reading silently.

Generally, only reading comprehension is measured on any state standardized test. However, for academic purposes, all types of comprehension should be measured with instruction in the classroom, because communication involves all three types of comprehension.

Text comprehension is generally taught through a series of comprehension strategies, which students use to scaffold their own learning and interdependence with text. The apprentice-to-expert theory holds true here. A teacher giving instruction in comprehension should always model what is going on inside her head while reading is occurring. These mental models, or mental maps, should be made directly and explicitly available while the text is being read so that students can see and understand how to train their own brain to read and comprehend text. As students see this repetition over and over, they can begin to track when their own comprehension is lagging. Without this type of repetitive instruction, comprehension will not become an independent task but will always rely on the master. Instead, the scaffolding, as in a mental model, should be adjusted gradually so that students use only those braces they need. As independence with text grows, the scaffolds are dismantled.

However, dismantling is also a repetitive process. While other foundational skills—phonemic awareness, phonics, and fluency—are gradually mastered, comprehension, like vocabulary acquisition, never really is. As students become better able to manipulate certain types of text, more difficult skills are added to the standards that students have to know and are expected to perform. The range, complexity, and quality of the text changes to accommodate the grade level and maturity of the student. For example, a kindergarten standard would require a student to recognize the structure of a poem as opposed to a story. A standard from grade 12 would require a student to analyze satire or multiple points of view in a poem. Comprehension instruction must match what is being assessed so that students are being prepared for further comprehension instruction and mastery.

While comprehension instruction includes many different components and types of text, the following are common guiding instructional practices that should always be included in lessons to understand text:

>> Making use of prior knowledge

>> Mental mapping and modeling of thoughts

>> Using graphic and semantic organizers

>> Generating and answering questions as text is being read

>> Recognizing text structure

>> Anticipating the purpose of reading

>> Summarizing ideas from reading

As with the other foundational skills, comprehension monitoring should take place as instruction is given, not just assessed at the end. When students begin to struggle with a specific skill or type of text, reteaching and redirection is needed immediately. This is so that comprehension skills can be mastered and students are able to move to the next level, whatever that may be. Effective instruction always includes direct explanation, modeling, guided practice (the monitoring of comprehension), and application. Assessment is not an end task here either; assessment must occur as the student is practicing. While there are multiple strategies that can be used, text comprehension instruction should always bridge the gap between the standard that is expected and the ability of each individual student. In this way, comprehension is not necessarily *taught*. Rather, it is developed over time.

Helping students learn to read literature and informational text

As can be seen from the previous sections, the comprehension of text is a process that occurs over time. It is not a destination as much as it is a journey for students in schools. Each of the foundational reading skills must be taught individually, with explicit and direct instruction, but they must also be incorporated into larger chunks of meaning and instruction. These instructional units immerse students into genres of writing. There are only two types of writing, or text: fiction and nonfiction.

>> **Fiction** is all work that is imaginative in nature. This includes literature, poetry, drama, fables, and myths. If it is not real and did not really occur or cannot occur, it is made up, or fiction. Generally, fiction is read for the purpose of enjoyment.

>> **Nonfiction** is all work that is real. This includes a huge range of work that is informational, or *expository,* in nature such as textbooks, speeches, reports, documentaries, and so on. Generally, nonfiction is read for the purpose of acquiring information about a topic.

Students will have standards for both types of writing throughout their academic career. Specific instructional practices must be taught that address the specific text formats and features of each type of writing. Each type of writing calls for the use of specific instructional strategies and methods so that students can comprehend the text. Even if they can read the words fluently, if they are unsure how to read a pamphlet, for example, comprehension may suffer because the information is formatted differently.

However, certain strategies and skills do apply to both types of writing. Both types of writing must be understood through a process of identifying the main idea and details, the summarizing of ideas, and the retelling of those concepts. Construction of the meaning of the text is generally understood when students can complete all of those tasks about any given text, whether fiction or nonfiction. The only exception might be with some types of poetry.

Developing students' writing skills

Just as students become more familiar with language—understanding that small chunks of sounds and letters can add up to larger meanings—students will also begin their own communicative processes where they start to write for meaning, using the proficiencies they have attained. Writing, like reading, is a developmental process that matches the type of instruction being given. So, as students learn what the letter "a" sounds like, they will begin to write that letter. As they learn phonics, they will begin to write words. As they learn new words, they will begin to write them. That instructional process must continue. As students are exposed to longer and more difficult kinds of text in stories and reports, they should be expected to model those types of reading in their own writing. Only in that way can they move from the apprentice level to the expert level in writing. It is not enough for writing to be a personal task—the taking of notes and recording of answers. Instead, writing should be a communication of ideas across all subjects and contents and should happen as often as the other kinds of communication, reading and speaking.

Early childhood writings are exemplified by simple stories with a few sentences and journal writing. Eventually, these stories build into paragraphs and then begin to model more difficult kinds of text as more examples of genres are taught. Students should be given daily opportunities to write and to record their process of learning. Examples include journals and reflections, but students should also have opportunities to write for the purpose of communicating with others— teachers and peers, family and friends. Writing will never become masterful if the teacher is the only recipient. The audience must include others in the outside world, the real world where reading and speech occur.

Improving students' understanding of the English language

In order to more effectively communicate through written words, students must be taught and allowed to practice the mechanics, spelling, and grammar rules that govern mastery of the English language. Most standardized tests have sections that test for this very thing. Each state plus College and Career Readiness Standards give specific outlines for the curriculum implementation of these skills.

Teaching these skills, though, is very different from the previously discussed foundational skills. While most beginning lessons focus on the use of simple punctuation, like using periods, later instructional lessons focus on clauses, phrases, and the analytical use of grammar and language skills. Instruction should be explicit and specific. However, instruction must also take into account that these types of skills are no longer foundational skills, as opposed to content knowledge. Content knowledge is taught in different ways and with different approaches than foundational reading skills. The foundational reading skills support the comprehension and ability of students to understand and exhibit content knowledge. Instructional lessons concerning language should also be modeled, but there should be an understanding that students have to know a concept, as opposed to only having to read and understand a concept. In other words, language conventions are not necessarily skills, as much as they are specific pieces of knowledge that must be learned and incorporated into the writing that students are performing in the classroom.

Advancing students' speaking and listening styles

Just as silent language mastery is important, so are speaking and listening. The attainment of these communication skills must be purposely taught, explicitly and directly. These skills involve listening critically to ideas and knowing the differences between formal and informal speech, which includes a variety of genres for different purposes and audiences.

Many state standards and College and Career Readiness Standards specifically address communication through media, such as listening to and comprehending speeches. Always remember that the purpose of learning to read isn't just to be able to look at words on a page and know what they mean. Communication revolves around speaking and listening, and reading and writing. Lessons that start in kindergarten must continue as students give presentations and speeches of their own work and ideas, and evaluate and analyze the work and ideas of their peers and others in the world. While some students will never read a book after they leave high school, comprehending what is spoken is a vital life skill that must be developed, and taught, within the language arts curriculum. Again, a good rule to remember is this: If students are supposed to be reading something for content and skill, then they should be able to model that with their own writing and speaking.

Conducting Reading and Language Arts Assessment

Reading and language arts assessments can take a variety of forms but can be divided into two different types: One assessment measures the attainment of knowledge or a set of curricula or standard, most often assessed through a standardized test yearly; the other is an assessment given multiple times a year, sometimes weekly or more, that measures how students are progressing—or failing to progress—toward language mastery. Both assessments must occur along the learning path, with the understanding that failure to master foundational reading skills will inhibit knowledge acquisition. In other words, failure to progress toward the mastery of language will affect standardized tests that measure content. If students cannot silently read and write well, even if they can verbally give content knowledge, they will likely fail a standardized test.

Knowledge of curricula and standards

These assessments must measure the progress that students are making toward a standardized set of knowledge-level or performance descriptors, usually determined by state, district, or another governing or chosen body. These assessments measure the attainment of knowledge as opposed to skill. Each state and College and Career Readiness Standards have practice tests, which often guide curriculum development for states, districts, and classrooms. These tests are designed to measure the standards that have been taught during a given period of time. Teachers have little or no influence over the tests, other than administering them.

Knowledge of language mastery

Teachers do, though, have complete influence over language mastery assessment. These assessments measure how students are progressing, or failing to progress, against a standard of language acquisition. These assessments measure the foundational reading skills, initially, but continue beyond those early childhood years into areas of fluency and comprehension. Failure of students to master the foundational reading skills will inhibit the growth of knowledge and can be seen most easily through assessment of fluency and comprehension. Further instruction is necessary to correct these foundational reading skills so that knowledge mastery can continue.

Sequences of instruction should include the corresponding sequence of assessments. In other words, if students cannot master a specific skill, then redirection and further instruction should take place immediately, not at the end of the year. For each foundational skill taught, immediate assessment should be given. While that can sometimes be as simple as having children recognize and read letters on a series of cards or read words from a list, checking for fluency and comprehension takes more work.

Running records

Running records, as an assessment tool, are the best way to measure all the foundational reading skills and can be adapted easily to check for a specific skill, as well as adapted for both age and developmental disability. While there are programs which can be purchased with ready-made materials, these can also be easily made by a teacher. Including running records during instruction gives teachers immediate knowledge of what should be taught next, or retaught. Running records can assess a variety of skills, including decoding of phonetic elements, miscues of words and sounds, oral reading behaviors leading to more fluid reading, and text difficulty for individual students, as well as more specific foundational reading skills.

During a running record, students are given a piece of preselected text to read. As the student reads, the teacher makes notes, based on a set of predetermined learning objectives. Analysis of the running records, and of a series of records, for an individual student can allow a teacher to determine which specific missing skill is causing decoding and comprehension problems.

Retelling analysis

Another assessment, *retelling analysis,* pinpoints more specifically problems that students are having with comprehension, as opposed to accuracy with words. As children progress through a mastery of the foundational reading skills, the retelling analysis can show the teacher which scaffolding techniques are needed to aid individual students with comprehension. During a retelling, a student tells the teacher what he remembers from a text. The text can be fiction or nonfiction, and can be directed to include specific elements of language or genre so that a quick check of attainment of standards is being given. Retellings are the best way to measure for all the content knowledge that students are expected to have and exemplify. Retellings are also quick ways to check for the content knowledge within writing samples, ensuring that all three forms of communication—written, spoken, and read—are being assessed.

Answering Reading and Language Arts Practice Questions

The Praxis is divided up into these areas:

>> Assessment and diagnostic teaching of reading

>> Reading development

>> Writing in support of reading

Assessment and diagnostic teaching of reading

These questions focus on the foundational skills of reading—how to teach as well as how to assess them. Another important component of this type of question focuses on the instruction that must be given when students do not progress in attaining a continued mastery.

Reading development

These questions focus on five different areas:

>> Phonemic awareness and oral language development

>> Phonics and the alphabetic principle

>> Word analysis skills and vocabulary development

>> Development of reading fluency and comprehension

>> Reading comprehension strategies across genres

Writing in support of reading

This area of the test has two different components:

>> The interdependence of reading and writing development

>> Reading and writing as tools for inquiry and research

Chapter 11

Mathematics Curriculum, Instruction, and Assessment

We talked earlier about the foundational terms and concepts of elementary math. If you feel like you have a good understanding of those, then now is a really good time for you to proceed with the mathematics part of your preparation for the Praxis Elementary Education: Curriculum, Instruction, and Assessment test.

Chapter 5, the chapter on math content knowledge, is the weapons warehouse on your warpath toward full preparation for your coming test. You are not in that warehouse right now. You are now in the training center that shows you how to use your weapons. If you see that you have dropped any of your weapons, you can go back to Chapter 5 to get them back.

Although the Chapter 5 preparation is a foundation for the principles discussed in this chapter, your understanding of the content knowledge chapter can be further improved by this one. We discuss many of the instruction methods you will need to know for your test, and learning those methods helps secure foundational knowledge not only for students, but also for teachers.

Calculating a Mathematics Curriculum

Planning a schedule and a methodology for an elementary mathematics course — and really any math course — needs to be rooted in an understanding of what concepts need to be understood before others can be learned. For example, in this book, we present math content knowledge before this chapter on application of the knowledge. A mathematics education is like a wall composed of many bricks that are made of smaller bricks, which are made of even smaller bricks, and so forth. A math teacher needs to have an understanding of what concepts are parts of bigger concepts in order to know what to teach first. The best way to develop a clear perspective on how to arrange a math curriculum accordingly is to thoroughly understand the concepts that are to be taught. The better you understand the math content and teaching methods, the better you will know what to teach when. This applies to arranging concepts within a lesson and also to arranging lessons within a time frame.

One of the major issues to consider in forming a mathematics curriculum is the potential for student misconceptions. Misunderstanding of foundational material can hinder a student's learning process, so a teacher needs to be ready to clear up misconceptions before proceeding to higher levels. A teacher's awareness of this too is best strengthened by a knowledge of content and instruction methods.

REMEMBER

The major purpose of modern elementary math is to help students relate mathematical concepts to the real world, which is why teachers need to focus on connecting math knowledge to things that go on in the world, including the learning of other school subjects. Math is not all about the numbers.

Providing Mathematics Instruction

This part of the chapter covers the meat of what you need to know about the mathematics section of the Praxis Elementary Education test. The instruction methods covered and the content foundation they are rooted in help you attain the pure knowledge and the basis for critical thinking that you need to take your test successfully. We are about to get into a large spectrum of elementary math teaching tools and methods. This is where you get to see a very clear view of what you need to know about elementary math for your test.

In many areas of math, manipulatives are very useful for learning about concepts. *Manipulatives* are objects students can use to understand numbers and how to work with them. A lot of the methods discussed in this section involve various types of manipulatives.

New methods for teaching math to elementary students have developed and become mainstream in recent times. The more modern methods are generally focused on giving students broader understandings of what is involved in approaches to math problems and why the approaches work the way they do. Traditional methods are still used, but strategies newer to the mainstream are designed to clarify mathematical concepts in general in order to make more sense of the traditional algorithms and to, in some cases, create simpler routes to answers to problems.

TIP

A modern mainstream approach to a type of problem should be taught before the traditional approach, because the modern algorithms typically create bases for student understanding of why the classic strategies work.

Teaching the major categories of numbers and operations

The most basic level of teaching math to elementary school students is teaching them what numbers are. Since base 10 is the system that is taught in American elementary schools and almost everywhere else, base-10 blocks are a powerful tool that can be used to teach elementary students the natures of base 10. This tool helps students understand place value and how it relates to the full value of a number. Base-10 sticks, base-10 chips, and other such manipulatives are also used to help students gain perspectives on the fundamental natures of numbers. *Base-10 blocks* are arguably the best of all the manipulatives because one type of unit block is used to form the tens blocks (rods) as well as hundreds blocks (flats) and thousands blocks (cubes). Base-10 blocks illustrate place value very effectively. However, other types of manipulatives also work well, and you can use very simple ones to demonstrate the principles of how to use manipulatives.

Using base-10 manipulatives to illustrate the natures of numbers

The following diagram illustrates the use of base-10 blocks to teach students the value of the number 24. The longer blocks represent tens, and the smaller blocks represent ones. When all the blocks are put together, students can see that 24 is two sets of ten plus four ones.

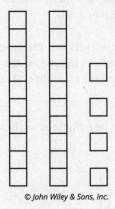
© John Wiley & Sons, Inc.

Places beyond the tens can also be represented by base-10 manipulatives. The following arrangement uses base-10 sticks. The largest represent hundreds, the next largest symbolize tens, and the smallest are representative of ones. The number presented by these base-10 sticks is 346.

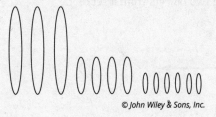
© John Wiley & Sons, Inc.

Fractions can also be represented by base-10 manipulatives. A type of chip, for example, could be given a value of 1/4. Other types of chips could be given other values. In the diagram here, the larger chips symbolize ones and the smaller chips denote 1/3 each. The value of the number the chips represent is 1 2/3.

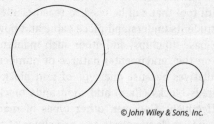

© John Wiley & Sons, Inc.

Base-10 manipulatives can be used for more than merely representing numbers. They can also be used for showing how operations work, making calculations, and demonstrating how properties of operations work and why they work the ways they do.

Helping students understand addition and subtraction

Four major operations can be performed with numbers, and there are different rules for performing them with the various types of numbers. Modern approaches to computation and enhancing understanding cover every possible combination. However, elementary math does not. We cover the major approaches for each combination used in elementary-level math.

Teacher instructions for elementary addition and subtraction cover very simple problems up to adding and subtracting decimal numbers with many digits. Those operations on the most basic level are well demonstrated and performed with the use of manipulatives, which can also be used at higher levels of addition and subtraction.

Consider the really basic addition problem 1 + 2. One square can be combined with 2 squares to get 3 squares.

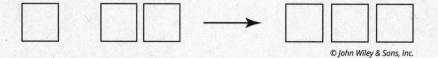

© John Wiley & Sons, Inc.

Basic subtraction can be shown similarly, except manipulatives are removed in the process.

The problem 3 − 2 can be worked by removing two objects from a set of 3.

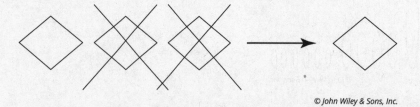

© John Wiley & Sons, Inc.

Addition with larger numbers is traditionally performed by lining up the numbers vertically, with columns of numbers that are in the same places, and adding the digits in each place. If the result of adding digits in a column goes beyond the base-10 limit, the resulting number's digit on the right is put on the sum line and the digit on the left is carried to the next place column, except the last column sum is written entirely on the sum line. The following problem presents the traditional method for adding 489, 286, and 134.

```
  21
 489
 286
+134
 909
```

When decimals are involved, the process is the same as long as the decimal points are lined up.

```
  21
 48.9
 28.6
+13.4
 90.9
```

Addition with multiple-digit numbers can also involve base-10 manipulatives. Objects with different sizes representing different places can be put together to get sums. Suppose you want to show a student how to add 231 and 412. You can ask the student to represent both numbers with base-10 objects and then combine the objects.

© John Wiley & Sons, Inc.

$$231 + 412 = 643$$

When base-10 manipulatives are used for adding and a place limit is exceeded, ten objects of a place can be put together and replaced by an object of the next highest place, or else counted together as an object representing a 1 in that place. Suppose a student is trying to add 38 and 24. She can use base-10 sticks or another type of manipulative.

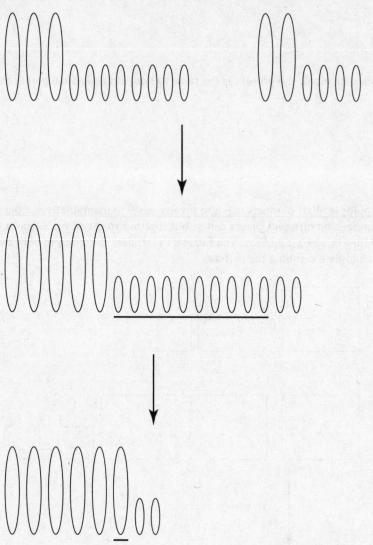

© John Wiley & Sons, Inc.

One of the advantages of base-10 blocks is that ten blocks representing units can be physically put together and attached to form one tens block, called a *rod*.

A common modern strategy of addition that does not involve the use of manipulatives is the *partial sums* method. It is also known as *partitioning*. A major advantage of the method is that it clearly illustrates the role and significance of place value in addition. This strategy entails adding place values as full numbers instead of representing them with single digits through the entire process. If the number 497 is added in partitioning, the 9 is written as 90 because that is what it represents, and 4 is written as 400 since that is its true meaning. The fully written values are what are really being added with the traditional method. With partial sums, the fully written values are added in groups based on place. Then, those sums are added to yield the answer to the problem.

$$427$$
$$+\underline{531}$$
$$400 + 500 = 900$$
$$20 + 30 = 50$$
$$1 + 7 = 8$$
$$900 + 50 + 8 = 958$$
$$427 + 531 = 958$$

As with addition, subtraction with multiple-digit numbers can be performed with manipulatives. To perform subtraction with that method, instead of adding the objects to each other, students can take away one type of object from both groups until there are none left to represent the *subtrahend*, the number being subtracted. Suppose you ask a student to find the answer to 437 − 215. Use of base-10 objects can reveal the difference.

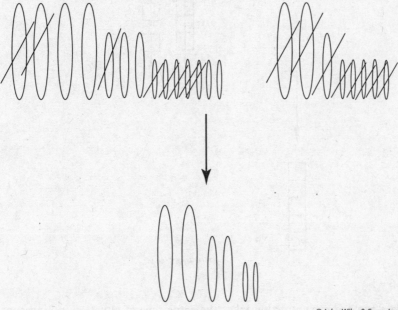

© John Wiley & Sons, Inc.

$$437 - 215 = 222$$

Base-10 blocks are a good choice for subtraction when a place value in the subtrahend is greater than its corresponding place value in the *minuend* (the number from which the subtrahend is subtracted) because of the shortage of blocks representing a place in the minuend in such problems. When the objects representing a place are used up, it is necessary to cut into the next-highest place value, and base-10 blocks are set up for that because some place objects are composed of smaller place objects. Suppose you want to teach a student the concepts involved in subtracting 15 from 20.

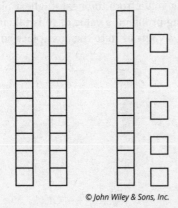

© John Wiley & Sons, Inc.

An issue with taking away blocks for this problem is that after one rod is taken from each set, all that remains is a rod in the first set and 5 unit blocks in the second set. However, because each rod is made up of 10 units, 5 of the units making up the remaining rod can be taken away.

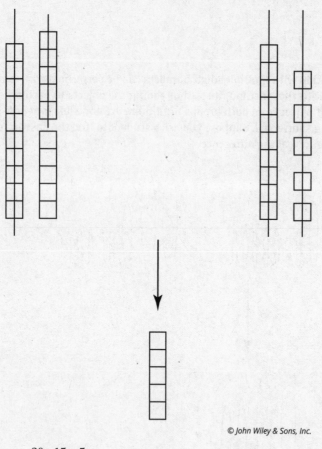

© John Wiley & Sons, Inc.

$20 - 15 = 5$

The standard method of subtraction takes the same type of situation into account. On a more basic level, the method simply involves putting the subtrahend under the minuend, lining up places vertically, and subtracting the bottom digits from the top digits.

$$\begin{array}{r} 975 \\ -\ 842 \\ \hline 133 \end{array}$$

The situation of a digit being subtracted from a lower digit in a multiple-digit subtraction problem can be worked out with the traditional method. It involves *regrouping*, which is making subtraction of a digit from a lower digit possible by taking value from the next-highest place value. Regrouping is also called "borrowing." In the following problem, a value of 10 is taken from the tens place by subtracting the 8 by one digit and giving a value of 10 to the ones place so the 2 can be turned into a 12.

$$\begin{array}{r} 7\,12 \\ 782 \\ -\ 524 \\ \hline 258 \end{array}$$

As with the traditional approach to addition with multiple-digit numbers, decimals do not change the process, aside from being there and needing to be lined up.

$$
\begin{array}{r}
\overset{7\,12}{} \\
78.2 \\
-\,52.4 \\
\hline
25.8
\end{array}
$$

A more modern teaching instruction for subtraction involving multiple-digit numbers without the use of manipulatives is called *counting up*. The method involves starting with the subtrahend and counting up to the minuend in steps that involve getting to round numbers that are easy to work with. After that, all the numbers that were added are combined, and their sum is the difference for the subtraction problem. That approach can be used for the previous subtraction problem, 782 – 524.

$$
\begin{array}{r}
524 \\
+\,6 \\
\hline
530 \\
+70 \\
\hline
600 \\
+100 \\
\hline
700 \\
+\,82 \\
\hline
782
\end{array}
$$

The counting up reached 782, the minuend in the subtraction problem. The next step is to add the numbers that have plus signs beside them.

$$
\begin{array}{r}
6 \\
70 \\
100 \\
+82 \\
\hline
258
\end{array}
$$

$$782 - 524 = 258$$

As shown previously, adding with decimals can be done with the traditional method. The partial sums method can also be used, with values represented after decimal points added in the process. An instruction strategy that can help students understand the nature of adding and subtracting decimal numbers uses sets of squares that can be shaded to represent portions of 10 or a multiple of 10. Those tools are very effective for students who are beginners at adding and subtracting with decimals. Suppose a student is adding 0.04 and 0.03. She can start with a set that has 4 of the 10 squares shaded and then shade 3 more. Next, she can count the total number of tenths that resulted.

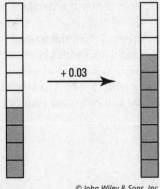

Sets that are 10 by 10 are called 100 *grids*. They can be used for adding and subtracting with numbers that have two digits after the decimal. When digits precede the decimal, the represented whole numbers can be combined, and fully shaded sets can also be used.

Fractions can be added or subtracted when they have common denominators. The traditional method of adding or subtracting fractions is to multiply the numerator and denominator of a fraction by the same number in order to get the necessary denominator, and to do that for every fraction for which it is necessary. Then, the numerators are added and the common denominator remains.

$$\frac{1}{4} + \frac{1}{2} = \frac{1}{4} + \frac{1(2)}{2(2)}$$
$$= \frac{1}{4} + \frac{2}{4}$$
$$= \frac{3}{4}$$

Subtraction involves the same method, except with subtraction instead of addition.

A popular and useful modern technique is to get *cross products* of the numerators and denominators. They are obtained by multiplying the numerator of the first fraction and denominator of the second fraction to get a product and then multiplying the denominator of the first fraction and the numerator of the second fraction to get a second product. Those two products become the new numerators, and the new denominator is the product of the denominators in the problem. The method works because of the principles involved in the classic method, but a shortcut is used.

$$\frac{2}{5} + \frac{1}{7} = \frac{2(7) + 1(5)}{5(7)}$$
$$= \frac{14 + 5}{35}$$
$$= \frac{19}{35}$$

$$\frac{3}{8} - \frac{1}{4} = \frac{3(4) - 1(8)}{8(4)}$$
$$= \frac{12 - 8}{32}$$
$$= \frac{4}{32}$$
$$= \frac{1}{8}$$

Instructing students on multiplication and division

Many of the major teaching strategies for multiplication and division parallel those of addition and subtraction. In all four areas, traditional methods are often used, but effective modern ones are employed as well to put focus on the elements of operations, the significance of those elements, and how they are connected. The modern methods help clarify the standard methods.

Simple multiplication is often demonstrated with manipulatives. Use of them helps students see with their eyes what multiplication is and how it works. They can watch objects actually multiply by a certain number, which can be shown by taking a given number of manipulatives and copying them a certain number of times. For example, to multiply 2 by 3, a student could use 2 objects and create a set of 3 of those sets. Then, the student can count the resulting number of objects.

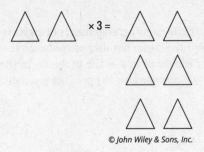
© John Wiley & Sons, Inc.

$$2 \times 3 = 6$$

Division with manipulatives is more of a challenge. One form of it is taking a certain number of objects and dividing them into equal groups. The number of objects in each group is the answer to the division problem. Consider the problem $6 \div 3$.

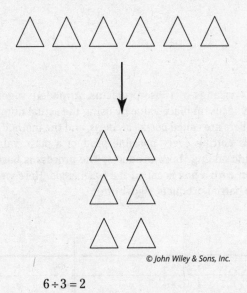
© John Wiley & Sons, Inc.

$$6 \div 3 = 2$$

The arrangement also demonstrates that $6 \div 2 = 3$.

The classic algorithm for multiplying multiple-digit numbers has one factor on top of the other. A digit in the bottom factor is multiplied by the top number, digit by digit, and then the next bottom factor digit goes through the same process. When place limits are exceeded, digits are carried as they are in classic addition. Since each digit in the bottom factor is in a place a notch up from the previous, a zero is put at the end of the second digit's product, two zeros at the end of the third's, and so forth. Then, the resulting products are added to give the answer to the problem. The addition is performed in accordance with the traditional model of multiple-digit addition. The following method shows the classic method for multiplying 326 and 483.

$$
\begin{array}{r}
1\ 2 \\
2\ 4 \\
1 \\
326 \\
\times\ 483 \\
\hline
978 \\
26080 \\
\underline{130400} \\
157458 \\
\end{array}
$$

$$326 \times 483 = 157,458$$

Traditional multiplication of decimal numbers with the same arrangements of digits is an identical process, except the product has a decimal point the same number of spaces to the left of the last digit as the number of digits there are after decimal places in the problem. In the following example, there are three digits after decimals in the problem, so the product has a decimal point placed three digits to the left.

$$
\begin{array}{r}
1\,2 \\
2\,4 \\
1 \\
32.6 \\
\times \quad 4.83 \\
\hline
978 \\
26080 \\
130400 \\
\hline
157.458
\end{array}
$$

$$32.6 \times 4.83 = 157.458$$

Notice the role place value plays in the workings of those problems. A modern algorithm for multiple-digit multiplication puts a heavy focus on place value by using the actual numbers represented by digits. Products of those numbers are called *partial products,* and the method is known as the *partial products algorithm.* It entails getting every possible product a place value in one number and a place value in the other, and adding those products. The process is based on the distributive property. Use of the algorithm with a box is called the *box method.* Here we multiply 326 and 483 again, but this time with the partial products algorithm.

$$326 \times 483$$

Place Values	400	80	3
300	120,000	24,000	900
20	8,000	1,600	60
6	2,400	480	18

$$120,000 + 24,000 + 900 + 8,000 + 1,600 + 60 + 2,400 + 480 + 18 = 157,458$$
$$326 \times 483 = 157,458$$

The classic method for dividing with multiple-digit numbers is *long division.* It involves putting the dividend in a long division symbol and dividing the divisor into the numbers formed by just some of the digits in the dividend, starting on the left. The maximum number of times the divisor goes into such a number is written above the last digit in the derived number, and the result is multiplied by the divisor and written under the dividend digits that were used. The difference of the number they form and the product written under it has the next digit in the dividend put right after it to form a new number, and then the process starts over. The process repeats at least until a resulting difference is less than the divisor or no digit from the dividend can be put after the difference. The remaining number is the *remainder,* or amount left over after the divisor can no longer be divided into any numbers. However, a decimal followed by zeros can be put to the right of the dividend, in which case the quotient can be a decimal number and no remainder needs to be given because the digits after the decimal represent the same quantity.

$$
\begin{array}{r}
130\,R\,14 \\
25\overline{)3264} \\
\underline{25} \\
76 \\
\underline{75} \\
14
\end{array}
$$

$$
\begin{array}{r}
130.56 \\
25\overline{)3264.00} \\
\underline{25} \\
76 \\
\underline{75} \\
140 \\
\underline{125} \\
150 \\
\underline{150} \\
0
\end{array}
$$

$3,264 \div 25$ is equal to 130 with a remainder of 14, or $130\frac{14}{25}$, which is equal to 130.56.

If a divisor has a decimal, the decimal can be moved all the way to the right. The number of places it is moved is the number of places the decimal in the dividend must be moved. Keep in mind that a whole number can be followed by a decimal point and an unlimited number of zeros.

$$
1.5\overline{)60} = 1.5\overline{)60.0} = 15\overline{)600}
$$

A different algorithm for division with multiple-digit numbers has become common in recent times and is perhaps easier to use. It also helps illustrate the reasoning involved in a process of division with multiple-digit numbers. The method is called *expanded notation,* and it uses *partial quotients,* numbers determined to add up to the answer in an expanded notation process. Instead of aiming for the maximum number of times a divisor goes into a number formed by digits in the dividend, a student can multiply the dividend by a number he knows will result in a product that is less than the dividend. The number he multiplied by is written to the right of the division symbol, which is different for this algorithm. The product is written under the previous number, the first of which is the dividend and after which all are differences. The product of the divisor and the number written to the right of the symbol is put under the previous difference, and the difference of that number and the new product is written. That difference becomes the number under which the next product goes. This process is repeated until a difference is less than the divisor. That difference is the remainder.

Suppose a student is instructed to divide 541 by 35. She could use the following procedure. There are multiple options for which numbers can be put to the right of the division symbol. As long as the process is followed correctly, the answer will be correct.

$$
\begin{array}{r|l}
35\overline{)541} & 10 \\
\underline{350} & \\
191 & 4 \\
\underline{140} & \\
51 & 1 \\
\underline{35} & \\
16 &
\end{array}
$$

35 does not go into 16 1 time or more, so 16 is the remainder. The sum of 10, 4, and 1, which are partial quotients, is 15, so the answer to the problem is 15 R 16, or $15\frac{16}{35}$.

Multiplication with fractions is traditionally performed by writing the product of the numerators over the product of the denominators.

$$
\frac{2}{7} \times \frac{1}{3} = \frac{2}{21}
$$

The classic division strategy with fractions is to multiply the dividend by the reciprocal of the divisor. The *reciprocal* of a fraction has the numerator and denominator in reverse positions.

$$\frac{2}{5} \div \frac{4}{7} = \frac{2}{5} \times \frac{7}{4}$$
$$= \frac{14}{20}$$
$$= \frac{7}{10}$$

An approach that can be used to demonstrate very simple multiplication of a whole number by a fraction is to show an image divided into sections, one of which is shaded, and then show that the number of shaded sections is increased until the original number of shaded regions is represented the given number of times. The following diagram shows that $3 \times \frac{1}{4} = \frac{3}{4}$. It also presents the fact that $3 \times \frac{1}{4} = 3$ of $\frac{1}{4}$.

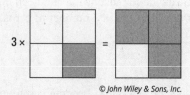
© John Wiley & Sons, Inc.

Actual objects can be used for the demonstration. For some examples, equally divided pizzas and pies, and constructed imitations of them, can be used to illustrate the principle.

Division of a whole number by a fraction can be illustrated through a strategy called the *conceptual approach.* The method entails using an object or image divided into equal sections and then dividing up those sections. For example, the quotient of 5 ÷ 1/2 can be revealed by starting with something like 5 rectangles.

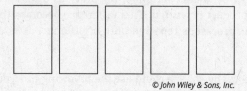
© John Wiley & Sons, Inc.

Then, each of the 5 rectangles can be divided into halves to show how many times 1/2 goes into 5.

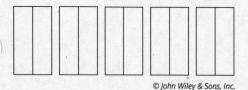
© John Wiley & Sons, Inc.

The result is 10 smaller rectangles. This shows that 1/2 goes into 5 a total of 10 times. The conceptual approach can also be presented by teachers and worked by students on number lines.

Rounding and estimating

When students perform operations, it is often a good idea for them to *estimate* the answer, which means to get an idea of the general ballpark area where it can be found, by working with *rounded* numbers. If a student multiplies 12 and 18, she can round both of them to the nearest 10, because they are two-digit numbers, and multiply the results. This will tell her that the answer is somewhere in the vicinity of 200, so if she ends up with an answer of 35 or 4,800, she can know that she made a mistake and needs to try again.

Numbers can be rounded to different places. Simply put, rounding a number to a given place is about putting a 0 in the next place immediately to the right and all places after it. Of course, 0's after a decimal point are understood after the last non-zero digit.

To round a number to the nearest 10 means to determine the nearest multiple of 10. Rounding a number to the nearest hundredth is rounding with the final digit being in the hundredths place. When rounding to a nearest place, if the digit in the place to the right is 5 or greater, a student should round up by increasing the value of the place to which he is rounding by 1. If the digit to the right is 4 or lower, he should keep the value of the place to which he is rounding.

58 rounded to the nearest 10 is 60.

53 rounded to the nearest 10 is 50.

14.53 rounded to the nearest tenth is 14.50, which equals 14.5.

Teaching the order of operations

When multiple operations are used in the working of a problem, there is an order in which the operations must take place. False orders can cause false answers, but the true order of operations, which is called the *order of operations*, results in true answers when the calculations involved are correct. The order of operations is often represented by the acronym PEMDAS, which represents the following order: parentheses, exponents, multiplication and division (from left to right), addition and subtraction (from left to right). The "parentheses" part of the acronym actually means all grouping symbols, starting with the innermost and working outward. The acronym has a long history of successfully helping students remember the order of operations.

$$
\begin{aligned}
[(5-2)^2 + 3 \cdot 4 - 6] \cdot 2 &= [3^2 + 3 \cdot 4 - 6] \cdot 2 \\
&= [9 + 3 \cdot 4 - 6] \cdot 2 \\
&= [9 + 12 - 6] \cdot 2 \\
&= [21 - 6] \cdot 2 \\
&= 15 \cdot 2 \\
&= 30
\end{aligned}
$$

Demonstrating the properties of operations

Use of manipulatives can help students understand that the properties of operations are not wild, random inventions of ancient thinkers. One of the purposes of modern instruction strategies is to show that math is about reality and that there are reasons for the rules beyond the fact that people said they are rules. Base-10 manipulatives can be used to clearly illustrate the properties of operations and why they are true. The activities generally involve arranging manipulatives in different groups and counting the totals to understand the equality that results from creating *equal sets*, which are various arrangements with the same objects. Teachers can show these exercises to students, and students can engage in the activities on their own or in groups.

The commutative property of addition can be shown with the use of manipulatives. Counters are used in the following example. It demonstrates that $3 + 2 + 1 = 2 + 1 + 3$. In both arrangements, the total number of counters is 6.

Arrangement 1: ● ● ●   ● ●   ●

Arrangement 2: ● ●   ●   ● ● ●

The associative property of addition can be illustrated in a similar manner, but it entails separating groups of objects in certain ways instead of changing the numbers of objects in them. This demonstration shows that $(3+2)+1 = 3+(2+1)$.

Arrangement 1: ● ● ●   ●
                ● ●

Arrangement 2: ● ● ●   ● ●
                         ●

The commutative property of multiplication can be demonstrated with counters or other manipulatives. This diagram shows that $3 \times 2 = 2 \times 3$.

Arrangement 1: ○ ○ ○
                ○ ○ ○

Arrangement 2: ○ ○
                ○ ○
                ○ ○

The associative property of multiplication works similarly, but it is about the way numbers are grouped, not ordered. The example here illustrates the fact that $(2 \times 3) \times 4 = 2 \times (3 \times 4)$.

Arrangement 1: △△ △△ △△ △△
                △△ △△ △△ △△
                △△ △△ △△ △△

Arrangement 2: △△△ △△△
                △△△ △△△
                △△△ △△△
                △△△ △△△

Finally, the nature of the distributive property can be presented in a way that clearly reveals its nature. We do a demonstration like this when we explain the distributive property in Chapter 5. It is an effective way of showing how and why the distributive property works. This illustration presents the fact that $2(3+4) = 2(3)+2(4)$. Both sides of the equation have a value of 14, so this illustration shows a way to arrange 14 manipulatives. If you have 3 sets of 2 blocks and add another 4 sets of 2 blocks, you now have 7 sets of 2 blocks.

□□ □□
□□ □□
□□ □□
    □□

The distributive property can also be illustrated in two arrangements. You can show how 2 sets of the sum of 3 blocks and 4 blocks have a total of the same number of blocks as the sum of 2 sets of 3 blocks and 2 sets of 4 blocks.

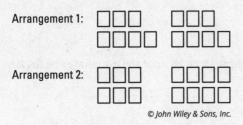
© John Wiley & Sons, Inc.

A teacher can point out that both arrangements have 2 sets of 3 and 2 sets of 4, as well as a total of 14.

The substitution property can be illustrated by putting two groups of manipulatives together and showing that the total number of objects does not change when one of the groups is rearranged as a sum or product. The following demonstrates that $2 + 3 = 2 + (2 + 1)$.

Arrangement 1: ●●   ●●●

Arrangement 2: ●●   ●●   ●

© John Wiley & Sons, Inc.

TIP

All the exercises we discuss in regard to properties of operations are about demonstrating how rearranging a set of objects does not change the number of objects in the set. Starting such an exercise with a random rearrangement of the objects followed by focus on the fact that the number of objects is still the same highlights the purpose and focus of the exercise and adds clarity to what it is used to teach.

Converting number forms

A number can be written in several forms. Elementary math focuses on the fraction, mixed number, decimal, and percent forms of numbers, and also the integer forms of numbers that are *integers*. Methods exist for converting among number forms.

Mixed numbers can be converted to improper fractions, which are fractions with a greater (in magnitude) numerator than denominator. Since the number of times 1 over a denominator goes into 1 is the denominator, the denominator in a mixed number times the integer, with the numerator added to the product, is the numerator that can go over the denominator to get an improper fraction. If the mixed number is negative, ignore the negative sign until the final step and then put it beside the improper fraction. Confusing enough? Here you see it in numeric form:

$$5\frac{1}{8} = \frac{8(5) + 1}{8}$$
$$= \frac{40 + 1}{8}$$
$$= \frac{41}{8}$$

That process can be reversed to convert an improper fraction to a mixed number. The maximum number of times the denominator goes into the numerator equals the integer in the resulting mixed number. The remainder goes over the improper fraction's denominator to form the fraction in the mixed number.

$$\frac{41}{8} = 5\frac{1}{8}$$

A fraction can be converted to a decimal through division of the numerator by the denominator.

$$3/4 = 4\overline{\smash{)}3.00} \begin{array}{r} .75 \\ \underline{28} \\ 20 \\ \underline{20} \\ 00 \end{array}$$

Another effective algorithm that is commonly used in modern times for converting fractions to decimals is multiplying the denominator by the number necessary to get a power of 10 (10, 100, 1000, and so on) and multiplying the numerator by the same number.

$$\frac{3}{4} = \frac{3(25)}{4(25)}$$
$$= \frac{75}{100}$$
$$= 0.75$$

To convert a decimal to a fraction, a student can write the fraction that the decimal represents. Then simplify the result if necessary.

$$0.75 = \frac{75}{100}$$
$$= \frac{3}{4}$$

A percent is an amount divided by 100, so converting a percent to a fraction is simply a matter of dropping the % and writing the number over 100.

$$11\% = \frac{11}{100}$$

From there, a student can write the fraction as the decimal that has the same meaning as the fraction.

$$\frac{11}{100} = 0.11$$

A percent can also be converted to a decimal as a result of dropping the % and moving the decimal two places to the left. The % means "divided by 100," and moving the decimal two places to the left has the same effect.

$$11\% = 0.11$$

The reverse of that process changes a decimal to a percent. Students can move the decimal point in a decimal number two places to the right, which is a way to multiply by 100. That can be undone with the introduction of a %.

$$0.11 = 11\%$$

Those rules can guide students all throughout the types of elementary number conversions.

Converting number forms can be used to compare values of numbers. Consider the question of whether $\frac{3}{8}$ is greater than, less than, or equal to 41%. The best way to approach a question like that is to put the numbers in the same form and then compare the results.

$$\frac{3}{8} = 0.375$$

$$41\% = 0.41 = 0.410$$

Since $0.375 < 0.410$, $\frac{3}{8} < 41\%$.

Use of a number line can add visual perspective to such problems and make working them easier for many students.

Looking for factors and multiples

A time-honored method for determining the factors of a whole number is the use of a *factor tree*, which is a presentation of two factors with a product that is a number being factored, factors that multiply to get those factors, and so forth, with the bottom numbers being all prime numbers that multiply by each other to get the top number being factored. The presentation of all prime numbers multiplied by each other to get the factored number is the *prime factorization* of the number. Consider the number 42 and how it can be factored.

© John Wiley & Sons, Inc.

The prime factorization of 42 is $3 \times 2 \times 7$. All factors of 42, other than 1, can be found through multiplying combinations of the prime factors of 42. Because $3 \times 2 = 6$, $3 \times 7 = 21$, $2 \times 7 = 14$, and $3 \times 2 \times 7 = 42$, and no other combinations of prime numbers times each other are possible, all the factors of 42 are 1, 3, 2, 7, 6, 21, 14, and 42.

A mainstream modern approach to finding all the factors of a number is the *rainbow method*, which starts with writing the number and 1 as the factors at the beginning and end of a set and connecting them with an arch. Then another combination of factors is written between them, and connected. The next combination is placed in such a way that the factors remain in numerical order. This process continues until no other factor pairs can be introduced. The following rainbow display shows the factors of 24.

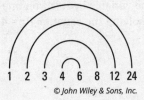

© John Wiley & Sons, Inc.

The greatest common factor (GCF) of two numbers can be found by listing the factors of both and identifying the largest one they have in common, as illustrated in Chapter 5, to define the greatest common factor. The ladder method is also effective, and it is much quicker and simpler. It also illustrates why a number is a GCF. Suppose a student is trying to find the greatest common factor of 16 and 24. The student can put 24 and 16 next to each other and draw an "L" under them. Then, she can write the lowest prime number that goes into both of them to the left of the "L." That number is 2. Next, she should write under the "L" the numbers that 2 has to be multiplied by to get 16 and 24. Those numbers are 8 and 12. The process needs to be repeated until the numbers at the bottom have no prime factors in common.

$$
\begin{array}{r|rr}
2 & 16 & 24 \\
2 & 8 & 12 \\
\hline
 & 4 & 3
\end{array}
$$

This is where things get interesting. The product of the numbers to the left of the "L" formations is the greatest common factor of 16 and 24. The product of the numbers on the left and the numbers on the bottom is the least common multiple (LCM) of 16 and 24.

Advancing students' algebraic thinking

After all that talk about numbers, it's time to talk about letters, though we have been using a lot of letters to talk about numbers. In this section, we are talking about letters that represent numbers.

Working basically with variables and expressions

The most basic use of algebra is using a letter, a *variable*, to represent a number. The next most basic algebraic action is perhaps multiplying that letter by a number to form another term, and the next is combining terms when it is possible to do so. That can only happen when the terms are like terms. To add like terms, students can combine the coefficients and keep the variable combinations the same.

$$
\begin{aligned}
5x + 2x &= (5+2)x \\
&= 7x
\end{aligned}
$$

Combining like terms is a process involved in simplifying algebraic expressions and solving algebraic equations. An algebraic expression can be simplified by putting like terms together and keeping unlike terms separated by addition or subtraction.

$$
\begin{aligned}
5y + 4 - 2y + 8 &= (5-2)y + (4+8) \\
&= 3y + 12
\end{aligned}
$$

Solving algebraic equations

Algebraic equations can be solved with the classic approach, which is to combine like terms on both sides, get the variable on one side if it is not already there, and then undo everything that is being done to the variable by doing the opposite. Anything done to one side must be done to the other side so the two sides stay equal. The goal is to get the variable by itself on one side of the equals sign. The following shows the standard method for solving the equation $8p - 4 = 12$.

$$
\begin{aligned}
8p - 4 &= 12 \\
8p - 4 + 4 &= 12 + 4 \\
8p &= 16 \\
\frac{8p}{8} &= \frac{16}{8} \\
p &= 2
\end{aligned}
$$

Another effective method for solving algebraic equations that is often employed in modern times is the use of a *bar model*, which has one quantity represented by a bar that is labeled with one side of the equation and a bar of equal length labeled with the other side of the equation. Quantities can be symbolically removed from both bars until nothing remains but the variable in one bar and its numerical value in the other. Suppose you want to show a student how to solve the equation $2x + 3 = 11$. You can use this bar model.

© John Wiley & Sons, Inc.

The top and bottom bars can be changed in the same ways and still be of equal length. They can both be reduced by 3 so that only $2x$ remains in the top bar.

© John Wiley & Sons, Inc.

Those bars can be cut in half so that only x remains in the top bar, which reveals the value of x in the bottom bar.

© John Wiley & Sons, Inc.

The remaining bars reveal that the value of x is 4.

Bar models can be used to represent algebraic equations derived from written language. If a problem says that four more than three times a number is 19, two sides of an equation are presented. One side is four more than three times a number, and the other side is 19. The first step in deciding how to translate English wording about an unknown quantity into an algebraic equation is to decide what is unknown. A variable can be used to represent it.

n: the number

Then, the English wording can be directly translated into mathematical language to show what is being done to the variable. What is described in the situation here is four added to three times *n*.

$3n + 4$

That is what is equal to 19.

$3n + 4 = 19$

A student can then use a bar model to solve the equation.

© John Wiley & Sons, Inc.

$$n = 5$$

The traditional method for solving algebraic inequalities includes the same types of steps that are used in traditional equation solving, except solving inequalities involves changing the direction of the inequality symbol if both sides are multiplied or divided by a negative number in the process or else switched.

$$3x + 3 < 24$$
$$3x + 3 - 3 < 24 - 3$$
$$3x < 21$$
$$\frac{3x}{3} < \frac{21}{3}$$
$$x < 7$$

A bar model can be used to solve an algebraic inequality, with one bar shorter than the other.

© John Wiley & Sons, Inc.

$$x < 6$$

The goal and focus of solving an equation or inequality is to get the variable by itself on one side of the equals sign.

REMEMBER

Finding formulas based on patterns

An algebraic equation can be a formula that represents a pattern. Say you're teaching students about an example of someone who makes $25 for babysitting plus another $10 for each hour of babysitting. A question asks how much money the babysitter would make for 5 hours on the job. The student can answer the question by making a table.

Babysitting Number of Hours	Number of Dollars Earned
0	25
1	35
2	45
3	55
4	65
5	75

The table shows that the money earned for 5 hours of babysitting would be $75. Another question that could be asked about the pay pattern is what formula could represent it. Two major components of the formula are the numbers 25 and 10 because they are part of what determines the amount of money earned. Also, the number of hours worked is part of what determines an amount of money earned, so it is part of the formula and must be represented by a variable because it varies and is unknown until a specific number is given for a particular situation. So, three parts of the formula are 25, 10, and a variable representing hours worked, which could be h. The amounts of money are in terms of dollars earned, so d would make a good variable for representing that quantity. The other terms come together and determine its value. Since 25 is always added, the formula involves $+25$. To what is it added? It is always added to the product of 10 and the number of hours. All of that together equals the value of d. Therefore, a formula that can represent the number of dollars earned for a number of hours of babysitting is $d = 10h + 25$. You can check every example in the table to see that the formula works.

Helping students weigh in on geometric and measurement principles

Measurements can apply to many things. Geometry is about measurements and the natures of figures that can be measured in various ways. However, the principle of measurement itself goes beyond geometry.

Revealing the natures of shapes

Understanding of elementary-level geometry is heavily centered on knowing the basic types of geometric shapes. A good way for students to learn the types of shapes is to compare them to each other by taking into account their *shared attributes*, or characteristics they have in common. A very effective tool students can use to reflect on shared attributes of geometric figures is a *shape hierarchy*, a diagram that presents geometric figure categories based on characteristics and connects types of shapes to others in terms of their common features. A shape hierarchy also illustrates how types of shapes are different from each other. The definitions of the types of shapes can be given with their names. The following is a polygon hierarchy.

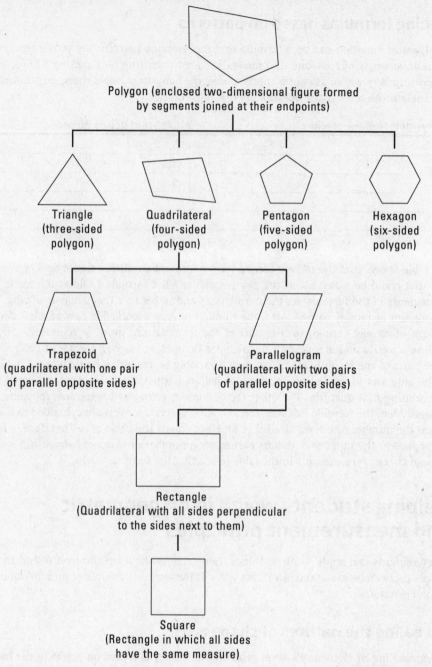

Polygon (enclosed two-dimensional figure formed
by segments joined at their endpoints)

Triangle
(three-sided
polygon)

Quadrilateral
(four-sided
polygon)

Pentagon
(five-sided
polygon)

Hexagon
(six-sided
polygon)

Trapezoid
(quadrilateral with one pair
of parallel opposite sides)

Parallelogram
(quadrilateral with two pairs
of parallel opposite sides)

Rectangle
(Quadrilateral with all sides perpendicular
to the sides next to them)

Square
(Rectangle in which all sides
have the same measure)

© John Wiley & Sons, Inc.

Basic geometric shapes can be put together to form composite figures. *Pattern blocks* are manipulatives students can use to understand shapes and how they can be put together to create composite figures and also other basic figures.

Measuring geometric figures

The blocks can also be used to demonstrate that the area of a figure is the same as the sum of the
figures that compose it. For example, the area of the following figure is the same as the sum of
the areas of the rectangle, square, and triangle that form it.

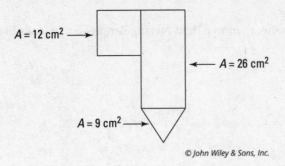

The area of the composite figure is the sum of $12\ cm^2$, $26\ cm^2$, and $9\ cm^2$, so it is $47\ cm^2$.

If the length and width of the rectangles were given and a base and corresponding height of the triangle were given, the areas of those figures could be determined without being stated directly. This is true because the area of a rectangle is length times width ($A = lw$) and the area of a triangle is one-half base times height ($A = \frac{1}{2}bh$).

The areas of some shapes can be determined and demonstrated with the use of square tile manipulatives. Use of them puts focus on the meaning of area and why certain formulas for it are what they are. For example, the following diagram represents a rectangle that is composed of square tiles which are 1 in.² each. The area of the rectangle can be determined in two ways. Each side of a tile is 1 inch, so the length and width of the rectangle can be found by counting tiles across length and width. The product of the length and width is the area of the rectangle. Also, the number of tiles is the number of square inches within the rectangle. When students study rectangle area with the use of square tiles, they can get a clear picture of what rectangle area is, the reason for the formula for it, and the true meaning of "$in.^2$."

The rectangle is composed of 12 tiles that each have an area of $1\ in.^2$. The rectangle formed by the 12 tiles is also $4\ in. \times 3\ in$. Both facts show that the area of the rectangle is $12\ in.^2$, and the diagram reveals how the two facts are connected.

Perimeter can be represented by the same type of arrangement. The number of tile lengths around the rectangle can be counted. The perimeter is that number of inches, 14 in.

Manipulatives can also be used for calculating, demonstrating, and studying surface area. A *net* is an arrangement of the two-dimensional figures that form a three-dimensional figure. Tiles and other objects can be used to form nets. The following image is a net of a right rectangular prism.

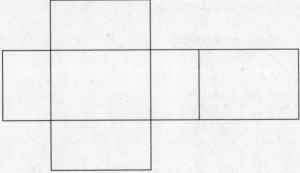

The tiles of the net can be put together to form a right rectangular prism that looks like this.

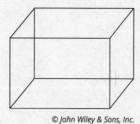

© John Wiley & Sons, Inc.

The surface area of the right rectangular prism is the sum of the areas of the tiles that form it. That is because the surface area of a right rectangular prism is the sum of the areas of its faces. Measuring the figures that form a net and then putting them together to form a three-dimensional object can very effectively help students understand the nature of surface area and how to find it.

The concept of volume can also be illustrated with manipulatives. Blocks and other three-dimensional objects of certain volumes can be put together to form larger objects. The volumes of the smaller objects combine to form the volume of the object they compose together. Suppose the cubic blocks that make up the largest cube are $125\ m^3$. Since 8 of the blocks form the greater cube, the greater cube has 8 time more volume. Its volume is $8 \times 125\ m^3$, or $1,000\ m^3$. That could be presented in connection with the fact that each smaller block is $5\ m \times 5\ m \times 5\ m$ and therefore the dimensions of the greater block are $10\ m \times 10\ m \times 10\ m$.

© John Wiley & Sons, Inc.

REMEMBER

Surface area is a two-dimensional form of measurement of three-dimensional objects.

Measurements beyond the shapes

Now it is time to talk about how time can also be measured. The amount of time that goes by between two given events is elapsed time. If you begin a study session for the Praxis Elementary Education test at 6:00 p.m. and study until 7:32 p.m., the elapsed time between the beginning of your session and the end is 1 hour and 32 minutes, or 92 minutes. An effective method elementary students can use to determine elapsed time is to work with a number line that has times of day for the coordinates. Not all the coordinates for times in between need to be labeled. The elapsed time from 6:00 p.m. to 7:32 p.m. is represented on the following number line. The first hour is represented as an increment, then 30 minutes is indicated. After that, 2 minutes remain. The sum of the labeled amounts of time is 1 hour and 32 minutes.

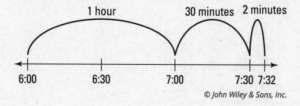

© John Wiley & Sons, Inc.

Unit rates involve ratios of measurements, such as miles per hour and dollars per gallon. Since multiple systems exist for each type of measurement, a unit rate can be converted to a form that uses a different system for each individual measurement. For example, a ratio of miles per hour can be converted to feet per second. Each measurement can be converted individually. Another method entails multiplying units by ratios that have values of 1 so that units can be canceled and the desired units can remain.

Suppose you want to show a student the value of 11 yards per minute in terms of feet per second. You could multiply by fractions that present ratios of measurements that have different units but are equal in value. For example, 3 feet is equal to 1 yard, so the fraction $\frac{3 \text{ feet}}{1 \text{ yard}}$ is equal to 1. Any value multiplied by 1 is equal to the original value. Anything times 1 is itself. Therefore, multiplying by $\frac{3 \text{ feet}}{1 \text{ yard}}$ does not change anything except the way something is written. If you multiply that and $\frac{11 \text{ yards}}{1 \text{ minute}}$, "yards" can be canceled while "feet" remains. That principle is key to the method. You want "feet" to remain, so you want to get rid of "yards." You can follow the same algorithm to get rid of "minutes" and keep "seconds," since you are looking for a value in terms of feet per second.

$$\frac{11 \text{ yards}}{1 \text{ minute}} \times \frac{3 \text{ feet}}{1 \text{ yard}} \times \frac{1 \text{ minute}}{60 \text{ seconds}} = \frac{33 \text{ feet}}{60 \text{ seconds}}$$

$$= \frac{11 \text{ feet}}{20 \text{ seconds}}$$

$$= \frac{11}{20} \text{ feet/second}$$

$$11 \text{ yards per minute} = \frac{11}{20} \text{ feet per second}$$

Proportions of measurements can be used to determine which measurements correspond to others in given situations. Suppose Aden makes $3 for every $2 Simon makes in Aden's lemonade stand business. Methods can be used for finding out the answers to questions such as how many dollars Simon acquired on a certain day in which Aden pulled in $24 for himself in the course of his business's lemonade-selling endeavors. One way to find the answer is to set up a proportion and cross multiply. The cross products of a true proportion are always equal. A variable can be used to represent the number of dollars Simon made on a day Aden made $24. This is an algebraic method, but algebra sneaks into geometry and measurement fairly often.

$$\frac{2}{3} = \frac{x}{24}$$
$$2(24) = 3x$$
$$48 = 3x$$
$$\frac{48}{3} = \frac{3x}{3}$$
$$16 = x$$
$$x = 16$$

Simon made $16.

Another algorithm for solving such problems is the use of a table that represents proportions. One ratio can be used to form other ratios that lead to the ratio in question. Each set of boxes next to each other shows what would be earned in a hypothetical situation. Aden's earnings increase by $3 every box down as Simon's increase $2 in each case. The last listing is $24 for Aden, and it is next to what Simon would make in that situation.

Aden's Earnings in Dollars	Simon's Earnings in Dollars
3	2
6	4
9	6
12	8
15	10
18	12
21	14
24	16

The table reveals that for every $24 Aden makes, Simon makes $16.

Locating points on the coordinate plane

The standard and modern algorithm for locating points on the coordinate plane is to start at the origin and then move horizontally along the x-axis a number of units. That number is the x-coordinate of the point. From there, a student can move vertically the number of units represented by the y-coordinate. That process will lead right to the point. For example, to find (3, 4) on the coordinate plane, a student can start at the origin, which is (0, 0). Next, she can move 3 units to the right and then 4 units up. The point where she arrives by following that algorithm is (3, 4).

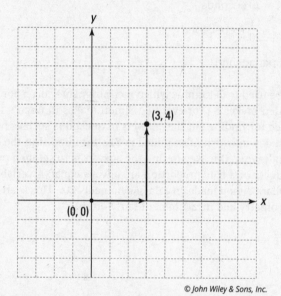

© John Wiley & Sons, Inc.

Expanding students' knowledge and skills concerning data, statistics, and probability

Data can be presented in various forms. For displays of data to have solid meaning and significance, they need to accurately reflect the natures of that to which they pertain. In other words, they need to be truly representative, and that requires being based on unbiased samples. When that is the case, data presentations such as bar graphs make accurate statistical indications.

Representing data

Bar graphs are a common and effective form of data presentation. They include bars, which are rectangles that correspond to data that is listed vertically. The categories to which those numbers apply are listed horizontally. The categories can be baseball tickets sold for each team in a year, jaywalking incidents in various cities, average hair lengths at universities, and all kinds of other such matters. The following is a bar graph representing the number of sandwiches sold per type of sandwich in Meadville in June, based on surveys. It is a display of categorical data.

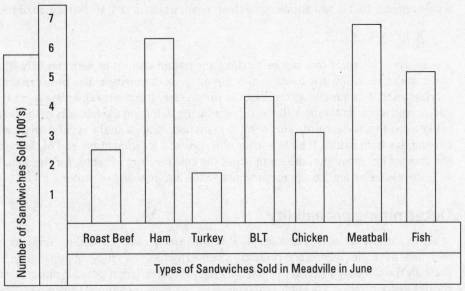

© John Wiley & Sons, Inc.

The bar graph shows that meatball sandwiches were the top type of sandwich sold in Meadville in June and that the number sold was approximately 700. Turkey was sold the least, at about 200.

Finding measures of center

The three measures of center of a data set, which are mean, median, and mode, can be found through the standard methods. Those are direct applications of the definitions of the words. Consider the following data set.

5 10 15 7 15 125

To find the mean, add the numbers and then divide by the number of numbers in the set.

$$\frac{5+10+15+7+15+125}{6} = \frac{177}{6}$$
$$= 29.5$$

The mean of the set of data is 29.5.

The mode of the set is the number that appears the most. No high-level, impressive trick here; students just simply spot the number that appears the most. However, putting the numbers in order can help if there are so many numbers that it is hard to tell which number is there the most. The mode of the data set in question right now is 15. It is in the data set twice while the others are there once each.

Median is the measure of center. A special trick for finding it has caught on since the rise of the standard approach. The standard method is to put the numbers in order and then pick out the one in the middle or determine the mean of the two that are in the middle. The following set has two numbers in the middle, in terms of value.

5 7 10 15 15 125

The two middle numbers are 10 and 15, and their mean is 12.5. Thus, 12.5 is the median of the data set.

A modern, mainstream approach to finding median without putting the numbers in order is to mark out the greatest number, then the lowest number, and then the second-highest number and second-lowest number, and so on, until no number remains but the middle number or two middle numbers. If there are two in the middle, find their mean, as with the traditional method. For this data set, a student would mark out numbers in this order: 125, 3, 15, 7. At that point, only 15 and 10 would remain. That is two numbers, so their mean, which is 12.5, is the median of the set of data.

$$\cancel{3} \ 10 \ 15 \ \cancel{7} \ 1\cancel{5} \ 12\cancel{5}$$

The measure of center that can best reflect the nature of a set of data can vary. However, it is never the mode unless the mode is also the mean or the median. The measure that best summarizes a set of data is always the mean or the median. It is the mean unless there is at least one *outlier*, which is a data number that is far outside the vicinity of the majority of the data. An outlier is like a dog that is clearly distant from the main pack of dogs. In the set of data we were just discussing, 125 is an outlier. It is far outside of the general location of the rest of the numbers. Since the data set has an outlier, the mean is not the best measure of center for the data. The median is. If there were no outlier, the mean would be the best measure of center.

Determining probability

Students can use visual aids to conceptualize the principles of probability. Spinners, coins, marbles, balls of varying colors, and cards are all effective tools for studying probability. They work in basically the same manner. All the manipulatives reveal different possible physical outcomes and the difference between a possible outcome and a favorable (qualifying) outcome. Those two principles together form the elements of probability, more technically called *theoretical probability*. It is the ratio of the number of qualifying outcomes to the number of possible outcomes.

To illustrate the concept, numbered cards could be put in a box.

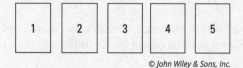
© John Wiley & Sons, Inc.

If the cards are shuffled and put in a box, and a student pulls out a random card without looking at the cards, the probability of pulling the 3 card is 1 in 5 because the 3 card is 1 of the cards and there are 5 cards. The exercise can show students that pulling a different card is a possible outcome but not a qualifying outcome, highlighting the meanings of the two concepts and how they are connected. The student and others watching the demonstration can see that the 3 card is 1 out of 5, so the probability of drawing it is $\frac{1}{5}$.

Experimental probability would be the actual ratio of the number of times a particular card is drawn to the total number of card drawings. Repeatedly drawing cards and accordingly changing the ratio based on the record of results can help students understand experimental probability.

Performing Mathematics Assessments

Elementary-level math assessments should be designed to accurately measure student progress and the effectiveness of instructional methods. Both formative and summative assessments should be used to help teachers improve instructional strategies. That includes designing strategies to prevent and correct student misconceptions of concepts and to reteach concepts when necessary. This ability is shaped by knowledge of course material and understanding of proper and effective methods for teaching it to elementary-level students.

Chapter 12

Science Curriculum, Instruction, and Assessment

S cience is an integral part of contemporary society, yet teachers often find themselves faced with less classroom time for science as reading/language arts and mathematics require more. How can you help ensure that our society continues to develop, encourage, and benefit from its scientists?

A balanced and focused curriculum lays the foundation for science education. Rigorous yet engaging instruction makes the education happen. Varied and timely assessments help ensure that all students are learning science content, processes, and methods of inquiry.

Establishing a Science Curriculum

The elementary science program should emphasize an approach that is both intellectually and literally (in other words, hands-on) engaging. Students need opportunities to learn science concepts while having direct experience with common objects, materials, and living things in their environment. They need the ability to explore the natural world in a safe and supervised yet independent manner.

Meeting the standards

Schools everywhere find themselves aligning their curricula to standards. A standards-based curriculum helps students prepare for the next grade(s) as well as for adulthood in a global society. National science organizations and educators have worked hard to establish standards for science education. These organizations include

>> American Association for the Advancement of Science (AAAS)

>> Council for Elementary Science International (CESI)

>> National Center for Science Education (NCSE)

>> National Institute for Science Education (NISE)

>> National Institutes of Health—Office of Science Education (NIHOSE)

>> National Science Foundation (NSF)

>> National Science Teachers Association (NSTA)

One widely used set of standards, the Next Generation Science Standards (NGSS), was compiled by the joint efforts of the National Research Council (NRC), NSTA, AAAS, and Achieve (an organization founded in 1996 by leading governors and business people).

The NGSS has three main parts:

>> **Practices:** Blend knowledge and skills to investigate and build theories, models, and systems; involve scientific inquiry and engineering design

>> **Crosscutting concepts:** Connect different domains of science and include patterns (predictions, similarities, differences); cause and effect; scale, proportion, and quantity; systems and system models; energy and matter; structure and function; stability and change; and the influence of science, engineering, and technology on society and the natural world

>> **Disciplinary core ideas (DCI):** Comprise the different contents of the four domains: physical sciences; life sciences; earth and space sciences; and engineering, technology, and applications of science

Selecting and organizing the material

In addition to meeting national standards such as the NGSS, many schools must align their curriculum to state standards. Administrators, teachers, and scientists work together to help establish these standards. In line with the standards, the curriculum should consider developmentally appropriate learner objectives, materials, scope, and technology.

The curriculum must also be appropriately focused and sequenced. An organized curriculum helps the student grasp the material and helps the teacher present the material in a time frame that may be shorter than before, as time requirements for reading/language arts and mathematics are increasing in many states and thus taking time away from other content areas.

It is essential that there is classroom time for both science concept and skill acquisition as well as for inquiry-based learning and meaningful assessments. Students must learn their grade-level's crosscutting concepts and disciplinary core ideas, including appropriate scientific vocabulary. Students need time to hone their investigation and experimentation skills. They need time to explore the uses of technology and instructional resources. They need time for formative and summative assessments.

TIP

Look at some of the components of the standards and ask yourself why it's important for students to learn them. For example, why do students need to know how to construct models? (*Hint:* Could your students demonstrate refraction without a model? Probably so, but modeling the concept helps clarify the real-world application. What about the phases of the moon? That would be hard to do without a 2D or 3D representation/model of the positions of the Earth, moon, and sun!)

Integrating science content

Scientists are involved and connected with other aspects of society, so it is entirely fit for science lessons to be involved with other content areas, the issue of classroom time aside. To learn and engage in science, skills are needed in reading, writing, speaking, and mathematics, and there are many ways to integrate science into other areas. For example, a math class may be engaged in solving a science-based problem, such as observing and collecting data and then tallying results. Reading/language arts classes may read science material as part of a lesson in nonfiction, from how night creatures see in the dark to why Pluto lost its status as a planet.

Lessons in history and social sciences may include studies of earlier science-related phenomena. For example, a class may study both the scientific processes and cultural significance of the X-ray work of Wilhelm Röntgen. The cause and means of the spreading of the bubonic plague may be studied in light of its effect on medieval Europe.

TIP

It is important to know how an instructional unit fits into the whole scope and sequence of a curriculum. Look at a sample unit, such as a third-grade one involving relationships among organisms in a food web. What prior knowledge and skills must students have to learn this unit? What skills must they take from this unit into other units? How can mathematics, reading/language arts, and history and social sciences be integrated with and help students' understanding of this unit?

Giving Science Instruction

Science instruction must be scholarly and rigorous yet interactive and fun. It must use multiple instructional strategies while covering science concepts, inquiry, and processes. It must span the domains of life science, Earth and space science, and physical science.

Delivering the message

Most educators favor a balanced method of instruction, one of guided inquiry, where the teacher facilitates instruction in important scientific concepts, relationships, processes, and mechanisms; and where the teacher provides students with the opportunities to be actively engaged in the discovery process, guiding them as needed through the steps. Some features of this method include small-group discussions, whole-class discussions, cooperative learning activities, experimentations, and research projects.

In order to ensure learning by all students, it is important to have a differentiated classroom, where instruction follows different methods, depending on the material and the learners. In addition to guided inquiry, some of these methods include direct instruction, scaffolding, modeling, reciprocal teaching, facilitative teaching, cooperative learning, and rehearsal learning, as discussed in Chapter 9.

TIP

When considering different methods of instruction for a particular unit or day, it is important to ask yourself some of the following questions. How will you begin the lesson? Will there be a point where you can have different students doing different things? How much direction do they need? Will some students need more than others? How will you end or wrap up the lesson? Will you need a follow-up? What method will you use?

Developing understanding of science concepts, inquiry, and processes

The field of science concepts is broad, embracing the crosscutting concepts of the NGSS. It's important for you to know how to help students understand these concepts as they apply them within and across domains. Science concepts also include personal and social perspectives of science as well as the history and nature of science. By engaging students in their science studies, you can help them understand and experience science as a part of their lives.

Students must also develop an understanding of scientific inquiry. The Biological Sciences Curriculum Study (BSCS) developed the 5 E's model illustrating the inquiry process: engage, explore, explain, elaborate, and evaluate.

The inquiry-based method lends itself particularly well to teaching scientific inquiry and its inherent processes, including variables, controls, observations, graphs, tables, charts, and models. Here are the steps of an instructional cycle, featuring the *5 E's*:

» **Discrepant event:** Something unusual or surprising presented to students that *engages* them and focuses their attention on a scientific phenomenon.

» **Question:** A phrase that defines (and specifically focuses) the point to be studied in terms of variables: *When does (the independent variable) affect (the dependent variable)?*

» **Inquiry:** A process that encompasses the *exploration,* the experiment(s), which should follow these steps:

- State the question.

- Make a hypothesis.

- Plan the investigation:

  Describe what is to be changed (the independent variable).

  Describe what is to be measured (the dependent variable).

  Indicate tools/means of measurement.

  Indicate controls; state constant variables.

- Collect and record data.

- Organize data; use charts, graphs, or tables.

- Analyze and *explain* data, summarizing the process and results.

- Conclude, using new knowledge to *elaborate* via predictions, implications, alternate explanations, future experiments, or further readings.

- Communicate, sharing the results and *evaluating* the experience to determine how much learning has taken place.

TIP

How might you go about teaching science as inquiry to second-graders? At this level, students need to be able to ask a simple question, complete a simple investigation, answer the question, and share the results. In one class, students used a finely calibrated balance scale to weigh a deflated balloon and an inflated one. They discovered that, even though they cannot see air, it has mass.

Making students' understanding of life science come alive

Concerned with the realm of organisms, life science can be made accessible to students through lessons involving concepts, facts, principles, models, and theories. As with the other domains, life science instruction can benefit from differentiated instruction as well as diverse visual, hands-on, and multimedia aids that technology and other resources can provide.

Regarding organisms, students need to be aware of their many characteristics. Organisms are composed of structures from cells to tissues to organs to systems, each of which has its function. Organisms may share any of zero to eight classifications in the taxonomy: domain, kingdom, phylum, class, order, family, genus, and species.

The life cycles of organisms are also a primary concern. Some understanding of reproduction and the passing on of genetic traits is necessary. Students may read about life cycles of mammals, and they may observe the life cycle of a plant, for example, by sowing a seed in a glass container and watching the plant change and grow.

Organisms live in and change in response to their environment. They may produce glucose or consume it; they may hibernate or migrate. Wherever they are, they are a part of a food web within their biome, and they are a part of natural selection.

Promoting students' conceptualization of Earth and space science

By teaching Earth and space science, you help students develop an understanding of the four main systems of Earth: the atmosphere (air), the biosphere (living things), the geosphere (rocks, minerals, and soil), and the hydrosphere (water). Students come to understand how an event that occurs in one Earth system often causes direct or indirect effects in other systems as well as its own.

Reaching for an understanding of what lies beyond Earth, students examine the interactions of Earth, the moon, and the sun. The components and configuration of the solar system come into the orbit of students' learning.

From the shifting of tectonic plates to the melting and cooling of rock, from the evaporation to the condensation and precipitation of water, cycles of change happen on Earth. Some of these changes students may observe, such as evaporation and condensation, and they may make models of them. Of extreme relevance today is the study of carbon dioxide (CO_2) and the greenhouse effect on Earth's weather patterns, its climate, its oceans, and its hydrology.

In covering Earth and space science, you also help students understand geologic history and fossils. You facilitate their learning about cloud formations, soil science, and oceanography.

Transforming students' knowledge of physical science

As with life and Earth and space science, physical science can be made accessible to students through lessons involving concepts, facts, principles, models, and theories. In physical science, students need to develop an understanding of matter, forces, motion, and energy.

In addition to these areas, interactive lessons can help students understand temperature and transfers of heat as well as wave properties of light and sound. Students can do experiments with magnetism and, under careful supervision, electricity.

Perhaps more than the other domains, physical science lends itself to hands-on, inquiry-based learning. Discovery lessons abound to help students grasp the essential concepts, from watching the chemical change of water as it evaporates to shining a light into a prism and observing as different wavelengths refract out into the colors of the spectrum.

TIP

What would you do if your students just didn't get a lesson, on, say, simple machines? Some approaches you might consider would be 1) a partial reteaching—depending on how they did on the assessment and how much time you have—with different examples, activities, or methods and 2) the use of different motivators—is the students' motivation intrinsic (they want to learn) or extrinsic (you're making them learn)?

Doing Science Assessments

Ongoing formative and summative assessments (covered in Chapter 9), as well as initial entry-level assessments, are a critical part of science education. Assessments answer the question, *Has the student mastered the content?* While mastery in science does include the ability to remember facts, more importantly it measures the ability to explain, analyze, and interpret scientific processes and phenomena.

Proceeding with content evaluation

Some assessments may take the traditional forms of multiple-choice, short-answer, and essay responses. The first two forms are useful in covering many content topics quickly, while the third form, essay responses, is useful for revealing students' in-depth understanding and application of material. Here, teachers must be able to distinguish between a student's knowledge of science and his writing ability, or lack thereof.

Additionally, other forms of content assessment demonstrate learning. These include checklists, discussion formats, games, homework, interviews, journals, laboratory techniques, portfolios, presentations, research papers, and science projects.

Conducting science inquiry assessments

As with essay-response assessments, assessments involving investigation and experimentation need careful evaluation to distinguish between student knowledge and linguistic ability. A student's physical limitations may also need to be considered. Assessment categories or questions should be grade-level and content appropriate. In general, the teacher needs to evaluate the degree to which students are able to independently follow the inquiry method: state the question, make a hypothesis, plan the investigation, collect and record data, organize the data, analyze and explain the data, conclude and elaborate on the findings, and evaluate the investigation.

Using science process indicators

Assessments involving science process skills must also be grade-level and content appropriate. Many teachers find checklists helpful when assessing student proficiency in science processes. Some process indicators include

» Classifying

» Communicating

» Constructing charts, graphs, and tables

» Constructing models

» Controlling variables

» Interpreting data

» Measuring

» Observing

» Presenting findings

» Researching

» Using instruments

» Using mathematics

TIP

It's important to consider the type of assessment you'll use to evaluate student progress at different intervals. When would you use formal assessments? When informal ones? When might both be helpful? For example, observation would tell you whether a student is correctly measuring something, and you could then check her off on that particular instrument or skill.

Chapter 13

Social Studies Curriculum, Instruction, and Assessment

Being a social studies teacher might seem like a daunting prospect. After all, the future of mankind is resting on your shoulders! If not for you, where are students going to learn how to find their way? How will they learn an appreciation for their ancestors? How will they figure out how to vote and whom to vote for? Sure, states give standards and guidelines, but the job still seems to be a huge one. Getting a little nervous and stressed? Don't worry, because help is on the way.

No, don't look up in the sky for Superman or Wonder Woman. Instead, the call is being answered by another superhero, the NCSS. These guys and gals won't show up with magic wands or crime scene kits, but they have some pretty amazing superpowers of organization. NCSS stands for the National Council for Social Studies, and they came up with a national curriculum standard framework that encompasses all that teachers should teach in ways that make it doable and easy. In other words, it makes sense to teachers who can help it make sense to students.

TIP

NCSS, the National Council for Social Studies, is an association devoted to social studies education and is affiliated with many state social studies councils across the nation. For more information, visit its website: http://www.socialstudies.org.

The Themes of Social Studies Standards

The standards are structured around ten themes of social studies. These themes set learning expectations and provide a purpose and organization for the exploration, knowledge, products, and processes that are included within the content of social studies. The framework doesn't add anything to the curriculum of a teacher. Rather, it takes the curriculum and organizes it in a way that is teachable and in a way that is developmentally appropriate and interesting for the students.

The themes give ideas for teaching, learning, and assessment and give consistency to a process that is of gargantuan proportions. Remember, you have to teach the entire history of the world and every culture that ever lived. If not you, then who? Don't look over your shoulder for a sidekick like Batman's Robin. With NCSS, you've got this covered on your own.

If you want a little help with all that content, check out the ten themes the council has determined are the most important guiding principles and ideas in social studies.

Culture

Human beings have created culture, and learn, share, and adapt to that culture. Culture is constantly changing, and students compare and contrast elements of their own culture with cultures across time and place. In the classroom, this theme involves the instruction of geography, history, sociology, and anthropology as well as multicultural topics across the curriculum. Literature, music, arts and artifacts, and food are often included under this theme, as well as religion and belief systems. Can you think of a better way to have a feast of all your favorite foods? Maybe a field trip to your favorite Mexican restaurant? While these ideas may seem silly, remember you may be the only person and your classroom the only place offering kids the opportunity to try something new.

Time, continuity, and change

In order for us to understand our here and now, we have to understand what has happened in the past. Understanding how our ancestors reacted to situations teaches us the causes and consequences of events and developments, and helps us to place these in the context of institutions, values, and beliefs of the periods in which they took place. Knowing how to read about, reconstruct, and interpret the past allows us to answer the questions that intrigue, challenge, and delight us. Children in early grades learn to locate themselves in time and space. Through a study of history, students in the upper grades continue to expand their understanding of the past and are increasingly able to apply the research methods associated with historical inquiry.

People, places, and environments

The theme of people, places, and environments teaches students to understand the relationship between human populations and the physical world. Learners examine changes in the relationship between peoples, places, and environments over time. Today's learners connect the past social, cultural, economic, and civic issues with the demands of modern cultures. In classrooms, this instruction typically involves geography, regional studies, and world cultures.

Individual development and identity

Our identity, as a person, is shaped by our culture, by groups, by institutional influences, and by lived experiences shared with other people both inside and outside our own culture throughout our development. In the classroom, this instruction looks at how important psychology, sociology, and anthropology are in the understanding of who we are. The study of individual development and identity helps students describe what is important in their own development as unique individuals.

Individuals, groups, and institutions

Not everything is about us! We must also look at the institutions, whether political, economic, or social organizations, that help us carry out, organize, and manage our daily affairs. Students should know how these institutions are formed, what controls and influences them, how they control and influence individuals and culture, and how institutions can be maintained or changed. In classrooms, instructional lessons are focused on sociology, anthropology, psychology, political science, and history.

Power, authority, and government

In order for students to be civic citizens, they must understand the foundations of political thought and the historical development of various structures of power, authority, and governance. This concept also requires knowledge of the evolving functions of these structures in contemporary U.S. society, as well as in other parts of the world, so that students understand the role of government and democracy. In this way, learners become more effective problem-solvers and decision-makers when addressing the issues and social problems encountered in public life. In the classroom, instruction on this theme usually involves lessons on government, politics, political science, civics, history, laws, and other social sciences.

Production, distribution, and consumption

A person may say: "Let's face it, life sometimes isn't fair. If it were, I wouldn't have to work for a living. Instead, I could lie on the beach all day. But, I have to work because I want things, and things cost money." In this theme, students understand that the goods they want involve both actions (working for a living) and consequences (making money lets them buy things). In exploring this theme, students confront questions about goods and economies, both local and global. Students gather and analyze data, as well as use critical thinking skills to determine how best to deal with the scarcity of all kinds of resources. In classrooms, instruction on this theme usually deals with the concepts, principles, and issues drawn from economics.

Science, technology, and society

Thought you were going to stay safe in your room only teaching about history and geography? Think again! Teaching social studies means you also have to teach science. Think about it: How did man come up with the amazing technological advantages we have today? The answer: through social and cultural change and the ways people interact with the world. Young children need to learn how science and technology influence, and have been influenced by, beliefs and knowledge from culture and how this affects them personally. In the classroom, instruction usually deals with the topics of history, geography, and civics and government.

Global connections

In today's world, being halfway across the globe is as easy as a plane ride or a Skype session. Global connections have intensified and have caused changes faced at the local, national, and international levels. Students need to be taught the global connections linking them to the world. This involves an analysis of the cost and benefits of increased global connections and evaluations of the tensions between national interests and global priorities. Understanding these concepts contributes to the development of possible solutions to emerging global issues that will affect future generations. In the classroom, instruction and lessons focus on geography, culture, economics, history, political science, government, and technology, but also may draw upon the natural and physical sciences and the humanities, including literature, the arts, and languages.

Civil ideas and practices

Being part of the world comes with a responsibility to take part in the changes that are coming. Students need an understanding of civil ideas and how civic practices are critical to full participation in society and are an essential component of education for citizenship. Learning how to apply civic ideas and become part of responsible civic action is essential to the exercise of democratic freedoms and the pursuit of the common good. Instruction and lessons usually focus on civics, history, political science, cultural anthropology, and fields such as global studies and law-related education, while also drawing upon content from the humanities.

Presenting Social Studies Instruction

Teaching such a broad curriculum requires a broad range of instructional strategies. You can't teach history in the same manner that you teach geography. While teachers of any subject need many instructional strategies, there are certain "tricks" that are best for each of the topics in social studies. At its most basic level, social studies instruction must be interactive. It can't be simply memorizing curriculum and content. Understanding the concepts of social studies means interacting with the content. It is not enough to look at civic responsibilities; students must practice civic responsibilities.

Embedding these lessons into your own classroom rules and responsibilities is a great place to start. Uncertain whether kids can really be role models for citizenship? One Internet search will bring you to "Kid President," whose ideas for civic leadership and national and global responsibility could teach adult politicians how to do a better job! Other active ideas are inviting guest speakers—from politicians to senior citizens—who may have personal stories to match those dry facts in the textbook. Social studies must be lived in order to be understood. Include voting in discussions about homework and tests—then make sure to live by those votes. Hey, it's democracy in action, right?

Remember that social studies can involve as many outside sources as a language arts lesson on research and report writing, as much experimentation as a science classroom, and as many hands-on activities as the math classroom. Instead of simply reading about the history, stage a role-play. Teaching culture? Then, include those art lessons instead of just looking at dry, boring pictures. When kids do things, they learn things.

Regardless of which teaching strategy and method you use to get kids more actively involved in the content, the fact is that there are certain skills that all students will need in order to understand the kind of information presented to them. And, if they need to know, you have to teach it to them. Following are the categories of specific skills needed for the content and the best teaching strategies to help your students understand that kind of material.

Improving students' social studies information processing skills

Social studies is probably the heaviest content course from all the disciplines, science included. So much of social studies must be known, rather than completed, as in a skill. That means that improving *how* students learn is as important as *what* they learn. Social concepts and social behaviors aren't listed on any curriculum guide, yet we still expect students to be able to think rationally and logically about the information presented to them. That, my friends, takes some steps on your part. Students will only become those logical creatures if they are taught logical processes and how to think in linear ways, to get from Point A to Point B using certain methods or skills. Processing large chunks of information is easier if the teaching methods and strategies match the type of skill needed. The strategies in the following sections help you teach students to think and to think about their thinking.

Metacognition

Thinking about thinking? Sounds a bit crazy, right? After all, doesn't everybody reflect on decisions and problem solving while they are in a situation? You'd be surprised to know most of your students act spontaneously, without any thinking at all! Actually, if you're in the classroom already, you know this is true. *Metacognition* is a strategy that helps students to think about thinking. It teaches them that their brain is a machine and can be programmed to help deal with the massive amounts of information they receive each day. Metacognition is the first strategy students need to learn so that other forms and methods of instruction can build on what they already know. What does this look like in a classroom? Metacognition involves such activities as

>> Setting goals for learning and behaving

>> Evaluating progress

>> Monitoring achievement of goals

>> Assessing when they understand the material

>> Taking action when they don't understand the material

If students are never taught metacognition strategies, they will never learn to be responsible for their own learning. Being actively involved in the process of learning is key for social studies. Remember, this is how civilization is created! Students should be involved in that creation.

Prior knowledge

Activating prior knowledge is another key strategy that must be taught. Since students are already part of the civilization and processes they are going to learn about, they already have knowledge of the subject. Connecting new ideas to old ideas is important so connections can be made. Brainstorming and KWL charts are first steps to this process and help students to deal with new information.

Collaboration

Social studies, perhaps more than any other discipline, involves learning how people work together to make new ideas. Bouncing ideas off one another and creating something new is how this civilization we live in came to be. This act of working together to create a new product is called the *collaborative process*. It doesn't involve students just sitting around chatting, although that's how it might seem when teachers eavesdrop! Rather, this type of thinking allows students to process new information from peers in order to solve problems and complete tasks.

This process also allows students to identify questions, issues, and problems. Then, students gather evidence and data to solve those problems, eliminating data that doesn't help the group get closer to the goal. Along the way to the product, students also get practice with these key skills:

>> **Decision-making skills:** Defining the problem helps students to hone in on the specific information they need. Information processing isn't just about being a sponge and absorbing all the facts. Rather, information processing allows students to process information, meaning to take it in, evaluate it, and reject it if necessary. This skill is key if students are ever going to categorize the vast amount of information they are going to learn in social studies classrooms.

>> **Problem-solving skills:** Problem solving may sound like it happens at the end of a project, but that's not quite true. In order for students to solve a problem, they have to identify the problem. Then, they have to devise a plan to solve the problem and explore possible solutions, rejecting those that don't get the group closer to the goal and keeping those that fix or address the problem. This process teaches both forward- and backward-thinking, two skills that are key in processing information.

Because much of social studies is linear, meaning it operates step by step, understanding those steps helps students understand how others who used those steps furthered civilization. Every piece of content that comes later first went through this exact process. Why were maps created in the first place? Because explorers had a problem — they kept getting lost! So, they used problem-solving skills to create a process we study today. And, you know what? The work of those early explorers certainly saves us a lot of time and trouble today. Plus, we all want know the quickest way to get to the mall!

>> **Thinking skills:** Aren't all these skills "thinking skills"? Technically, yes, but there are a few more you have to include. Students also need to understand how to ask questions, analyze answers and facts, interpret data, and judge and evaluate consequences. Remember, you're teaching them *how* to think, not what to think. Teaching them how to think allows them to tackle the concepts in social studies, which often include issues of morality and ethics. If students aren't taught how to think, they'll take every fact as the truth and every proposal as a completed act. While we want the kids to follow the rules, we also need to make them understand how rules were created and why it is important to follow them.

You're probably saying, "Wait a minute! None of these skills has anything to do with content." You're right . . . but teaching social studies content is useless until you teach your students how to think in an academic and active way. The time spent will be earned back when students are better able to learn what you have to teach.

Positioning students' understanding of geography

Teaching geography shows the important distinction between teaching what needs to be taught and what needs to be learned. Students learn geography because it is important to know as a life skill, not just because it is on the standards or guidelines. While very few students will grow up and become a geographer, all of them will live on planet Earth and need to understand that dynamic, interactive relationship. Teaching geography isn't just teaching how to use maps and atlases. Rather, it involves teaching two main concepts of learning: human–environment interaction and spatial understanding.

Human–environment interaction is a method that studies how humans interact with and affect the environment. This involves looking at how people adapt to, depend on, and modify the environment to fulfill a human need or desire. Earth's ecosystems are not static; they are constantly changing, and many of those changes are the result of human interference. Understanding this teaches students to be better stewards of the one natural resource that cannot be replicated, our planet.

It's also important that students learn *spatial understanding* and geography helps with those connections. Spatial understanding, or *spatial awareness,* is an understanding of an individual's proximity to other people or objects and involves times, whether time of day or time period in history. Knowing physical space and location helps a child to connect his or her own body and personality to the entire content that is social studies — where we are and why we are where we are. Helping a child to see his or her small part in the large world is empowering, and a geographical awareness helps with the context of facts that are presented.

Developing students' conceptualization of history

Teach the history of the entire world, from dinosaurs until today. No problem, right? Clearly, no one human being knows *all* of history. Volumes of books and hundreds, if not thousands, of websites aren't enough to contain all that history. And, more is being discovered every day. To be honest, you just can't teach it all, and it doesn't matter what content guidelines state. No child will know every fact of history. Rather, children need to learn the facets of history.

To understand the facets of history, students need to think big, rather than little. They need to think in terms of ideas. This also helps them understand their space and spot in the world and why we even study the subject of social studies in the first place. Here's an example of what needs to be taught about history and how to teach history:

>> First, think in terms of **concepts.** Knowing the big picture about a subject will help the smaller details fit into place. It's not helpful to know the United States is a democracy without first teaching this lesson: Rules are hard to follow. Rules made by one person for an entire group of people are hard to follow. Sometimes, people have better ideas, and their ideas aren't listened to by the leader.

>> Next, students have to be taught **generalizations.** They need to know that there are different kinds of governments, ones that allow rules (democracies) and ones that don't (dictatorships, monarchies). These are generalizations, statements about the relationships between concepts. Generalizations organize and summarize information about broad ideas or topics.

Understanding the concept of monarchies by connecting that to what the students go through every day can help them to understand the historical concept of what led to the United States being a nation and writing a set of rules where everybody has a vote.

>> Finally, students can be taught **facts,** true and verifiable pieces of data. Facts are specific and limited and focus learning on the topic at hand. This process also helps students understand the categories of new information and where, in their brains and lives, they should place this information. The facts are the building blocks to generalizations and are used to support ideas. If you only fling out random facts at students, don't expect that learning to be long-term. Rather, they will remember it for a test or quiz, and then promptly forget it and never learn the *why* of needing the fact in the first place.

Why do we need a set of rules where everybody has a vote? Looking at the facts of monarchies and dictatorships helps the students understand the freedoms guaranteed under the Constitution, like Freedom of Speech, which means we, the people, can speak out against those rulers who don't listen to us. Hopefully, though, once students understand this process, they don't revolt like those patriots from long ago. That might take the next strategy to the extreme!

TIP

Roleplaying and simulations are great strategies to use when teaching history. They allow a set of issues to be discovered. When students act out and watch historical scenes, they get a better sense of how complex an issue is than they can by reading about one viewpoint presented in a textbook. These activities allow students to construct a mental map that paints a living picture of the time period as well as the very human people who lived during that time. Blending a historical background with the problems and solutions that historical figures faced intensifies and accelerates learning. It leads students to integrate new facts in a synergistic way. Now, that is knowledge in action! Did you think history could only be dry, boring recitations of battles and facts? History takes on an entirely new meaning when those issues are given to young people to figure out. Don't be surprised if their ideas are more creative and better than those of the heroes from history they learn about.

Improving students' awareness of government, civics, and economics

While history is the learning of content from long ago, government, civics, and economics are topics that occur to students, and their families, on a daily basis and have direct consequences that students can immediately see. The kinds of strategies that students need for developing awareness involve connecting the content to them personally and individually. The following strategies can make the content relevant and real to the students, in ways that show how they can interact with content, as opposed to being a passive recipient of knowledge. Here, and only here, what they do can change what is being learned. That's a powerful lesson for students and teachers.

Modeling

Modeling is when teachers provide students with clear examples of how things are supposed to work by showing them, step by step, the process that an adult takes. This allows the teacher to take a complex concept and break it down into manageable steps. *Thinking aloud,* or "think-alouds," while completing a task shows the students that not all content is set in stone. While there are certain facts that must be learned, government, civics, and economics are fluid and flexible, allowing learning at the pace of the individual students. For example, do you vote every time there is an election? If not, what a great lesson for students. Thinking aloud about where to vote and the steps involved in making a voting decision is a great modeling lesson.

Community-based instruction

Community-based instruction is a method of teaching that uses real-life settings to connect content for students. Many think this means hopping on a bus for a field trip. While that is one way to include community-based instruction, it doesn't have to be as elaborate as renting buses and meeting rooms. Instead, it's a hands-on approach to learning things that happen outside of school and, let's face it, most economics happens outside of school. Unless you count the lunchroom, students get very little practice handling money. Setting up a small store in the classroom and having students complete "work" for "money" is one small example. Don't start printing your own counterfeit coins, though! There are plenty of other ways to make this happen, such as inviting representatives from the community into the classroom — perhaps a bank teller who can describe a typical day or a representative from the electric company who can explain why bills are higher in the winter. It is functional learning at its best and shows students the daily rules that are often never explained to them.

Service learning

Service learning is an approach where students actually get to serve in the community where they live. This is perhaps, at first glance, the hardest to do, but it can be accomplished in small, but meaningful ways. Writing letters to members of the local government on behalf of issues that affect students is one way to accomplish this, as is volunteering around the school, like in the library or with custodians to help pick up trash on the school grounds. Service learning goes a step beyond traditional approaches to teaching and puts the child directly in the environment to make a difference.

Teaching the principles of anthropology and sociology

Anthropology and sociology blend social studies with science with a specific focus on understanding why and how people interact with one another. If you've always wanted to know why children act the way they do, now's your chance! Sorry, that secret is still well-kept, but learning why *humans* act the way they do is a bit easier. Think of your favorite CSI crime show and apply those same principles to history, and you'll have an understanding of the how and why of teaching sociology.

Inquiry teaching, or *inquiry-based teaching,* is a teaching strategy often used in science classrooms, but it works well for social studies, too. In this type of learning, the teacher presents a problem to the students and guides them on the way to answers. This is the opposite of traditional methods of teaching, where the teachers have all the answers. With this type of teaching, there are many possible answers, and the answer is only as important as the journey taken to acquire it. In other words, the process is just as important as the product.

The *process for inquiry,* or *inquiry process,* follows many of the same steps as the process of meta-cognition, with some differences in terms, but the concept is the same. Thinking, and acting, follow a set of procedures to get desired results. The steps in the inquiry process are:

1. Create a question, either student-teacher or teacher-directed.

2. Obtain supporting evidence, such as sources, resources, and research.

3. Analyze evidence to determine whether it furthers thinking to the desired outcome.

4. Connect the knowledge learned during the investigation to the original problem or question.

5. Find an answer and justify the data.

Another similar teaching method used to teach anthropology is the *deductive method,* another favorite of cop and mystery shows. In deductive instruction, the teacher introduces a concept and students then practice the concept, guiding their own learning to deduce connections and knowledge. An example of this might involve different art techniques used by various cultures. Rather than simply watching a presentation of artwork, students might be given the raw materials, given some instructions, and allowed to complete the process on their own, connecting their learning with how other cultures also learned the same technique.

What all these strategies from all these topics of social studies have in common is this — they are dirty and messy and fun! Social studies is not meant to be learned at a desk with a slate of facts, but to be lived and experienced. So, roll up your sleeves, trade your pantyhose or neckties for some comfortable clothes, and dig in! Who knows what you'll learn?

Social Studies Performance Assessment

Most classes focus on assessments that are either formative or summative, and that information is certainly needed. While most teachers may suppose that social studies is more inclined toward summative assessments, the opposite is really true. How can that be, you ask? Surely we all remember teachers who had us memorize lists of facts and figures related to social studies and then spew those out on a test. Really, though, what do you remember about that *content?* Probably not much.

There will always be a place to assess the big picture and the steps needed to get there, which is what summative assessments do. However, for the purposes of social studies, a different type of assessment is needed in order to gauge the thinking processes that have been taught. Remember, social studies isn't just about the content, it's the how and why of civilization.

That "how and why" requires a type of formative assessment, a type of assessment that measures content and the thinking required to cement that content into the habits and structures of those tiny humans you're in charge of. This type of assessment is called a *performance assessment,* and it evaluates the individual growth and development taking place in the classroom.

What performance assessments measure

A performance assessment, also called *authentic assessment,* involves a set of tools that a summative assessment cannot include. Performance assessments measure:

>> What children know and can do on a daily basis in the classroom. How else to measure concepts like economy except to see examples of it at work, embedded in the habits of the learners?

>> What progress children make through the process of learning a new skill. Let's face it, democracy is not a definition to be learned, but a style of living and government to be seen and developed.

>> Where children are developmentally in the processes required for knowledge. Geography is not simply looking at a map and knowing where something is. It involves a complicated process of reading, seeing, and synthesizing information to come up with a correct answer.

Performance assessments measure the whole child, her progress as well as her performance. They create a balance between what students know and what they can do with their knowledge. If social studies can't remain in the classroom, neither can student knowledge. Social studies requires that students become interactive in their world, making changes. Performance assessment involves combining content knowledge, information processing skills, development of work habits, and performance tasks.

Data measuring techniques

Performance assessments include many different types of measurements, and any or all of them can be used within a classroom setting easily. Performance assessments leave behind the old testing method of multiple-choice answers as a way to express knowledge. Instead, teachers use these different data-measuring techniques to assess what is being learned by the students:

>> **Rubrics:** Rubrics are used to measure holistically, that is, by looking at a whole product instead of single indications of knowledge. Rubrics measure standards of performance, as opposed to specific skill and knowledge sets. Rubrics often involve many dimensions, which rate performance of academic standards. Rubrics take into account the developmental aspects of children while setting in place expectations for standards.

>> **Checklists:** Does the notion that a simple checklist could be an assessment sound too good to be true? Well, it's true! Developmental checklists are quick ways to walk around and use

observational data to determine whether or not skills are being used. Checklists can be lifesavers in classrooms where many activities are going on and many students are involved. Checklists allow you to hone in on specific skills and determine at a glance who needs help and in which areas.

» **Portfolios:** You may think that only artists keep their work in a portfolio, but think again. All kinds of work can be kept, and it doesn't have to be a task for the teacher. Portfolios are collections of work and can be focused on specific skills, like making of maps, or specific themes, like a unit in history. Having students keep track of their own learning and seeing the proof of classroom learning is a powerful tool. It's also powerful for teachers, who can get so bogged down in the daily planning of a classroom that the big picture is hard to see. Portfolios allow teachers to see work over time and to see the growth in a student's learning.

» **Summary reports:** Summary reports are ways for teachers and students to reflect on learning. While we often instruct students to reflect on their own processes, we discover, as teachers, that we're just too tired or busy to do the same. The time taken to reflect on what worked well or didn't work at all makes a nice comparison with student reflections on the same unit of work. It also gives you a better sense of what types of remediation may need to be involved. If students can't write simple reflections of learning, as an informal piece of writing, then transfer of classroom activities to long-term academic knowledge isn't likely to occur.

Other examples involve projects, whether group or single; various written assessments; demonstrations; experiments; ranking scales; and holistic scales.

Chapter 14

Art, Music, and Physical Education Curricula, Instruction, and Assessment

S ometimes relegated to after-school activities, art and music, and even physical education, seem less valued today than ever before. Yet, more studies exist today than ever before that demonstrate how all three contribute significantly to the development of a child's mind and body.

The arts and physical education are an important part of a balanced curriculum. Instruction in these areas helps children lead balanced lives. Assessment of student work, including performances and exhibitions, gives students a sense of what they know, helps teachers with ongoing curriculum and instructional improvement, and provides administrators with a reliable means of attending to the standards.

Building Art, Music, and Physical Education Curricula

Studies have shown that engagement in the arts helps students improve in many important areas, including problem-solving, self-expression, and cooperative behavior. Likewise, research in physical education shows it helps students improve in areas including memory, attention, and various social skills. School systems must find ways to keep, instill, and integrate art, music, and physical education into the curricula.

Rising to the standards

Addressing the standards is a major concern when planning a curriculum. Content standards in art and music generally include the following:

>> Concepts, terminology, and overall ability to process, explain, and analyze visual or auditory information

>> Creative expression of artistic processes and skills and presentation or performing of them

>> Cultural and historical context of works of art or music

>> Aesthetic judgment of works of art or music

>> Awareness of ethics involved in art or music belonging to another

>> Introduction to or familiarity with different technological media and resources

>> Integration of art or music content into other subject areas

As with art and music, physical education standards vary somewhat from state to state. When you design a curriculum for physical education, it is important to remember that even activities considered appropriate for a grade-level may not be appropriate for all children in that level. Motor skills are not guaranteed by age but develop through varied practice, which is why a *multi-activity* approach is the best for a physical education curriculum. It is an approach that allows for the development of different skills as well as for the inclusion of different abilities.

Content areas for physical education are many and diverse. They include the following:

>> Locomotor skills

>> Body management skills

>> Manipulative skills

>> Aerobic capacity

>> Muscular strength

>> Flexibility

>> Rhythmic skills

>> Health and fitness concepts

>> Body composition

>> Self-responsibility

>> Social interaction

In making time for all these areas of content, planners must sometimes remember that recess and play may provide curriculum opportunities as well as organized classes and sports.

Scoping and sequencing the material

In addition to addressing standards, curriculum planners in art and music must account for equipment, materials, facilities, books, electronic media, teacher time, and community resources. At the classroom level, teachers are directly involved in curriculum implementation, including:

>> Preparing and presenting activities that align with the standards

>> Ensuring the logical flow or sequence of instruction

>> Making sure students know specifically what is expected of them and receive specific feedback for what they do

>> Fairly assessing student work

>> Helping students assess their own work

>> Managing time, including coordinating with other teachers for integrated study

>> Working with parents or members of the community regarding student performances

The scope and sequence of a physical education curriculum must first and foremost consider the students' physical capabilities, and what is developmentally appropriate for them at any given time. In the case of special needs students, the teacher needs to consider not only what is developmentally appropriate but also what is possible and yet still meets the standards. Learning must afford universal access, and learning must be safe. Finally, because physical education happens in front of others, it is especially important that the learning environment is inclusive, supportive, and respectful.

Use of equipment and facilities is also an important consideration in organizing the curriculum. Planners must work with what is there, and what is there must often be shared between many classes. Sometimes coordination with city or county facilities is necessary as well as beneficial. For example, a field trip may be made to a local park; in such instances, of course, proper authorization must be obtained and safe supervision provided.

As with art and music, assessments for physical education should be scheduled in the three basic time frames of a unit—initial, mid or ongoing, and final—so that instruction may be reviewed and adapted as needed. Students should be able to start at an instructional point that is best for them, have the opportunity to receive and improve with feedback, and know how they have progressed and what they have achieved.

It is also important to remember that some assessments for physical education may be conducted with those of other subjects. For example, a physical education standard that involves rolling a ball different times with different forces and comparing resultant speeds may meet a science standard involving force and motion.

TIP

As discussed in Chapter 9, matters of curriculum, instruction, and assessment often overlap. When thinking of one, it is often helpful to consider its effect on and how it is affected by the other two. For example, in addition to playing instruments, what kinds of media and technologies would you use in a unit on music of other cultures? How would you go about obtaining these additional materials? Which instructional strategies would be involved in their use? What type(s) of assessment might be involved?

Making connections with other subject areas

There are wide applications of art and music in other subject areas, particularly reading/language arts and history/social sciences. Stories, biographies, and various histories can help students understand the effect their own creations may have on other people.

Additionally, reading or writing about the art and music of a time period can help students appreciate and understand art and music as well as strengthen their grasp on historical or literary concepts. For example, the Realism movement in European art of the latter half of the 19th century can be shared in history/social science classes with a discussion of democratic movements in Europe at that time. Computer software may aid in the application of color theory, studied in art class, to such vocational courses as interior decoration or fashion design. A kindergarten music class may play simple instruments from other cultures and integrate lessons on rhythms and tempo with cultural studies. Moving (dancing) to the music can align with physical education standards related to body management and rhythmic skills.

There are many ways of integrating physical education with other subjects. Students in the lower primary grades may use the gym to physically advance from one station to another based on directions of a map or on addition, subtraction, multiplication, or division calculations, thus aligning with history (map-reading) and mathematics standards. In another physical education/mathematics integration, students in upper primary grades may focus on heart-rate intensity in connection with aerobic capacity by using mathematic functions involving decimals and positive and negative integers.

TIP

Some state publications now have tables illustrating different subject standards aligning with one activity. These publications may be extremely helpful for curriculum designers and teachers alike. It's relatively easy to find these publications on the Internet and well worth your time to read through the charts or tables, imagine your students engaged in several of the interdisciplinary activities, and understand the standards they are aligned with.

Supplying Instruction on Art, Music, and Physical Education

All students should have opportunities to increase their knowledge of art, music, and physical education concepts and to advance in terms of creativity, self-expression, accomplishment, and social and cultural awareness. Coordination with curriculum designs and with assessment methods is essential for teachers to ensure that each student progresses as much as possible.

Crafting students' understanding of art and design media and tools

Many instructional strategies may be used to develop students' skills and knowledge base in art, particularly in the production of art. Use of the Developmentally Appropriate Practice (DAP) is advised to accommodate differences in student skill level, background, and rate of development and achievement.

The use of demonstration and example followed by guided student practice and eventual independence is beneficial for the understanding of the elements and design principles of art, which include

>> Line

>> Color

>> Space

- » Shape and form
- » Texture
- » Balance
- » Proportion
- » Emphasis
- » Movement
- » Variation
- » Unity

While guiding instruction in a skill or process, teachers must remember to respect students' self-expression. A positive emphasis on the creative process at the elementary level opens the door for students to discover and learn about self-expression as well as starts them on the road to respecting it in others.

As student learning levels and available resources allow, teachers should introduce students to and guide them in the use of electronic media, including videos, digital cameras, and photo software. Technology is increasingly a part of all aspects of modern life, including artistic aspects. From observing (through video re-creation) how artists lived and worked in the past to working in a new medium today, technological advances are making many things possible for artists, and necessary for them to be aware of.

Advancing students' perspectives on musical elements

As with art, music education requires the teaching of concepts as well as the encouraging of creativity and the developing of appreciation for the work of others. Among the elements of music, students need an understanding of melody and harmony, rhythm and tempo (including note values and measures), forms and compositions, voice and instrument parts, and an awareness of the place of music and musicians in history. Students also need to consider aesthetic valuations and ethics in music.

Teaching strategies such as lecture and direct instruction may work for introducing a concept and as a precursor to student involvement. Similarly, demonstration should precede student practice. Feedback should always accompany student activity.

Indirect methods, such as facilitating individual or group/ensemble work, are ideal for music education. With teacher feedback and guidance, students can improve, achieve individual success, and learn from each other. Experiential learning allows students to be actively involved as they experience and feel the effects of music on themselves and others. Reflective follow-ups including journals, logs, and group discussions can in turn provide a bridge to summative assessments, including those involving performances.

TIP

Have you ever played a percussion instrument? If so, can you remember how you were taught? Was it beneficial? If not, how might you go about teaching a lesson on it? Hint: If your students have actual instruments, it helps to try one out first yourself. Internet research and instructional videos are helpful. Put yourself in your students' place: Follow the sequence of your own instruction, from concept and skill acquisition to self-expression and assessment.

Conditioning students' awareness of physical education principles

Instructional activities in physical education are directly tied to students' *locomotor* skills. These skills, in order from first-attained to last, are walking, running, hopping, leaping, sliding, galloping, skipping, and jumping.

Also of concern to curriculum planners are *body management* skills, which involve agility, balance, coordination, flexibility, and strength. Some specific skills include

>> Spatial awareness

>> Pathways

>> Levels

>> Speeds

>> Force

>> Directions

When teaching skills for games and sports, it is important to consider the four basic levels. The first is *precontrol*, where the child is not in control of the movement or equipment and, for example, cannot dribble a ball. Next comes *control*, where with intense focus, the child has a measure of control; movement may be stiff and repetitious. The child can dribble the ball but not while moving or against an opponent. Third is the *utilization* level, where the intense focus is replaced by flow and the child, for example, can dribble a basketball with an opponent present. Finally comes *proficiency*, where complex movements seem natural. The child can dribble the ball while moving and change course to avoid an opponent.

When teaching social skills, there are two essential approaches to communicating rules and desired actions. One way to manage behavior is the *proactive* method, which works to reward desired behavior and prevent inappropriate actions. Proactive strategies include

>> **Prompting:** For example, "Please remember to put your basketballs back in the box."

>> **Positive interaction:** For example, "That was nice of you, Tony, to pass the ball to Zach and compliment him on his shot."

>> **Avoiding differential treatment:** For example, "I will wait for the class [not just Rachel and Sonia] to calm down."

Alternatively, there are times when *reactive* methods may be necessary. Reactive strategies include

>> **Nonverbal responses:** For example, giving Lori a jump-rope after she kicks the basketball in seeming frustration

>> **Person-to-person dialogue:** For example, asking to meet with Tommy after class after he says he doesn't want Howard on his team

>> **Extinction:** For example, ignoring Carlo when he interrupts another student and, looking at the student, asking him to please repeat what he said

TIP

Different instructional strategies may be used in approaching the same standard. For example, one fourth-grade standard involves balancing with a partner while sharing a common base of support. The teacher may use a lecture-demonstration strategy, where the task is described and shown via a visual aid; the teacher may pose the task as a question, using a problem-solving strategy in asking the pairs if they can perform the task; or the teacher may use stations with task cards, where the pairs read their directions and seek to implement them.

Engaging in Art, Music, and Physical Education Assessments

Assessment of student work in art, music, and physical education takes many forms as standards involve both individual and group situations, concept-learning, and performances. Self- and peer-assessments are important evaluative considerations. In all cases, every effort should be made to ensure that assessments are valid, reliable, and as objective (in other words, concept-based) as possible.

Looking for understanding, analysis, and creative expression in art and music

Students in art and music need to understand the basic elements and principles. Evaluating student understanding of such concepts may be accomplished through short- or constructed-answer tests such as:

>> Vocabulary

>> Fill-in-the-blank

>> True-false

>> Multiple choice

>> Matching

Teachers need to be certain that students grasp the fundamental concepts before moving on to units that combine basic elements or involve more complex principles or skills. Checklists and observations may be sufficient if the components of such are comprehensive and clear to both teacher and student.

Assessments also include student art works and performances, projects, portfolios, research assignments, and discussion formats. Presentations may be related to units on the study of artists or musicians and their influence on culture, or vice versa.

It is important to remember that these assessments should be as objective and fair as possible. Teachers need to establish or use valid rubric or rating scales, and students need to be aware of the components of these scales so that when, for example, they work on a composition, they know what things they need to be aware of or include and so may achieve their goals.

Testing the strength of progress in physical education

Physical education assessments help teachers identify students' psychomotor skill levels as well as those involving fitness, health, and social interaction. From grasping concepts to grasping physical objects, students are expected to be able to describe, demonstrate, distinguish, explain, follow, interact, participate, perform, and resolve, to name a few of the myriad actions listed in many standards. It's not surprising then that many types of assessments are helpful. Some examples of assessments include

>> Checklists

>> Essay questions

>> Exit/entrance tickets

>> Homework

>> Journals

>> Logs

>> Peer observations

>> Portfolios

>> Selected-response/forced-choice items such as multiple-choice

>> Self-assessments

>> Student demonstrations

>> Student displays

>> Student illustrations

>> Teacher observations

>> Videotaping

TIP

A formative assessment gives you a great opportunity to advance and encourage student development. An important part of this assessment is feedback that positively acknowledges and reinforces the specific concept or skill a student is working on. For example, for a unit on baseball, when a student makes good contact, feedback such as "You kept your eyes on the ball and your head down — Nice!" is much more helpful than "You're progressing wonderfully!"

4
Praxis Elementary Education Practice Tests

IN THIS PART . . .

Take a full-length practice Praxis 5017 or 5018 test.

Review the answers to the practice test and determine your mastery level.

Study explanations of answer choices to determine any gaps in understanding.

Use information from your practice test to devise a study plan.

Chapter 15

Practice Test: Praxis Elementary Education - 5017

ere's the test before the test. This is your chance to show if your hard work has paid off. To get the most out of this testing experience, there are a few things you can do to help:

>> **De-gadgetize.** No cellphone, tablet, TV remote, and so on. Feel free to use your calculator during this practice test, since you will have access to an on-screen calculator on test day.

>> **Find a distraction-free zone where you can take the test.**

Once the environment is ready, prepare your mind:

>> **Watch the time.** You have roughly 1 minute per question, so don't get bogged down on any one question.

>> **Focus on the subject area or concept you're being tested on.** Tune in to key words or triggers that help you locate the correct answer.

>> **Answer every question.**

>> **Stay focused on your goal.** Keep in mind the score you want to achieve and know that you can!

Refer to Chapter 3 for more detailed test day strategies and instructions.

TIP

If you want to practice taking the test electronically, as you will on test day, go to www.dummies.com and use your PIN code to activate the online access that accompanies the purchase of this book. (Instructions are in the Introduction.) You'll find another test for your studying enjoyment and strategizing. You can answer the questions digitally, and the software tabulates correct and incorrect responses. This summary provides you with a snapshot of which areas you excel in and which areas you may need to review again.

Answer Sheet

The test is divided into five areas. You have two hours to answer all the questions. During the actual test, there is no stopping point between different subject areas. Some questions have more than one correct answer. In those cases, select all correct options.

Section 1: Reading and Language Arts

1. Ⓐ Ⓑ Ⓒ Ⓓ	9. Ⓐ Ⓑ Ⓒ Ⓓ	17. Ⓐ Ⓑ Ⓒ Ⓓ	25. Ⓐ Ⓑ Ⓒ Ⓓ	33. Ⓐ Ⓑ Ⓒ Ⓓ
2. Ⓐ Ⓑ Ⓒ Ⓓ	10. Ⓐ Ⓑ Ⓒ Ⓓ	18. Ⓐ Ⓑ Ⓒ Ⓓ	26. Ⓐ Ⓑ Ⓒ Ⓓ	34. Ⓐ Ⓑ Ⓒ Ⓓ
3. Ⓐ Ⓑ Ⓒ Ⓓ	11. Ⓐ Ⓑ Ⓒ Ⓓ	19. Ⓐ Ⓑ Ⓒ Ⓓ	27. Ⓐ Ⓑ Ⓒ Ⓓ	35. Ⓐ Ⓑ Ⓒ Ⓓ
4. Ⓐ Ⓑ Ⓒ Ⓓ	12. Ⓐ Ⓑ Ⓒ Ⓓ	20. Ⓐ Ⓑ Ⓒ Ⓓ	28. Ⓐ Ⓑ Ⓒ Ⓓ	36. Ⓐ Ⓑ Ⓒ Ⓓ
5. Ⓐ Ⓑ Ⓒ Ⓓ	13. Ⓐ Ⓑ Ⓒ Ⓓ	21. Ⓐ Ⓑ Ⓒ Ⓓ	29. Ⓐ Ⓑ Ⓒ Ⓓ	37. Ⓐ Ⓑ Ⓒ Ⓓ
6. Ⓐ Ⓑ Ⓒ Ⓓ	14. Ⓐ Ⓑ Ⓒ Ⓓ	22. Ⓐ Ⓑ Ⓒ Ⓓ	30. Ⓐ Ⓑ Ⓒ Ⓓ	38. Ⓐ Ⓑ Ⓒ Ⓓ
7. Ⓐ Ⓑ Ⓒ Ⓓ	15. Ⓐ Ⓑ Ⓒ Ⓓ	23. Ⓐ Ⓑ Ⓒ Ⓓ	31. Ⓐ Ⓑ Ⓒ Ⓓ	39. Ⓐ Ⓑ Ⓒ Ⓓ
8. Ⓐ Ⓑ Ⓒ Ⓓ	16. Ⓐ Ⓑ Ⓒ Ⓓ	24. Ⓐ Ⓑ Ⓒ Ⓓ	32. Ⓐ Ⓑ Ⓒ Ⓓ	

Section 2: Mathematics

1. Ⓐ Ⓑ Ⓒ Ⓓ	7. Ⓐ Ⓑ Ⓒ Ⓓ	13. Ⓐ Ⓑ Ⓒ Ⓓ	19. Ⓐ Ⓑ Ⓒ Ⓓ	25. Ⓐ Ⓑ Ⓒ Ⓓ
2. Ⓐ Ⓑ Ⓒ Ⓓ	8. Ⓐ Ⓑ Ⓒ Ⓓ	14. Ⓐ Ⓑ Ⓒ Ⓓ	20. Ⓐ Ⓑ Ⓒ Ⓓ	26. Ⓐ Ⓑ Ⓒ Ⓓ
3. Ⓐ Ⓑ Ⓒ Ⓓ	9. Ⓐ Ⓑ Ⓒ Ⓓ	15. Ⓐ Ⓑ Ⓒ Ⓓ	21. Ⓐ Ⓑ Ⓒ Ⓓ	27. Ⓐ Ⓑ Ⓒ Ⓓ
4. Ⓐ Ⓑ Ⓒ Ⓓ	10. Ⓐ Ⓑ Ⓒ Ⓓ	16. Ⓐ Ⓑ Ⓒ Ⓓ	22. Ⓐ Ⓑ Ⓒ Ⓓ	28. Ⓐ Ⓑ Ⓒ Ⓓ
5. Ⓐ Ⓑ Ⓒ Ⓓ	11. Ⓐ Ⓑ Ⓒ Ⓓ	17. Ⓐ Ⓑ Ⓒ Ⓓ	23. Ⓐ Ⓑ Ⓒ Ⓓ	29. Ⓐ Ⓑ Ⓒ Ⓓ
6. Ⓐ Ⓑ Ⓒ Ⓓ	12. Ⓐ Ⓑ Ⓒ Ⓓ	18. Ⓐ Ⓑ Ⓒ Ⓓ	24. Ⓐ Ⓑ Ⓒ Ⓓ	30. Ⓐ Ⓑ Ⓒ Ⓓ

Section 3: Science

1. Ⓐ Ⓑ Ⓒ Ⓓ	5. Ⓐ Ⓑ Ⓒ Ⓓ	9. Ⓐ Ⓑ Ⓒ Ⓓ	13. Ⓐ Ⓑ Ⓒ Ⓓ	17. Ⓐ Ⓑ Ⓒ Ⓓ
2. Ⓐ Ⓑ Ⓒ Ⓓ	6. Ⓐ Ⓑ Ⓒ Ⓓ	10. Ⓐ Ⓑ Ⓒ Ⓓ	14. Ⓐ Ⓑ Ⓒ Ⓓ	18. Ⓐ Ⓑ Ⓒ Ⓓ
3. Ⓐ Ⓑ Ⓒ Ⓓ	7. Ⓐ Ⓑ Ⓒ Ⓓ	11. Ⓐ Ⓑ Ⓒ Ⓓ	15. Ⓐ Ⓑ Ⓒ Ⓓ	19. Ⓐ Ⓑ Ⓒ Ⓓ
4. Ⓐ Ⓑ Ⓒ Ⓓ	8. Ⓐ Ⓑ Ⓒ Ⓓ	12. Ⓐ Ⓑ Ⓒ Ⓓ	16. Ⓐ Ⓑ Ⓒ Ⓓ	20. Ⓐ Ⓑ Ⓒ Ⓓ

Section 4: Social Studies

1. Ⓐ Ⓑ Ⓒ Ⓓ	5. Ⓐ Ⓑ Ⓒ Ⓓ	9. Ⓐ Ⓑ Ⓒ Ⓓ	13. Ⓐ Ⓑ Ⓒ Ⓓ	17. Ⓐ Ⓑ Ⓒ Ⓓ
2. Ⓐ Ⓑ Ⓒ Ⓓ	6. Ⓐ Ⓑ Ⓒ Ⓓ	10. Ⓐ Ⓑ Ⓒ Ⓓ	14. Ⓐ Ⓑ Ⓒ Ⓓ	
3. Ⓐ Ⓑ Ⓒ Ⓓ	7. Ⓐ Ⓑ Ⓒ Ⓓ	11. Ⓐ Ⓑ Ⓒ Ⓓ	15. Ⓐ Ⓑ Ⓒ Ⓓ	
4. Ⓐ Ⓑ Ⓒ Ⓓ	8. Ⓐ Ⓑ Ⓒ Ⓓ	12. Ⓐ Ⓑ Ⓒ Ⓓ	16. Ⓐ Ⓑ Ⓒ Ⓓ	

Section 5: Art, Music, and Physical Education

1. Ⓐ Ⓑ Ⓒ Ⓓ	4. Ⓐ Ⓑ Ⓒ Ⓓ	7. Ⓐ Ⓑ Ⓒ Ⓓ	10. Ⓐ Ⓑ Ⓒ Ⓓ	13. Ⓐ Ⓑ Ⓒ Ⓓ
2. Ⓐ Ⓑ Ⓒ Ⓓ	5. Ⓐ Ⓑ Ⓒ Ⓓ	8. Ⓐ Ⓑ Ⓒ Ⓓ	11. Ⓐ Ⓑ Ⓒ Ⓓ	14. Ⓐ Ⓑ Ⓒ Ⓓ
3. Ⓐ Ⓑ Ⓒ Ⓓ	6. Ⓐ Ⓑ Ⓒ Ⓓ	9. Ⓐ Ⓑ Ⓒ Ⓓ	12. Ⓐ Ⓑ Ⓒ Ⓓ	15. Ⓐ Ⓑ Ⓒ Ⓓ

Section 1: Reading and Language Arts

1. Which of the following are examples of summative assessments? (Choose all that apply.)

   (A) teacher observations

   (B) cumulative examination

   (C) term paper

   (D) jigsaw teaching

2. Which of the following are examples of formative assessments? (Choose all that apply.)

   (A) exit ticket

   (B) think–pair–share

   (C) mid–term exam

   (D) a research paper

3. A fourth-grade teacher asks her students to write three predictions for what they believe will happen in Chapter 2 of *Tales of a Fourth Grade Nothing* by Judy Blume. At which level of Bloom's Taxonomy is the activity?

   (A) knowledge

   (B) comprehension

   (C) analysis

   (D) synthesis

4. A fifth-grade teacher notices that his students are having difficulty choosing text to include as evidence in an extended response question. He decides to model for students how he would find textual evidence. He gives his students the text he is using and then explains why he would choose various quotes in his response. Finally, he explains and models for students how he would formulate his own response to the given question. Which of the following best describes this teaching method?

   (A) reciprocal teaching

   (B) think–aloud

   (C) direct instruction

   (D) a jigsaw

5. A second-grade student is having difficulty sounding out the words "coat," "boil," and "loud." The teacher can best address the needs of the student by offering direct instruction in which of the following?

   (A) blends

   (B) digraphs

   (C) graphemes

   (D) diphthongs

6. A second-grade teacher's students are whisper-reading with a partner. What reading skill is being reinforced by this instructional method?

   (A) decoding

   (B) fluency

   (C) phonics

   (D) comprehension

7. Mrs. Fitzsimmons, a fourth-grade teacher, had the following objective for her students in the previous day's lesson.

   Students will be able to define, label, and identify text features of various nonfiction texts.

   Which of the following assessments would **best** determine whether students have mastered the skill?

   (A) Have students fill in a KWL chart on text features.

   (B) Give students a formal exam.

   (C) Conference with each student and ask why he has learned about text features.

   (D) Give students an entrance ticket with various text features for them to identify.

8. A student is using a variety of strategies, including using pictures, to help him decode words on his own. He is also able to make predictions based on the pictures he sees in his text.

   At which stage of literacy is this student?

   (A) emergent reader
   (B) early reader
   (C) transitional reader
   (D) fluent reader

9. Mrs. Simpkins, a fifth-grade teacher, has just finished a writing conference with one of her students. She has asked the student to revise the ending of his mystery story. She has specifically asked him to create two alternate endings that they will discuss at their next conference. At which level of Bloom's Taxonomy is the task that Mrs. Simpkins has posed to her student?

   (A) comprehension
   (B) application
   (C) synthesis
   (D) evaluation

10. A kindergarten teacher asks a student to tell her all the sounds in the word "cat." Which skill is the teacher formatively assessing with the given student?

    (A) segmentation
    (B) onset and rime
    (C) syllabication
    (D) isolation

11. Which type of figurative language is illustrated in the following sentence?

    Allison ate apricots, anchovies, and asparagus.

    (A) personification
    (B) assonance
    (C) alliteration
    (D) metaphor

12. A sixth-grade student is writing a paper about the importance of school uniforms. The student is engaging in which type of writing?

    (A) expository
    (B) persuasive
    (C) narrative
    (D) informational

13. A fourth-grade student is conferencing with her teacher about a narrative she has been working on. She has asked her teacher to listen closely to the ending and offer feedback about clarifying and expanding. The student is engaged in which stage of the writing process?

    (A) prewriting
    (B) proofing
    (C) revising
    (D) publishing

14. A fifth-grade student is writing an expository essay about the similarities and differences between polar bears and grizzly bears. He should begin the writing process by using which of the following graphic organizers?

    (A) Venn diagram
    (B) flow chart
    (C) KWL chart
    (D) web

15. Through observation, a kindergarten teacher recognizes that several of her students do not comprehend that each letter of the alphabet is connected to a specific sound. Through these observations, the teacher recognizes that this group of students is having difficulty with which phonetic skill?

    (A) phonemes
    (B) graphemes
    (C) concepts of print
    (D) alphabetic principle

GO ON TO NEXT PAGE

16. Which of the following word meanings can be determined based on a structural analysis?

    (A) mischief

    (B) plateau

    (C) disagreeable

    (D) vivid

17. A second-grade teacher notices a student is having difficulty decoding words such as "block," "grapes," and "split." Which skill needs to be retaught and reinforced with this student?

    (A) diphthongs

    (B) consonant blends

    (C) consonant digraphs

    (D) onset and rime

18. A kindergarten teacher notices a student has difficulty creating a list of rhyming words, such as "man" and "can," when given the ending -an. This child needs further instruction in which of the following areas?

    (A) phonological awareness

    (B) onset and rime

    (C) alphabetic principle

    (D) phonics

19. A sixth-grade teacher is meeting with each of his students to discuss what each student believes are his or her own strengths and weaknesses in reading. Which method is the teacher utilizing?

    (A) formative assessment

    (B) summative assessment

    (C) conferencing

    (D) reciprocal teaching

20. A first-grade teacher is introducing the concept of inference with students by using picture cards. She has just shown a picture card of a crying girl standing over an ice-cream cone on the ground. Which question would best introduce the concept of inference?

    (A) What flavor do you think the ice cream is?

    (B) How is this girl feeling?

    (C) What time of day is it?

    (D) What might have just happened?

21. An eighth-grade teacher is giving a unit assessment on the major events of the Revolutionary War. Which method is the teacher utilizing?

    (A) formative assessment

    (B) summative assessment

    (C) high stakes testing

    (D) collaborative learning

22. A teacher shows his students the following paragraph to assess their editing skills. Which of the following errors can the students find in the paragraph? Choose all that apply.

    Over the weekend, my family and I will go out for diner at a fancy restaurant downtown. Everyone are anxious and excited to go. My brother and I are especially excited to go because we haven't never been to a fancy restaurant. We even have to wear ties and dress shoes.

    (A) a misspelled word

    (B) a double negative

    (C) a punctuation error

    (D) a subject/verb agreement error

23. Many early primary teachers label objects in their classrooms, such as "garbage can," "teacher's desk," and "computer." What instructional method are these teachers employing in this situation?

    (A) giving students access to high-frequency words

    (B) developing specialized vocabulary

    (C) creating a word wall

    (D) fostering a print-rich environment

24. What activity would **best** build student understanding that nouns are people, places, and things?

    (A) Have students list all the words they can that begin with a given letter.

    (B) Match pictures of places with their names.

    (C) Cut out and sort pictures that are people, places, and things.

    (D) Go outside and have students observe and record various things in nature.

25. A third-grade teacher reads the following sentences from a student's narrative about a trip to Florida.

We flew on a plane. It was really exciting. When we got there we went to the beach and swam in the ocean.

What strategy would the teacher use to best help the student improve the narrative?

(A) Suggest the student research beaches in Florida.

(B) Ask the student to bring in pictures from the trip.

(C) Ask the student questions about the trip.

(D) Tell the student to provide more information about the plane ride.

26. Mrs. Williams, a first-grade teacher, is interested in finding out which of her students have mastered the "long a" sound. Which formative assessment would **best** measure this instructional goal?

(A) Have students list as many words as they can that contain the "long a" sound.

(B) Have students cut out pictures of items that have the "long a" sound and make a collage.

(C) Have students cut out pictures of some items that have the "long a" sound and some items that do not have that sound, sort the items, and glue them to separate sheets of paper.

(D) Have students bring in items from home that have the "long a" sound and share what they've brought with the class.

27. Ms. Kennedy, a kindergarten teacher, wants to begin to develop her students' oral communication skills. Which activity would best assist Ms. Kennedy in reaching this goal?

(A) Have students read books aloud to a partner.

(B) Have students express ideas using complete sentences.

(C) Have students present on a topic to the class.

(D) Have students listen to books read aloud by the teacher.

28. Which of the following is a measurable objective?

(A) Students will be able to enjoy adding adjectives to various sentences.

(B) Students will be able to underline adjectives within given sentences.

(C) Students will be able to know a variety of adjective examples.

(D) Students will be able to comprehend what an adjective is and how to use one in a sentence.

29. What is the first step of curriculum planning?

(A) Become familiar with the standards that are to be taught.

(B) Create objectives for each lesson.

(C) Find ways to connect lessons to multiple subject areas.

(D) Look at or create a final assessment for the given unit of study.

30. Which activity would best suit the needs of an intrapersonal learner?

(A) a nature walk

(B) think-pair-share

(C) journal reflection

(D) using manipulatives

31. Which of the following are examples of cooperative learning strategies? (Choose all that apply.)

(A) think-pair-share

(B) think-aloud

(C) reciprocal teaching

(D) jigsaw

32. Which of the following are benefits of read-alouds? (Choose all that apply.)

(A) development of a student's fluency level

(B) development of a student's listening skills

(C) development of a student's oral communication skills

(D) model provided of reading with expression and tone

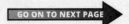

33. In what situation would the use of a double journal be most beneficial?

(A) writing similarities between characters on the left and differences on the right

(B) writing quotes from a text on the left and thoughts about the quotes on the right

(C) writing character names on the left and descriptions of those characters on the right

(D) writing what is known and what the student wants to know about a character

34. Which of the following is an example of a literal level of comprehension question?

(A) What do you think will happen next?

(B) What happened before the dog ran away?

(C) Do you like this story better than the last story we read? Why?

(D) What happened because the dog ran away?

35. A kindergarten teacher is asking a student to find the title of a book. She is also asking the student to identify the front and back covers of that same book. What is she most likely assessing? (Choose all that apply.)

(A) alphabetic principle

(B) phonological awareness

(C) readiness for reading

(D) concept of print

36. Which of the following methods would assist in increasing student engagement? (Choose all that apply.)

(A) Call on students not paying attention.

(B) Connect the lesson to real-life situations.

(C) Utilize a variety of instructional techniques.

(D) Regularly administer pop quizzes.

37. Which of the following is the least invasive behavior intervention?

(A) Write the student's name on the board and continue teaching.

(B) Stand next to the child and continue teaching.

(C) Stop the lesson and wait for the child to correct the behavior.

(D) Tap on the child's desk with a pencil and continue teaching.

38. In which situation would homogenous grouping be most appropriate?

(A) a jigsaw activity about Abraham Lincoln

(B) a guided reading group

(C) a think-pair-share where students make predictions about the class read-aloud

(D) a science experiment about erosion

39. What is one way that a teacher could maximize student learning time?

(A) Teach procedures for activities at the beginning of the school year.

(B) Have extra work packets available for early finishers.

(C) Offer after-school extra-help sessions.

(D) Give students more than enough time to complete group work activities.

Section 2: Mathematics

1. A math teacher gives her students the following problem as part of a class assignment. Which of the following concepts is the teacher most likely trying to help her students understand?

   A cross country runner kept a record of all the places in which he finished in races in a season. He finished in the following places:

   1, 3, 2, 2, 4, 3, 2, 1

   Which place did he come in the most?

   (A) mean

   (B) median

   (C) mode

   (D) range

2. Students in a class are learning basic geometric shapes. Creating which of the following could best help the students understand the figures by illustrating the similarities and differences among the figures?

   (A) set of pattern blocks

   (B) arrangement of square unit tiles

   (C) cube formed from base-10 blocks

   (D) shape hierarchy

3. A student is asked to locate (3, 5) on a coordinate plane, but the student points to (5, 3). Which TWO of the following types of mistakes are most likely why the student gave an incorrect answer?

   (A) assuming the indication of a third axis

   (B) confusing the x-coordinate with the y-coordinate

   (C) having a misconception of the location of the origin

   (D) confusing the x-axis with the y-axis

4. A teacher gives each of his students 24 counters and asks each student to arrange the counters in 6 rows of 4, 2 rows of 12, 3 rows of 8, and 1 row of 24. Which of the following math concepts is the teacher most likely helping his students learn?

   (A) length and width

   (B) factoring

   (C) sequencing

   (D) commutative property of addition

5. A teacher plans to give her class the following problem. Which of the following concepts do the students need to have learned first in order to understand how to work the problem?

   $$12p - 3 = 11p$$

   (A) combining like terms

   (B) defining variables

   (C) associative property of addition

   (D) cancellation

6. For a classroom project, students divide into groups, and each group creates a rectangle of a specified length and width. Each group determines the area of its rectangle. Then, the students put all the rectangles together to form a rectangular solid. Which of the following concepts are the students most likely exploring?

   (A) volume

   (B) surface area

   (C) shape hierarchy

   (D) size ratios

GO ON TO NEXT PAGE

7. Students in a math class are asked to convert 15 miles per hour to a unit rate expressed in feet per second. One student wrote the following:

$$\frac{15\text{ miles}}{1\text{ hour}} \times \frac{5,280\text{ feet}}{1\text{ mile}}$$

What should the teacher instruct the student to multiply what he has written by in order for the student to determine the correct answer to the problem?

(A) (1 hour)/(60 minutes) · (1 minute)/ (60 seconds)

(B) 60 seconds

(C) (1 mile)/(5,280 feet)

(D) (1 hour)/(60 seconds)

8. Which of the following student activities would be most effective for introducing students to the distributive property with the example of evaluating $2(3 + 7)$?

(A) multiplying 2 by 10

(B) forming 3 groups of 2 counters and adding 7 counters to the set

(C) multiplying 2 by 7 and adding 3 to the result

(D) combining 3 groups of 2 counters with 7 groups of 2 counters and then using the same set to form 10 groups of 2 counters

9. The students in a math class have three upcoming lessons on geometric measurements.

Lesson A: Surface areas of rectangular solids

Lesson B: Measures of segments

Lesson C: Areas of rectangles

In which of the following orders should the lessons be taught?

(A) A, C, B

(B) B, A, C

(C) B, C, A

(D) A, B, C

10. Students in a class put cubes of the same size and shape in a rectangular solid until the rectangular solid is completely filled with the cubes. What concept are the students most likely exploring?

(A) surface area

(B) face area

(C) volume

(D) transformation

11. Which of the following activities best demonstrates that 3/4 is 3 of 1/4?

(A) combining 1 base-10 block with a set of 3

(B) taking a pizza divided into 4 equal slices and removing 1 slice, then another slice, and then another slice, and putting together the removed slices to form 3/4 of what the students had at the beginning

(C) taking a pie divided into 4 equal slices and removing 1 slice, leaving 3 of the original 4 slices

(D) dividing students up into groups of 4 and having 3 students in each group sit down while 1 remains standing

12. Students in a class are given the following equation, in which R represents an exact number of functional units. Which of the following problems could be presented based on the equation?

$$40 \div 4 = R$$

(A) Forty T-shirts are divided equally among 4 people. How many T-shirts does each person get?

(B) An amount of $4 is divided equally among 40 people. How much money does each person get?

(C) Forty pounds of ice cream are divided among 4 people. How many people in the group are there for every pound of ice cream?

(D) Four cats are divided among 40 people. How many cats does each person get?

13. A teacher uses the following models to illustrate some of the principles involved in a type of mathematical procedure. What type of procedure is the teacher most likely teaching her students?

$x + 3$

10

x

7

(A) solving algebraic equations

(B) calculating length

(C) algebraic division

(D) segment similarity

14. A teacher gives her students a set of data during a lesson. Which of the following questions about the data are appropriate for helping the students understand concepts of central tendency?

Select **all** that apply.

(A) Which number appears the most in the set?

(B) What do you get when you add all the numbers and divide the sum by the number of numbers?

(C) What is the largest number in the data set?

(D) What is the difference between the largest number and the smallest number?

15. A teacher presents the following figure to her class and asks the students to determine the area of the figure. The figure is composed of a triangle sharing a side with a rectangle. All width, length, and height measures are available to the students. Which is the best method the teacher could instruct the students to use?

© John Wiley & Sons, Inc.

(A) Paint the figure and determine how much paint was used. Then determine how much area was covered based on the amount of paint.

(B) Use a formula, involving strictly multiplication, for the area of the type of figure and apply the formula.

(C) Use the appropriate formulas to determine the area of the rectangle and the area of the triangle separately. Then add their areas.

(D) Find the area of the figure that would exist if the triangle were a rectangle with a width the same as the triangle's height.

16. Students in a class are given sheets of paper with ten rows of natural numbers 1 through 100. The students are asked to circle the 2 in the first row and then every second number after it in that row. They are then asked to circle the 3 in the next row and then every third number after it in that row. The process is repeated for one number higher in each next row. Which of the following concepts are the students most likely exploring?

(A) factors

(B) equivalent sets

(C) the relationship between addition and subtraction

(D) multiples

GO ON TO NEXT PAGE

17. A student worked the following multiplication problem on a board. In which type of action did the student make a mistake in working the problem?

$$
\begin{array}{r}
722 \\
\times\,14 \\
\hline
2918 \\
7320 \\
\hline
10238
\end{array}
$$

(A) multiplying a number of ones by a number of tens

(B) adding the tens column

(C) multiplying a number of tens by a number of hundreds

(D) adding the hundreds column

18. A teacher gave her students the following problem.

Janet has 4 more than twice the number of oranges Mark has. The total number of oranges Janet and Mark have together is 13. How many oranges does Janet have?

If a student uses the variable g to represent the number of oranges Mark has, what should the student be instructed to use to represent the number of oranges Janet has, in order to write an equation based on the situation?

(A) $4g + 2$

(B) $2g + 4$

(C) $13 - 2g$

(D) $6g$

19. Two students were asked to add the numbers of students in three classrooms. The students who added the numbers added them in different orders but got the same sum. What property was the teacher most likely trying to illustrate for her students?

(A) commutative property of addition

(B) distributive property

(C) associative property of addition

(D) substitution property

20. For the purpose of teaching students a lesson on writing formulas based on patterns, a teacher presented the following table to her students.

Number of Sides	Interior Angle Sum (Degrees)
3	180
4	360
5	540

The table shows the interior angle sums of polygons based on their number of sides. Which of the following correctly presented tables would be best for the teacher to use in conjunction with the first table to illustrate how to determine a formula based on the pattern?

(A)

Number of Sides	Interior Angle Sum (Degrees)
3	90(2)
4	90(4)
5	90(6)

(B)

Number of Sides	Interior Angle Sum (Degrees)
3	180
4	180 + 180
5	360 + 180

(C)

Number of Sides	Interior Angle Sum (Degrees)
3	180(1)
4	180(2)
5	180(3)

(D)

Number of Sides	Interior Angle Sum (Degrees)
3	180(3 – 2)
4	180(4 – 2)
5	180(5 – 2)

21. Which of the following situations involves getting a wrong answer as a result of incorrect use of a base system?

   (A) concluding that the elapsed time between 2:45 p.m. and 3:15 p.m. on the same day is 70 minutes

   (B) determining that $4.65 − $1.20 is $345

   (C) getting a false product of $6\frac{7}{40}$ from trying to multiply $3\frac{1}{5}$ by $2\frac{7}{8}$

   (D) forming the conclusion that 6 yards is equal to 2 feet

22. A teacher gives her students the following expression to evaluate. Which of the following should she instruct her students to do first?

   $$9(4+7\cdot2)-5$$

   (A) Add 4 and 7.

   (B) Subtract 5 from 9.

   (C) Multiply 7 by 2.

   (D) Add 4 and 2.

23. A teacher gave her class the following word problem.

   A milk company's crates hold 4 jugs of milk each. How many crates will a driver for the company need to transport 22 jugs of milk?

   Many of the students gave the answer $5\frac{1}{2}$, 5 R 2, or 5.5. Students who gave such answers need practice in which of the following?

   (A) converting fractions to decimals

   (B) using number sense

   (C) rounding

   (D) determining remainders

24. Which of the following exercises would be best for a class to do in order to gain understanding of the difference between prime and composite numbers?

   (A) Factor a set of numbers and make a list of numbers in the set that have two factors and a list of numbers that have more than two factors.

   (B) Represent a set of prime numbers and a set of composite numbers with base-10 blocks.

   (C) Identify types of polygons with prime numbers of sides and compare them to polygons with composite numbers of sides.

   (D) Divide composite numbers by prime numbers.

25. Which of the following strategies should a teacher instruct his students to use to best help them determine the answer to the following algebraic word problem?

   Bob has 7 more stamps than Fred. The sum of the numbers of stamps Bob and Fred have is 27. How many stamps does Fred have?

   (A) Use a variable to represent the number of stamps Fred has, use a different variable to represent the number of stamps Bob has, write two equations to illustrate the situation, and solve for one variable to determine the other.

   (B) Try various combinations of numbers with a sum of 27 until the combination that works is identified. Select the lower number.

   (C) Use a variable to represent the number of stamps Fred has, write an expression using that variable to represent the number of stamps Bob has, add the two expressions and set the sum equal to 27, and solve the equation.

   (D) Try various combinations of numbers with a sum of 27 until the combination that works is identified. Select the higher number.

GO ON TO NEXT PAGE

26. A teacher instructs her students to use square unit tiles to form a rectangle and then count the number of tiles on each side of the formed rectangle. Which of the following concepts is the teacher most likely helping her students explore?

(A) rectangle area

(B) rectangular solid surface area

(C) rectangular solid volume

(D) composite figure area

27. A teacher gives students in a group a different number of counters each and asks the students to write down the number of counters he or she has. The teacher then asks the students to put their counters together and divide them up equally. What concept is the teacher most likely helping the students understand?

(A) mean

(B) median

(C) mode

(D) range

28. Which of the following instructional methods would best help students grasp the concept of area?

(A) Divide the volume of a right rectangular solid by its height.

(B) Square the measure of the side of a square.

(C) Calculate the amount of elapsed time involved in decorating a geometric figure with glitter.

(D) Give students square unit tiles and ask them to form a rectangle. Then ask the students to count the number of tiles and compare it to what they get when they multiply the number of tiles along the length by the number of tiles along the width.

29. Which of the following would be the best formative assessment of students' understanding of how percents are related to fractions?

(A) Write a fraction on the board. Then ask students to divide the numerator by the denominator and move the decimal in the quotient two places to the right and put a percent sign by the result.

(B) Give students a fraction in which the denominator is a factor of 100. Ask the students to multiply the denominator by the number necessary to get 100 and multiply the numerator by the same number. Ask the students to write the product of the numerator and the number on a piece of paper.

(C) Have students write reports on percentages concerning population demographics.

(D) Instruct students to memorize a list of fraction to percent conversions and give a short quiz on the list.

30. Which of the following concepts must students understand before learning about probability?

(A) ratios

(B) manipulatives

(C) odds

(D) excluded values

Section 3: Science

1. A ball that is resting on top of an inclined plane has energy. What type of energy does that ball have?

   (A) radiant energy

   (B) gravitational potential energy

   (C) electrical potential energy

   (D) thermal energy

2. A science teacher wants to teach a lesson on changes in a state of matter due to pressure or temperature. Which of the following labs would best teach this concept?

   (A) adding a drop of food coloring to a warm cup of water without stirring

   (B) adding a cube of ice to a warm cup of water

   (C) allowing a cool cup of water to sit, undisturbed, until it reaches room temperature

   (D) mixing cold water and hot water

3. A teacher wants to instruct students in proper methods for gathering scientific data. As part of an experiment to introduce reliable sources of data for investigative purposes, she has the students gather information on how other students feel about the health and nutritional content of their school lunches. What type of data do the students gather?

   (A) observational data

   (B) nutritional measurements

   (C) anecdotal evidence

   (D) secondary data

4. As part of an experiment, the students in Mr. John's class have been watching cocoons mature on a life path. When a cocoon opens and a student observes the new butterfly fluttering its wings, she states this fluttering is important so the butterfly can next break free of the cocoon. The student is using two scientific processes in her statement. What are they?

   (A) observation and measurement

   (B) observation and experimentation

   (C) inference and communication

   (D) observation and inference

5. As part of an anticipatory set for a new unit of study, a teacher took his shoes off and slid across the tile floor in only his socks until he came to a gradual stop. Which force was the teacher showing to the students?

   (A) momentum

   (B) centrifugal

   (C) inertia

   (D) friction

6. Which is one of the most important things to consider when teaching science?

   (A) Science should be taught through processes because the concepts will be easier to understand if they are grounded in genuine inquiry.

   (B) Always teach the facts because that is what students will be tested on for state assessments.

   (C) Only focus on the content because science content has already been proven and can never change.

   (D) Teach the laws of science. Students who stay grounded in proven theories will have an easier time understanding larger concepts.

GO ON TO NEXT PAGE

7. As part of a unit on the water cycle, a teacher has divided the class into cooperative learning groups and assigned each group to complete a presentation. Their presentation is to identify the importance of their component of the water and describe what would occur on the planet if this component were to be changed in some way due to global warming. This is an example of which of the following stages of Bloom's Taxonomy?

(A) comprehension

(B) evaluation

(C) application

(D) synthesis

8. The area of science that includes the study of meteorology, astronomy, and oceanography is which of the following?

(A) natural science

(B) earth science

(C) life science

(D) behavioral science

9. In a science classroom, students have been given four different flowers by their teacher. They are asked to examine the structure of the flower, identify all the parts, and compare the differences between them. After this, students are then directed to develop a generalization on the plants using their knowledge of the plant kingdom. They have to determine the type of habitat each flower could exist in and how the flower might affect insects. What form of teaching style does this lesson model?

(A) reflective

(B) inductive

(C) deductive

(D) introspective

10. The word "taxonomy" refers to what area of scientific study?

(A) reproduction, in the understanding that each gene must have specific characteristics and traits

(B) classification, in the understanding that each species belongs to a family which exhibits similar traits

(C) ecosystems, in the understanding that a biological community has organisms interacting with a physical environment

(D) paleontology, with the understanding that all matter is derived from earlier life on Earth

11. Which of these would be the best way to explain heat conduction to students?

(A) People feel heat when they touch a hot mug or bowl.

(B) People feel heat when they stand near a heater.

(C) People feel heat when they stand in the sun.

(D) People feel heat when they stand near a heater and feel the hot air blowing on them.

12. Which of the following does **not** contribute to the process of the rock cycle, or the cycling of rocks in the environment?

(A) metamorphism

(B) weathering and erosion

(C) mineral dissolution

(D) crystallization

13. Which of these depicts a chemical process?

(A) soil being eroded through water runoff

(B) iron forming rust on submerged ships

(C) the melting of icebergs

(D) the eruption of the Yellowstone Grand Geyser

14. Use this diagram to answer the question that follows:

The Carbon Cycle

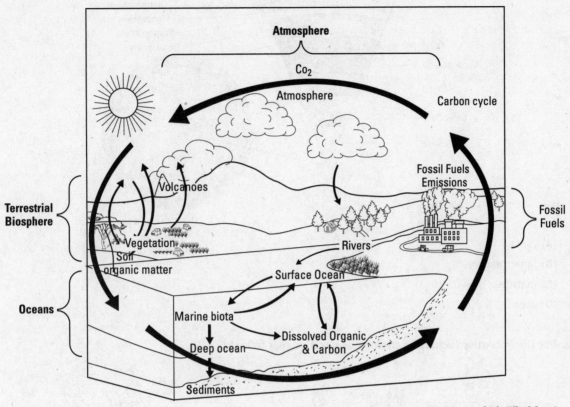

© John Wiley & Sons, Inc.

In understanding the carbon cycle, which of the following is not considered a main reservoir of carbon?

(A) atmosphere

(B) fossil fuels

(C) oceans

(D) dissolved organic carbons

GO ON TO NEXT PAGE

15. Based on the following diagram, which of these is the thickest layer?

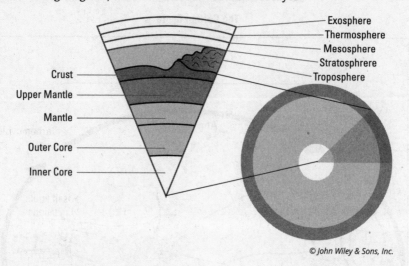

Exosphere
Thermosphere
Mesosphere
Stratosphrere
Troposphere

Crust
Upper Mantle
Mantle
Outer Core
Inner Core

© John Wiley & Sons, Inc.

(A) crust

(B) upper mantle

(C) mantle

(D) core

16. Use the following diagram to answer the question that follows:

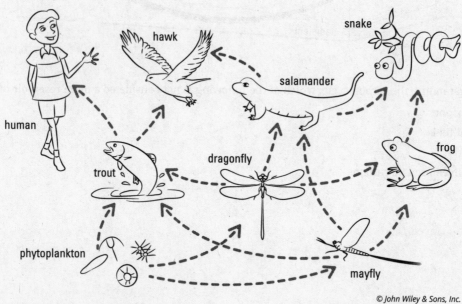

snake

hawk

salamander

human

frog

dragonfly

trout

phytoplankton

mayfly

© John Wiley & Sons, Inc.

It would be most correct to say that energy in this food web flows in which direction?

(A) The energy is flowing upward.

(B) The energy is flowing downward.

(C) There is no flow of energy represented.

(D) Energy is flowing in both directions, upward and downward.

17. Use this diagram to answer the question that follows:

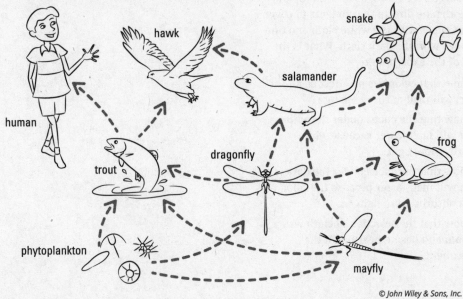

© *John Wiley & Sons, Inc.*

Which of the following is the most likely short-term outcome if, due to pollution, phytoplankton were eliminated from this pond and this food web?

(A) Photosynthesis would kick in, creating more food sources.

(B) The food web, as illustrated here, would collapse as dragonflies, trout, and mayflies have no other recognized food source.

(C) Salamanders would become a new food source to fill in the gaps of the food chain.

(D) Dragonflies would adapt and begin eating mayflies to fill in the gaps of the food chain.

18. As part of an experiment about sound, a teacher sends two students to the end of a school hallway and tells them to have a conversation, neither whispering nor yelling. The remaining students observe that they can hear the voices, even though they cannot understand the specific words being said. What is the best way to explain this phenomenon?

(A) Sound travels through any medium, including air and water.

(B) Human voices are unique conductors of sound.

(C) Echoes moving down the hallway cause the sound to be heard.

(D) Sound will travel in any direction until it hits a receiver, where it stops.

19. As part of an experiment on electricity, a teacher brings in a string of Christmas lights. When she randomly removes one light, the rest of the strand also turns off. What concept is she most likely trying to exemplify?

(A) that a string of lights is part of a series of electric currents that are connected by the wire

(B) that the light the teacher pulled was the circuit breaker for the entire string

(C) that electricity occurs in a parallel circuit

(D) that electricity is a safety hazard and should only be handled by adults

GO ON TO NEXT PAGE

20. As part of an experiment, a teacher gives each student several ice cubes, a white cloth, and a dark cloth. She directs the students to cover one set of cubes with the white cloth and one set of cubes with the dark cloth. What is the purpose of the experiment?

(A) to show that color has no effect as all the cubes will melt at the same rate

(B) to show that the cubes under the white cloth will melt faster because white absorbs more light

(C) to show that the cubes under the dark cloth will melt faster because the color black absorbs more light

(D) to show that the selection of cloth was random and has no bearing on the experiment

Section 4: Social Studies

1. A fifth-grade student has just finished reading a text about the settling of the colony of Jamestown, Virginia. After he reads, he remarks that this is new information for him. He explains that his past experiences led him to believe that the Pilgrims were the first permanent settlers, and their colony was the first attempt at colonizing the new world. What comprehension strategy is the student demonstrating with his comments?

   (A) inferential reading and thinking

   (B) summarizing

   (C) metacognition

   (D) observation

2. In order for students to be civic citizens, they must understand political thought processes and the historical development of governance. Which of the following situations would help them to understand the concept of democratic governance?

   (A) A formal system of democratic government is necessary to create laws, to establish order, and to provide security for citizens by a law of majority.

   (B) Governments are established so that a ruling body can be created in order to control a large population and protect citizens from harm.

   (C) In order for culture to be maintained and treasured, a government must be created that joins people together and establishes their right to enjoy a commonly created culture.

   (D) The underlying purpose of a government is to protect the properties and the lives of its citizens, even if individual liberties have to be sacrificed.

3. Spatial organization is important for students to understand the organization of people, places, and environments that exist in the world. All of the following topics are essential to understand spatial organization, except:

   (A) the location of the seven major continents

   (B) the compass rose

   (C) the land areas and living conditions of deserts

   (D) an understanding of water, which covers 70 percent of the earth's surface and provides 97 percent of the world's water supply

4. A fourth-grade teacher wants her students to understand that human characteristics can consist of many components, including values, religious beliefs, language systems, political structure, economic methods, and socioeconomic status. Which of the following lesson ideas would be the best way for her to introduce this concept?

   (A) The teacher introduces maize to the students, showing that growing of corn in the arid climate of the Southwest uses the resources of the desert and allows those Native Americans to make adobe homes and use the plants of the maize corn in many ways.

   (B) The teacher introduces the Socratic Method to the students, helping them to see that the culture of Greek and Roman civilization favored wisdom and rational inquiry.

   (C) The teacher introduces the explorers Juan Ponce de Leon and Fernando De Soto to help the students understand that the colonization of the Americas took many forms and was not solely instigated by British rule.

   (D) The teacher introduces the Inuit people of the Arctic North to the class in a slide show, displaying artifacts of clothing made from animal skins, homes made of ice, money made of fur, and travel by dog sled.

GO ON TO NEXT PAGE

5. Which lesson would **not** fit into teaching students about anthropology, sociology, and psychology?

(A) Students virtually visit a local museum, comparing the lives of pioneer settlers to their modern lives.

(B) Students read a biography of Chief Black Hawk.

(C) Students elect a student council in their own classroom by giving speeches, voting, and establishing a government.

(D) Students create a family tree and research the use of family name crests.

6. When comparing the Iroquois and the Cherokee Native American people, the students learn about how food is obtained. What type of anthropology are they studying?

(A) linguistic

(B) physical

(C) biological

(D) cultural

7. A third-grade teacher is going to assess his students on the social studies unit he has been teaching. The unit involves the dance and music of the Ojibwa, a Native American tribe whose culture is important in the local area. He wants to make sure that the students are prepared for the end-of-the-year state assessment concerning this unit of historical information. Which of the following assessments should he use in preparation for the test?

(A) Place students into groups to research and then model a specific dance or type of music.

(B) Place students into groups and then use a checklist to determine which content is being discussed.

(C) Assign each student a specific piece of music or dance to research and then have them present their findings to the class.

(D) Give students a vocabulary test with content terms for music and dance.

8. What is the highest level of Bloom's Taxonomy reached when a student diagrams and compares the checks and balances of the legislative, executive, and judicial powers of the U.S. government?

(A) evaluation

(B) analysis

(C) synthesis

(D) knowledge

9. As an elementary teacher, you are teaching a unit on map-making skills. You want your unit to address all the learning intelligences. Which of the following activities would satisfy the needs of a verbal/linguistic learner?

(A) have students go outside and draw a map of the school grounds

(B) teach the students a song about different map components

(C) have students draw a map of their bedroom, with a legend

(D) read passages about biographies of important historical mapmakers and explorers

10. When studying local history, you take your class on a field trip to the local historical library which has artifacts and exhibits of your community and the founding of the town. What instructional strategy is this an example of?

(A) scaffolding of instruction

(B) primary source utilization

(C) a unifying presentation

(D) visual representations

11. A fifth-grade teacher is presenting information on early civilizations. As part of the introduction, the teacher reads the chapter from the textbook to the students and then paraphrases the text. What instructional strategy is the teacher using?

(A) scaffolding of instruction

(B) cooperative learning

(C) whole class instruction

(D) deductive learning

12. A third-grade teacher just completed a the-matic study of states, including important cities and flags. Which of the following types of assessment would be the most beneficial in planning instruction for the next unit: state capitols?

(A) observation

(B) summative

(C) formative

(D) performance

13. The anticipatory set that a second-grade teacher could use to engage an elementary classroom about learning directions would be:

(A) to give students a treasure map, with directions, to a class prize which can be found on the playground

(B) to have students complete a map of the classroom

(C) to deliver a speech about the importance of using maps when traveling

(D) to have students watch a documentary about Christopher Columbus and the discovery of the New World

14. A multicultural approach to teaching social studies at the elementary level should include

(A) an understanding of how news in one part of the world can influence political events in another part of the world.

(B) looking at examples from every con-tinent in every unit in order to fairly promote every race and culture.

(C) comparing how people from differ-ent cultures have responded, and still respond, to similar life events, such as war, famine, and weather, for example.

(D) an understanding that every culture is similar and that no culture is superior to another.

15. A social studies teacher needs to adapt his social studies instruction for a group of stu-dents who are significantly below grade level in reading. Which of the following actions, on the part of the teacher, is appropriate?

(A) using instructional materials with less difficult concepts

(B) teaching only the most important con-cepts, the ones most likely to appear on a state standardized test

(C) using instructional materials with a lower reading level

(D) placing students into groups so that the higher readers can help the lower readers understand the more difficult text

16. A teacher wants to use a token system to teach and motivate students during an economy unit. Which of the following actions would best support this approach?

(A) providing tokens as symbolic reinforce-ment for work completed by students and then allowing the students to purchase materials, such as pencils, or classroom privileges, such as free com-puter time or extra library time

(B) distributing tokens as reinforcement for positive behavior

(C) explaining to students that tokens can be collected and then traded for bonus points on assignments

(D) giving students a token as an appre-ciation of kindness witnessed in the classroom and around school and then showcasing the student with the most tokens earned on parent night

GO ON TO NEXT PAGE ▶

17. A teacher wants to most accurately describe the central goal of the Women's Suffrage Movement in the United States. How should she best introduce this concept?

(A) by introducing Abraham Lincoln and the Emancipation Proclamation, which essentially outlawed slavery

(B) by showing students a graph that explains the glass ceiling

(C) by reading a biography of famous women in history, including scientists, mathematicians, and other female leaders in the field

(D) by telling students that the class is going to read a whole-class novel of their choice, and then allowing only the boys to have a vote

Section 5: Art, Music, and Physical Education

1. A first-grade art class is practicing drawing lines and shapes with accuracy. Which other subject area is the teacher most likely integrating with this lesson?

   (A) history

   (B) science

   (C) reading/language arts

   (D) music

2. During music, a kindergarten teacher is having the whole class sing "It's a Small World" from memory for a creative-expression standard. Which assessment type is she most likely using?

   (A) norm-referenced

   (B) diagnostic

   (C) summative

   (D) formative

3. Which of the following activities is most appropriate for a second-grade physical education class?

   (A) dribble a basketball and pass it to a moving partner

   (B) pass a volleyball while stationary to a stationary partner

   (C) catch a rolled ball while moving and throw it back to a stationary partner

   (D) bounce a ball while stationary and catch it

4. The sixth-grade art class needs to have lessons that meet a standard of aesthetic valuing. Which of the following is most likely to help the class meet this standard?

   (A) small discussion groups that focus on new works of art and what they say about the students' current culture(s)

   (B) small discussion groups that focus on pencil drawings that use different values to suggest dimension, shape, and so forth

   (C) both Choice (A) and Choice (B)

   (D) neither Choice (A) nor Choice (B)

5. A fourth-grade teacher is having her music class keep journals as an assessment on how they evaluate the way practice has improved their performance. Which of the following activities is the teacher most likely having the class do in conjunction with their journals?

   (A) describe a piece of music according to its elements, using appropriate vocabulary

   (B) read, write, and play diatonic scales well

   (C) identify and describe music from diverse cultures

   (D) explain the criteria for judging a musical performance

6. A first-grade teacher is having students show their understanding of an element of art by mixing two primary colors in tempura paint to get a different secondary color. Which type of assessment measure is the teacher most likely using?

   (A) diagnostic

   (B) constructed response

   (C) performance-based

   (D) process-focused

7. A kindergarten teacher is doing a formative assessment in physical education, having the class "jump," "hop," or "slide" as she says each word. Which standard is the teacher most likely addressing?

   (A) knowledge of psychological concepts

   (B) knowledge of movement concepts

   (C) knowledge of physical fitness concepts

   (D) knowledge of improving performance

GO ON TO NEXT PAGE

8. A third-grade teacher is having a music class use flashcards with sixteenth notes, single eighth notes, paired eighth notes, quarter notes, quarter rests, half notes, dotted half notes, and whole notes on them. Which part of the curriculum's scope and sequence is the teacher most likely addressing?

(A) notate and perform rhythmic patterns

(B) notate and perform treble-staff melodies

(C) make appropriate physical responses to music

(D) describe and perform on pitched and nonpitched instruments

9. An art class of sixth-graders has just finished a summative assessment, and the teacher realizes she needs to go over radial balance in a more engaging way. Which lesson might prove most effective?

(A) having each student look at beautiful examples of radial balance

(B) having each student work with a balance scale to understand what balance means

(C) having each student use an app that allows each one to make his or her own image

(D) none of the above

10. In music, a fifth-grade teacher is conducting a summative assessment by having her students write an essay comparing the sounds of the same song when sung by a tenor and when sung by a bass. Which part of the music curriculum's scope and sequence is the teacher most likely addressing?

(A) distinguishing tone

(B) understanding major and minor chords

(C) distinguishing different measures

(D) understanding dynamics

11. A third-grade physical education class is working on complex movements. They take turns going to different stations, finding a card there, and doing the activity written on the card. Which other subject area is the teacher most likely integrating with this lesson?

(A) history

(B) science

(C) reading/language arts

(D) music

12. A second-grade teacher is conducting a formative assessment in art by having her students discuss photographs of different sculptures and who might have created them. Which part of the curriculum's scope and sequence is the teacher most likely addressing?

(A) understanding the principles of design

(B) understanding the relationship of art and culture

(C) understanding how to use materials in a safe manner

(D) understanding how to solve a visual arts problem with imagination

13. A kindergarten teacher is doing an informal, formative assessment in music that involves children identifying how sound is produced in different instruments. Which other subject area is the teacher most likely integrating with this lesson?

(A) social studies

(B) reading/language arts

(C) math

(D) science

14. As part of a physical education assessment of students' understanding of aerobic capacity, a fifth-grade teacher is having students measure and record their heart rates before and after vigorous activities. Which type of assessment tool is the teacher most likely using?

(A) project

(B) structured observation

(C) selected response

(D) essay question

15. A first-grade physical education class is working in pairs, very gently tossing a ball back and forth to a partner. Which of the following standards is the teacher LEAST likely addressing?

(A) motor skill development

(B) anatomical basis of movement

(C) fitness planning

(D) social development

Chapter 16

Answers and Explanations for 5017 Practice Test

After you finish the practice test sections in Chapter 15, take some time to go through the answers and explanations in this chapter to find out which questions you missed and why. Even if you answered the question correctly, the explanation may offer a useful strategy that helps you improve your performance.

Answers for Section 1: Reading and Language Arts

1. **B and C.** This question requires an understanding of the difference between formative and summative assessment. Summative assessments are given to students at the end of a particular unit and are used to assess student achievement. *Cumulative examinations* and *term papers* both fall into this category. Choice (A) is incorrect because *teacher observations* are formative assessments. They are used throughout the learning process as an informal tool to gauge learning. Choice (D) is incorrect because *jigsaw teaching* is neither a summative nor formative assessment. Jigsaw teaching is an instructional strategy that educators may utilize to enhance student learning on a particular subject.

2. **A and B.** The question requires an understanding of the differences between formative and summative assessments. Formative assessments are different methods of assessment that

educators utilize throughout the learning process in order to assess a student's progress toward mastery of a given skill. *Exit tickets,* short evaluations traditionally used at the end of a day's lesson to evaluate whether or not a student has mastered the day's objective, and *think-pair-shares,* discussions between students that can quickly be observed by teachers to determine a level of mastery toward a particular objective, are both examples of formative assessment. Choices (C) and (D) are both examples of summative assessment because they are given at the end of a given instructional period and are used to assess student achievement.

3. **B.** The question requires an understanding of Bloom's Taxonomy and the different types of questions and activities at each particular level. *Comprehension* is the second level of Bloom's Taxonomy. At this level, students need to be able to read given material and demonstrate their basic understanding through various activities, such as predicting, organizing, and summarizing. Choice (A) is incorrect because the *knowledge* level requires basic recall and retell skills, such as "Who is the main character?" or "Match the character on the left to his/her description on the right." Choice (C) is incorrect because the *analysis* level requires the manipulation of information for a specific purpose. At the analysis level, students might be asked about the theme of the book and to cite specific incidents within the text that support that theme. Choice (D) is incorrect because the *synthesis* level asks the student to make a change to the material and create alternatives. At the synthesis level, students might be asked to make a change to the plot and rewrite a section of the text based upon that plot change.

4. **B.** The question requires an understanding of different instructional models that educators utilize to best convey information to students. A *think-aloud* occurs when a teacher models aloud for a student her own thinking as she attempts to solve a complex problem or difficult task. This teacher has noticed that students do not know how to find appropriate text to defend an argument. Choice (A) is incorrect because *reciprocal teaching* occurs when students take on the role of the teacher in a small group setting. Choice (C) is incorrect because *direct instruction* occurs when a teacher delivers a lecture to students while they take notes based on the information being delivered. Choice (D) is incorrect because a *jigsaw* occurs when different students in a class learn different pieces of material about a given topic. They then deliver that new information to a different group of students who have all studied a different piece of the material.

5. **D.** The question requires an understanding of the foundations and terminology of early literacy instruction. *Diphthongs* are two vowels in the same syllable that create one unique sound. In "coat," the diphthong is "oa," and in "boil," the diphthong is "oi." Choice (A) is incorrect because *blends* are pairs of adjacent consonants that still hold their own unique sound. Choice (B) is incorrect because *digraphs* are two adjacent consonants that produce one sound, different than each letter's individual sound. Choice (C) is incorrect because *graphemes* are single letters or groups of letters that produce one sound. Each letter of the alphabet is an example of a grapheme.

6. **B.** The question requires an understanding of what fluency is and how to develop that skill within early readers. *Fluency* is a reader's ability to read at a certain speed with appropriate accuracy and expression. Whisper-reading is a minimally invasive instructional technique that teachers utilize to increase a student's fluency rate. Choice (A) is incorrect because *decoding* is a series of phonetic strategies readers are taught to assist in the pronunciation of unknown written words. Choice (C) is incorrect because *phonics* is the connection of a sound with a particular letter or group of letters. Choice (D) is incorrect because *comprehension* is an understanding of the material presented in a given text.

7. **D.** The question requires an understanding of how to choose an assessment strategy that fits the goal of an educator. An *entrance ticket* is a formative assessment that consists of a variety of questions that allow a teacher to quickly determine which students have mastered an objective and which students still need further instruction. Choice (A) is incorrect because a *KWL chart* is traditionally used prior to teaching a lesson and its function is to assess what

students already know about a given topic. Choice (B) is incorrect because a formal exam is a summative assessment that is given at the end of a unit, not after a single objective is taught. Choice (C) is incorrect because while conferencing with each student would be helpful, it would be too time consuming for Mrs. Fitzsimmons. It would not be the best use of her instructional time.

8. **B.** The question requires an understanding of the stages of teaching literacy and what occurs at each stage. An *early reader* is becoming a more independent reader. The student still relies heavily on a book's pictures to give clues, but the student has also developed a variety of decoding skills to assist in the reading process as well. Choice (A) is incorrect because *emergent readers* have not yet developed decoding skills and rely almost exclusively on pictures within a text. Choice (C) is incorrect because *transitional readers* begin to focus less on pictures in text and have almost mastered decoding skills. They are beginning to utilize various comprehension strategies in their reading. Choice (D) is incorrect because *fluent readers* read independently and have confidence in both their decoding and comprehension skills.

9. **C.** The question requires an understanding of Bloom's Taxonomy and the different types of questions and activities at each particular level. At the *synthesis* level, students are asked to revise work and compose a new piece based on those revisions. Choice (A) is incorrect because the *comprehension* level asks students to perform tasks such as predicting and summarizing. At the comprehension level, students are not asked to manipulate material in a new way. Choice (B) is incorrect because at the *application* level, students are asked "how would you" do something. If Mrs. Simpkins asked her student to simply think about how to alter the ending, that would be an example of an application question. Choice (D) is incorrect because *evaluation* requires students to rank and justify responses. If Mrs. Simpkins asked the student to also rank the endings in order and give a reason for the ranking, that would be an example of evaluation.

10. **A.** The question requires an understanding of key terminology necessary for early literacy instruction. *Segmentation* is the breaking apart of a word into each particular letter sound. Choice (B) is incorrect because *onset* is the initial sound in a word, while *rime* is the ending sound in that same word. Choice (C) is incorrect because *syllabication* is the breaking apart of words with more than one syllable into each individual syllable. Choice (D) is incorrect because *isolation* occurs when a student is asked to identify a single sound within a word, not all the sounds independently.

11. **B.** The question requires an understanding of figurative language. *Assonance* is the repetition of a vowel sound at the beginning of words in a sentence. Choice (A) is incorrect because *personification* is giving living qualities to a nonliving object. Choice (C) is incorrect because *alliteration* is the repetition of a consonant sound at the beginning of words in a sentence. Choice (D) is incorrect because *metaphor* is the comparison of two unlike items.

12. **B.** The question requires an understanding of different kinds of writing. *Persuasive* writing occurs when the author is attempting to influence the thoughts or actions of the reader. Choice (A) is incorrect because *expository* writing occurs when the author is attempting to inform or give information to the reader. Choice (C) is incorrect because *narrative* writing occurs when the author is attempting to entertain the reader through a story. Choice (D) is incorrect because *informational* writing occurs when the author is attempting to give information to the reader about a given topic.

13. **C.** The question requires an understanding of the writing process and how best to navigate a student through that process. At the *revision* stage, authors seek input from others and make changes to the content of a given piece of writing. Choice (A) is incorrect because *prewriting* occurs at the beginning of the writing process, before a draft has been created. Choice (B) is incorrect because *proofing* or editing looks strictly at the mechanics of a piece, not the content. Choice (D) is incorrect because *publishing* occurs when the final draft of the piece is complete.

14. A. The question requires an understanding of how to assist students in creating clear writing. A *Venn diagram* is a graphic organizer that allows students to compare and contrast two particular items. Choice (B) is incorrect because a *flow chart* is used when discussing a sequence of events. Choice (C) is incorrect because a *KWL chart* is used prior to instruction about a given topic to determine what students already know and what students want to know about the topic. Choice (D) is incorrect because a *web* is used to brainstorm a lot of information about one central topic.

15. D. The question requires an understanding of the fundamentals of early literacy instruction. The *alphabetic principle* involves understanding that there is a connection between a letter sound and a written letter. Choice (A) is incorrect because *phonemes* are units of sound that have meaning. Phonemes apply strictly to sound. Choice (B) is incorrect because *graphemes* are written letters. Graphemes apply strictly to print. Choice (C) is incorrect because *concepts of print* relate only to the written letter and not sound.

16. C. This question requires an understanding of structural analysis. Structural analysis is the ability to determine the meaning of an unfamiliar word based on using familiar parts (a prefix, suffix, or base word). "Disagreeable" is the only word in the group that contains multiple word parts that can be determined based on structural analysis. It can be broken apart into its prefix (dis), base word (agree), and suffix (able) in order to determine its meaning. Choice (A), "mischief," has a prefix (mis), but its meaning cannot be determined strictly using the word parts. Choices (B) and (D), "plateau" and "vivid," respectively, do not have prefixes, root words, or suffixes to assist in determining meaning. Those words' meanings can best be determined through the use of context clues.

17. B. The question requires an understanding of early literacy terminology. A *consonant blend* is a pair of adjacent consonants, such as "bl," "gr," and "sp" that maintain their own unique sounds. Choice (A) is incorrect because a *diphthong* is a pair of vowels, such as "ou" and "oi" that have a unique sound, different than the sound of either independent vowel. Choice (C) is incorrect because a *consonant digraph* is a pair of adjacent consonants, such as "ph" and "sh" that create a new sound when put together. Choice (D) is incorrect because *onset* is the first sound in a given one-syllable word, and *rime* is the second sound in that same word.

18. B. The question requires an understanding of early literacy terminology and instructional practices. An *onset* is the first sound in a one syllable word, such as "m" in man or "c" in can. The *rime* is the second sound, which in this example is "-an." Choice (A) is incorrect because *phonological awareness* is an individual's ability to hear and tell the difference between different phonetic sounds. Choice (C) is incorrect because the *alphabetic principle* is the knowledge that each letter of the alphabet has a unique name and sound. Choice (D) is incorrect because *phonics* is the relationship between individual letters or groups of letters and the sounds that accompany them.

19. A. The question requires an understanding of different kinds of assessments and when/how to utilize each type. *Formative assessment* is an informal way for teachers to gather important data about students throughout the learning process. Choice (B) is incorrect because *summative assessments* are given at the end of a particular unit of study and are used to assess student achievement. Choice (C) is incorrect because *conferencing* is not a type of assessment. Conferencing is used to discuss next steps in a process with students on an individual basis. Choice (D) is incorrect because *reciprocal teaching* is when students take on the role of instructor in a small group setting.

20. D. The question requires an understanding of inferences and instructional cues and methods teachers can utilize to build student skills in the area. An inference is a conclusion that can be drawn beyond the information given. Choice (D) requires students to think beyond what they see in the picture and draw a conclusion about what could have happened to make the ice cream drop. Choice (A) is incorrect because it asks students to make a guess that does not ask them to draw a conclusion. Choice (B) is incorrect because the information can be seen in the picture. It does not require students to draw their own conclusions. Choice (C) is incorrect because it, too, fails to ask students to draw a conclusion. The information is in the picture for them.

21. **B.** *Summative assessments* are formal assessments that are administered at the end of a particular unit of study, in this case, a unit on the Revolutionary War. Choice (A) is incorrect because *formative assessments* are used during an instructional period, not after it has been completed. Choice (C) is incorrect because *high stakes tests* are standardized tests, such as the ACT and SAT, that are uniform for all test-takers and can have substantial implications. Choice (D) is incorrect because *collaborative learning* is a system of learning in which students work together toward a common goal.

22. **A, B, and D.** The question requires an understanding of the mechanics and conventions of standard English. Choice (A) is correct because the word "dinner" has been spelled incorrectly as "diner." A *double negative*, Choice (B), occurs when two negatives appear in the same sentence. An example of a double negative is found in Sentence 3, "We haven't never been. . . ." A *subject/verb agreement error*, Choice (D), occurs when the subject and verb of a sentence do not agree in number. "Everyone are anxious . . ." is an example because it should read, "Everyone is anxious." Choice (C) is incorrect because there are no errors in punctuation at any point within the piece.

23. **D.** The question requires an understanding of early literacy instructional methods that increase awareness that every object has a corresponding written word. Creating a *print-rich environment* allows students to see, all the time, that daily objects have a printed partner. Choice (A) is incorrect because *high-frequency words* are words that students will encounter on a frequent basis in their own reading. Choice (B) is incorrect because *specialized vocabulary* relates to a particular subject area. Choice (C) is incorrect because *word walls* are visual representations and cues of high-frequency words students will begin to encounter in their reading.

24. **C.** The question requires an understanding of the best instructional methods to teach a given concept. When introducing nouns, having students find and sort nouns on their own gives them a tactile representation of different nouns they encounter regularly. Having them sort them based on types of nouns helps them further understand that there are subcategories in the larger realm of nouns. Choice (A) is incorrect because students will focus on the letter, not the part of speech of the word they are writing. Choice (B) is incorrect because this method addresses only the subcategory of places, not people and things. Choice (D) is incorrect because this method addresses only the subcategory of things, not people and places.

25. **C.** The question requires an understanding of what instructional techniques to employ when attempting to have students expand their written responses. Asking the student about the trip will remind the student of the experience and resurface certain events that will help make the writing stronger and more detailed. Choice (A) is incorrect because research about beaches will not make a personal story stronger. Choice (B) is incorrect because while asking the student to bring in pictures of the trip might be helpful, it is time consuming. The teacher wants to get the student writing in more detail immediately. Choice (D) is incorrect because the teacher wants the student to recall the information on his own, not tell the student exactly what needs to be expanded upon. By answering questions, the student comes to the conclusion of what is important on his own, not by being told how to make the piece better.

26. **C.** The question requires an understanding of formative assessments and how to use them to measure results within the classroom. Having students sort from a finite number of pictures allows them to demonstrate their knowledge of the skill in a measurable fashion. Choice (A) is incorrect because students do not yet have the necessary independent spelling and writing skills to allow them to create a list independently of a specific type of word. Choice (B) is incorrect because it gives students too many options to choose from and can be an overwhelming task. When tasks become overwhelming, they do not always accurately gage student understanding of a given topic. Choice (D) is incorrect because it gives students an infinite number of items to choose from and the assessment then becomes immeasurable.

27. **B.** The question requires an understanding of the development of oral communication skills at the primary level. Asking students to express their thoughts and ideas in complete sentences is grade appropriate and assists in the development of the basic skills of communication with others. Choice (A) is incorrect because reading books aloud is not age appropriate for a kindergarten classroom. This option is better suited for older students. Choice (C) is incorrect because it is also not age appropriate. At the kindergarten level, students should not be delivering presentations to their class about a given topic. Choice (D) is incorrect because engaging in a read-aloud develops listening skills rather than oral communication skills.

28. **B.** The question requires an understanding of verbs that illustrate a student's measurable progress toward a given objective. Asking students to "underline" adjectives is measurable because it clearly indicates a student's understanding and can be measured by accuracy or inaccuracy. Choice (A) is incorrect because "enjoy" is not a measurable verb. Choice (C) is incorrect because one cannot measure how much an individual "knows" about a given topic. Choice (D) is incorrect because "comprehend" cannot be measured in any concrete fashion.

29. **A.** The question requires an understanding of the logical steps to follow when going through the curriculum planning process. It is most important to become familiar with and understand the standards that are to be addressed prior to completing other steps in the curriculum planning process. In order to best complete the other steps, one must fully understand the standards to address. Choice (B) is incorrect because creating objectives for singular lessons needs to come after one knows the standards and what students will need to know for the assessment process. Choice (C) is incorrect because it should be the final step in the process. Finding ways to connect to other curriculum is important, but should be a secondary step in the process. Choice (D) is incorrect because the assessment can be created only after one fully understands the standards being addressed throughout the unit.

30. **C.** The question requires an understanding of the multiple intelligences and instructional strategies that fit the needs of each learning intelligence. *Journal reflection* allows students to work individually and connect to themselves through personal writing. Choice (A) is incorrect because *taking a nature walk* would be most beneficial for a naturalist learner. Choice (B) is incorrect because a *think-pair-share* would be most beneficial for an interpersonal learner. Choice (D) is incorrect because *using manipulatives* would be most beneficial for a kinesthetic learner.

31. **A and D.** The question requires an understanding of cooperative learning and the methods that best execute this instructional strategy. A *think-pair-share* requires students to cooperatively engage in a conversation with a peer about a given topic. A *jigsaw* requires students to cooperatively engage in a group-teaching task, where each student becomes an expert on a piece of a topic and then shares his expertise with the rest of the group. Choice (B) is incorrect because *think-aloud* is an instructional strategy teachers use to help students see their thinking as they perform a given task. Choice (C) is incorrect because *reciprocal teaching* puts students in the teacher's role.

32. **B and D.** The question requires an understanding of the benefits of reading aloud to students. When students are read aloud to, listening skills become more developed because students must simply listen to a text and develop an understanding based on what they have heard. Reading aloud also allows students to hear what a good reader sounds like. They are able to hear different tones and expressions and apply them to their own reading in the future. Choice (A) is incorrect because fluency is developed when the child reads the text aloud, not when the child listens to someone else read a text aloud. Choice (C) is incorrect because students are not engaging in oral communication when listening to a read-aloud.

33. **B.** The question requires an understanding of instructional practices that can be used to evaluate a student's understanding of a given text. Double-entry journals are a practice that allows students to write down parts of text that are confusing, interesting, humorous, or thought provoking. Through those entries, a teacher can get a glimpse into the child's thinking in regards to a given text. Choice (A) is incorrect because a Venn diagram would be the best way to compare and contrast characters. Choice (C) is incorrect because a character web would be the best way to give descriptions of specific characters within a text. Choice (D) is incorrect because a KWL chart would be the best way to write what is known and what a student wants to know about a character.

34. **B.** The question requires an understanding of questioning strategies and the different levels of comprehension that are addressed using those strategies. The literal level of comprehension is the most basic level of questions and can be answered by simply looking back in the text. Choice (A) is incorrect because it requires students to interpret what has already been said in the text and make an evaluation based on what they already know. Choice (C) is incorrect because it requires students to critically analyze two texts and determine what their preference is between the two texts. Choice (D) is incorrect because it is a cause-and-effect question that requires students to interpret the events and relationships between events within a text.

35. **C and D.** The question requires an understanding of early literacy instructional practices. Students indicate a *readiness for reading* and having a *concept of print* when they are able to identify a variety of parts of books with a variety of different texts. They are able to understand that books are read from left to right and understand that printed words have meaning. Choice (A) is incorrect because the *alphabetic principle* is the recognition that written letters have a corresponding sound. Choice (B) is incorrect because *phonological awareness* is the association of sound with corresponding letters and letter pairs.

36. **B and C.** The question requires an understanding of what instructional practices allow for the most beneficial student outcomes. When a teacher connects a lesson to real life experience, students can more easily relate to the topic and see how it can affect their own lives. When a teacher utilizes multiple techniques when delivering a lesson, it allows the teacher to engage the most students possible by touching on a variety of learning intelligences. Students are more likely to find engagement with a topic when they feel their learning style is being addressed and recognized. Choice (A) is incorrect because the practice negatively draws attention to students and will likely cause them to become more disengaged. Choice (D) is incorrect because while pop quizzes can be beneficial in certain situations, they are an instructional practice that should be used on a limited basis and do not directly increase student engagement in a particular lesson.

37. **B.** The question requires an understanding of a variety of classroom management techniques. Proximity to a misbehaving student allows for the flow of a lesson to continue, yet allows the student to know the behavior is unacceptable. Least invasive interventions call minimal, if any, attention to the student's misbehavior. Choice (A) is incorrect because the action stops the flow of teaching and gives unnecessary attention to the student's misbehavior.

Choice (C) is incorrect because it, too, stops the flow of teaching and now completely focuses the attention of the class on the misbehaving student. Choice (D) is incorrect because even though it does not stop the flow of the lesson, it calls unnecessary attention to the student's misbehavior.

38. **B.** The question requires an understanding of both homogenous and heterogeneous grouping strategies. Homogenous groups include students all at the same instructional level, while heterogeneous groups include students at a variety of instructional levels. Guided reading groups should always include students at the same instructional level, because students are reading a text that is specified for their instructional reading level. Choice (A) is incorrect because students are teaching one another in a jigsaw activity and it would be beneficial to have students at higher levels assisting those at lower instructional levels. Choice (C) is incorrect because think-pair-shares are quick assessments where students at differing instructional levels can teach one another. Choice (D) is incorrect because instructional levels do not factor into this type of grouping.

39. **A and B.** The question requires an understanding of best practices of time management. As in Choice (A), when procedures are explicitly taught, it allows more work time for students throughout the school year because expectations have been clearly established. Taking the time to teach those procedures at the beginning of the year allows for less time with procedures throughout the rest of the year. Choice (B) also works because students who finish early can continue to work, maximizing their learning time. Choice (C) is incorrect because it is not directly maximizing in-class work time. Choice (D) is incorrect because giving students too much time to complete a task can lead to behavior problems and wasted classroom time.

Answers for Section 2: Mathematics

1. **C.** The *mode* of a set of data is the number that is in it in the highest number of instances, and that is what the teacher asked about in this case. None of the other choices are defined by how many times they appear in the data.

2. **D.** A *shape hierarchy* is a categorical arrangement of illustrated shapes. The categories are based on shape similarities, and the hierarchy shows which shapes do and do not fit certain characteristics. The other choices show characteristics of shapes but do not focus on similarities and differences among them.

3. **B and D.** In a coordinate pair, the first number is the x-coordinate and the second number is the y-coordinate. The x-axis is horizontal, and the y-axis is vertical. Confusing the x-coordinate with the y-coordinate without confusing the axes will very likely lead a student to move vertically based on the value of the x-coordinate and horizontally based on the value of the y-coordinate instead of the reverse, which is the correct method. If a student confuses the x-axis with the y-axis without confusing the coordinates, the student will be highly likely to move vertically based on the first coordinate and horizontally based on the second. Nothing in the situation would make Choice (A) likely to happen. Choice (C) is something that could happen, but missing where both coordinates are 0 on the coordinate plane is not as likely a mistake as reversing coordinate values, because students at that level are much more familiar with the difference between 0 and other numbers than they are with the difference between coordinate plane x and y representations.

4. **B.** All of the arrangements involve pairs of *factors* of 24 and illustrate why they have a product of 24. Choice (A), *length and width*, is an aspect of each arrangement, but it is not a focus

of them. It can also vary from student to student because how far apart the counters are spaced is not relevant to the exercise. Choice (C), *sequencing*, could be an issue to study if the distances between counters were measured and focused on and had a pattern of increase or decrease, but nothing in the question suggests either issue. Choice (D), *commutative property of addition*, is incorrect because the exercise does not highlight adding a set of numbers in more than one order.

5. **A.** To solve the equation, a student would have to combine p terms to get the variable in one place. Choice (B) is incorrect because the equation already exists and what the variable represents is irrelevant to the problem. Choice (C) is not a principle involved in the solving of the equation because no changes in merely the way added terms are grouped need to take place. Choice (D) is a principle that does not take place in the solving of the equation because no term has to be combined with its opposite to get 0.

6. **B.** The described situation is the formation of a net that is assembled into a rectangular solid. Nets are used to illustrate the concept of *surface area* and to calculate it. When the areas of the faces are known, they can be combined for students to determine the value of a solid's surface area. Choice (A) is incorrect because it is not necessary to know the area of every face of a rectangular solid to determine its *volume*. Choice (C), *shape hierarchy*, is insufficient for illustrating or calculating surface area. Choice (D) is incorrect because *size ratios*, or how sizes compare to each other, are irrelevant to a focus on the concept of surface area.

7. **A.** Multiplying by Choice (A) correctly will result in a product expressed in feet per second if all possible unit cancellations are made. Both unit rates in Choice (A) have a value of 1. Therefore, other unit rates can be multiplied by them without resulting in change of value. Multiplying by 1 does not change value. Multiplying by any of the other choices and making all possible unit cancellations would not result in a product expressed in feet per second.

8. **D.** This arrangement would show that combining 3 groups of 2 and 7 groups of 2 results in $7 + 3$ groups of 2. It would illustrate that $2(3 + 7) = 2(3) + 2(7)$, which is a demonstration of the distributive property. None of the other choices even involve correct application of the distributive property.

9. **C.** Segment measure is used to calculate rectangle area when the formula is applied, and rectangle area is at the root of rectangular solid surface area. Understanding of segment measure is necessary for conceptualization of rectangle area, and knowledge of the nature of rectangle area is needed for understanding surface area of rectangular solids. The other choices contradict that.

10. **C.** Cubes are three-dimensional and therefore have *volume.* The exercise involves combining units of space to form a bigger unit of space, and the measure of an amount of space is volume. Choices (A) and (B), *surface area* and *face area*, are two-dimensional concepts, so filling up space with cubes would not illustrate them. Choice (D), *transformation*, is incorrect because the exercise does not focus on changing the position or size of any figure.

11. **B.** The activity puts focus on 1/4 of the pizza 3 times and results in assembly of 3/4 of the full pizza. The activity in Choice (B) clearly shows each part of the equation $3 \cdot \frac{1}{4} = \frac{3}{4}$, thereby showing detail by detail that 3/4 is 3 of 1/4. None of the other choices involve focusing on both 1/4 and 3.

12. **B.** The answer to the question that Choice (B) asks is $0.10 per person. That is a functional unit. Partial T-shirts, partial people, and partial cats are not functional units because T-shirts, people, and cats only serve their functions when they count as full units.

13. A. The models are bar models, which are used for solving algebraic equations and illustrating the principles involved. The second bar model is a reduction of the first, and it illustrates how removing three from both the top and bottom row leaves only *x* and its value. The bar model presentation does not illustrate any of the other choices, though it does involve a change in length. Choice (B) is a length principle, but nothing indicates the length of the bar models or how much one changed from the other. Also, bar models are not intended for studying length. They are designed specifically to illustrate algebraic equation solving.

14. A. The three measures of central tendency are mean, median, and mode. Choice (A) asks for the mode, and Choice (B) asks for the mean. Choice (C) asks for the largest number, and Choice (D) asks for the range. Largest number and range are not measures of central tendency.

15. C. Rectangle area has a formula, as does triangle area. Those formulas can be used to calculate the area of the rectangle and the triangle, and the sum of their areas is the area of the composite figure they form together. Choice (A) is incorrect because the amount of paint used on a surface can vary. No formula exists for determining area accurately based on amount of paint used. Choice (B) is incorrect because there is no universal formula for the area of such a composite figure. Choice (D) is incorrect because it will give you too much area.

16. D. In the first row, the students are to circle only multiples of 2. In the next row, they are supposed to circle only multiples of 3. Every row is set up to display the multiples of a number, and it is a different number for each row. The exercise is all about multiples. It does not focus on any of the other choices.

17. A. The student multiplied the 4, a number of ones, by 3, a number of tens, and showed that he got 11 by writing a 1 in the first product row and carrying a 1. He should have gotten 12, as would be indicated by putting a 2 in the product row and carrying the 1. No mistakes were made in the other answer choices.

18. B. $2g$ represents twice the number of oranges Mark has, and $2g + 4$ represents 4 more than that, which is what Janet has. Choice (A) represents 2 more than 4 times the number of oranges Mark has, Choice (C) symbolizes twice the number of oranges Mark has less than 13, and Choice (D) represents $(4 + 2)$ times Mark's number of oranges.

19. A. The situation entails adding numbers in different orders and getting the same sum. That is the focus of the exercise. The principle that addition works that way is the *commutative property of addition*. Choice (B) is incorrect because multiplication was not part of the problem, Choice (C) is wrong because the exercise does not focus on how the numbers are grouped, and Choice (D) is false because no substitution of one expression for another one of equal value takes place in the exercise.

20. D. All the tables give true indications of the pattern, but Choice (D) is the table that gives the clearest indication of what changes from one number of sides to another. It shows a specific arrangement in which the only thing that changes from one to the next is the first number in the parentheses, and that number is revealed to always be the same as the number of sides. The other choices show changes in numbers but do not reveal specifically what is causing them to change from one instance to another. Choice (D) indicates specifically what causes the changes.

21. A. The system of time we generally use, which has 60 seconds per minute and 60 minutes per hour, is not a base-10 number system. The next minute after 2:59 p.m., for example, is 3:00 p.m., not 2:60 p.m. The change to 3:00 happens at the 60th minute after 2:00 and not the 100th minute. 315 − 245 is 70, but 3:15 p.m. comes 30 minutes after 2:45 p.m. on the same day, not 70 minutes. Choice (B) is incorrect because U.S. currency uses base 10. Choice (C) is wrong because it results from an incorrect fraction multiplication strategy. The method is wrong for any base system. Choice (D) is incorrect because it results only from lack of understanding how to convert units of measurement. A number of yards is always less than the number of feet for the same distance. That is the case no matter what number base system is used.

22. **C.** The first step in the order of operations is to work inside grouping symbols, such as parentheses. Within parentheses, the order of operations still applies. Multiplication comes before addition, so 7 must be multiplied by 2 inside the parentheses before the addition indicated within the parentheses or anything else takes place. That is why the other choices are wrong.

23. **B.** This is a problem for which students would need to think beyond just the operation rules. They need to also consider the fact that an entire crate is needed, even if only part of it is used. The answer the students should have gotten is therefore 6. Remainders and fractions do not apply to crates. The aspect of number sense shown to be lacking is an understanding of how to apply numbers to real-world situations. The remainder, fraction, or decimal suggests that an extra, whole crate needs to be used.

24. **A.** Choice (A) is an exercise in separating prime numbers from composite numbers based on the definitions of prime and composite numbers. It clearly shows a distinction between the prime and composite numbers that students work with and what makes them different from each other. None of the other choices would as clearly illustrate what separates prime numbers from composite numbers.

25. **C.** The best way to begin working an algebraic word problem is to use a variable to represent an unknown. If another unknown can be represented by an expression that uses the same variable, that is the best thing to do next because only one equation is necessary for determining the value of only one variable. Choice (A) is incorrect because using a second variable makes working problems more complicated and often impossible, though it can be necessary at levels beyond the elementary school level. For the problem in question, only one variable is necessary, and only one equation (with its varying forms) is possible. Choice (B) is incorrect because the process is much more tedious than Choice (C) and does not illustrate principles of algebra. Choice (D) is incorrect because composite figures involve more than one shape; in this instance, only a rectangle was formed.

26. **A.** This is a common exercise for helping students understand area. The number of square unit tiles is the same as the number of square units (whichever square unit each tile has for an area) the formed rectangle has for an area. Also, the product of the numbers of tiles the formed rectangle has covering its length and width is the number of square units in the formed rectangle's area. Choice (B) is wrong because the exercise focuses on the area of just one rectangle formed by the tiles. Nothing is suggested regarding a three-dimensional figure formed by tiles. Choice (C) is incorrect since the exercise illustrates the nature of area and does not focus on volume or any other three-dimensional measure. It only involves two dimensions.

27. **A.** The *mean* of a set of data is the sum of the numbers divided by the number of numbers. The exercise illustrates the definition of mean and how to calculate it. The number of counters each student has at the end of the exercise is the sum of the numbers of counters the students had originally divided by the number of students, or the number of original numbers of counters. That calculation gives the mean of the original numbers of counters. The exercise illustrates none of the other choices.

28. **D.** This exercise illustrates what area means, how the area of a rectangle can be calculated, and how the meaning and calculation are connected. Choices (A) and (B) are methods that can be used to find area, but they do not help students understand what area is. Choice (C) would give students a very basic idea of what area is, but Choice (D) would give students a much better understanding of the elements of area and why a formula for calculating it with accuracy is what it is.

29. **B.** This exercise would help students understand that a percent is a number out of 100 and also the connection between that number and a fraction that expresses the same percent. Choice (A) would help students learn how to calculate percents based on fractions but would not be very effective for helping them understand what percents are. In other words, it would help students grasp a method of conversion but would not help them conceptualize the "why" of the process. Choice (C) would give students an added perspective on what percents mean, but it would do very little to help them understand how or why a percent can be written as an exact fraction. Choice (D) would enhance knowledge of which fractions are equal to which percents, but it would do hardly anything to illustrate why the conversions are what they are.

30. **A.** Probabilities are *ratios,* so students need to understand ratios to conceptualize what probability means and how to express it. The principle of ratio is an inherent component of the meaning and calculation of probability. Choice (B) is incorrect because even though *manipulatives* can help students understand probability, they are not absolutely necessary for it. Choice (C) is wrong because although understanding *odds* would help students grasp probability, it is not necessary for students to understand odds first. Odds are not at the root of what probability is. Choice (D) is incorrect since understanding *excluded values* is completely unnecessary for conceptualizing what probability is. They are not inherent components of the definition or calculation of probability.

Answers for Section 3: Science

1. **B.** Potential energy is an energy that an object has due to its relation to some other force or system. *Gravitational potential energy* is related to the force of gravity being expended on the ball, which will roll when released. *Electrical potential energy*, Choice (C), would be correct if the ball were electrified, rather than perched on a plane. Choice (A) is incorrect because *radiant energy* requires light, so the ball would need to be powered by solar panels rather than perched on the plane. *Thermal energy*, Choice (D), requires heat. Even if the ball were heated, that would not necessarily inspire movement.

2. **B.** Choice (B) would take a solid, an ice cube which is frozen, and cause change by adding a liquid, the warm water at a higher temperature. Choice (A) is diffusion of matter, by adding a color to a clear liquid and watching the color change. Choices (C) and (D) are both measures of temperature, but they do not create or cause a change in the state of matter. In both examples, liquid water just remains liquid water, although at different temperatures.

3. **C.** Since the students gathered data from stories told to them, that evidence is *anecdotal* in nature. Choice (A), *observational data,* would be appropriate if the students were told to witness other students' choices as far as healthy eating. Choice (B), *nutritional measurements,* would be appropriate if students were allowed to analyze the content of foods served, which is not really possible within a school setting. Choice (D), *secondary data,* is not correct because the students went straight to the source they were given — other students — making the data collection primary rather than secondary.

4. D. By watching the process, the student is involved in direct *observation* of the event. By stating why this is important, she is making an *inference* about the event, that the process is necessary in the life cycle, since the information was not made available before. Seeing the process allowed her to make an inferential guess based on the action she saw. Choice (A) is not correct because no *measurement* was taking place, either the time of the cocoon budding open or the length of the cocoon, for example. Choice (B) is incorrect because no elements were added to gauge a reaction, which would have been necessary for *experimentation*. Choice (C) is incorrect because the answer lacks the observational note and because the student was not necessarily sharing information, or *communicating*; she was only guessing as to why the action was occurring.

5. D. The teacher is showing the students the force of *friction*, which occurs when two objects come in contact with one another (socks and floor) and then slide, causing those objects to have an interaction of opposing forces, eventually causing the teacher to stop sliding. Choice (A), *momentum*, is not correct because that would mean the object would gain a force by staying in motion, such as rolling down a hill. Choice (B), *centrifugal*, is not correct because the objects were not in force due to movement away from the center of something, such as swinging a bat. Choice (C), *inertia*, is not correct because the teacher did move and did not remain still, such as would be the case with an object in inertia, resisting motion.

6. A. Teaching facts, content, and laws will be easier if students understand how those can be applied to broader concepts they are learning. Teaching students the processes of inquiry and investigation yields a stronger base of learning. Choice (B) is incorrect as tests should measure knowledge; knowledge is not gained for assessment purposes, but for its own sake. Choice (C) is incorrect because content can and will change depending on new scientific breakthroughs, which constantly occur. Choice (D) is incorrect because theories are not learnable if a basis in science content and concepts is not instilled first.

7. C. Because students are demonstrating what they already know and using that knowledge to postulate on a change in the process, the students are applying their knowledge, *application*. Choice (A) is incorrect because more than *comprehension* is being used. Comprehension would only measure that the students knew the importance of their component. Choice (B), *evaluation*, is incorrect because no judgements are involved nor are solutions offered. Choice (D), *synthesis*, is incorrect because students are not creating a new product.

8. B. *Earth science* is concerned with the study of those processes that affect the planet Earth, such as weather, water, and movement in the solar system. Choice (A), *natural science*, involves a study of the physical world, such as biology and chemistry. Choice (C), *life science*, deals with living specimens and is a branch of natural science. Choice (D), *behavioral science*, involves learning about human and animal behavior.

9. C. *Deductive* learning allows students to look at data and make generalizations on what is observed. Choice (A) is incorrect because *reflective* learning requires looking back at an action and making judgements. Choice (B) is incorrect because *inductive* learning would have required students to make their own rules about the experiment. For example, they would not have been given a set of directions, but simply given the plants and told to make generalizations of any kind. Choice (D) is incorrect because *introspective* learning involves one's own personal learning and how that learning causes a personal change in knowledge, such as the metacognition process of learning.

10. B. Taxonomy refers to classifying animals within domains and kingdoms according to their physical traits. Choice (A) is incorrect in that *reproduction* has nothing to do with classification of organisms, other than asexual and sexual classifications. Choice (C) is incorrect because *ecosystems* do not have classification systems; rather, they entail how things are related in biological communities. Choice (D) is incorrect because *paleontology* is the study of fossils, not the scientific theory that all creatures were related to earlier life forms.

11. **A.** Conduction requires a transfer of heat through direct contact with an object, such as skin to the hot mug or bowl. Choices (B) and (C) are incorrect because there is no direct contact with the skin. Choice (D) is incorrect because the moving air is an example of convection, the movement of air due to temperature.

12. **C.** *Mineral dissolution* is a consequence of the rock cycle, but is not a contributing process because it does not add materials back to the process. Choices (A), (B), and (D), *metamorphism*, *weathering and erosion*, and *crystallization*, respectively, all contribute to the process of creating and changing materials in a way that furthers the cycle.

13. **B.** Rust forms when iron and mater mix, creating iron oxide. This is a chemical process. Choice (A) may or may not have chemical changes, but the sentences imply that erosion is due to runoff. Choice (C) is simply a physical process. No chemical changes occur. Choice (D) is an action or a reaction. The eruption itself does not cause a chemical change.

14. **D.** An understanding of how to read charts and graphs cannot be taken for granted. Studying the illustration shows that dissolved organic carbons are not considered a main reservoir, whereas Choices (A), (B), and (C) are. Rather, dissolved organic carbons are one component of the main reservoir, the ocean.

15. **D.** An understanding of how to read charts and graphs is important. Studying the illustration shows that the question does not address the specific layers, but instead combines the terms "outer core" and "inner core" into "core." Choices (A), (B), and (C) are not as thick, according to the representation, as the combined inner and outer cores.

16. **A.** The nature of a food web is to show that energy flows upward, from smaller organisms to larger organisms as they are eaten, which is represented in this illustration. Further evidence would be the directional nature of the arrows. Choice (B) is incorrect as the arrows are not downturned and food webs do not show larger organisms passing down energy because the energy comes from the attainment of food and nutrition. Choice (C) is incorrect since the arrows represent the process of the food chain, and in that food is energy. Choice (D) is incorrect because the arrows are only one-directional, rather than having an arrowhead at both ends, and because food webs, in this representation, are not symbiotic.

17. **B.** An understanding of how to read charts and graphs cannot be taken for granted. Studying the illustration shows that dragonflies and mayflies have no other food source other than phytoplankton, and trout relies on all three as a food source. Polluting the pond will effectively kill off most of the food chain. Choice (A) is incorrect because photosynthesis is not part of the illustration and cannot be counted on to heal the effects of the pollution. Choices (C) and (D) are incorrect because the question asks for "short-term" outcomes. Any adaptation that might occur would be long-term and would require generations of adaptive behavior.

18. **C.** Echoes bouncing off the empty walls in the hallway cause the sound to be carried for longer distances. Choice (A) is incorrect as it is not necessarily true. While sound does carry in air and water, it does not travel through any medium. Choice (B) is incorrect because it would not explain how the sound would travel down the hall. Choice (D) is incorrect because sounds do not "stop" when they hit something that receives them. Sound waves do stop, and the waves can also weaken over space and air, causing them to be unheard or "received" by any object.

19. A. Showing the students that the string of lights is connected through a series could have been done by pulling any random light, which the teacher did. Choice (B) is incorrect because the teacher would have to have known that particular light was a circuit breaker. Choice (C) is incorrect as it is not always true. Choice (D) is incorrect because although safety is a concept taught in science, it is not likely the teacher's main focus with this demonstration.

20. C. Dark colors, such as black, do absorb more heat and light. Choice (A) is incorrect because color does affect the outcome. Choice (B) is incorrect because white reflects, rather than absorbs, light and heat. Choice (D) is incorrect because the color of cloth was the intended, specific control in the experiment and is therefore not random.

Answers for Section 4: **Social Studies**

1. C. *Metacognition* is thinking about thinking. When the student uses his knowledge to correct previous knowledge, he is considering his previous thinking and assimilating his new knowledge. Choice (A) is incorrect because *inferential reading and thinking* would have occurred if the student had made a conclusion based on the information, or suggested some conclusion that showed he was "reading between the lines" about why one colony was successful and the other was not. Choice (B) is incorrect because *summarizing* would have occurred if the student gave only factual information and did not include any personal thoughts about how the information impacted him. Choice (D) is incorrect because *observation* would have occurred if the student gave an insight about the actions that occurred or simply noted the new information, without connecting it to previous knowledge.

2. A. *Democracy* is a system of government that seeks to provide for the security of all citizens and to accommodate the wishes of the *majority* of the population via voting. Choice (B) is not correct because democracy is not created in order to control large populations; size is unimportant in democratic processes. Choice (C) is incorrect because governance is not overtly concerned with culture or the protection of culture. Choice (D) is incorrect because democracy does not include the sacrifice of individual liberties; rather, democracy seeks to secure rights for all citizens.

3. B. A *compass rose* is for giving more precise directions on a map, pointing to the cardinal points of north, south, east, and west. The compass rose would assist in the reading of a map, but it would not give students an understanding of where and how they exist in the world. Choices (A), (C), and (D) give students knowledge about the major areas and locations of the world they inhabit.

4. D. Choice (A) is about the study of geography and how humans adapted to the geography. Choice (B) is the study of ancient civilization and the development of inquiry and knowledge. Choice (C) is the study of exploration and colonization of the Americas. Only Choice (D) shows the way of life of a people and how those people were impacted in every way by their environment, using their resources for food, shelter, and trade.

5. C. Choice (C) would be part of a lesson for the practice of citizenship. Choices (A), (B), and (D) all focus on helping students understand the lives and culture of other groups of people from the past as well as having students investigate their own personal identities, the aim of teaching sociology, psychology, and anthropology.

6. D. *Cultural anthropology* is the study of ancient and modern cultures and groups of people and includes issues of food gathering, political organizations, religion, and the arts, among other components. Choice (A) is incorrect because *linguistic anthropology* is the study of how humans communicate. Choice (B) is incorrect because *physical anthropology* is the study of human development over time. Choice (C) is incorrect because *biological anthropology* is the study of the noncultural aspects of humans and near-humans, such as apes.

7. **D.** Choice (A) is a performance assessment and not likely to give indications of specific content learned. Choice (B), as a checklist, is best used to determine content at a glance, but gives no indication of whether or not that content would then be transferable to a state assessment, whose format is usually multiple-choice. Choice (C) is not an assessment, but an activity. Only Choice (D) could be used to check student comprehension of the content, including specific terms likely to be used on a state assessment.

8. **B.** The student project shows *analysis* of thought in which the student recognizes patterns, organizes parts, identifies components, and clarifies potential misunderstandings. A project of *evaluation*, Choice (A), would judge the checks and balances process. A project of *synthesis*, Choice (C), would create new knowledge from the process. A project of *knowledge*, Choice (D), would just show the checks and balances of the governmental process.

9. **D.** Choice (D) would interest students who gain knowledge through reading and communication. Choice (A) would address the naturalistic learner. Choice (B) would address the musical intelligence learner. Choice (C) would address the intrapersonal learner.

10. **B.** Choice (B) is a type of social studies instruction that includes actual items from the time period or place being studied and includes primary source documents, such as artifacts, maps, and clothing. Choice (A), scaffolded learning, would involve setting up structures for learning to occur to help students connect to content. Choice (C) would be the answer only if all learning that occurred centered on the artifacts found in the museum, rather than the museum serving as just an example of what the teacher was teaching. The artifacts in the museum might serve as visual representations, Choice (D), but the lesson included many examples of primary source artifacts, as opposed to simply looking at artifacts, which might have included looking at pictures rather than taking a field trip.

11. **A.** By reading the text to the students and then paraphrasing the text, the teacher is *scaffolding instruction* by providing supports for those students whose comprehension levels might not allow them to read and comprehend the text or concepts at this level. *Cooperative learning*, Choice (B), can only be applied if students are placed into a group to complete a task or learn a concept. *Deductive learning*, Choice (D), would only apply if the teacher then had the students practice some concept after the introduction. Choice (C), *whole class instruction*, is incorrect because while the teacher is presenting information to the whole class, it is simply a presentation of text and does not involve instruction or modeled practice.

12. **B.** A *summative assessment* would be the best assessment, providing the necessary data the teacher needs in order to plan for a new unit of instruction, using those decisions to guide the new unit. *Observation* and *performance assessments*, Choices (A) and (D), would be extremely difficult to plan since the data set needed for each student is large, including all the states as well as concepts like state pride and state recognition. A *formative assessment*, Choice (C), is not used at the end of a unit, but during a unit, to guide instruction in the process.

13. **A.** The purpose of an anticipatory set is to get students excited about an upcoming lesson while connecting that lesson to them personally. Giving students a treasure map would link students' prior knowledge of the playground and spatial understanding with new knowledge, using directions to find an object. Choice (B) would be a culminating activity showing

knowledge gained after the unit. Choice (C) is a necessary part of instruction, and Choice (D) would fit better within a theme on exploration, rather than following simple directions.

14. **C.** A broad view of teaching social studies is the understanding that people are influenced by, and influence, their physical surroundings on this planet Earth. Choice (A) is too broad a concept, and students are likely to be unfamiliar with world events and how those events might influence political change. Choice (B) is not necessarily a possibility. For example, when studying a unit on the U.S. Constitution, it would be confusing to read and compare constitutions from around the world. That would be more appropriate for later grades. Choice (D) does not promote multicultural understanding because all cultures are not similar. A multicultural approach looks at commonalities, but also includes how cultures uniquely face adversities and challenges.

15. **C.** Choice (C) is an appropriate reading comprehension strategy to use when encountering students with lower reading levels. Choices (A) and (B) are not appropriate because they take away content from the students. A teacher's job is to help students access the content, not remove content which he or she disagrees with or feels is too hard or too easy for students. Choice (D) does not help all students access content, as other students should not be held accountable to provide instruction within the classroom.

16. **A.** A definite reward system is the best means of using the token system, where tokens represent money, which is then used as barter in the classroom. Choices (B) and (C) tie the concept of economies to behavior, which is not a component of the concept of economy. Choice (D) is not correct because it allows grades to be changed based on economic rewards, which would most certainly bring complaints from parents and administrators.

17. **D.** Teaching about the suffrage movement specifically addresses a woman's right to vote. Choice (D) allows the class to get a feel of it from both sides. Choices (B) and (C) do address the rights of women, but do not address voting. Choice (A) does not address the topic in any way, as it is directed toward a different time period in history and a different concept.

Answers for Section 5: Art, Music, and Physical Education

1. **C.** Printing legibly and forming letters with accuracy is part of first grade reading/language arts. Choice (A) might be likely if the class were composed of older students studying writing styles used by different cultures. Choice (B) might be likely if the class were composed of older students producing only lines in connection with making charts. Choice (D) might be likely if the class were composed of older students working on music notation.

2. **D.** Having the students sing together is an efficient way for the teacher to assess how the students are progressing toward the goal. Choice (A) refers to a test that measures students against a "norm" and includes such tests as the SAT, Iowa Basic Skills Test, and other standardized tests. Choice (B) would more likely involve a song such as "Twinkle, Twinkle," or the birthday song, which more students are likely to have heard and thus (at least partially) memorized. Choice (C) is wrong because it's hard to assess mastery of individual students when they're all singing together as a class.

3. **B.** In second grade, students begin to combine body-management skills, such as force and direction, components of Choice (B). The movement is at the later stages of the *control* level.

Choice (A) is a movement at the *proficiency* level and is most appropriate for fourth grade. Choice (C) is a movement at the *utilization* level and is most appropriate for third grade. Choice (D) is a movement at the earlier stages of the *control* level and is most appropriate for kindergarten or early first grade.

4. **A.** In describing how different current works of art reflect their culture(s), students are analyzing and making (value) judgments about the works. Choice (B) would be for a lesson in the element of color, as value is a property of color that refers to how light or dark something is. Choice (C) is wrong because Choice (B) does not align with a standard of *aesthetic* valuing. Choice (D) is wrong because Choice (A) *does* align with a standard of aesthetic valuing.

5. **B.** Learning to read, write, and play diatonic scales (consisting of seven pitches, five whole steps and two half) well gives students a sense of improvement through practice. Choice (A) and Choice (C) both describe instruction more likely to be used in conjunction with a more formal type of assessment rather than a personal (performance) journal. Choice (D) also describes instruction more likely to be used in conjunction with a more formal type of assessment and is more likely to be part of an aesthetic standard.

6. **C.** The teacher is evaluating the students' ability to demonstrate their understanding of colors and how they may be combined. Choice (A) describes assessment types used at the start of a unit to discover what students may already know. Choice (B) describes such assessment types as fill-in-the-blank and short answer. Choice (D) includes such assessment types as portfolios or journals, gauging students' ability to see progress in and assess their own work.

7. **B.** Students learn the vocabulary associated with these movements. Choice (A) involves the children gaining an awareness of how physical activity makes them feel emotionally. Choice (C) involves the children gaining an awareness of how physical activities make them feel physically. Choice (D) involves the children performing activities for increasing periods of time.

8. **A.** Different lengths (durations) of notes and rests are used to notate rhythms. Choice (B) involves pitch. Choice (C) would more likely involve performances, including line and circle dances. Choice (D) refers to comparing and playing percussion instruments such as a marimba or xylophone (pitched) and a cymbal or drum (nonpitched).

9. **C.** The class needs a hands-on approach, such as creating their own radial-balance designs (center-focused designs based on a circle, such as those made by a kaleidoscope). Choice (A) is not an example of active, or engaged, learning. Choice (B) does not directly relate to balance based on a circle and so is not the most effective lesson here. Choice (D) is incorrect because Choice (C) is, in fact, an effective lesson.

10. **A.** Different voice parts (such as soprano, alto, tenor, and bass) and instrument types are part of the element of tone (also referred to as *timbre*). Choice (B) describes part of the element of melody and harmony. Choice (C) describes part of the element of rhythm. Choice (D) is also part of the element of melody and harmony and pertains to how loud or soft the music is.

11. **C.** The teacher is incorporating a lesson on action verbs. Choice (A) might be likely if the class were discussing how the movement was related to dances, say, of different cultures. Choice (B) might be likely if the class were taking measurements related to their movements or generally studying the effects of their movements. Choice (D) might be likely if the class were moving in relation to music being played instead of to a written word.

12. **B.** The class is involved in a unit on the cultural context of visual art. Choice (A) might be likely if the class were discussing only such topics as (a sculpture's) balance, proportion, or pattern, and not also who the sculptor might have been. Choices (C) and (D) describe a unit where students are actively engaged in creating art.

13. **D.** The assessment involves the production of sound, which is in the domain of science. Choice (A) would be involved if the teacher focused on cultural differences in music instead of (physically) experiencing music. Choice (B) would be involved if the teacher focused on oral expression or listening. Choice (C) would be involved if the teacher focused on counting or moving to different rhythmic patterns.

14. **B.** The teacher would be closely observing the students' accuracy in measuring and recording. Choice (A) would be more likely to involve the whole unit, not just the part involving measurement. Choice (C) involves tests such as multiple choice and true/false. Choice (D) is an effective tool for assessing students' ability to apply facts, not observe and record them.

15. **C.** If the children were engaged in a more vigorous activity, then this standard might be addressed via students discussing changes they noticed in their bodies. Choice (A) is likely to happen by the body movements the children are engaged in. Choice (B) is likely to occur by having the students explain that the attachment of arm muscles to arm bones helps a person throw. Choice (D) is likely to be addressed by having each member of a pair be courteous to each other.

Answer Key

Section 1: Reading and Language Arts

1. B and C	9. C	17. B	25. C	33. B
2. A and B	10. A	18. B	26. C	34. B
3. B	11. B	19. A	27. B	35. C and D
4. B	12. B	20. D	28. B	36. B and C
5. D	13. C	21. B	29. A	37. B
6. B	14. A	22. A, B, and D	30. C	38. B
7. D	15. D	23. D	31. A and D	39. A and B
8. B	16. C	24. C	32. B and D	

Section 2: Mathematics

1. C	7. A	13. A	19. A	25. C
2. D	8. D	14. A	20. D	26. A
3. B and D	9. C	15. C	21. A	27. A
4. B	10. C	16. D	22. C	28. D
5. A	11. B	17. A	23. B	29. B
6. B	12. B	18. B	24. A	30. A

Section 3: Science

1. B	5. D	9. C	13. B	17. B
2. B	6. A	10. B	14. D	18. C
3. C	7. C	11. A	15. D	19. A
4. D	8. B	12. C	16. A	20. C

Section 4: Social Studies

1. C	5. C	9. D	13. A	17. D
2. A	6. D	10. B	14. C	
3. B	7. D	11. A	15. C	
4. D	8. B	12. B	16. A	

Section 5: Art, Music, and Physical Education

1. C	4. A	7. B	10. A	13. D
2. D	5. B	8. A	11. C	14. B
3. B	6. C	9. C	12. B	15. C

Chapter 17

Practice Test: Praxis Elementary Education - 5018

ere's the test before the test. This is your chance to show if your hard work has paid off. To get the most out of this testing experience, there are a few things you can do to help:

>> **De-gadgetize.** No cellphone, tablet, TV remote, and so on. Feel free to use your calculator during this practice test, since you will have access to an on-screen calculator on test day.

>> **Find a distraction-free zone where you can take the test.**

Once the environment is ready, prepare your mind:

>> **Watch the time.** You have roughly 1 minute per question, so don't get bogged down on any one question.

>> **Focus on the subject area or concept you're being tested on.** Tune in to key words or triggers that help you locate the correct answer.

>> **Answer every question.**

>> **Stay focused on your goal.** Keep in mind the score you want to achieve and know that you can!

Refer to Chapter 3 for more detailed test day strategies and instructions.

TIP

If you want to practice taking the test electronically, as you will on test day, go to www.dummies.com and use your PIN code to activate the online access that accompanies the purchase of this book. (Instructions are in the Introduction.) You'll find another test for your studying enjoyment and strategizing. You can answer the questions digitally, and the software tabulates correct and incorrect responses. This summary provides you with a snapshot of which areas you excel in and which areas you may need to review again.

Answer Sheet

The test is divided into four areas. You have 150 minutes to answer all the questions. During the actual test, there is no stopping point between different subject areas. Some questions have more than one correct answer. In those cases, select all correct options.

Section 1: Reading and Language Arts

1. Ⓐ Ⓑ Ⓒ Ⓓ	11. Ⓐ Ⓑ Ⓒ Ⓓ	21. Ⓐ Ⓑ Ⓒ Ⓓ	31. Ⓐ Ⓑ Ⓒ Ⓓ	41. Ⓐ Ⓑ Ⓒ Ⓓ
2. Ⓐ Ⓑ Ⓒ Ⓓ	12. Ⓐ Ⓑ Ⓒ Ⓓ	22. Ⓐ Ⓑ Ⓒ Ⓓ	32. Ⓐ Ⓑ Ⓒ Ⓓ	42. Ⓐ Ⓑ Ⓒ Ⓓ
3. Ⓐ Ⓑ Ⓒ Ⓓ	13. Ⓐ Ⓑ Ⓒ Ⓓ	23. Ⓐ Ⓑ Ⓒ Ⓓ	33. Ⓐ Ⓑ Ⓒ Ⓓ	43. Ⓐ Ⓑ Ⓒ Ⓓ
4. Ⓐ Ⓑ Ⓒ Ⓓ	14. Ⓐ Ⓑ Ⓒ Ⓓ	24. Ⓐ Ⓑ Ⓒ Ⓓ	34. Ⓐ Ⓑ Ⓒ Ⓓ	44. Ⓐ Ⓑ Ⓒ Ⓓ
5. Ⓐ Ⓑ Ⓒ Ⓓ	15. Ⓐ Ⓑ Ⓒ Ⓓ	25. Ⓐ Ⓑ Ⓒ Ⓓ	35. Ⓐ Ⓑ Ⓒ Ⓓ	45. Ⓐ Ⓑ Ⓒ Ⓓ
6. Ⓐ Ⓑ Ⓒ Ⓓ	16. Ⓐ Ⓑ Ⓒ Ⓓ	26. Ⓐ Ⓑ Ⓒ Ⓓ	36. Ⓐ Ⓑ Ⓒ Ⓓ	46. Ⓐ Ⓑ Ⓒ Ⓓ
7. Ⓐ Ⓑ Ⓒ Ⓓ	17. Ⓐ Ⓑ Ⓒ Ⓓ	27. Ⓐ Ⓑ Ⓒ Ⓓ	37. Ⓐ Ⓑ Ⓒ Ⓓ	47. Ⓐ Ⓑ Ⓒ Ⓓ
8. Ⓐ Ⓑ Ⓒ Ⓓ	18. Ⓐ Ⓑ Ⓒ Ⓓ	28. Ⓐ Ⓑ Ⓒ Ⓓ	38. Ⓐ Ⓑ Ⓒ Ⓓ	48. Ⓐ Ⓑ Ⓒ Ⓓ
9. Ⓐ Ⓑ Ⓒ Ⓓ	19. Ⓐ Ⓑ Ⓒ Ⓓ	29. Ⓐ Ⓑ Ⓒ Ⓓ	39. Ⓐ Ⓑ Ⓒ Ⓓ	49. Ⓐ Ⓑ Ⓒ Ⓓ
10. Ⓐ Ⓑ Ⓒ Ⓓ	20. Ⓐ Ⓑ Ⓒ Ⓓ	30. Ⓐ Ⓑ Ⓒ Ⓓ	40. Ⓐ Ⓑ Ⓒ Ⓓ	

Section 2: Mathematics

1. Ⓐ Ⓑ Ⓒ Ⓓ	10. Ⓐ Ⓑ Ⓒ Ⓓ	19. Ⓐ Ⓑ Ⓒ Ⓓ	28. Ⓐ Ⓑ Ⓒ Ⓓ	37. Ⓐ Ⓑ Ⓒ Ⓓ
2. Ⓐ Ⓑ Ⓒ Ⓓ	11. Ⓐ Ⓑ Ⓒ Ⓓ	20. Ⓐ Ⓑ Ⓒ Ⓓ	29. Ⓐ Ⓑ Ⓒ Ⓓ	38. Ⓐ Ⓑ Ⓒ Ⓓ
3. Ⓐ Ⓑ Ⓒ Ⓓ	12. Ⓐ Ⓑ Ⓒ Ⓓ	21. Ⓐ Ⓑ Ⓒ Ⓓ	30. Ⓐ Ⓑ Ⓒ Ⓓ	39. Ⓐ Ⓑ Ⓒ Ⓓ
4. Ⓐ Ⓑ Ⓒ Ⓓ	13. Ⓐ Ⓑ Ⓒ Ⓓ	22. Ⓐ Ⓑ Ⓒ Ⓓ	31. Ⓐ Ⓑ Ⓒ Ⓓ	40. Ⓐ Ⓑ Ⓒ Ⓓ
5. Ⓐ Ⓑ Ⓒ Ⓓ	14. Ⓐ Ⓑ Ⓒ Ⓓ	23. Ⓐ Ⓑ Ⓒ Ⓓ	32. Ⓐ Ⓑ Ⓒ Ⓓ	41. Ⓐ Ⓑ Ⓒ Ⓓ
6. Ⓐ Ⓑ Ⓒ Ⓓ	15. Ⓐ Ⓑ Ⓒ Ⓓ	24. Ⓐ Ⓑ Ⓒ Ⓓ	33. Ⓐ Ⓑ Ⓒ Ⓓ	
7. Ⓐ Ⓑ Ⓒ Ⓓ	16. Ⓐ Ⓑ Ⓒ Ⓓ	25. Ⓐ Ⓑ Ⓒ Ⓓ	34. Ⓐ Ⓑ Ⓒ Ⓓ	
8. Ⓐ Ⓑ Ⓒ Ⓓ	17. Ⓐ Ⓑ Ⓒ Ⓓ	26. Ⓐ Ⓑ Ⓒ Ⓓ	35. Ⓐ Ⓑ Ⓒ Ⓓ	
9. Ⓐ Ⓑ Ⓒ Ⓓ	18. Ⓐ Ⓑ Ⓒ Ⓓ	27. Ⓐ Ⓑ Ⓒ Ⓓ	36. Ⓐ Ⓑ Ⓒ Ⓓ	

Section 3: Social Studies

1. Ⓐ Ⓑ Ⓒ Ⓓ	6. Ⓐ Ⓑ Ⓒ Ⓓ	11. Ⓐ Ⓑ Ⓒ Ⓓ	16. Ⓐ Ⓑ Ⓒ Ⓓ	21. Ⓐ Ⓑ Ⓒ Ⓓ
2. Ⓐ Ⓑ Ⓒ Ⓓ	7. Ⓐ Ⓑ Ⓒ Ⓓ	12. Ⓐ Ⓑ Ⓒ Ⓓ	17. Ⓐ Ⓑ Ⓒ Ⓓ	22. Ⓐ Ⓑ Ⓒ Ⓓ
3. Ⓐ Ⓑ Ⓒ Ⓓ	8. Ⓐ Ⓑ Ⓒ Ⓓ	13. Ⓐ Ⓑ Ⓒ Ⓓ	18. Ⓐ Ⓑ Ⓒ Ⓓ	23. Ⓐ Ⓑ Ⓒ Ⓓ
4. Ⓐ Ⓑ Ⓒ Ⓓ	9. Ⓐ Ⓑ Ⓒ Ⓓ	14. Ⓐ Ⓑ Ⓒ Ⓓ	19. Ⓐ Ⓑ Ⓒ Ⓓ	24. Ⓐ Ⓑ Ⓒ Ⓓ
5. Ⓐ Ⓑ Ⓒ Ⓓ	10. Ⓐ Ⓑ Ⓒ Ⓓ	15. Ⓐ Ⓑ Ⓒ Ⓓ	20. Ⓐ Ⓑ Ⓒ Ⓓ	25. Ⓐ Ⓑ Ⓒ Ⓓ

Section 4: Science

1. Ⓐ Ⓑ Ⓒ Ⓓ	6. Ⓐ Ⓑ Ⓒ Ⓓ	11. Ⓐ Ⓑ Ⓒ Ⓓ	16. Ⓐ Ⓑ Ⓒ Ⓓ	21. Ⓐ Ⓑ Ⓒ Ⓓ
2. Ⓐ Ⓑ Ⓒ Ⓓ	7. Ⓐ Ⓑ Ⓒ Ⓓ	12. Ⓐ Ⓑ Ⓒ Ⓓ	17. Ⓐ Ⓑ Ⓒ Ⓓ	22. Ⓐ Ⓑ Ⓒ Ⓓ
3. Ⓐ Ⓑ Ⓒ Ⓓ	8. Ⓐ Ⓑ Ⓒ Ⓓ	13. Ⓐ Ⓑ Ⓒ Ⓓ	18. Ⓐ Ⓑ Ⓒ Ⓓ	23. Ⓐ Ⓑ Ⓒ Ⓓ
4. Ⓐ Ⓑ Ⓒ Ⓓ	9. Ⓐ Ⓑ Ⓒ Ⓓ	14. Ⓐ Ⓑ Ⓒ Ⓓ	19. Ⓐ Ⓑ Ⓒ Ⓓ	24. Ⓐ Ⓑ Ⓒ Ⓓ
5. Ⓐ Ⓑ Ⓒ Ⓓ	10. Ⓐ Ⓑ Ⓒ Ⓓ	15. Ⓐ Ⓑ Ⓒ Ⓓ	20. Ⓐ Ⓑ Ⓒ Ⓓ	25. Ⓐ Ⓑ Ⓒ Ⓓ

Section 1: Reading and Language Arts

1. There are three reasons for writing for an audience. These reasons include

   (A) writing to entertain, writing to learn, and writing to persuade

   (B) writing to entertain, writing for reflection, and writing to persuade

   (C) writing for reflection, writing to inform, and writing to persuade

   (D) writing to entertain, writing to inform, and writing to persuade

2. Which of the following terms is not a figurative language device?

   (A) onomatopoeia

   (B) irony

   (C) metaphor

   (D) personification

3. What is a definition of "tone" in writing?

   (A) the author's personality as reflected in the text

   (B) how the reader feels about the text

   (C) how the author feels about the subject

   (D) the point of view of a text

4. An argumentative essay should include which of the following components?

   (A) a statement of agreement or disagreement followed by supporting reasons and examples

   (B) a statement of agreement or disagreement followed by feelings and personal experiences

   (C) a personal opinion followed by feelings

   (D) a thesis statement followed by supporting details

5. What is the difference between rime and rhyme?

   (A) There is no difference other than the spelling of the two words.

   (B) A rime is a part of a syllable focused on the vowels and the consonants and the rest of the syllable that follows; rhyme is a repetition of sounds most often found in the final syllable.

   (C) Rime is a repetition of sounds most often found in the final syllable; rhyme is a part of a syllable focused on the vowels and the consonants and the rest of the syllable that follows.

   (D) Rime is only considered within the genre of poetry, while rhyme is considered with the genre of music and song lyrics.

6. Use the following poem to answer this question.

   ### The Red Wheelbarrow
   by William Carlos Williams

   so much depends upon

   a red wheel barrow

   glazed with rain water

   beside the white chickens.

   This poem is an example of what common stanza?

   (A) couplets

   (B) triplets

   (C) quatrains

   (D) sestets

7. A first-grade student listened to a story being read by the teacher about a boy who lost his baseball glove. After the story, the student shares that he also lost something. He relates feelings of being angry at losing something he cared about. What stage is this student demonstrating in the interpretation of literature?

(A) the development stage

(B) the beginning stage

(C) the stage of critical analysis

(D) the reflection and response stage

8. Two students are sharing stories in an elementary classroom, discussing their new library books and showing one another interior illustrations. What stage of literary appreciation are these students demonstrating?

(A) understanding that pleasure and profit come from literature

(B) losing oneself in a story

(C) finding oneself in a story

(D) venturing beyond self

9. In a literary or narrative text, what is the purpose of the exposition?

(A) The exposition describes the most vital plot points on which the action hinges.

(B) The exposition concludes the events and problems of a story.

(C) The exposition describes events of the story that cause the main character to be challenged in obtaining a goal of some kind.

(D) The exposition introduces the characters, the setting, and a description of the central conflict of a story.

10. A brochure is an example of what genre of literature?

(A) fictional poetry

(B) fictional narrative

(C) nonfiction expository

(D) research expository

11. What is the primary purpose of teaching figurative language?

(A) helping students to understand that some ideas are abstract in nature

(B) because much of the language of poetry includes figurative language

(C) so that symbolism of fictional stories can be understood

(D) because so much figurative language occurs on assessments

12. A kindergarten teacher reads a picture book aloud to her students as a way to start every day. As she reads, she pauses after each page and asks a student to retell something important that occurred either in the text or from the illustration. Which foundation of literacy is this teacher demonstrating?

(A) the alphabetic principle

(B) early print concepts

(C) comprehension

(D) phonemic awareness

13. A fourth-grade student is reading a story about the sport: hurling. When she reaches an unknown word, *camogie,* she reads that this is a similar sport for girls. She is able to decipher from the clues that this sport uses sticks and balls and infers that the male sport uses the same equipment, but has different rules and procedures. Which word recognition strategy is she displaying with her description and inferencing?

(A) word structure clues

(B) syntactic clues

(C) context clues

(D) antonym clues

GO ON TO NEXT PAGE

14. When reading an article about how to improve his golf game, a fifth-grade student used which of the following two context clues to determine the meaning of the unknown italicized words in the following sentence: Young players should concentrate on their *alignment*, or body placement to the target line of the ball, as a way to improve *range.*

(A) sequential and analogic clues

(B) syntactic and semantic clues

(C) symbolic and syntactic clues

(D) symbolic and analogic clues

15. When a second-grader reads a poem with expression and uses rhythm in a smooth way, he is demonstrating which reading principle?

(A) poetic expression

(B) fluency

(C) phonemic awareness

(D) oral smoothness

16. When a fourth-grade student sees the word "equator" when reading and then automatically states, "Oh, yeah, that's the imaginary line dividing the Earth into northern and southern hemispheres. We learned about that in Social Studies," what foundational literacy development stage is she demonstrating?

(A) fluency

(B) comprehension

(C) word identification

(D) concepts of print

17. What are Dolch words?

(A) a list of the most frequently used English words, often divided up by grade levels

(B) words that children are encouraged to memorize whole, by sight

(C) words that can be instantly recognized when reading, without having to think about them

(D) words that should be learned by the end of first grade

18. A fourth-grade student reads an article on the first "real" Thanksgiving and remarks how surprised she is that those first settlers did not eat turkey, mashed potatoes, and pumpkin pies like we do today. Then, she remarks that such a meal would have been hard to cook without having a stove and microwave. What comprehension strategy is she demonstrating?

(A) summarizing

(B) metacognition

(C) cause and effect

(D) inferential thinking

19. Developmental writing is considered to have eight different stages. Which of these answers represents that progression?

(A) making pictures to represent text; becoming aware of how letters sound; making strings of random letters; connecting letters to sounds correctly; being able to make beginning sounds; being able to make ending sounds; being able to make middle sounds; spelling single-consonant words

(B) pictures to represent text; becoming aware of how letters sound; making strings of random letters; connecting letters to sounds correctly; using inventive spelling; being able to spell beginnings, middles, and ends of words; using transitional words between thoughts; standard spelling

(C) making alphabetic representations for sounds; scribbling nonsense words; being able to make beginning sounds; being able to make ending sounds; being able to make middle sounds; spelling single-consonant words; spelling double-consonant words; spelling multiple-consonant words

(D) scribbling representations of letters; making actual letterlike symbols; putting together strings of letters to represent words; being able to make letters represent beginning sounds; making consonants that represent words; being able to spell beginnings, middles, and ends of words; using transitional words and phrases; standard spelling

20. Silent reading comprehension involves two important skills. What are they?

   (A) print skills and making-meaning skills

   (B) making-meaning skills and fluency

   (C) listening skills and making-meaning skills

   (D) speaking skills and making-meaning skills

21. What is inventive, or invented, spelling?

   (A) spelling that is considered appropriate when teaching creative writing, such as poetry, in order to achieve a specific affect

   (B) the practice of spelling words the way students hear them, even if this means the spelling is incorrect

   (C) spelling words according to traditional rules rather than phonetically

   (D) a transitional form of spelling whereby students are corrected in writing and made to correctly spell wrong words

22. A fourth-grade teacher has selected a book to read aloud to his students on the topic of African savannas. Before reading the book, he asks the students what they already know about this topic and then generates some questions about things they would like to learn. After reading the book, he revisits the questions with the students and finds answers for the questions, and then generates some details about new information learned. What reading strategy is this teacher using to aid comprehension of text?

   (A) reciprocal teaching

   (B) direct instruction

   (C) KWL strategy

   (D) use of graphic organizers

23. Why is teaching visual imagery an important part of comprehension?

   (A) because good readers make mental images when they read and connect text to real situations

   (B) to connect reading to the "art" of the fine arts

   (C) so that students can prepare for more difficult text in other genres that heavily relies on imagery

   (D) because imagery is a standard of academic learning across all disciplines

24. Having instruction in print concepts, letter knowledge, and the alphabetic principle is necessary in order for what to occur?

   (A) phonemic awareness

   (B) fluency

   (C) decoding

   (D) comprehension

GO ON TO NEXT PAGE

It little profits that an idle king,

By this still hearth, among these barren crags, Matched with and aged wife, I mete and dole Unequal laws unto a savage race,

That hoard, and sleep, and feed, and know not me.

I cannot rest from travel: I will drink

Life to the lees: all times I have enjoyed

Greatly, have suffered greatly, both with those

That loved me, and alone; on shore, and when Through scudding drifts the rainy Hyades

Vexed the dim sea: I am become a name;

For always roaming with a hungry heart

Much have I seen and known; cities of men

And manners, climates, councils, governments, Myself not least, but honoured of them all;

And drunk delight of battle with my peers,

Far on the ringing plains of windy Troy.

25. This poem is an example of which type of poetry?

(A) blank verse

(B) cinquain

(C) elegy

(D) sonnet

26. The format of this first stanza of the poem represents an example of which of the following dramatic elements?

(A) a call to action on the part of the audience

(B) foreshadowing

(C) a dramatic dialogue

(D) an interior dramatic monologue

27. A diary is an example of what kind of source?

(A) survey

(B) primary

(C) secondary

(D) tertiary

28. Which of these is a common pattern of nonfiction?

(A) exposition, rising action, resolution

(B) metaphor and simile

(C) cause and effect

(D) symbolism and meaning

29. What would be the correct way to write "tomato" in the plural form?

(A) tomatos

(B) tomatos or tomatoes

(C) tomatoes

(D) tomato's

30. What is the correct part of speech designation for the underlined word?

Flying makes me very nervous.

(A) predicate noun

(B) object noun

(C) object pronoun

(D) gerund

31. In the sentence, "The tired, green-eyed boy lazily tossed the rubber ball for the energetic golden retriever," which word is categorized as a compound adjective?

(A) tired

(B) green-eyed

(C) rubber ball

(D) golden retriever

32. In the following sentence, what part of speech is the word "similarly"?

The two girls were similarly attired.

(A) adjective

(B) preposition

(C) adverb

(D) verb

33. A kindergarten teacher says /t/ /i/ /n/ to his students and asks them what he is saying. He suggests they do the same thing and sound out a word. What is this an example of?

(A) phoneme segmentation

(B) phoneme blending

(C) phoneme addition

(D) phoneme identification

34. Which of the following is the best example of an activity that would promote alphabetic awareness?

(A) talking with someone

(B) singing a song

(C) playing with plastic letters

(D) listening to a story

35. An elementary teacher is reading *If You Give a Mouse a Cookie* by Laura Joffe Numeroff. The teacher is using dialogic reading to find the answers to questions like:

Who has ever eaten a homemade chocolate chip cookie? Did it make you thirsty?

Who has a pet?

How hard do you work to take care of your pet?

In conducting the reading lesson this way, what is the teacher establishing for his students?

(A) He is establishing extended time for comprehension to occur.

(B) He is providing a chance for oral comprehension as the students talk about what is happening in the text.

(C) He is preparing them for state standardized testing and the kinds of questions that will be asked.

(D) He is helping them to make a connection between what they are reading and their actual life experiences.

36. Read the following excerpt from a first-grade student.

"Mikl is mi fadr nam. He tak me swm he tak me bal. He is fune."

What does this writing example reflect?

(A) The child uses invented spelling to deliver the message.

(B) The child has a firm grasp of proper sentence structure.

(C) The child has a firm grasp of vowel sounds.

(D) The child needs to focus on alphabetic principle in future writing examples.

GO ON TO NEXT PAGE

37. Joni is a student who has difficulty remembering some of the letters in the words when she reads. These are familiar words and should be easy to read. What does this indicate?

(A) Joni has difficulty with traditional spelling rules.

(B) Joni has not mastered letter-sound correspondence.

(C) Joni is not using context clues to help her solve unknown and unfamiliar words.

(D) Joni has not mastered the Dolch word list for her grade.

Use the following story to answer Questions 38–40.

The Grasshopper and the Ant

One summer day, a grasshopper and an ant were in the woods. The grasshopper played all day long, skipping and singing. The ant worked very hard all day, collecting food.

Exasperated at the end of a long and tiring day, the ant said, "Grasshopper, all you do is play. You need to work. You should put away food for the winter." The grasshopper looked at the ant and smilingly said, "There's time for work, and there's time for play. Work is no fun. I like to play. I can work another day."

All summer, the ant worked very hard. He put away food for the winter while the grasshopper played every day, all day long, and didn't put away any food for the winter.

Soon, it was winter. The leaves fell from the trees. The grass turned brown and fell from the stalk. The air turned chilly. The snow started to fall and it was very cold. Freezing and hungry, the grasshopper knocked on the ant's door. He said, "Dear ant, I'm so hungry. It's so cold. What should I do? Might you take me in? You surely have enough food for the both of us because you worked so hard this summer."

The ant thought for a moment and answered, "I thought about your wise words this summer when I was working so hard and you were playing so hard, and I decided you were right. There is time for work, and there is time for play. This summer I worked and you played. Now, I will play and you will work." The ant smiled at the grasshopper and soundly closed the door in his face.

38. Which of the following is the underlying moral of this passage?

(A) A fair face is of little use without sense.

(B) A little common sense is often worth more than cunning.

(C) Advice prompted by selfishness should not be heeded.

(D) Diligence survives hard times that are sure to come.

39. "The Ant and the Grasshopper" comes from which famous collection of stories?

(A) Mother Goose Nursery Rhymes

(B) Grimm's Fairy Tales

(C) Hans Christian Andersen's Tales

(D) Aesop's Fables

40. Since fables were supposed to teach morals based on a Judeo–Christian context, why did the ant not allow the grasshopper into its home or share its food?

(A) The grasshopper was supposed to represent evil and evil things must be shunned.

(B) The story was written for children and parents did not want to encourage their children to take in strangers.

(C) The story was written during a time of plague and allowing strangers into the home was unthinkable.

(D) The Christian value of hard work and a moral work ethic overrode any sympathetic feelings toward other creatures in order to teach an important lesson.

For Questions 41 and 42, read each sentence. Determine whether one of the sentences or phrases contains grammatical, word use, or punctuation errors. If so, choose the letter of that part of the sentence. If there are no errors, choose D.

41. Identify the error.

> A) The students are going on a field trip next week. B) All the students brought back their permission slip, accept for Hector. C) Hector will remain behind with another class. D) No error.

(A) The students are going on a field trip next week.

(B) Each student brought back their permission slip, accept for Hector.

(C) Hector will remain behind with another class.

(D) No error

42. Identify the error.

> A) When I was at camp, a wasp stung my arm: B) right away, I placed mud on the C) site, and the swelling decreased immediately. D) No error.

(A) When I was at camp, a wasp stung my arm:

(B) right away, I placed mud on the

(C) site and the swelling decreased immediately.

(D) No error.

43. Read the sentence. Select the answer choice that best represents standard English without altering the meaning of the original sentence and which best communicates using style and tone.

The first robotic inventions were actually long ago, in 1737, when French inventor Jacques de Vaucanson built a robotic duck that could flap its wing, paddle in the water, and even eat grain.

(A) The first robotic invention occurred in 1737 when French inventor Jacques de Vaucanson built a robotic duck that could flap its wing, paddle in the water, and even eat grain.

(B) The first robotic invention was, actually, long ago, in 1737, when French inventor Jacques de Vaucanson built a robotic duck that could flap its wing and paddle in the water and even eat grain.

(C) In 1737, the first robotic invention occurred long ago when French inventor Jacques de Vaucanson built a ridiculous robotic duck that could flap its wing, paddle in the water, and even eat grain.

(D) The first robotic invention was in 1737 and it was made by French inventor Jacques de Vaucanson when he built and designed a duck that looked like a real duck because he wanted it to flap its wing, paddle in the water, and even eat grain just like the ducks he owned.

44. Read the sentence, which has some parts underlined, followed by four answer choices. Select the answer choice that best represents standard English without altering the meaning of the original sentence and which best communicates using style and tone.

Josh and Tom spent all day walking along a new hiking trail they discovered, and they were almost too exhausted to return to base camp for the night.

(A) they were almost

(B) were

(C) each almost were

(D) was almost

GO ON TO NEXT PAGE ▶

45. Consider the following passage.

What do you get when you cross a lion with a tiger? A liger! Ligers have a thick mane like that of a lion and stripes like those of a tiger. There are not a lot of ligers in the world because tigers and lions don't usually get along. There are no ligers in the wild, although several have been born in captivity.

Which of the following choices is the best summary of this passage?

(A) The author feels as if ligers should be protected from extinction.

(B) Humans should not take science into their own hands and create new creatures.

(C) Ligers are rare because they blend characteristics of two different animals, lions and tigers.

(D) Ligers are rare, but it is just a matter of time before they are reintroduced back into the wild.

46. Consider the following passage.

How far back does your family tree go? An ancient skull in Africa suggests that the human family might go back much further than thought. A skull discovered in the desert of Chad in 2001 is estimated to be between 6 and 7 million years old. This skull, that of a hominid, might not be a direct ancestor of humans. Instead, the human timeline might resemble an actual tree with lots of branches representing lots of different species in different places.

This passage indicates that

(A) Human ancestors might go back as far as 7 million years ago.

(B) Human ancestry can never really be determined.

(C) The newest research field for this type of work is in Africa.

(D) Humans are direct descendants of the creature represented by the skull, a hominid.

47. Consider the following passage.

Bethany Hamilton has lived in Hawaii her whole life. She dreamed of becoming a professional surfer and was in the water all of the time. One day, when she was 13 years old, Bethany went swimming with her first friend so they could practice catching some waves. Unexpectedly, a tiger shark attacked Bethany and bit her arm off. Bethany almost died and spent a week in the hospital. Less than a month after the attack, Bethany was back in the ocean, swimming and working towards her dream of becoming a professional surfer. Bethany had decided that nothing was going to stand in the way of her dream!

The author's main reason for writing this passage is to

(A) inform readers of how dangerous surfing can be.

(B) persuade readers that oceans can be dangerous places filled with wild creatures.

(C) inform readers of how to become a professional surfer.

(D) describe an inspiring account of a girl who overcame tremendous obstacles to realize her dreams.

Today, humans rule the Earth, but that wasn't always the case. Millions of years ago, dinosaurs ruled the Earth. Dinosaurs became extinct long before humans ever existed. At some time in the past, an unknown catastrophic event made dinosaurs extinct. Dinosaurs lived all over the world, when the Earth was one giant continent. The weather was warmer, and the temperature was hotter. Small mammals and birds lived alongside crocodiles and other reptiles. There was plenty to eat. No one is really sure when or why dinosaurs became extinct. There are many theories, but none have ever been proven.

48. The main idea of this passage is that

(A) the Earth was a much different place during the time of dinosaurs.

(B) dinosaurs and humans could never have lived alongside one another.

(C) humans are the cause of climate change and the extinction of many plant and animal species.

(D) dinosaurs would never have ruled the Earth if humans had lived during the same time period.

49. According to the text, which of the following best describes how the dinosaurs became extinct?

(A) The continents drifted apart, separating species from specific nutrition.

(B) It is unknown how the dinosaurs became extinct.

(C) An asteroid occurred.

(D) Humans came in control of Earth and pushed the dinosaurs to extinction.

Section 2: Mathematics

1. What is the value of x in the following proportion?

$$\frac{12}{x} = \frac{20}{5}$$

   (A) 5
   (B) 8
   (C) 4
   (D) 3

2. Which of the symbols could be placed in the space between the two following numbers to form a true inequality?

$$7\frac{2}{5} \qquad 7.41$$

   (A) <
   (B) >
   (C) ≤
   (D) ≥

3. A coin will be flipped three times. What is the probability that it will land on heads all three times?

   (A) $\frac{1}{3}$
   (B) $\frac{1}{8}$
   (C) $\frac{1}{6}$
   (D) $\frac{1}{9}$

4. In which place is the 2 in the following number?

   934.8127

   (A) hundredths
   (B) thousandths
   (C) ten thousandths
   (D) tenths

5. John is paid $10 per hour to paint a house, $6 per half hour to paint another house, and $3 per 15 minutes to paint a third house. If John spends the same number of hours, represented by N, painting each house, which of the following equations correctly represents the amount John makes for painting all three jobs?

   (A) $10 \times N + 6 \times N + 3 \times N$
   (B) $\frac{1}{8} \times 19N$
   (C) $10 \times N + 6 \times 2 \times N + 3 \times 4 \times N$
   (D) $10 \times N + 6 \times 4 \times N + 3 \times 2 \times N$

6. What is the mean of the following set of numbers?

   5 10 6 14 5

   (A) 8
   (B) 6
   (C) 5
   (D) 9

7. Which of the following equations represents the associative property of multiplication?

   (A) $(2+8)+7 = 2+(8+7)$
   (B) $2 \times 8 \times 7 = 7 \times 2 \times 8$
   (C) $2(8+7) = 2(8) + 2(7)$
   (D) $2 \times (8 \times 7) = (2 \times 8) \times 7$

8. Angles 1 and 2 in the following diagram are both which type of angle?

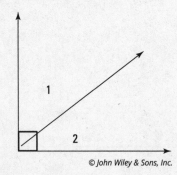

© John Wiley & Sons, Inc.

   (A) acute
   (B) right
   (C) obtuse
   (D) straight

9. Which of the following is equal to 7.5834×10^3?

   (A) 0.0075834

   (B) 7,583.4

   (C) 75.834

   (D) 758.34

10. Which of the following inequalities has a solution that is represented by the following graph?

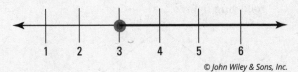
© John Wiley & Sons, Inc.

   (A) $2x > 6$

   (B) $2x - 5 \geq 1$

   (C) $4x < 12$

   (D) $3x + 5 \leq 14$

11. What is the greatest common factor of 56 and 84?

   (A) 7

   (B) 14

   (C) 12

   (D) 28

12. If $3p - 7 = 14$, what is the value of $2p + 14$?

   (A) 3

   (B) 7

   (C) 28

   (D) 16

13. In which quadrant of the coordinate plane is the point $(-5, 12)$?

   (A) I

   (B) II

   (C) III

   (D) IV

14. A boat leaves its port at 5:30 a.m. and returns to the port at 12:15 p.m. the same day. What is the elapsed time between the boat's departure and return?

   (A) 11 hours and 25 minutes

   (B) 6 hours and 15 minutes

   (C) 7 hours and 15 minutes

   (D) 6 hours and 45 minutes

15. The following right rectangular solid has a length of 12 m, a width of 4 m, and a height of 5 m. What is the volume of the figure?

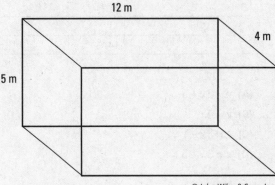
© John Wiley & Sons, Inc.

   (A) 32 m^3

   (B) 240 m^3

   (C) 210 m^3

   (D) 160 m^3

16. If $|2x| = 8$, which of the following could be a value of x?

   (A) 8

   (B) −4

   (C) 2

   (D) −8

17. At a cookie party, 120 cookies were divided equally among 30 students. How many cookies did each student get?

   (A) 4

   (B) 9

   (C) 3

   (D) 12

GO ON TO NEXT PAGE

18. Marcie is 3 years older than twice Bill's age. The sum of their ages is 33. How old was Bill 5 years ago?

(A) 10

(B) 15

(C) 18

(D) 5

19. Which of the following equations relates x and y according to the pattern represented in the following table?

x	y
1	8
2	11
3	14
4	17

(A) $y = 2x + 5$

(B) $y = 4x$

(C) $y = 3x - 1$

(D) $y = 3x + 5$

20. The following lines intersect to form right angles. What type of relationship do the lines have with each other?

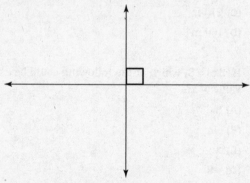

© John Wiley & Sons, Inc.

(A) parallel

(B) not on the same plane

(C) perpendicular

(D) same line

21. What is the solution to the following inequality?

$$4x + 11 > 27$$

(A) $x < 3$

(B) $x > 3$

(C) $x > 4$

(D) $x > 9.5$

22. Which of the following is a correct label for the following figure?

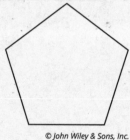

© John Wiley & Sons, Inc.

(A) convex pentagon

(B) concave pentagon

(C) convex hexagon

(D) concave octagon

23. Which of the following is equal to $7(p + 5)$?

(A) $7p + 5$

(B) $7p + 35$

(C) $7p + 12$

(D) $35p$

24. The only prime factors of a number are 2, 5, and 7. Which of the following could be the number?

(A) 35

(B) 210

(C) 42

(D) 140

25. What is the value of $\dfrac{5p - qr}{qr^2}$ if $p = 4$, $q = 1$, and $r = 5$?

(A) 3

(B) $\dfrac{3}{5}$

(C) 5

(D) $\dfrac{2}{3}$

26. What is 38.452 rounded to the nearest tenth?

(A) 38.5

(B) 38

(C) 38.4

(D) 38.45

27. Which of the following is NOT a composite factor of 90?

(A) 10

(B) 45

(C) 3

(D) 15

28. What property is demonstrated by the following equation?

$$15 + 5 + 7 = 5 + 15 + 7$$

(A) associative property of addition

(B) commutative property of addition

(C) distributive property

(D) transitive property

29. 285.496 decameters is equal to how many centimeters?

(A) 0.285496

(B) 28.5496

(C) 28,549.6

(D) 285,496

30. The ratio of boys to girls in a class is 3:2. If there are 18 boys in the class, how many girls are in the class?

(A) 2

(B) 12

(C) 17

(D) 8

31. The following rectangle has a length of 20 inches and a width of 8 inches. What is the perimeter of the rectangle?

(A) 160 in.^{2}

(B) 28 in.

(C) 56 in.

(D) 28 in.^{2}

32. What is the value of h in the following equation?

$$9h - 7 = 65$$

(A) 8

(B) 72

(C) 6

(D) 58

33. What is the least common multiple of 12 and 4?

(A) 24

(B) 48

(C) 36

(D) 12

34. If Steve averages 9 kilometers per hour on a jog, how many meters per second does he average?

(A) 9,000

(B) 150

(C) 5

(D) 2.5

35. If $w^3 = 64$, what is the value of w?

(A) 4

(B) 8

(C) 16

(D) 64

GO ON TO NEXT PAGE

36. The net in the following diagram is composed of six 3-centimeter-by-3-centimeter squares. If the net were arranged to form a cube, what would be the surface area of the cube?

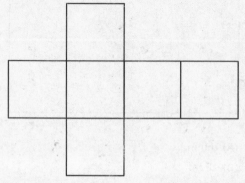

© John Wiley & Sons, Inc.

(A) 54 cm^2

(B) 27 cm^3

(C) 36 cm^3

(D) 9 cm^2

37. Which of the following is equal to $12x + 3 + 5x - 2$?

(A) $17x + 5$

(B) $17x + 1$

(C) $18x$

(D) $7x + 5$

38. In the number 578.324, the 8 represents a value that is how many times greater than the value represented by the 4?

(A) 20

(B) 2

(C) 2,000

(D) 200

39. Which of the following statements about the following bar graph is NOT true?

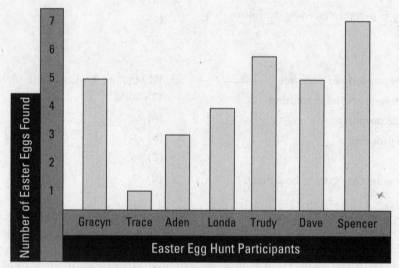

© John Wiley & Sons, Inc.

(A) Dave and Gracyn found the same number of eggs.

(B) Trace found the lowest number of eggs.

(C) Londa found more eggs than Trudy.

(D) Spencer found the most eggs.

40. What is the value of the following expression?

$$17 - 3(8 - 2 \times 3)^2 + 5$$

(A) 5

(B) 33

(C) 61

(D) 10

41. A bag contains 2 orange marbles, 4 blue marbles, 1 yellow marble, and 3 red marbles. If Luca randomly pulls a marble out of the bag, what is the probability that the marble will be either blue or red?

(A) $\frac{3}{25}$

(B) $\frac{7}{20}$

(C) $\frac{2}{5}$

(D) $\frac{7}{10}$

Section 3: Social Studies

1. According to the graph, each of the following is true EXCEPT

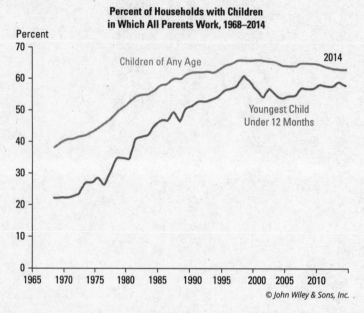

**Percent of Households with Children
in Which All Parents Work, 1968–2014**

© John Wiley & Sons, Inc.

(A) In households where all parents work, there have always been fewer households where the youngest child is under 12 months than in others.

(B) In 1970, there was about a 15 percent difference between working-parent households where the youngest child was under 12 months than in others.

(C) In households where all parents work, the gap between all households with children and households where the youngest child is under 12 months than in others was widest in 2005.

(D) The percent of households with children in which all parents work appears to be leveling off.

2. Which of the following is true regarding the Suez Canal?

(A) It connects the Red Sea and the Mediterranean Sea.

(B) It reduces travel-distance for ships by over 4,000 miles.

(C) It is over one hundred years old.

(D) All of the above

3. How many major territorial acquisitions (over 200,000 square miles) contributed to the current United States?

(A) 4

(B) 5

(C) 6

(D) 7

4. Which of the following is the most likely reason for John Hancock signing his name so large on the Declaration of Independence?

(A) so that King George III of Great Britain could read the signature without his spectacles

(B) He was responsible for writing most of the document.

(C) As president of the Continental Congress, he was the first person to sign the document.

(D) to demonstrate his defiance of Great Britain

5. The Indus River Valley Civilization is best known for which of the following major contributions?

   (A) urban planning

   (B) terraced farming

   (C) cuneiform script

   (D) aqueducts

6. Which of the following pieces of legislation, intended to prevent physical conflict, instead led to it?

   (A) Elementary and Secondary Education Act (1965)

   (B) Fugitive Slave Act (1850)

   (C) Homestead Act (1862)

   (D) Federal Reserve Act (1913)

7. Where would you find a continental divide?

   (A) at a deep-sea depth

   (B) at a shallow undersea depth

   (C) at a low land elevation

   (D) at a high land elevation

8. All of the following were intended effects of the Marshall Plan EXCEPT

   (A) a removal of trade barriers

   (B) a discouraging of labor unions

   (C) a stop to the spread of communism

   (D) a modernization of industry

9. The title is missing from the following chart. Which of the following is the best title for the chart's information?

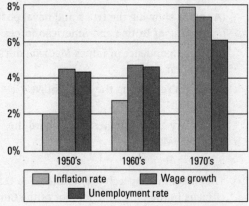

© John Wiley & Sons, Inc.

   (A) Money Supply

   (B) Economic Indicators

   (C) Consumer Price Index

   (D) Business Cycle

10. Which branch of the federal government has the power to declare war?

    (A) Judicial

    (B) Executive

    (C) Legislative

    (D) Military

11. Which Native American tribe is most often associated with the Trail of Tears?

    (A) Cherokee

    (B) Iroquois

    (C) Apache

    (D) Cheyenne

12. Select all of the following that are generally considered to be negative effects of globalization.

    (A) loss of domestic industries

    (B) spread of technology to rural areas

    (C) increase of work opportunities

    (D) dominance of foreign institutions

GO ON TO NEXT PAGE

13. A teacher requires students to use at least one primary resource for a project involving the War of 1812. Which of the following sources could the students use?

    (A) maps showing the troop and naval positioning of British and American forces

    (B) correspondence of James Madison during the war

    (C) a film reenacting the Battle of New Orleans

    (D) a diary entry from a sailor aboard the U.S.S. *Monitor*

14. The freedom of speech is guaranteed to U.S. citizens in the First Amendment of the Constitution. Which of the following describes the exceptions to this freedom?

    (A) making libelous statements

    (B) creating a danger

    (C) both A and B

    (D) There are no exceptions.

15. Where would you most likely find a moraine?

    (A) any place there is or has been a glacier

    (B) only on land

    (C) only undersea

    (D) both A and B

16. Among social issues and events from the late 1950s through the 1970s, which of the following is viewed mainly as a questioning of authority?

    (A) the Counterculture

    (B) the Great Society

    (C) the Bay of Pigs

    (D) the Montgomery bus boycott

17. A government takes a hands-on approach to its economy, determining prices as well as production and distribution. Which of the following describes this system?

    (A) a market economy

    (B) a planned economy

    (C) a mixed economy

    (D) a traditional economy

18. Alienation of the worker, in the sense of the worker not being fulfilled by his or her work, is a concept attributed to which of the following?

    (A) Auguste Comte

    (B) Adam Smith

    (C) Karl Marx

    (D) John Maynard Keynes

19. Select all of the following which occurred following the end of WWII.

    (A) The Jewish people were granted land that would become Israel.

    (B) Russia became a part of the Soviet Union.

    (C) The Ottoman Empire collapsed.

    (D) The United Nations was formed.

20. Which of the following is NOT a benefit of using inquiry-based learning in Social Studies?

    (A) It offers a student-centered experience.

    (B) It assures thorough content coverage.

    (C) It helps develop critical thinking.

    (D) It provides many opportunities for interdisciplinary study.

21. Which of the following is NOT an example of the probable impact of humans on the environment?

    (A) a rise in solar activity

    (B) a loss of coral reefs

    (C) a rise in sea levels

    (D) a loss of species

22. Which of the following is true regarding the Articles of Confederation?

    (A) It was not an actual constitution.

    (B) It was ratified right after the signing of the Declaration of Independence.

    (C) It featured state's rights.

    (D) It was written primarily by Thomas Jefferson.

23. A cross-cultural psychologist is starting a new study. Which of the following questions is the psychologist most likely to explore?

   (A) What are some of the differences between the ways Australian and Polynesian people dress?

   (B) How open to new experiences are the hunting peoples of Greenland?

   (C) How much extroversion exists across the different castes of India?

   (D) What different social clues do people in the U.S. and China rely on?

24. What was Hannibal's military target when he crossed the Alps?

   (A) Rome

   (B) Madrid

   (C) Lisbon

   (D) Carthage

25. Which was the first state to grant women the right to vote?

   (A) California

   (B) Wyoming

   (C) New York

   (D) Kansas

Section 4: Science

1. Which of the following describes the correct order of the interior sections of Earth, from the ground inward?

   (A) mantle, crust, inner core, outer core

   (B) crust, mantle, inner core, outer core

   (C) crust, mantle, outer core, inner core

   (D) outer core, inner core, mantle, crust

2. Which of the following is the name for the process by which light energy is converted into chemical energy?

   (A) photosynthesis

   (B) respiration

   (C) carbon dating

   (D) mitosis

3. Select all of the following that characterize carbon dioxide, or CO_2.

   (A) mixture

   (B) compound

   (C) solution

   (D) molecule

4. Which of the following is NOT involved in the scientific collection of data?

   (A) tools

   (B) variables

   (C) models

   (D) trials

5. Wind power has been proposed and successfully used as an alternative energy source. Which of the following is a negative effect of using wind power?

   (A) The turbines are not space-efficient.

   (B) The turbines are a threat to wildlife.

   (C) The cost of using wind power has been increasing.

   (D) It is not a renewable resource.

6. According to the illustration, which of the following explains the effects of human poisoning of animals?

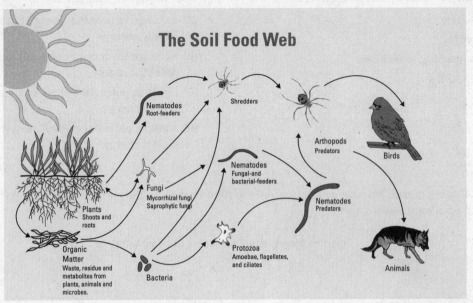

© John Wiley & Sons, Inc.

(A) The number of large, predatory arthropods would increase.

(B) The number of birds would increase.

(C) The number of fungi would stay about the same.

(D) all of the above

7. Where did the term *quasar* come from?

(A) from the Greek for *galaxy*

(B) from the Latin for *star*

(C) from the name of the scientist who first discovered quasars

(D) from a shortening of the phrase *quasi-stellar radio source*

8. Where in the Periodic Table of the Elements would you find the noble gases?

(A) the far left column

(B) the far right column

(C) the middle of the first full row

(D) the middle of the last full row

9. Which of the following is NOT a human genetic disorder?

(A) color blindness

(B) poliomyelitis

(C) Down syndrome

(D) neurofibromatosis

10. Which of the following is a benefit associated with the mineral zinc?

(A) helps eyes and skin

(B) helps teeth and bones

(C) helps the immune system

(D) helps the nervous system

GO ON TO NEXT PAGE

11. All of the following forces are involved in the formation of sedimentary rock EXCEPT

(A) cooling

(B) eroding

(C) compacting-cementing

(D) depositing

12. A rollercoaster car going from the top of a loop downward is an example of

(A) a change in potential energy but not in kinetic energy.

(B) a change in kinetic energy but not in potential energy.

(C) a gain in potential energy and a loss in kinetic energy.

(D) a loss in potential energy and a gain in kinetic energy.

13. The following chart is missing descriptions on the right explaining the plotted lines. What do the plotted lines most likely show?

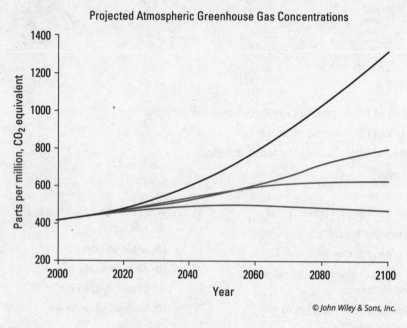

Projected Atmospheric Greenhouse Gas Concentrations

(A) different levels of projected emissions in reverse proportion to concentration levels

(B) different levels of projected emissions in direct proportion to concentration levels

(C) different costs of fossil fuels depending on available resources

(D) none of the above

14. Which of the following is NOT a characteristic of amphibians?

    (A) They are cold-blooded.

    (B) They have backbones.

    (C) They have scales.

    (D) They spend some of their time on land and in water.

15. Which of the following is most likely to be found in shells?

    (A) $CaCO_3$

    (B) $CuSO_4$

    (C) NH_3

    (D) $NaHCO_3$

16. Select all of the following that are true regarding sea ice.

    (A) When melting, it does not raise sea levels.

    (B) It is studied by scientists observing climate-change effects.

    (C) It provides a habitat for algae and fish.

    (D) Continued loss will not measurably affect weather patterns.

17. Which scientist is credited with the discovery of X-rays?

    (A) Wilhelm Roentgen

    (B) Marie Curie

    (C) Antonie van Leeuwenhoek

    (D) Heinrich Hertz

18. Select all of the following functions served primarily by a plant's stems.

    (A) help with a plant's energy acquisition

    (B) help with a plant's growth in height

    (C) help with a plant's nutrition

    (D) help with a plant's stability

19. Which of the following forces causes a pendulum to keep swinging?

    (A) friction

    (B) electromagnetism

    (C) contact

    (D) gravity

20. Which is the highest layer of Earth's atmosphere where birds have been found flying?

    (A) troposphere

    (B) stratosphere

    (C) mesosphere

    (D) thermosphere

21. The primary function of the human endocrine system is to

    (A) protect the body from infection.

    (B) regulate growth and development.

    (C) provide strength and movement.

    (D) serve as the body's main control center.

22. Which of the following is most important for weather forecasting?

    (A) barometer

    (B) thermometer

    (C) wind gauge

    (D) Kelvin scale

23. What happens when light passes through a prism?

    (A) The light is reflected, with the longest wavelength at the top.

    (B) The light is reflected, with the shortest wavelength at the top.

    (C) The light is refracted, with the longest wavelength at the top.

    (D) The light is refracted, with the shortest wavelength at the top.

GO ON TO NEXT PAGE

24. Which of the following involves an exchange between human body systems and the environment?

   (A) photosynthesis

   (B) bio-waste

   (C) leucine

   (D) all of the above

25. Select all of the following that can be determined by studying the rock record where radioactive elements are missing.

   (A) the exact age of a fossil

   (B) the relative age of a fossil

   (C) the exact ages of rocks found in different places

   (D) the relative ages of rocks found in different places

DO NOT TURN THE PAGE UNTIL TOLD TO DO SO **STOP** DO NOT RETURN TO A PREVIOUS TEST

Chapter 18

Answers and Explanations for 5018 Practice Test

After you finish the second practice test sections in Chapter 17, take some time to go through the answers and explanations in this chapter to find out which questions you missed and why. Even if you answered the question correctly, the explanation may offer a useful strategy that helps you improve your performance.

Answers for Section 1: Reading and Language Arts

1. **D.** There are three reasons or purposes for writing, and all text can be fit into one of these purposes: *writing to entertain, writing to inform,* and *writing to persuade.* Choice (A) is incorrect because readers can read to learn, but writers do not write to learn. That is not a purpose of the writing process. Choice (B) is incorrect because *writing for reflection* is a personal type of writing and is generally not shared with an audience. Choice (C) is incorrect for the same reason.

2. **B.** *Irony* is considered to be within tone, or expression, of a text rather than an element of figurative language, which describes one thing by comparing it to something else. Irony can be used in a humorous way for comparisons, but that would be the tone of the work.

3. **C.** Author's tone is best described as the words the author uses to show his or her opinions or feelings about a topic or content. Choice (A) is incorrect as the author's personality is known as voice. Choice (B) is incorrect as the feelings created in the reader are known as the mood of a text. Choice (D) is incorrect as the point of view of an author is referred to as the author's purpose.

4. **A.** An argumentative essay should begin with a statement of agreement or disagreement followed by the necessary details of reasons and examples to support the opinion. Choices (B) and (C) are incorrect because argumentative essays must include more than opinions and feelings. Details must be supported by logical reasons, not just opinions. Choice (D) is a statement regarding essay writing in general, not argumentative writing specifically.

5. **B.** These are the correct definitions of rime and rhyme. Choice (A) is incorrect because each word has a separate definition, and the terms do not mean the exact same thing. Words with rime can rhyme, but that is not always true. Words can have many rimes, according to how many syllables they have, but the rhyme is dependent on the inclusion of a matching sound in another word. Choice (C) is incorrect because the definitions are switched. Choice (D) is incorrect in that rhyme is most certainly used in poetry.

6. **A.** *Couplets* are two lines of verse that form a unit. Choice (B) is incorrect because a *triplet* is three lines of poetry that rhyme. Choice (C) is incorrect because a *quatrain* is a stanza of four lines, which usually alternately rhyme. Choice (D) is incorrect because *sestets* are six lines of poetry, usually the last six lines of a sonnet.

7. **D.** Readers who draw connections between text and their own personal experiences are reflecting upon personal knowledge, and the response connecting the story to the reader's own life is within the *reflection and response stage* of literature. Choice (A) is incorrect because the *development stage* is where readers begin to make connections with printed word, but usually only to ask clarifying questions as opposed to making personal connections. Choice (B) is incorrect because the *beginning stage* generally is an introduction to text with little personal response from the reader, other than declarations of opinion about the pleasure received from the text. Choice (C) is incorrect because the *critical analysis stage* involves the reader judging and analyzing text and examining the connections that might, or might not, be personally related.

8. **A.** In this initial stage of literacy appreciation development, students learn that literacy can be a social experience and that text can bring individual pleasure. Choice (B) is incorrect because, in the *losing oneself in a story* stage, the act of reading becomes a means of escape and does not involve social aspects, but instead focuses on individual connections. Choice (C) is incorrect because, in the *finding oneself in a story* stage, students try and make personal and relevant connections between the characters and events and themselves, rather than simply seeking pleasure. Choice (D) is incorrect because, in the *venturing beyond self* stage, students use text to understand larger issues happening in the world around them and how they fit into that picture.

9. **D.** An *exposition* is an introduction to a story, where the main characters, the setting, and often the central problem are discussed. Choice (A) is incorrect as this describes a part of the story known as the climax. Choice (B) is incorrect as the conclusion of the story is known as the resolution. Choice (C) is incorrect as these central plot events of the story are referred to as rising action in a story.

10. **C.** Brochures are *nonfiction*, in that they give real and true information. *Expository* is writing that is informative in nature. Choices (A) and (B) are incorrect in that they are *fictional* in nature, meaning the information is creative and not true as regards to events and information that is usable and correct. Choice (D) is incorrect because research expository would be text that is more descriptive in nature than a brochure, such as a nonfiction book, essay, and so forth.

11. A. The primary reason to teach figurative language is so that students can understand that some ideas presented in text are abstract in nature and may be outside their present knowledge. Connections made through figurative language connect the abstract to more easily relatable topics. Choices (B) and (C), while true, are incorrect because neither is the only reason to teach figurative language. Figurative language occurs in nonfiction, in TV commercials, and so forth — it can be in any type of text, not just fiction. Choice (D) is incorrect because assessment expectations are never purposes for instruction; instruction drives the assessment.

12. C. Because the teacher pauses after each page to focus on details from the text and illustration, she is helping the students to pay attention to details that build on understanding the nature of stories, which have plot lines. Choice (A) is incorrect because the *alphabetic principle* focuses on written letters and symbols. By listening to the story, the students aren't seeing the letters and symbols in a meaningful way. Choice (B) is incorrect because *early print concepts* involve introducing text to students by pointing out how to hold a book, how to turn pages, and so on, not by asking clarifying questions. Choice (D) is incorrect. While the teacher is reading the text aloud, which supports *phonemic awareness,* the clarifying questions go a step beyond simply hearing the sounds and transition to meaning making.

13. C. Using *context clues* is a process where a reader uses words, meaning, and content in surrounding sentences to decipher unknown words. Choice (A) is incorrect because the word has no word parts that are recognizable when looked at separately, which would be *word structure clues.* Choice (B) is incorrect because *syntactic clues* are used to decipher meaning from the structure of the sentence. Since the sentence is not given, this answer choice would not be the best one. Choice (D) is incorrect because *antonym clues* give readers hints by telling the opposite, or contrast, of a word and is often signaled by the words *whereas, unlike,* or *as opposed to.*

14. B. *Semantic and syntactic clues* use content and the structure of the sentence to help define the meaning of unknown words; because the definition of alignment is given and separated by commas, this uses syntactic clues, and the definition helps to define range using semantic clues. Choices (A) and (D) are incorrect because *analogic clues* draw connections between known and unknown words and both words were unknown. Choice (C) is incorrect because *symbolic clues* use known images to figuratively express an idea, usually in thematic works. This informational sentence has no figurative expressions.

15. B. *Fluency* is the ability to read text smoothly and with expression, without stumbling over words. Choice (A) is incorrect because the term *poetic expression* simply refers to poetry in general. Choice (C) is incorrect because *phonemic awareness* focuses on the sounds of individual letters in regards to words. Choice (D) is incorrect because the term *oral smoothness* simply means speaking well, not reading well.

16. B. *Comprehension* occurs when students see a word and automatically connect meaning to the word. Choice (A) is not correct because *fluency* would involve the student reading aloud, rather than stating connections. Choice (C) is not correct because *word identification* involves the recognition of words, or word parts, without meaning necessarily attached. Choice (D) is not correct as *concepts of print* refers to the structure of books, text, and stories without meaning being attached to particular words.

17. A. This list of words was composed by William Edward Dolch and corresponds to words most often used in grade-level text. Choice (B) is incorrect because this is the definition of sight words. Choice (C) is incorrect as this is another way to say "sight words." Choice (D) is incorrect because Dolch is a list of words that are divided by grade level and do not necessarily focus on the first grade only.

18. D. By going a step beyond basic comprehension recall and stating that such a meal would have been hard to make, she is inferencing that the settlers would have had to use other methods of cooking, even though those specific methods are beyond her knowledge. Choice (A) is incorrect because *summarizing* just states what was in the text, without additions of thoughts or personal reflections. Choice (B) is incorrect. If the student had simply stopped at stating she didn't know these facts and they were new to her, that would have been *metacognition*, thinking about her thinking. She added to that, which involved a higher-level thinking process, *inferential thinking*. Choice (C) is incorrect because *cause and effect* traces a process or progression of some event.

19. **D.** There are specific phases that developmental, or beginning, writers experience. The first stages involve making symbols to represent sounds and letters with a progression to meaning-making through beginning sounds, and then consonants representing letters, and finally a standard spelling that can be read and understood. Choices (A) and (B) are not correct because pictures and illustrations are not part of development alphabetic writing. Choice (C) is not correct because nonsense words are not part of meaning-making with text.

20. **A.** In order for silent comprehension to occur, students must possess both print skills (phonemic awareness, word analysis, word recognition, spelling, fluency) and making-meaning skills (word meaning, background knowledge, connection of words to complex ideas). Choice (B) is not correct because fluency alone simply means speed and accuracy, whether oral or silent. Choice (C) is not correct because it focuses on listening comprehension, not silent comprehension. Choice (D) is incorrect because it focuses on oral comprehension.

21. **B.** Inventive spelling is a method of teaching spelling where students spell what they phonetically hear and then transition to more traditional forms of spelling gradually, over time and practice. Choice (A) is not correct because invented spelling is not considered to be a creative writing format; rather, it is a transitional phase whereby students become more traditional spellers. Choice (C) is not correct as this is the definition for conventional spelling. Choice (D) is not correct as students are not necessarily "corrected" with inventive spelling. It is understood by the teacher that the phase is transitional and students will learn to spell more correctly through immersion in text and through direct instruction in appropriate spelling phases.

22. **C.** First, the teacher led a discussion about what the students already *knew* (K). Then, he asked them what they would like to, or *wanted* (W) to, learn. Finally, he discussed what other *learning* (L) had occurred. Choices (A) and (B) are not correct because these are teaching strategies, not reading comprehension strategies. Choice (D) is incorrect because a specific graphic organizer may or may not have been employed in the class-led discussion. When students become more skillful, they could be asked to generate a graphic organizer, which is frequently used in KWL to aid independent comprehension.

23. **A.** Good readers must be able to create mental models and connect what they read to what they know about their world. Teaching students to make these mental models improves overall comprehension of all text. Choice (B) is incorrect because visual imagery is not connected to teaching art. Art involves physical representations, while visual imagery is a comprehension strategy. Choice (C) is incorrect because all text relies on images, not only "harder" text. Choice (D) is incorrect because "imagery" is a strategy, as opposed to a standard of learning that can be assessed or measured.

24. **C.** In order for students to *decode* unknown words, they must understand print concepts and have knowledge of letters and the alphabetic principle so that unknown words lead to meaning-making through connecting sounds to letters to words. Choice (A) is incorrect because *phonemic awareness* simply means listeners can hear the sounds, not that they can use those sounds to break apart unknown words. Choices (B) and (D) are incorrect because *fluency* and *comprehension* focus on meaning-making of entire sentences and text, either oral or silent, and involve much more complex processes than those described in the question.

25. A. A *blank verse* is a type of poem written in unrhymed iambic pentameter, usually resembling speech. Choice (B) is not correct because a *cinquain* is a poem with only five lines. Choice (C) is not correct because an *elegy* is a sad and thoughtful poem about the death of someone. Choice (D) is not correct because a *sonnet* is a poem with 14 lines and usually has an identifiable rhyme scheme.

26. D. This first stanza is the speaker's reflection and resembles a speech a person might make if alone, or the thinking occurring inside his head. This is an example of a *dramatic monologue,* a character speaking alone. Choice (A) is not correct because the speaker never directly addresses the audience of the poem. Choice (B) is incorrect because *foreshadowing* is a literacy device where an author hints about events to come. Choice (C), *dramatic dialogue,* is incorrect because there is only one speaker in the poem, not two.

27. B. A *primary* source is an original source material that has not been adapted in any way. Choice (A) is incorrect because a *survey* is generally a questionnaire of opinions, rather than a direct source of information. Choice (C) is incorrect because *secondary* sources are written after the event and only comment on and discuss the event. Choice (D) is incorrect because a *tertiary* source simply collects information, such as in an almanac.

28. C. *Cause and effect* is frequently used in nonfiction text that discusses relationships between causes and events. Choice (A) is a common pattern in fiction text. Choices (B) and (D) are literary devices, not patterns.

29. C. Because "tomato" is a noun that ends with an –o, a vowel, it must have an ending of –es, rather than just –s. Choices (A) and (B) are incorrect, but are frequent misspellings. Choice (D) is incorrect because an apostrophe shows ownership, not an increase in number.

30. D. A *gerund* is a noun formed from a verb by adding –ing to the end. Choice (A) is incorrect because a *predicate noun* is a noun or noun phrase that generally follows the verb "to be." Choice (B) is incorrect because an *object noun* is generally found after the verb. Choice (C) is incorrect because an *object pronoun* is a personal pronoun used as the object in a sentence.

31. B. *Green-eyed* is a compound adjective because it combines two words into one, separated by a hyphen in this example. Choice (A) is incorrect because *tired* is an adjective of quality and consists of one word. Choice (C) is incorrect because *ball* is the noun, with *rubber* as an adjective describing what kind of ball. Choice (D) is incorrect because *golden retriever* is a noun.

32. C. "Similarly" is an adverb because it describes the verb, "attired." Choice (A) is incorrect because adjectives describe nouns, not verbs. Choice (B) is incorrect because prepositions immediately precede nouns or pronouns, not verbs. Choice (D) is incorrect as "similarly" does not show the action of the noun.

33. B. *Phoneme blending* is providing a sequence of spoken phonemes and then using them to sound out and form words. Choice (A) is incorrect because *phoneme segmentation* is breaking apart the sounds of words for decoding purposes. Choice (C) is incorrect because *phoneme addition* is when you add a phoneme to the beginning or ending of word. Choice (D) is incorrect because *phoneme identification* asks students to identify a single sound in a word.

34. C. Alphabetic principle is knowing letter names and being able to recognize the symbols of the alphabet. *Playing with plastic letters* would enhance recognition of those symbols. Choices (A), (B), and (D) are incorrect because they do not focus specifically on the letters of the alphabet.

35. **D.** In order for comprehension to occur, students must be taught to make connections between the text and their actual life experiences. Students using prior knowledge of their own life aids in this. Choice (A) is incorrect as comprehension is not tied to the amount of time spent, as opposed to strategies used. Choice (B) is incorrect in that students are discussing their own life experiences, as opposed to focusing solely on text in the story. Choice (C) is incorrect in that state standardized testing should never be a purpose for any lesson.

36. **A.** In this example, the child uses what letter skills she has to deliver a message, creating unusual, but effective, spellings. Choice (B) is incorrect in that there is a sentence formatting mistake. Choice (C) is incorrect in that there are vowel mistakes. Choice (D) is incorrect in that there were no specific alphabetic mistakes, only spelling mistakes.

37. **B.** Because Joni does not recognize all of the letters in words, especially words that are familiar and should be easy, she is having a problem remembering the individual letters and the sounds they represent. Choice (A) is incorrect because traditional spelling has many "rule breakers" and "rule followers" and is generally used to teach writing skills, as opposed to reading skills. Choice (C) is incorrect in that familiar and easy words should not need context clue analysis. Context clues, as a strategy, are used for unfamiliar and more difficult words. Choice (D) is incorrect because there is no indication that the words are from a specified list, or whether Joni has already mastered those words.

38. **D.** The ant's attitude and actions show the value of having a good work ethic, which is useful when eventual hard times occur, such as the winter. Choice (A) is not correct because the grasshopper seems to have sense; he just enjoys playing more than working. Choice (B) is not correct because neither the grasshopper nor the ant show cunning in the story. Choice (C) is not correct because the ant's advice was not directed by selfishness, but rather a desire for the grasshopper to beware.

39. **D.** The story should be easily recognizable as a fable because of its moral lesson, and Aesop is the oldest and most well-known collection of such tales. Choice (A) is incorrect because the story is not a rhyming tale. Choices (B) and (C) are incorrect because the story is not a fairy tale, in which there are magical and imaginary beings and legends.

40. **D.** Fables are designed to teach a lesson, and the ant's hard work would have been seen as a virtue while sharing food would have taught another lesson about emulating the grasshopper's behavior. Choice (A) is incorrect because the grasshopper was not written as an evil character, but one who is simply unthinking. Choice (B) is incorrect in that the fables were not necessarily written for children, but were written as short and meaningful texts, usually full of Biblical and political symbolism which would only have been apparent to adults. Choice (C) is incorrect because Aesop lived in ancient Greece and was a storyteller, collecting stories from the countryside. It is unknown when the story was actually composed.

41. **B.** The word "accept" should be "except." "Accept" means to receive something, while "except" means not including something. Choices (A) and (C) are not correct because there are no errors within those sentences. Choice (D) is not correct because there was an error with the paragraph.

42. **D.** The sentence is grammatically correct. Choice (A), with the colon, is correct because two independent clauses can be joined by a colon. Choice (B) is correct with no errors. Choice (C) uses "site" correctly as location.

43. **A.** Choice (A) is the sentence which most succinctly, and correctly, rewords the original sentence. Choice (B) is incorrect in that it has too many commas in the beginning and lacks commas for the list at the end. Choice (C) is incorrect because it lacks style and has the

addition of the word "ridiculous," which changes the tone from informational to judgmental. Choice (D) is incorrect because it adds information not given about the inventor wanting the duck to look like ducks he owned.

44. **A.** Choice (A) is correct because the subject and verb agree in number. Choice (B) is incorrect because it changes the meaning of the sentence by leaving out the word "almost." Choices (C) and (D) are incorrect because they don't agree in number.

45. **C.** Choice (C) is the only answer that provides a short summary, a brief statement of the main points of the paragraph. Choices (A) and (B) are incorrect because they have judgment or opinion in them, which summaries do not contain unless it is the stated or inferred opinion of the author. Choice (D) is not correct because it contains misleading information, that ligers live in the wild.

46. **A.** The passage suggests that this skull is one of the oldest ever found and points to ancestors of humans as long ago as 6 to 7 million years. Choice (B) is not correct because the article does not state or infer that human ancestry will remain a mystery. Choice (C) is not correct as the article only suggests that the skull was found in 2001, not that it is the newest find in the field. Choice (D) is not correct because it directly opposes the article, which only states that the skull "might" be a direct ancestor of humans.

47. **D.** The author's tone in the piece lets the reader know that he or she admires Bethany, which is more than just providing information about a shark attack. Choice (A) is incorrect because only one incident is described, and the actual event is only briefly discussed. Choice (B) is incorrect because only one dangerous creature is discussed, and the author uses no persuasive techniques. Choice (C) is incorrect because no advice or information is given on how to actually become a surfer.

48. **A.** The main idea of this passage is that the time of dinosaurs was much different, in terms of weather, temperature, and living species, than it is during the time of humans. Choices (B), (C), and (D) are all judgment calls, with inferences that are not supported by the text.

49. **B.** The passage states in two different places that, while there are many theories, no theory has proven the reason as to dinosaur extinction. Choice (A) is not correct as the article states this is why fossils are found all over the world, not as the cause of extinction. Choice (C) in incorrect because the article states the catastrophic event was "unknown." An asteroid would be a known event. Choice (D) is incorrect as the passage states the dinosaurs lived on Earth before humans.

Answers for Section 2: Mathematics

1. **D.** When a fraction is set equal to a fraction, you can cross multiply and get equal cross products. Then, you can solve the resulting equation involving equal cross products.

$$\frac{12}{x} = \frac{20}{5}$$
$$12(5) = 20(x)$$
$$60 = 20x$$
$$\frac{60}{20} = \frac{20x}{20}$$
$$3 = x$$
$$x = 3$$

The answer is 3, as you can see by plugging 3 in for x in the original equation. None of the other choices result from correctly solving the equation, so none of them can produce a true equation by being substituted in for x.

2. **A.** The best way to compare two numbers is to put them in the same form. For example, you can write $7\frac{2}{5}$ as 7.4 because $\frac{2}{5} = 0.4$. The number 7.4 is the same as 7.40, which is less than 7.41. Giving the numbers the same number of digits after the decimal helps make that clear. Since the answer is <, it cannot be any of the other choices. They all contradict the correct answer.

3. **B.** The probability that multiple events will all happen is the product of their individual probabilities. Every time a coin is flipped, the probability that it will land on heads is $\frac{1}{2}$. That is the probability of getting heads for all three coin tosses.

$$\frac{1}{2} \times \frac{1}{2} \times \frac{1}{2} = \frac{1}{8}$$

Choice (A) is 1 over the number of coin tosses. Choice (C) is 1 over the sum of the denominators of the individual probabilities. Choice (D) is 1 over the square of the number of coin tosses.

4. **B.** The third place after the decimal in a decimal number is the thousandths place. Choice (A) is the place of the 1, Choice (C) is the place of the 7, and Choice (D) is the place of the 8.

5. **C.** The amount of money John makes for all three jobs is the sum of what he makes for each job. The amount he makes for the first job is $10 times the number of hours. The second job makes John $6 times 2 times the number of hours. The 2 is multiplied there because there are 2 periods of half an hour in every hour. The third job makes John $3 times 4 times the number of hours, since each hour has 4 periods of 15 minutes. Since N represents the number of hours John spends working on each job, the sum of the amounts of money John makes for each job is $10 \times N + 6 \times 2 \times N + 3 \times 4 \times N$. Choice (A) fails to consider the number of payment periods that are in an hour. Choice (B) is the product of $\frac{1}{2}$ and $\frac{1}{4}$ multiplied by the sum of the dollar per period amounts times N. Choice (D) switches around where the 2 and the 4 are multiplied.

6. **A.** The mean of a set of data is a ratio of the sum of the numbers and the number of numbers. In this case, the sum of the numbers is 40. The number of numbers is 5. The quotient of $\frac{40}{5}$ is 8. Choice (B) is the median of the set of data. Choice (C) is the mode. Choice (D) is the range.

7. **D.** The associative property of multiplication is the principle that the way numbers are associated when only multiplied does not make a difference in the product. In Choice (D), the 8 and 7 are grouped together on the left while the 2 and 8 are grouped together on the right. The two sides are equal regardless because they both equal 112. Choice (A) demonstrates the associative property of addition. Choice (B) illustrates the commutative property of multiplication. Choice (C) represents the distributive property.

8. **A.** Angles 1 and 2 form a right angle together. That means they are both less than 90 degrees. They are also both greater than 0 degrees. Therefore, they are acute angles. No angle can be both an acute angle and any of the other choices.

9. **B.** When a number is multiplied by a 10 with a whole number exponent, the value can be written by a simple moving of the decimal to the right the number of places that is the same as the exponent. In this case, the decimal needs to be moved to the right three places because

the exponent for 10 is 3. The result of moving the decimal in 7.5834 three places to the right is 7,583.4. It is, therefore, none of the other choices.

10. **B.** The graph represents $x \geq 3$, which is the solution to Choice (B) and none of the other choices. A solid filled in circle on a number line represents including the corresponding number. Since $\geq$ means "greater than or equal to," the 3 is included. Thus, the interior of the circle is darkened. The line is darkened to the right of 3 because the graph represents 3 and all numbers that are greater.

$$2x - 5 \geq 1$$
$$2x - 5 + 5 \geq 1 + 5$$
$$2x \geq 6$$
$$\frac{2x}{2} \geq \frac{6}{2}$$
$$x \geq 3$$

11. **D.** By writing a whole number as a product of two factors and breaking those factors down into products of factors, and so on, you can get the prime factorization of the number. From there, you can multiply every combination of prime number factors to find the other factors of the original number. If you do that with 56 and 84, you can see that $56 = 2 \times 2 \times 2 \times 7$ and $84 = 2 \times 2 \times 3 \times 7$. Those prime factorizations can help you find every factor of 56 and 84. The largest number that is a factor of both is 28.

12. **C.** The solution to the first equation is 7, so 7 is the value of p.

$$3p - 7 = 14$$
$$3p - 7 + 7 = 14 + 7$$
$$3p = 21$$
$$\frac{3p}{3} = \frac{21}{3}$$
$$p = 7$$

Since p has a value of 7, you can put 7 in for p in $2p + 14$ to determine the value of the expression.

$$2p + 14 = 2(7) + 14$$
$$= 14 + 14$$
$$= 28$$

Choice (A) is just the coefficient in the original equation. Choice (B) is the value of p and thus the solution to the original equation. Choice (D) is the sum of 2 and 14 and not helpful to this solution.

13. **B.** In Quadrant II, every point has a negative x-coordinate and a positive y-coordinate. Quadrant II is the only quadrant where that type of combination exists. Therefore, $(-5, 12)$ is in Quadrant II. Also, you can find the point by moving 5 units to the left of the origin, $(0, 0)$, and then 12 units up. That will land you in Quadrant II. It is the quadrant that is left of the y-axis and above the x-axis.

14. **D.** You can count up whole numbers of hours from 5:30 a.m. and then count minutes. 11:30 a.m. is 6 hours later, 12:00 p.m. is 30 minutes after that, and 12:15 is another 15 minutes ahead. The sum of 6 hours, 30 minutes, and 15 minutes is 6 hours and 45 minutes. Remember that our system of time is not purely base 10. You cannot subtract 530 from 1215 to get the answer to the problem. Doing so would result in Choice (A). Choice (B) neglects the 30 minutes from 11:30 a.m. to 12:00 p.m. Choice (C) can result from minor calculation errors that produce a wrong answer.

15. B. The formula for the volume of a right rectangular solid is $A = l \times w \times h$, so the area of the right rectangular solid in this case is $12\,\mathrm{m} \times 4\,\mathrm{m} \times 5\,\mathrm{m}$, or $240\,\mathrm{m}^3$. Choice (A) is the perimeter of two of the bases, Choice (C) is the sum of the dimensions times 10, and Choice (D) is one of the lateral areas.

16. B. Only two numbers have an absolute value of 8. They are 8 and −8.

17. A. To find the answer, divide 120 by 30 since 120 cookies were divided into 30 groups.

$$\frac{120 \text{ cookies}}{30 \text{ students}} = 4 \text{ cookies/student}$$

The other choices were randomly thought up and do not result from proper division.

18. D. The first thing to determine is Bill's age now. You can use a variable to represent it. If Bill's current age is x, then Marcie is 3 more than twice that, or $2x + 3$. The sum of those two expressions is 33. That situation can be represented by an equation, and you can solve the equation to find Bill's current age.

$$x + 2x + 3 = 33$$
$$3x + 3 = 33$$
$$3x + 3 - 3 = 33 - 3$$
$$3x = 30$$
$$\frac{3x}{3} = \frac{30}{3}$$
$$x = 10$$

Bill is presently 10. Five years ago, his age was 5 less than that, so he was 5. Choice (A) is Bill's current age. Choice (B) will be Bill's age in 5 years. Choice (C) is $33 - 5(3)$, which does not lead to the answer.

19. D. Since you have a list of choices, you can try them until one works. You can put all of the x and y combinations into each equation. All of the combinations work for Choice (D). They all make the equation true. Also, you can see that the y values go up 3 from one to the next. If you go back to 0 for x, you get 3 less than what you get when x is 1. That means if x is 0, y is 5. Therefore, 5 is the constant (number without a variable) in an equation in which y is on the left and x and a constant are on the right. The 5 is added to something times x, and the result is y. The next question is what is multiplied by x. To find out, look at the row where x is 1. What is 1 multiplied by to get a number to which 5 can be added to get 8? The number is 3.

$$8 = 3(1) + 5$$
$$y = 3x + 5$$

The equation is therefore $y = 3x + 5$. None of the other equations work for all of the x and y combinations, and no proper reasoning supports them.

20. C. Perpendicular lines are defined as lines that intersect to form right angles. Choice (A) is incorrect because parallel lines never intersect. Choice (B) is wrong because lines that are not on the same plane never intersect. Choice (D) is wrong because a line cannot intersect itself. Lines have to intersect to be perpendicular, and they have to form right angles.

21. **C.** To solve an inequality, get the variable by itself on one side of the inequality sign by doing the opposite of what is being done to it, and look at the result.

$$4x + 11 > 27$$
$$4x + 11 - 11 > 27 - 11$$
$$4x > 16$$
$$\frac{4x}{4} > \frac{16}{4}$$
$$x > 4$$

22. **A.** The figure is a *polygon* because it is completely enclosed, and it is formed entirely by segments joined at their endpoints. It has five sides, so it is a *pentagon.* It is *convex* because no two sides come together and point inward. Therefore, the figure is a convex pentagon. Choice (B) is incorrect because the figure is convex. Choice (C) is wrong because a hexagon has six sides. Choice (D) is incorrect because an octagon has eight sides and the figure in question is convex.

23. **B.** As proven by the distributive property, $7(p + 5) = 7(p) + 7(5)$, or $7p + 35$. Choice (A) results from simply adding the 5 and not multiplying 7 by it. Choice (C) has a second term that results from adding 5 to 7 instead of multiplying 7 by 5. Choice (D) is the result of multiplying 7, p, and 5. There is no reason to do that.

24. **D.** You can break down the factors of each choice until you find which one only has 2, 5, and 7 for prime factors. The answer is Choice (D) because $140 = 2 \times 2 \times 5 \times 7$. Choice (A) does not have 2 for a factor. Choice (B) has a prime factor of 3, and so does Choice (C).

25. **B.** You can put the numerical values of p, q, and r in for the variables and simplify the result.

$$\frac{5p - qr}{qr^2} = \frac{5(4) - (1)(5)}{(1)(5^2)}$$
$$= \frac{20 - 5}{25}$$
$$= \frac{15}{25}$$
$$= \frac{3}{5}$$

The other choices can result from misrepresenting variable values and other miscalculations.

26. **A.** The tenths place is the first place to the right of the decimal, so your answer should have exactly one digit to the right of the decimal. Since the digit that comes after the 4 in the tenths place is 5 or more, because it is 5, you need to round the tenths place up. Therefore, the digit in the tenths place needs to be 1 higher than 4. That means the tenths place digit should be changed to 5 and no digits should follow. Choice (B) is the original number rounded to the nearest whole number, Choice (C) is a result of rounding down instead of up, and Choice (D) is the original number rounded to the nearest hundredth.

27. **C.** By breaking down the factors of 90 until you get a prime factorization, you can see that the prime factorization of 90 is $2 \times 3 \times 3 \times 5$. All the factors of 90 are products of combinations of those prime factors. All the choices are factors of 90, but the only one that is not a composite factor is Choice (C). The number 3 is a prime number, so it is not composite. A *composite number* is a whole number that has more than two factors. It is impossible for a prime number to be a composite number, and 3 is a prime number because it has exactly two factors, 1 and itself.

28. **B.** The commutative property of addition is the principle that the order in which numbers are added does not affect their sum. That is illustrated by the equation. None of the other choices are demonstrated by the given equation.

29. **D.** A decameter is 10 meters, a meter is 10 decimeters, and a decimeter is equal to 10 centimeters. Therefore, a decameter is $10 \times 10 \times 10$ centimeters, or 1,000 centimeters. Any number of decameters is the same as 1,000 times that many centimeters. Thus, 285.496 decameters is 285,496 centimeters. To multiply a decimal number by 1,000, you can simply move the decimal three places to the right. For every 10 you multiply a decimal number by, move the decimal one place to the right. Also, you can make a list of the metric prefixes in order. Every space you move down from bigger units to smaller units requires that you multiply by 10 to compensate. If you move down three prefixes, as you do in this case, you multiply the number by $10 \times 10 \times 10$, or 1,000. The other choices involve moving the decimal incorrectly.

30. **B.** You can set up a proportion to figure out the unknown number. You can represent the number of girls in the class with a variable such as g and solve a proportion that has it. The proportion 3:2 is equal to the proportion 18 to some number. You can write ratios as fractions that can be used in proportions. A proportion is a statement that one ratio equals another.

$$\frac{3}{2} = \frac{18}{g}$$
$$3g = (18)(2)$$
$$3g = 36$$
$$\frac{3g}{3} = \frac{36}{3}$$
$$x = 12$$

The value of g is 12, so the number of girls in the class is 12. Also, you determine what you must multiply 3 by to get 18 and multiply 2 by the same number. That number is 6, and $2 \times 6 = 12$.

31. **C.** The perimeter of any polygon is the sum of the measures of its sides. Since opposite sides of a rectangle have the same measure, the perimeter of a polygon is twice the length plus twice the width.

$$p = 2l + 2w$$
$$= 2(20) + 2(8)$$
$$= 40 + 16$$
$$= 56$$

Choices (A) and (C) are wrong because they do not result from proper application of a perimeter formula and also because perimeter is a distance, so it is one-dimensional. Perimeter is not given in square units. Choice (B) results from adding the length and the width. That gives half the perimeter, not the full perimeter.

32. **A.** To solve an equation, get the variable by itself on one side by undoing everything that is being done to it. You undo those operations by performing the opposite operations on both sides of the equation.

$$9h - 7 = 65$$
$$9h - 7 + 7 = 65 + 7$$
$$9h = 72$$
$$\frac{9h}{9} = \frac{72}{9}$$
$$h = 8$$

You can check the solution by putting it in for the variable and seeing if it results in a true equation.

$$9(8) - 7 = 65$$
$$72 - 7 = 65$$
$$65 = 65$$

The value of h is 7 because that is the value of h that makes the equation true. Choice (B) is the value of the right side when 7 is added to it. Choice (C) is a random idea for a wrong choice. Choice (D) is the result of subtracting 7 from 65 instead of adding it. That is a false step in the solving process, and it would not complete the solving process even if it were a correct step.

33. **D.** You can write out the first few multiples of 12 and 4 and see that 12 is the lowest multiple both numbers have. You can also immediately identify 12 as a multiple of 4 and conclude that, since 12 is also a multiple of itself, the least common multiple of 12 and 4 is 12. All of the other choices are common multiples of 4 and 12, but 12 is the lowest one.

34. **D.** Take the ratio $\dfrac{9 \text{ km}}{1 \text{ hour}}$ and change the numerator and denominator to the necessary units. A distance of 9 km (kilometers) is 1,000 times that many meters because every kilometer is 1,000 meters. An hour is 60 minutes, and a minute is 60 seconds, so an hour is 60×60 seconds, or 3,600 seconds.

$$\frac{9 \text{ km}}{1 \text{ hour}} = \frac{9,000 \text{ m}}{3,600 \text{ seconds}}$$
$$= \frac{2.5 \text{ m}}{1 \text{ second}}$$
$$= 2.5 \text{ meters/second}$$

You can also multiply $\dfrac{9 \text{ km}}{1 \text{ hour}}$ by ratios that use the units you want to use but also equal 1. Multiplying by a value of 1 does not produce a new value. Anything times 1 equals itself.

$$\frac{9 \text{ km}}{1 \text{ hour}} \times \frac{1 \text{ hour}}{3,600 \text{ seconds}} \times \frac{1,000 \text{ m}}{1 \text{ km}} = \frac{9,000 \text{ m}}{3,600 \text{ seconds}}$$
$$= 2.5 \text{ m / second}$$

Choice (A) is merely the number of meters in 9 kilometers. Choices (B) and (C) are just random and wrong.

35. **A.** You can use the prime factorization of 64 to determine what value can be cubed, or set to the third power, to get 64. The prime factorization of 64 is $2 \times 2 \times 2 \times 2 \times 2 \times 2$, so 2×2 is what can be set to the third power to get 64. The value of 2×2 is 4.

$$4^3 = 4 \times 4 \times 4$$
$$= 64$$

Choice (B) is the square root of 64, not the cube root. Choice (C) is the square of the cube root of 64. Choice (D) is exactly 64, not the cube root of it.

36. **A.** Every square has an area of $3 \text{ cm} \times 3 \text{ cm}$, or 9 cm^2. There are six squares of that area making up the net, so the net has an area of $(9 \text{ cm}^2)(6)$, or 54 cm^2. The six squares of the net can be put together to form a cube, which will have a surface area equal to the area of the net. The other choices result from false operations with 3 cm square sides.

37. **B.** Only like terms can be combined, and like terms are either constants or variable terms with exactly the same variables and each variable having only one exponent in the full

expression. In the expression $12x + 3 + 5x - 2$, $12x$ and $5x$ are like terms that can be added to get $17x$, and 3 and -2 are like terms that can be added to get 1. Thus, $12x + 3 + 5x - 2$ is equal to $17x + 1$. The other choices result from false combination methods.

38. **C.** The 8 is in the ones place, so it represents 8. The 4 is in the thousandths place, so it represents 4 thousandths, which can be written as $\frac{4}{1,000}$ or 0.004.

$$8\sqrt{0.004} = 2,000$$

The other choices can result from using false representations of the digits in question.

39. **C.** The bar graph indicates the following numbers of Easter Eggs found for the participants in the hunt.

Gracyn: 5

Trace: 1

Aden: 3

Londa: 4

Trudy: 6

Dave: 5

Spencer: 7

Trudy found more eggs than Londa, so Londa did not find more eggs than Trudy. Choice (A) is true, so it is an incorrect answer. Dave and Gracyn both found 5 eggs. Choice (B) is an incorrect answer because Trace really did find the lowest number of eggs. He found 1. Everybody else found more than that. Choice (D) also makes a true statement. Spencer found the highest number of eggs.

40. **D.** Finding the value of the expression requires following the order of operations, which you can do by using "PEMDAS," which stands for "Parentheses (and other grouping symbols), Exponents, Multiplication and Division (from left to right), Addition and Subtraction (from left to right)." If you perform those operations correctly in the correct order, you can find the value of the expression.

$$
\begin{aligned}
17 - 3(8 - 2 \times 3)^2 + 5 &= 17 - 3(8 - 6)^2 + 5 \\
&= 17 - 3(2)^2 + 5 \\
&= 17 - 3(4) + 5 \\
&= 17 - 12 + 5 \\
&= 5 + 5 \\
&= 10
\end{aligned}
$$

The other answer choices result from using the incorrect order in the order of operations.

41. **D.** The probability of a single event is a ratio of the number of favorable (qualifying) outcomes to the number of possible outcomes. The probability that one or another given event will happen is the sum of their individual probabilities. In this case, there are 10 marbles. That is the number of possible outcomes. There are 4 blue marbles in the bag, so the probability of randomly choosing a blue marble is $\frac{4}{10}$. The bag contains 3 red marbles, thus the probability of randomly choosing a red marble is $\frac{3}{10}$. The sum of $\frac{4}{10}$ and $\frac{3}{10}$ is $\frac{7}{10}$, Choice (D). Choice (A) is the number of red marbles over the random number 25. Choice (B) results from adding the denominators of the two individual probabilities instead of just the numerators. Choice (C) is the simplified form of the probability of picking a blue marble.

Answers for Section 3: Social Studies

1. **C.** The gap was widest at the outset of the data collected, in 1968, where all parents worked in about 4 out of 10 households. The halfway point was reached around 1980, and now it's more than 6 out of 10.

2. **D.** Finished in 1869, the Egyptian canal allows ships to pass between Europe and South Asia without having to go around Africa.

3. **C.** These acquisitions include the 1783 Treaty of Paris (original thirteen colonies), 892,135 sq. mi; the 1803 Louisiana Purchase, 827,987 sq. mi; the 1845 annexation of Texas, 389,166 sq. mi; the 1846 Oregon Treaty (with Great Britain, for the Oregon Territory), 286,541 sq. mi; the 1848 Mexican Cession (for California, Utah, Nevada, and Arizona), 529,189 sq. mi; and the 1867 purchase of Alaska, 591,000 sq. mi.

4. **C.** There was a lot of blank space (as no one else had signed yet), and the size of Hancock's signature is comparable with examples of it. Choice (A) is mythical. Choice (B) is incorrect because it was Thomas Jefferson who was primarily responsible (assisted by Benjamin Franklin, John Adams, Roger Sherman, and Robert Livingston). Choice (D) is not the correct choice because it signifies a less emotional reason.

5. **A.** Located in what is now Pakistan and India, this civilization is also noted for its recognition of the importance of hygiene in the urban environment. Choice (B) is attributed to ancient China. Choice (C) arose in ancient Sumer. Choice (D) first arose in Mesopotamia and on Minoan Crete.

6. **B.** This legislation, part of the Compromise of 1850, was meant to avoid war by appeasing Southern states by requiring all states to turn in (escaped) slaves; however, the legislation served instead to solidify Northern opposition to slavery and was one of the causes of the Civil War. Choice (A) involves federal funding of public schools. Choice (C) led to the (European–American) settling of the western territories by granting 160 acres of free land to homesteaders who would live there for five years and make improvements to it. Choice (D) created the Federal Reserve banking system, essentially giving power to the government to control currency.

7. **D.** A continental divide is an imaginary line on a land's high spot where river systems on either side of it drain into different oceans.

8. **B.** Also known as the European Recovery Plan, the 1947 Marshall Plan was established to help countries recover from WWII devastation and gave $13 billion in aid to those countries agreeing to its conditions. These stipulations did not appeal to the communist Soviet Union, which consequently refused the aid.

9. **B.** The chart shows, from the 1950s through the 1970s, the three economic factors that most affect the stability of the Social Security Trust Funds. Choice (A) is an economic indicator referring to how much money is available. Choice (C) is an economic indicator referring to the average change, over time, of consumer prices (in other words, what money will buy). Choice (D) refers to the long-term, overall pattern involving the ups and downs of an economy (growth, recession, recovery, and so on).

10. **C.** The power to declare war and appropriate funds for war belongs to Congress. The Executive branch (headed by the President) supplies the Commander-in-Chief of the military (the President). The military is not a branch of the federal government but part of the Executive branch (the Department of Defense).

11. **A.** In the 1830s, the U.S. government forced tribes from the Southeastern United States to leave their homes and walk, at gunpoint, to the Oklahoma Indian Territory. The forced march involved the Cherokee, Muscogee, Chickasaw, and Seminole tribes. The Iroquois were from the Northeast, the Apache from the Southwest, and the Cheyenne from the Great Plains.

12. **A and D.** The negative effects are generally considered to be those where local control is diminished. Choice (B) and Choice (C) are generally considered to be positive effects.

13. **B.** Madison was the President during the war. Choices (A) and (C) are secondary sources. Choice (D) involves a Civil War vessel, an ironclad.

14. **C.** The Constitution sanctions neither libel nor the creating of danger when none is present, such as falsely shouting "Fire!" in a crowded theatre.

15. **A.** Moraines are glacial deposits; they may be on top of, inside, or at the sides or end of a glacier, or where a glacier was. Moraines may occur both on land and undersea, such as when drifting ice melts, sending glacial deposits into the sea.

16. **A.** This movement was a social reflection of the era's political and civil unrest. Choice (B) refers to President Johnson's reforms, including Medicaid and Medicare. Choice (C) refers to the failed, 1961 U.S. military action in Cuba. Choice (D) goes well beyond the questioning of authority. It refers to protests in Montgomery, Alabama, resulting from the 1955 arrest of Rosa Parks, which had such far-reaching effects as the rise in prominence of Martin Luther King, Jr., a Supreme Court decision outlawing segregation on buses, and the potential of achieving social and political success through nonviolent mass protest.

17. **B.** Socialist governments exhibit this type of economy. Choice (A) involves a free-price, hands-off approach and is exhibited by capitalist countries. Choice (C) uses features of both a market and a planned economy. Choice (D), an older system, depends on traditions within a culture.

18. **C.** *Marx's* focus here was in regards to workers under a capitalistic system, which he claimed caused workers to have little creativity in and less control over what they did, which was often piecemeal work that did not allow the worker the satisfaction of seeing work through from start to finish. *Comte,* Choice (A), founded positivism, a sociology theory stating that information should be gained only by using the scientific method. *Smith,* Choice (B), developed a theory based on *laissez-faire,* where a culture's economy will essentially guide itself (with little or no government control) by the inherent needs and skills of its people. *Keynes,* Choice (D), believed the government should step in whenever it was necessary to help its economy stabilize or grow.

19. **A and D.** Israel became a country in 1948. The United Nations was established in 1945; its founders sought to improve on the failed League of Nations, created after WWI. The Soviet Union was formed in 1924 as a result of the Russian Revolution (1917). The Ottoman (or Turkish) Empire sided against France, Russia, and Great Britain in WWI. The Ottomans were defeated along with Germany, and when the war ended, the British occupied what are now Iraq, Palestine, Jordan, Syria, and Lebanon.

20. **B.** If student interest is driving areas of study, content coverage will suffer. To counter this effect, educators use *discovery learning,* where inquiry is used to have students *discover* the necessary content. Learning how to formulate questions, collect data, and make connections and conclusions develops critical thinking, especially when student interest is central and when other areas of study are included, a feature that also helps meet curriculum needs.

21. **A.** Solar flares are related to the sun's magnetic field. Between human activities and climate change (rising ocean temperatures), less than half the world's coral reefs are considered to be healthy. In addition to melting icecaps, rising ocean temperatures lead to the rise of sea levels. Most scientists tend to agree that the extinction rate has been accelerated because of humankind.

22. **C.** Authority of the central government, such as to levy taxes and regulate commerce, came largely with the ratification of the U.S. Constitution in 1787. The Articles of Confederation was in fact the first written constitution of the U.S., but it wasn't ratified until 1781, when differences could be ironed out following its somewhat hasty drafting during wartime (1775–1777). The final version was drafted by John Dickinson of Pennsylvania.

23. **D.** The U.S. has an individualistic culture, whereas China's is collectivist. How we think about others plays a role in how we interact with them. Choice (A) would be asked by a cultural anthropologist, not psychologist. Choices (B) and (C) involve just one culture; (C) certainly involves more than one sub-culture but is not the most likely choice here.

24. **A.** Hannibal, the head of the Carthaginian army, led it east from Iberia (now Spain and Portugal), over the Alps (in 218 BCE, with elephants!), and then down into Italy, intending to conquer the Roman Empire (which he did not succeed in doing).

25. **B.** Wyoming passed the measure as a state in 1890 (it was also the first to have done so as a territory in 1869). California passed the measure in 1911, New York in 1917, and Kansas in 1912. The passage of the 19th Amendment to the Constitution granted this right in 1920 to women in every state.

Answers for Section 4: **Science**

1. **C.** The *crust* extends down only about 50 kilometers (km). The upper and lower *mantles* then reach depths of 2,900 km. The liquid *outer core* reaches inward to 5,100 km, and the solid *inner core* to 6,370 km.

2. **A.** Plants and other organisms use energy from the sun, along with carbon dioxide and water, to produce glucose and oxygen via *photosynthesis.* While producing carbon dioxide and water, Choice (B), *respiration,* does not require sunlight. Choice (C), *carbon dating,* is a method of measuring and calibrating a radioactive isotope of Carbon (Carbon-14) to determine the age of such things as fossils. Choice (D), *mitosis,* is essentially the part of the cell cycle where the nucleus is divided.

3. **B and D.** A *compound* is a pure substance whose molecules contain atoms of different elements. Therefore all compounds are *molecules,* but not all molecules (such as O_2) are compounds. Choice (A), a *mixture,* is formed when two or more substances are combined but do not form a new substance. Choice (C), a *solution,* is a mixture where one substance is evenly distributed throughout another substance, such as air, a solution of gases.

4. **C.** A *model* is used to explain the phenomenon or data *after* it has been collected. Proper *tools* help ensure the data is accurate; proper management of the independent (unchanging) and dependent (changing) *variables* ensures reliable cause-effect results; and repeated *trials* help ensure the trustworthiness of the data.

5. **B.** Hundreds of thousands of birds and bats are killed each year by wind turbines. The industry is aware of and working on this problem. Solutions include choosing sites not in flyways; radar and GPS tracking that would slow or stop the turbines when approached; ultrasonic acoustics (to repel bats); not running turbines when wind speed is low; and designing new turbine shapes. Choice (A) is incorrect: One large turbine can power over 500 homes. Choice (C) is incorrect: The cost has been decreasing since 1980. Choice (D) is incorrect: As long as the sun produces heat energy for Earth, there will be wind.

6. **D.** With fewer animals consuming predatory arthropods, their numbers would increase. More predatory arthropods would increase the numbers of *their* consumers, the birds. More predatory arthropods would decrease the number of the smaller, shredder arthropods, which would increase fungi; however, more predatory arthropods would decrease the number of large nematodes, which would increase the number of smaller nematodes, which would decrease fungi.

7. **D.** Quasars were discovered when radio telescopes picked up point sources of radio waves. It is now believed that quasars are extremely bright centers of very distant galaxies. Their energy source is probably due to the presence of a massive black hole, where gravity is so strong (because of the condensed mass) that neither matter nor radiation can escape. The Greek for *galaxy* is *galaxias.* The Latin for *star* is *stella.* Quasars were discovered by Maarten Schmidt in 1963.

8. **B.** Originally called inert gases, the noble gases (helium, neon, argon, krypton, xenon, radon) are in group 18 of the table. Choice (A) is comprised of the alkali metals. Choice (C) is comprised mostly of transition metals. Choice (D) is comprised mostly of actinides (metallic elements from number 89 to 103).

9. **B.** *Poliomyelitis* is caused by a virus. *Color blindness,* Choice (A), which is actually a color vision deficiency, occurs most often due to missing or damaged genes on the X chromosome. Therefore males, who have only one X chromosome, are more likely to be affected. Choice (C), *Down syndrome,* results from part or all of an extra chromosome 21. Choice (D), *neurofibromatosis,* referring to several conditions that often lead to tumors, results from an affected dominant gene. Therefore, there is a relatively high probability of the condition(s) being passed from parent to child.

10. **C.** Found in dairy products, red meat, fish, and nuts, zinc is also associated with growth. Choice (A) is associated with vitamin A. Choice (B) is associated with vitamin D and calcium. Choice (D) is associated with vitamins B1, B3, and B6, plus magnesium and potassium.

11. **A.** The cooling of magma (inside the earth) or lava (outside) produces igneous rock. Sedimentary rock forms when eroded sediment is deposited and then compacted and often cemented together.

12. **D.** The car has the most potential energy (an effect of the car's mass and *height*) at the top. As it goes downward, the car's potential energy decreases and its kinetic energy (an effect of the car's mass and *speed*) increases.

13. **B.** The chart shows CO_2 concentration levels of the future going up as future emission levels go up. As of now, greenhouse-gas concentration has not been directly linked to the cost of fossil fuel.

14. **C.** Amphibians have a permeable skin that allows gases and molecules to pass through. Some common amphibians include frogs, toads, newts, and salamanders. The features of amphibians are somewhere between those of fish and reptiles.

15. **A.** Calcium carbonate is the substance that gives most shells their hardness. Limestone, made up of the shells of countless marine organisms, is mostly $CaCO_3$. Choice (B) is the chemical formula for copper sulfate, also known as blue vitriol, which can be found in plants and soil. Choice (C) is the formula for ammonia gas, which can be found in water, soil, and air. Choice (D) is the formula for sodium bicarbonate, also known as baking soda, which can be found in mineral springs.

16. **A, B, and C.** Choice (A) is true because sea ice is formed from ocean water to begin with. Choice (B) is true largely regarding the spiral of rising temperatures. Sea ice reflects the sun's radiation, thus keeping Arctic temperatures low. But rising temperatures melt sea ice; less sea ice means more radiation and thus heat, which will melt more sea ice. . . . Choice (C) is true because the ice, while helping to keep water temperatures from becoming too warm, also helps to keep water temperatures from becoming too cold. The sea ice also provides hunting and breeding grounds for marine mammals and birds. Choice (D) is NOT true because, over time, warmer Arctic temperatures will most likely push the jet stream north, which will affect weather patterns for the whole planet.

17. **A.** Roentgen discovered X-rays (*X* for *unknown*) in 1895. A year later, Marie Curie discovered that the air around uranium rays could conduct electricity and found how to precisely measure radiation. She coined the term *radioactivity* (which itself had been discovered earlier in 1896 by Henri Becquerel). Antonie van Leeuwenhoek invented the microscope. Heinrich Hertz discovered radio waves in 1886.

18. **B and C.** Strong stems help a plant grow taller and help water and nutrients move to the ends of the plant. Choice (A), energy acquisition, is a function primarily of a plant's leaves. Choice (D), stability, is a function primarily of a plant's roots.

19. **D.** Once the mass (the weight or *bob*) is displaced (set in motion), gravity will keep the mass oscillating in a regular manner. Choice (A) will eventually *stop* the swinging. Choice (B) involves objects with opposite or like charges, such as in the opposite attraction (pull) between an electron (negative) and a proton (positive). Choice (C) involves physical contact between objects; friction is a contact force.

20. **B.** A species of vulture (Rüppell's) was found at 37,000 feet, in the lower levels of the *stratosphere*. With very few exceptions, however, birds fly in the lowest atmospheric level, the *troposphere*, also home to Earth's weather patterns. Choice (C), the *mesosphere*, reaches to about 50 miles above Earth and is where shooting stars burn up. Choice (D), the *thermosphere*, extends to about 400 miles and has a very low air density. Satellites and the space shuttle orbit in this layer. It also absorbs much of the sun's UV radiation and contains many highly charged ions (thus the *ionosphere*) and almost all the aurora (Southern and Northern Lights).

21. **B.** The endocrine system is made up of the glands that secrete hormones. Choice (A) is the main function of the immune system. Choice (C) pertains to the muscular system. Choice (D) pertains to the nervous system, including the brain and spinal cord.

22. **A.** *Barometers* measure atmospheric pressure, changes in which are the primary indicators of (impending) weather patterns. *Thermometers* (air temperature) and *wind gauges* (wind direction and speed) are used primarily to measure existing conditions. Also used for existing conditions, the *Kelvin scale* measures temperature, with absolute zero at 0 degrees (or −273 degrees Celsius).

23. **C.** As light moves from air to glass, it changes speeds. This change causes a change in direction (refraction) as the different wavelengths (colors) exit the glass at different speeds. Red, with the longest wavelength, is scattered least, so it is at the top. Light that is reflected is "bounced back" by an object (such as a mirror).

24. D. Choice (A), *photosynthesis*, is involved as the carbon dioxide humans exhale is used by producers (plants) to make glucose and oxygen, which humans consume. Choice (B), *bio-waste*, is involved as excretory matter is processed by decomposers (such as bacteria and fungi). Choice (C), *leucine*, is one of the nine essential amino acids (all of which end in *–ine* except tryptophan), involved as humans use amino acids to produce proteins. Leucine has many plant-based sources, including seaweed, whole-grain rice, sesame seeds, sunflower seeds, turnip greens, figs, raisins, and olives.

25. B and D. Without radiometric dating (which can determine absolute age), all dating must be relative. Choice (B) is usually determined by using the principle of *superposition*, where, in an undisturbed rock sequence (of layers) the older fossils are lower than the more recent. Thus, a fossil in a lower layer is older than one in a higher layer. Choice (D) can be determined, for example, when the same kind of fossil is found in rocks from different places: The rocks would be of the same (relative) age.

Answer Key

Section 1: Reading and Language Arts

1. D	14. B	27. B	40. D
2. B	15. B	28. C	41. B
3. C	16. B	29. C	42. D
4. A	17. A	30. D	43. A
5. B	18. D	31. B	44. A
6. A	19. D	32. C	45. C
7. D	20. A	33. B	46. A
8. A	21. B	34. C	47. D
9. D	22. C	35. D	48. A
10. C	23. A	36. A	49. B
11. A	24. C	37. B	
12. C	25. A	38. D	
13. C	26. D	39. D	

Section 2: Mathematics

1. D	12. C	23. B	34. D
2. A	13. B	24. D	35. A
3. B	14. D	25. B	36. A
4. B	15. B	26. A	37. B
5. C	16. B	27. C	38. C
6. A	17. A	28. B	39. C
7. D	18. D	29. D	40. D
8. A	19. D	30. B	41. D
9. B	20. C	31. C	
10. B	21. C	32. A	
11. D	22. A	33. D	

Section 3: Social Studies

1. C	8. B	15. A	22. C
2. D	9. B	16. A	23. D
3. C	10. C	17. B	24. A
4. C	11. A	18. C	25. B
5. A	12. A and D	19. A and D	
6. B	13. B	20. B	
7. D	14. C	21. A	

Section 4: Science

1. C	8. B	15. A	22. A
2. A	9. B	16. A, B, and C	23. C
3. B and D	10. C	17. A	24. D
4. C	11. A	18. B and C	25. B and D
5. B	12. D	19. D	
6. D	13. B	20. B	
7. D	14. C	21. B	

5

The Part of Tens

Chapter 19

Ten Common Misconceptions Concerning Curriculum, Instruction, and Assessment

Teachers are supposed to know everything about every subject and every student in every situation. Right? It may feel like that on any given day, but teachers are human beings, too! Errors and confusion occur to the very best teachers, especially in today's times. Changing rules and the nation's "race to the top" has left even the most veteran teachers scratching their heads when confronted with new challenges. With all the hype and news concerning educational progress and lack of progress, there are bound to be some misunderstandings and false impressions about the true nature of teaching.

This list of the ten most common misconceptions concerning curriculum, instruction, and assessment focuses on the biggest mistaken beliefs that new teachers have, and maybe even some veteran teachers, too. Hopefully, the list will clear up some misunderstandings you may have about your new profession and heal some misapprehensions you may have about your educational and professional future.

Myth #1: Teachers are supposed to know everything

One of the biggest myths and fallacies new teachers encounter is the idea that they must know everything about their subject and students at all times. Unless you're a computer teaching a classroom of robots led by an administration of machines, that just isn't going to happen. Every part of the process of teaching includes humans, and humans are prone to error. "To err is human," right? Don't be afraid to make mistakes and don't think you have to know everything straight out of the gate. Becoming a master teacher takes years of development, and even the oldest practicing teachers in the school will still tell you they learn something new every day! Instead, embrace those moments when students ask you a question you can't answer. Show them what learning looks like. Learning is a process, and young people too often think that adults have learned it all. What a great opportunity to model what growth means! When a parent or administrator asks you a question you just don't have the answer to, tell him you'll work on finding out. Being a teacher is a lot like the 1970s superhero Stretch Armstrong. You'll be pulled in a thousand directions, but you never have to feel as if you need to be Mr. or Ms. Know-It-All. S-t-r-e-t-c-h and be flexible, and you'll find yourself looking forward to those moments when you can learn something new, just like the students you're teaching. Never feel as if you have to know it all—because you never will. Instead, be open to change and new experiences.

Myth #2: All curriculum is mandated, so teachers don't really need to be subject experts

Teachers should most certainly know and follow any curriculum guides coming their way, but those guides can't take the place of knowledgeable experts in the field. Teachers must continue to learn and know more about the subjects they teach in a world that is rapidly changing. While it may seem as if only science teachers need to worry about this, this statement is true across all subjects and all curricula.

Being an effective teacher does mean being able to teach, but it also means knowing what the subject is about. You're not going to know everything straight out of the gate, and no one expects you to. Also, don't walk into teaching thinking you know everything you need to about your subject. Mostly, don't rely on the school or district to provide you with a comprehensive guide for professional development. You'll need, and want, to become the best teacher you can, and that means constantly learning and knowing more about your subject. Read the novels the kids are reading. Go to lectures and museums on topics that interest you. Take a dance class. Learn a new language. Part of being a professional teacher is helping the kids to see the larger world. That means that you have to become more knowledgeable about the world around you. Teachers don't just teach. They also learn . . . and that is a never-ending process.

Myth #3: If it isn't part of the mandated and accepted standards, don't teach it

Those mandated guides are certainly subjects and topics that need to be taught, but they are not necessarily all-inclusive, like a Jamaican resort. While you do have to teach those topics, don't get so wrapped up in the curriculum that you forget to take a look around you. Your subject—your curriculum—is happening in the world every day and everywhere. Teachable moments must be embraced *as* they occur. The latest news stories concerning The Lost Colony of Roanoke Island are a perfect example. While the textbooks and curriculum guide may take years to catch up, history is happening right now that can put to rest a lot of questions and stimulate a lot of interest. You don't have to take a semester to teach it, but taking moments to show students how the curriculum connects to the world builds learners and not just little robots who can spout facts.

Myth #4: Students who can't keep up have to be left behind

Keep in mind the word "guide" that comes with pacing guides and standards. Those guides aren't mile markers for student progress. Rather, they are points that direct instruction and are there to guide teachers. The realistic truth is that not every student is able to keep pace with the guides that have been developed. An even more realistic truth is that very few of them learn at the levels set forth, especially those with adapted abilities, traumatic life issues, or language learners. Those exceptions make up a huge percentage of today's classrooms. The guides should be used by teachers like beacons in the darkness. Aim for them; hope to hit them; but have a plan in place . . . just in case.

Teaching is about both breadth and depth. If you just aim for those guides without assessing what's going on in the students' heads, you may find you're the only one ready at the end of the line. A teacher's job isn't just about spouting curriculum; instead, it is about creating learning opportunities. The military has a saying and philosophy that says, "We leave no man behind." This is a saying that every teacher and administrator should adopt as well. Students can't be left behind because they will never catch up. The learning of an individual is always more important than the words on a page and guides in a book.

Myths #5 and #6: Direct instruction is best; cooperative learning means losing control

You may be inclined to believe that direct instruction is the best teaching style, and cooperative learning is the best way to lose total control of a class. Both statements are inaccuracies, and both fall in line with *strategies* of teaching. Neither direct instruction nor cooperative learning is a method or style of teaching; rather, they are strategies that teachers use for different results. One teaching style may be to use humor to make a point. Another may entail being a strict disciplinarian. Instructional strategies may impact behavior in the classroom, but a behavior management plan should include a variety of teaching strategies so neither the students nor the teacher become bored. Students who sit and listen to direct instruction all day may start to exhibit troublesome behavioral problems.

REMEMBER

Mixing it up and practicing new styles is what keeps each day interesting. Don't be afraid to try new strategies and don't be afraid to fail. Teaching is an art form, and that means there will be failures. Learn from your mistakes and make the next time using a strategy even better because you know what the pitfalls are going to be.

Myth #7: Differentiated instruction is only for students with IEPs or language barriers

While differentiated instruction is often used, in legal terms, to denote instruction that must be different because of learning disabilities (resulting in Individualized Education Programs [IEPs]) or language barriers (English Language Learners [ELL], English as a Second Language [ESL], English Speakers of Other Languages [ESOL]), the truth is that most instruction should be differentiated, especially during the elementary years. Students in this age group are still developing unique personalities and tastes and have to be exposed to a wide variety of instructional methods and strategies. Any time any child is lagging behind or not grasping concepts, differentiated instruction should occur. It doesn't have to get to the level of setting up an RTI (Response to Interventions), but varying instruction for a particular child because of a difficulty in learning isn't an exception. It's the *rule* of teaching. Every student has the potential to succeed and the right to the best education. If a student isn't achieving success, the teacher has to step in and teach differently. One style and size do not fit all. Master teachers are those who rarely even need to glance at IEPs or other forms and mandated interventions, because they already know what every student needs and are working hard to provide it.

Also keep in mind that there are students who are ahead of the other students. They require our differentiation techniques as well so that they can be continually challenged and perform at their highest level.

Myth #8: All instruction should be geared toward standardized or state assessment

It might be more appropriate to say that all instruction should be geared toward *assessment* and leave out the words "state" and "standardized" altogether. Assessment is a necessary part of teaching, as are curriculum and instruction. And, all instruction should be geared toward assessment, but it is the assessment you do in the classroom that counts the most and is the most impactful on learning. Instead of thinking of assessment in terms of what it tells others, remember it's supposed to be in terms of what it can tell *you*—about the students who are learning in front of you and the teacher who is working hard every day. Instruction is aimed toward assessment, and it may be better to think of them in terms of cause and effect. Great instruction is the cause and the effect is what the kids are learning.

Myth #9: Teaching to the test results in better test scores and smarter students

First, it is largely illegal for teachers to teach content that they know will be on a test. Most tests have guides and statements stating this exact thing. Doing such a thing violates ethical and moral codes, and many states have guidelines in place for this occurrence. Teaching to a test in this way could mean a lifelong loss of licensure or, even worse, criminal charges. While students should be taught *how* to take a test, the curriculum on a test is the result of a year-long study of work. Those teachers who embrace this concept have much smarter students in the long run and better test scores because those students have embedded the knowledge and retained it.

REMEMBER

Learning something just for a test only plugs into short-term memory, not the long-term skills and thought processes that teachers truly develop with lessons. Great teachers get great results, no matter the test given.

Myth #10: The main purpose of a classroom assessment is for grading purposes

While classroom assessments can be taken into account for grading purposes, the primary purpose of an assessment is to provide information to the teacher. Assessments should never be used as a "gotcha" moment, as in surprising students with a quiz if you think they didn't do their reading assignment. A situation like this speaks to behavior management control issues or, perhaps, the complexity of an assignment. While it is true that students who don't study for a test certainly won't pass it, it is also true that these same children didn't learn the curriculum when it was being taught. The real problem, then, isn't necessarily with testing; instead, it lies with the one who is struggling in class. Teachers should know well ahead of any formal test how a student will perform. While there are always surprises in life, most teachers know which kids struggle with content and with assessment.

And One to Grow On: Test scores indicate the effectiveness of teachers

A test score is an indication of many things. It can indicate a lack of an effective curriculum guide. It can indicate struggling students. It also can indicate a lack of effectiveness on the part of a teacher. However, test scores must always be tied back to what occurs in the classroom between a teacher and a student. There are always many levels when looking at data, and every one of those have to be considered when looking at a test score. This statement is not designed to protect teachers, though.

If test scores from an entire class are low, then that certainly points to a teacher who is not adequately doing the job she was contracted for and is being paid for. If test scores are low across a building, though, a larger picture needs to be drawn. This could point to a lack of professional development or a lack of administrative leadership, or both. Low test scores across a district obviously point the arrow in a new direction.

Data collection is a complicated task, and reading that data requires a high level of knowledge and sophistication. Regardless of how news stories direct the slant, bad test scores usually have many factors to blame. While teachers always have to be cognizant of public perception, test scores are also an opportunity to learn. Teachers and administrators can often request more particular knowledge about a test. Looking at failing and succeeding data in a classroom under your direct supervision gives you a clearer insight into your own successes and failures. Remember, assessment is supposed to point to learning and lack of learning. That learning and lack of learning don't always have to point to students. They also need to point to teachers so a better idea is given about the particular methods and strategies that need to be refined.

While many teachers are frightened of test data and tend to steer clear of it when it hits the schools, the opposite should really happen. Teachers should become knowledgeable about how data is collected, measured, and disseminated. Only through such a process can a clear picture be shown of what testing is really all about.

Chapter 20

Ten Major Areas of Confusion in Math

Many math concepts are often confused for others, and in this chapter, we cover ten of the most common examples. Think of the times in your past when you may have thought, "I almost had the answer, but I confused this one idea with that other one!" This chapter is about helping you avoid such situations when you take the Praxis Elementary Education test. The test focuses on teaching methods and not very much on mathematical computation, but you still need to understand computation to answer the math questions about teaching. Getting a firm grip on the ten issues covered here will help you in your quest for mathematical invincibility.

Thinking 1 Is Prime and 2 Is Composite

A *prime* number is a whole number that has exactly two factors. Those two factors are the number itself and 1. A *composite* number is a whole number that has more than two factors. The false belief that 1 is a prime number is extremely common because the only factor of 1 is 1. However, that is only one factor. The number 1 does not have two factors, so it is not prime. It isn't correct to say that the factors of 1 are 1 and itself. The factor of 1 is 1, which is itself. The number 1 is only one number. It does not count as its own factor twice. In summary, 1 is not a prime number. It has only one factor.

A composite number is a whole number that has at least three factors—itself, 1, and another whole number. A common misconception is that 2 is a composite number. It is not. It is a prime number. The misunderstanding is based on the fact that 2 is an even number. All positive even numbers are composite, except 2. The only two factors of 2 are itself and 1. That makes 2 a prime number.

2 is a prime number. 1 is not a prime number.

REMEMBER

Viewing Surface Area as Three-Dimensional

Surface area can be a tricky concept because it is a two-dimensional measurement of three-dimensional figures. It is easily confused with volume, which is a three-dimensional measurement of three-dimensional figures. Keep in mind that surface area is a type of area. It is not a measure of how much space is in a figure. It is how much area is on the surface of a figure. Surface area is expressed in terms of square units (m^2, $in.^2$, cm^2, and so forth), not cubic units (m^3, $in.^3$, cm^3, and so on). Volume can be expressed in cubic units, but surface area cannot.

Misusing the Distributive Property

The distributive property is very often misunderstood and misused. The principle of it is that a number times a sum is equal to the sum of the products of the number and each addend. For example, $3(5 + 7) = 3(5) + 3(7)$. The most frequent mistake made with the distributive property is multiplying the outside number by only the first addend and then just adding the other addends. For example, many people are likely to conclude that $3(5 + 7) = 3(5) + 7$. The 3 needs to be multiplied by the 5 and also the 7.

TIP

When using the distributive property, visualize multiplying the outside term by every inside term before you start writing.

Confusing GCF with LCM

Factors are often mistaken for multiples, and vice versa. The misunderstanding is especially common in dealing with greatest common factor (GCF) and least common multiple (LCM). Those two terms are frequently mistaken for each other. When working with those concepts, remember that GCF is a factor and LCM is a multiple. A factor is a number that goes into another one, and a multiple of a number can be reached by multiplying the number by a whole number. A factor of 50 is 5, and a multiple of 50 is 100. Understanding that difference is the key to knowing the difference between GCF and LCM. You can also think about the "G" and the "L." What would be the point of finding a least common factor or a greatest common multiple? The least common factor of any two whole numbers is 1, and there is no limit on the common multiples of two numbers. Focusing on the first and last letters of GCF and LCM can help you stay clear on the difference between the two terms.

Solving for Something Other than a Variable

People often work to solve an equation or inequality and come to a conclusion about a term that is not the variable. For example, the final line of an equation solution may be something like $-x = 8$ or $2y = 10$. Solving for a variable should end with conclusions such as $x = -8$ and $y = 5$. It is the values of the variables that are in question. Terms such as $-x$ and $2y$ are not variables. They just contain variables. Solving for a variable is about determining the value of just the variable.

REMEMBER

An equation is not solved until the variable is completely by itself on one side of the equal sign.

Assuming a Middle Number Is a Median

The median of a set of data is the middle number or the mean (average) of the two middle numbers, in terms of value. When the numbers are in numerical order, the median is the middle number or mean of the two middle numbers in terms of physical order. If the numbers are out of order, looking for what is physically in the middle is not effective. If you see a set of data that is not in numerical order and you are trying to find the median, you need to either put the numbers in order and look for the middle or look for what is in the middle in terms of value.

REMEMBER

A median is physically in the middle of a set of data only when the data is in numerical order.

Misunderstanding Operations with Fractions

Getting common denominators is necessary for adding and subtracting fractions, but it is not necessary for mere multiplication or division with fractions. False ideas about this difference are at the root of a lot of incorrect use of fractions. Finding common denominators for multiplying and dividing with fractions is not a bad thing aside from being unnecessarily time-consuming and increasing the chances of error. The opposite is also true: Not finding common denominators for adding and subtracting fractions is a cause of major trouble when a calculator is not involved. Common denominators cause varying numbers of the same entity to be combined. Just as you can add 3 apples and 2 apples to get 5 apples, you can also add 3 sevenths and 2 sevenths to get 5 sevenths. That is why common denominators work for fraction addition and subtraction. However, that principle does not apply to fraction multiplication or division. Those operations do not require common denominators.

Mixing Up Perimeter and Area

Confusing perimeter with area is a lot like mixing up surface area and volume. Perimeter is a one-dimensional measure of a two-dimensional figure. Area is a two-dimensional measure of a two-dimensional figure. Because perimeter is a one-dimensional measure, a measure of distance, it is expressed in units such as meters and inches. Area is not distance. It is the amount of room within a two-dimensional figure, so it is expressed in square units, such as km^2 and ft^2. In elementary math, perimeter and area are measures asked for in regard to rectangles and triangles. They are measures concerning the same types of figures, and that is at the root of the common confusion. Just keep in mind that perimeter and area are different types of measures for the same types of figures.

TIP

When dealing with perimeter, visualize unraveling the path around the figure and forming a line segment with it. That will help you keep in mind that perimeter is a measure of distance, which is one-dimensional.

Lacking Perspective on Place Value

What causes so much confusion about operations with multiple-digit numbers is lack of perspective on what the digits in the numbers represent. Many people tend to think of the number 395, for example, as a 3, a 9, and a 5. However, there is more to the picture. It is important to think in terms of what each digit represents. What is fully represented by 395 is a 300, a 90, and a 5.

Understanding that is the key to fully conceptualizing what happens when numbers are carried or regrouped ("borrowed") in operations. If the 9 in 395 is correctly marked out and replaced by an 8 during subtraction, it is not because 1 was taken from 9 and given to the 5 to form 15. What really happens in that situation is that 10 is taken from 90 and added to the 5 to get 15. When you look at it that way, the process makes much more sense. Having a full perspective on that general principle makes it easier for you to answer questions about what a student needs to do or did incorrectly in working a problem.

Misconceiving the "MDAS" in "PEMDAS"

The "MD" in the acronym PEMDAS represents "multiplication and division from left to right, whichever comes first." The "MD" is often incorrectly seen as just "M" followed by "D." The two letters are actually counted together as one. It is not correct to do all multiplication and then do all division unless they are presented in that order in a problem. The correct method is to move from left to right and do both multiplication and division as they are encountered. For $30 \div 3 \cdot 5$, one should divide 30 by 3 first and then multiply the result by 5. It is not correct to multiply 3 by 5 first and divide 30 by the product. That would result in the false value of 2, when the correct value is 50. The same is true of the "AS." Addition and subtraction should be performed as they are encountered, going from left to right. The addition does not have to precede all subtraction. In PEMDAS, the "MD" and "AS" represent single phases of computation.

Index

F

fables, 66
facilitative teaching, 184
factor tree, 239
factors
  defined, 94
  explained, 97
  looking for, 239–240
Fahrenheit, 130
fairy tales, 66
falling action, 79
fantasies, 66
fascism, 147
fault lines, 123
fiction, 66, 216
figurative language, 77
figurative shapes, 152
final draft, 70
first law of thermodynamics, 130
first person, 81
fission, 132
flashback, 79
fluency, reading with, 64, 213–214
folk tales, 67
food chain, 120–122
food webs, 120–121
footnotes, 71
form, 152
formal balance, 153
formative assessments, 187–190
formulas, 105–106, 243
fossil fuels, 125
fossils, 127, 128
fractions
  adding or subtracting, 230
  common denominator, 99
  converting, 237–238
  converting percents to, 101
  converting to decimals, 101
  defined, 92
  misunderstanding operations with, 389
  mixed numbers, 100
  operations with, 99–100
  proportions, 100
  reciprocal of, 234
  reduced (converted to simplest form), 99
fragment, sentence, 73
free verse, 67
freezing, 129

friction, 133
frustrational level, 63
fulcrum, 131
fusion, 132

G

galaxies, 128
Gardner, Howard, 180
gas giants, 128
GCF (greatest common factor), 98, 239, 388
general knowledge clues, 78
generalizations, history, 265
geography
  basic ideas of, 138–139
  categories of, 139–140
  Content Knowledge Test (5018), 34
  cultural, 140
  how students are helped by studying, 139
  maps, globes, and other tools, 141–143
  physical, 139
  questions, 11
  teaching, 264–265
  themes of, 140–141
geological maps, 142
geometric sequence, 98
geometry. *See also* shapes
  basic concepts of, 106–107
  shape measurements, 110–111
  teaching, 243–248
    elapsed time, 246–247
    locating points on the coordinate plane, 248
    measuring geometric figures, 244–246
    natures of shapes, 243–244
geometry and measurement
  CIA test (5017), 10
  Content Knowledge Test (5018), 33
global connections, 261–262
globes, 141
glucose, 118
Golgi apparatus, 118
government
  civics, and economics, 11, 34
  overview, 146–147, 261
  teaching, 266
gradual release of responsibility, 183
graduated cylinder, 134
graphemes, 203
graphic organizers (visualizing), 64

physical education *(continued)*
nutrition and, 163–164
other academic subjects and, 164–165
practice questions, 27
answers, 28
psychological and social aspects of, 165
questions, 11
physical factors, cultural factors and, 138
physical geography, 139
physical maps, 142
physical science
Content Knowledge Test (5018), 34
energy, 130–131
interactions between energy and matter, 131–132
laws of force and motion, 133
questions, 10
states of matter, 129–130
transforming students' knowledge of, 256
Piaget, Jean, 179
pie charts, 115
pistil, 118
pitch, 157
place, as theme of geography, 140
place value, 100, 389–390
planes, 113
plans, scientific, 134
plate movement, 123
plot, 79
poetry, 67–69
point of view, 81
points
on coordinate plane, 113, 248
defined, 106
political maps, 142
political science, 146
pollen, 118
polygons
concave, 108
convex, 108
defined, 107
irregular, 109
regular, 109
types of, 108
polynomials, 103
polyphony, 158
portfolios, 269
positive interaction, 276
positive space, 152

potential energy, 130
power, political, 261
pre-assessments, 188
precipitation, 125
preconceived notions, 195
precontrol, 276
predicate of a sentence, 73
prediction, scientific, 134
Preparing to Take a Praxis Test webinars, 54
prepositions, 73
pre-writing, 69
primary colors, 152
primary sources, 70, 145
primatologists, 149
prime factorization, 98, 239
prime meridian, 142
prime numbers, 97, 387
print concepts, 62
prior knowledge
defined, 64
social studies, teaching, 263
probability, 250
experimental, 116
overview, 115–116
process for inquiry, 267
processes, geographical, 141
product, of multiplication, 94
production of goods, 261
proficiency, 276
progress monitoring (interim assessments), 188–189
prompting, 276
pronouns, 73
properties of operations, 95–97
proportions
algebraic, 104
in art, 153
fractions, 100
prose, 67
pulley, 131
"The Purple Cow" (Burgess), 68

Q

quadrants of coordinate plane, 113
quadrilaterals, 107
quartiles, 115
quatrains, 68

recessive traits, 119

reciprocal, of fractions, 234

reciprocal teaching, 184

reflection

  light, 132

  of a shape, 110

refraction, 132

regions, 141

registering for the test, 51

regrouping, 228

regular polygons, 109

rehearsal learning, 185

relationship concepts, 161

relative location, 140

reliability of scores and outcomes, 192

remainder, 232

remediation, 196

repetition, in art, 153

representational shapes, 152

reproduction, 119

reproductive organs, 118

rereading, in general, 64

resolution, 79

respiratory organs, 118

Response to Intervention (RTI), 172

reteaching, 196

retelling, 64, 219

review, 56

rhyme scheme, 67

rhymes, 62

rhythm

  in art, 153

  in music, 157

rhythmic skills, 162

ribosomes, 118

right angles, 108

right rectangular prism, 109

right triangle, 108

rime, 62

rising action, 79

road map, 142

rocks, 123–125

rotation of shapes, 110

rounding, 102, 234–235

rubrics, 268

running records, 63, 218

S

scaffolding, 62

scaffolding instruction, 183

scales, musical, 157

scatterplots, 115

science. *See also specific sciences*

  assessments, 198, 256–257

  concepts, inquiry, and processes, 254

  content knowledge, 198

  curriculum, 198, 251–253

  food chain, 120–122

  instruction, 198, 253–256

  life science principles, 117

  medicine, 135

  music and, 160

  physical, 129–133

  reproduction, 119

  short- and long-term changes, 120

  today, 133

  what things are made of, 117–119

science and technology in society, Content Knowledge Test (5018), 34

science concepts, inquiry, and processes

  CIA test (5017), 10

  Content Knowledge Test (5018), 33

science fiction, 67

science process indicators, 257

science section, CIA test (5017), 10, 22, 23, 295–300, 320, 352–356

science section, Content Knowledge Test (5018), 44–46, 373–376

scientific methods, 134

screw, 131

scribbles, 72

second draft, 69, 70

second law of thermodynamics, 131

second person, 81

secondary colors, 152

secondary sources, 70, 145–146

sedimentary rocks, 123

segmenting sounds, 62

segments, 106

selected-response questions, 11

self- and peer-reflection and evaluation, 189

semantic clues, 63

sentence fragment, 73

Notes

Notes

About the Authors

Carla Kirkland is founder and CEO of The Kirkland Group, a consulting firm headquartered in Ridgeland, Mississippi, that has provided services to school districts for over 20 years. Mrs. Kirkland is a lifelong educator who has served as a teacher, curriculum specialist, educational consultant, and mentor. Providing professional development, technical assistance, and standardized test preparation to multiple school districts, Mrs. Kirkland speaks to the hearts of teachers and students throughout the country. She resides in Mississippi with her husband.

Chan Cleveland currently serves as executive vice president of The Kirkland Group. Mr. Cleveland has taught elementary, middle, and high school English, and he has worked in several capacities at the Mississippi Department of Education. With over 16 years experience as an educator, he has created, reviewed, and revised language arts standard documents for multiple school districts and education organizations across the southern region. Mr. Cleveland has assisted students and teachers with attaining positive results on the Praxis, ACT, and subject area assessments for grades K-12. He holds English degrees from Jackson State University and Mississippi College.

Dedication

Carla Kirkland's Dedication: This book is dedicated to my two children, Malcolm and Alexia. I love you both, and remember to trust in God with all your heart.

Chan Cleveland's Dedication: This book is dedicated to my four children, Kacie, Cornelius, Dylan, and Jayden. Be strong and courageous. I love you all unconditionally.

Authors' Acknowledgments

We would like to thank God for the opportunity to write *Praxis Elementary Education For Dummies*. This book would not have been possible without the management and written contributions of Juana Brandon. She worked tirelessly on this project from start to finish. Spencer Powers, Victoria Ford, and C.C. Thomas provided written contributions for this book. We are grateful for Courtnie Mack and Cerissa Neal, who assisted us with editing and revising throughout the entire process. The entire Wiley Publishing team is second-to-no-one in quality, professionalism, and support. Tim Gallan, Lindsey Lefevere, and Tracy Boggier of Wiley Publishing were always providing helpful advice and feedback from beginning to end.

Publisher's Acknowledgments

Acquisitions Editor: Tracy Boggier
Project Editor: Tim Gallan
Copy Editor: Christine Pingleton
Technical Editor: Carolyn Obel-Omia
Art Coordinator: Alicia B. South

Production Editor: Siddique Shaik
Cover Image: ©gojak/iStockphoto

Apple & Mac

iPad For Dummies, 6th Edition
978-1-118-72306-7

iPhone For Dummies, 7th Edition
978-1-118-69083-3

Macs All-in-One For Dummies,
4th Edition
978-1-118-82210-4

OS X Mavericks For Dummies
978-1-118-69188-5

Blogging & Social Media

Facebook For Dummies, 5th Edition
978-1-118-63312-0

Social Media Engagement For Dummies
978-1-118-53019-1

WordPress For Dummies, 6th Edition
978-1-118-79161-5

Business

Stock Investing For Dummies,
4th Edition
978-1-118-37678-2

Investing For Dummies, 6th Edition
978-0-470-90545-6

Personal Finance For Dummies,
7th Edition
978-1-118-11785-9

QuickBooks 2014 For Dummies
978-1-118-72005-9

Small Business Marketing Kit
For Dummies, 3rd Edition
978-1-118-31183-7

Careers

Job Interviews For Dummies, 4th Edition
978-1-118-11290-8

Job Searching with Social Media
For Dummies, 2nd Edition
978-1-118-67856-5

Personal Branding For Dummies
978-1-118-11792-7

Resumes For Dummies, 6th Edition
978-0-470-87361-8

Starting an Etsy Business For Dummies,
2nd Edition
978-1-118-59024-9

Diet & Nutrition

Belly Fat Diet For Dummies
978-1-118-34585-6

Mediterranean Diet For Dummies
978-1-118-71525-3

Nutrition For Dummies, 5th Edition
978-0-470-93231-5

Digital Photography

Digital SLR Photography All-in-One
For Dummies, 2nd Edition
978-1-118-59082-9

Digital SLR Video & Filmmaking
For Dummies
978-1-118-36598-4

Photoshop Elements 12 For Dummies
978-1-118-72714-0

Gardening

Herb Gardening For Dummies,
2nd Edition
978-0-470-61778-6

Gardening with Free-Range Chickens
For Dummies
978-1-118-54754-0

Health

Boosting Your Immunity For Dummies
978-1-118-40200-9

Diabetes For Dummies, 4th Edition
978-1-118-29447-5

Living Paleo For Dummies
978-1-118-29405-5

Big Data

Big Data For Dummies
978-1-118-50422-2

Data Visualization For Dummies
978-1-118-50289-1

Hadoop For Dummies
978-1-118-60755-8

Language & Foreign Language

500 Spanish Verbs For Dummies
978-1-118-02382-2

English Grammar For Dummies,
2nd Edition
978-0-470-54664-2

French All-in-One For Dummies
978-1-118-22815-9

German Essentials For Dummies
978-1-118-18422-6

Italian For Dummies, 2nd Edition
978-1-118-00465-4

Math & Science

Algebra I For Dummies, 2nd Edition
978-0-470-55964-2

Available in print and e-book formats.

Available wherever books are sold. **For more information or to order direct visit www.dummies.com**

Anatomy and Physiology For Dummies,
2nd Edition
978-0-470-92326-9

Astronomy For Dummies, 3rd Edition
978-1-118-37697-3

Biology For Dummies, 2nd Edition
978-0-470-59875-7

Chemistry For Dummies, 2nd Edition
978-1-118-00730-3

1001 Algebra II Practice Problems
For Dummies
978-1-118-44662-1

Microsoft Office

Excel 2013 For Dummies
978-1-118-51012-4

Office 2013 All-in-One For Dummies
978-1-118-51636-2

PowerPoint 2013 For Dummies
978-1-118-50253-2

Word 2013 For Dummies
978-1-118-49123-2

Music

Blues Harmonica For Dummies
978-1-118-25269-7

Guitar For Dummies, 3rd Edition
978-1-118-11554-1

iPod & iTunes For Dummies, 10th Edition
978-1-118-50864-0

Programming

Beginning Programming with C
For Dummies
978-1-118-73763-7

Excel VBA Programming For Dummies,
3rd Edition
978-1-118-49037-2

Java For Dummies, 6th Edition
978-1-118-40780-6

Religion & Inspiration

The Bible For Dummies
978-0-7645-5296-0

Buddhism For Dummies, 2nd Edition
978-1-118-02379-2

Catholicism For Dummies, 2nd Edition
978-1-118-07778-8

Self-Help & Relationships

Beating Sugar Addiction For Dummies
978-1-118-54645-1

Meditation For Dummies, 3rd Edition
978-1-118-29144-3

Seniors

Laptops For Seniors For Dummies,
3rd Edition
978-1-118-71105-7

Computers For Seniors For Dummies,
3rd Edition
978-1-118-11553-4

iPad For Seniors For Dummies,
6th Edition
978-1-118-72826-0

Social Security For Dummies
978-1-118-20573-0

Smartphones & Tablets

Android Phones For Dummies,
2nd Edition
978-1-118-72030-1

Nexus Tablets For Dummies
978-1-118-77243-0

Samsung Galaxy S 4 For Dummies
978-1-118-64222-1

Samsung Galaxy Tabs For Dummies
978-1-118-77294-2

Test Prep

ACT For Dummies, 5th Edition
978-1-118-01259-8

ASVAB For Dummies, 3rd Edition
978-0-470-63760-9

GRE For Dummies, 7th Edition
978-0-470-88921-3

Officer Candidate Tests For Dummies
978-0-470-59876-4

Physician's Assistant Exam For Dummies
978-1-118-11556-5

Series 7 Exam For Dummies
978-0-470-09932-2

Windows 8

Windows 8.1 All-in-One For Dummies
978-1-118-82087-2

Windows 8.1 For Dummies
978-1-118-82121-3

Windows 8.1 For Dummies, Book + DVD
Bundle
978-1-118-82107-7

ℯ Available in print and e-book formats.

Available wherever books are sold. **For more information or to order direct visit www.dummies.com**

For Dummies is the global leader in the reference category and one of the most trusted and highly regarded brands in the world. No longer just focused on books, customers now have access to the For Dummies content they need in the format they want. Let us help you develop a solution that will fit your brand and help you connect with your customers.

Advertising & Sponsorships

Connect with an engaged audience on a powerful multimedia site, and position your message alongside expert how-to content.

Targeted ads • Video • Email marketing • Microsites • Sweepstakes sponsorship